S0-AEH-306

GREAT TRUE SPY STORIES

From the age of the ancient Greeks, all the way to modern times, the human race has engaged in espionage and intelligence-gathering activities. This extraordinary volume collects the best and most interesting tales from all over the world, creating a fascinating portrait of these activities.

Collected by spy expert Allen Dulles, here is a book that will satisfy aficionados of the art of espionage as well as anyone who enjoys a good story.

⊞ ESPIONAGE/INTELLIGENCE LIBRARY ⊞

THE AMERICAN BLACK CHAMBER
   by Herbert O. Yardley
HIGH TREASON
   by Vladimir Sakharov with Umberto Tosi
WILDERNESS OF MIRRORS
   by David C. Martin
THE PHILBY CONSPIRACY
   by Bruce Page, David Leitch, and Phillip Knightley
THE ATOM BOMB SPIES
   by H. Montgomery Hyde
THE DECEPTION GAME
   by Ladislav Bittman
PORTRAIT OF A COLD WARRIOR
   by Joseph B. Smith
INSIDE THE KGB
   by Aleksei Myagkov
VERY SPECIAL INTELLIGENCE
   by Patrick Beesly
TOP SECRET ULTRA
   by Peter Calvocoressi
THE STORM PETRELS
   by Gordon Brook-Shepherd
THE SPYMASTERS OF ISRAEL
   by Stewart Steven
ABEL
   by Louise Bernikow
HITLER'S SECRET WAR IN
SOUTH AMERICA, 1939–1945
   by Stanley E. Hilton
THE PENKOVSKIY PAPERS
   by Oleg Penkovskiy

GREAT
TRUE
SPY
STORIES

EDITED
BY
Allen Dulles

Ballantine Books . New York

Library of Congress Catalog Card Number: 66-20733

ISBN 0-345-30181-1

This edition published by arrangement with Harper & Row
Publishers, Inc. in association with the K. S. Ginger Co., Inc.
Manufactured in the United States of America
First Ballantine Books Edition: June 1982

Acknowledgments

"Stealing the Plans," from *Ten Thousand Eyes*, by Richard Collier. Copyright © 1958 by Richard Collier. Reprinted by permission of Curtis Brown, Ltd. All rights reserved.

"The Spy the Nazis Missed," by Edward P. Morgan. Reprinted by permission of *True, The Man's Magazine* (July, 1950). Copyright 1950, Fawcett Publications, Inc.

"Cicero—The Case of the Ambassador's Valet," from *Operation Cicero*, by L. C. Moyzisch. Copyright 1950 by L. C. Moyzisch. Reprinted by permission of Coward-McCann, Inc.

"The Rise and Fall of a Soviet Agent," by Edward R. F. Sheehan, *The Saturday Evening Post*, February 15, 1964. Copyright © 1964 by The Curtis Publishing Company. Reprinted by permission of the author.

"The Playboy Sergeant," from "The Playboy Sergeant Who Spied for Russia," by Don Oberdorfer, *The Saturday Evening Post*, March 7, 1964. Copyright © 1964 by Don Oberdorfer. Reprinted by permission of the author and Theron Raines Agency.

"The Colonel Turns West," from *The Penkovskiy Papers*, by Oleg Penkovskiy, with an Introduction and Commentary by Frank Gibney. Copyright © 1965 by Doubleday & Company, Inc. Reprinted by permission of the publisher.

"Spymaster George Washington," from *A Peculiar Service*, by Corey Ford. Copyright © 1965 by Corey Ford. Reprinted by permission of Little, Brown & Co.

"The Spy on the Postage Stamp," from "Technical Operations" in *The Case of Richard Sorge*, by F. W. Deakin and G. R. Storry. Copyright © 1966 by F. W. Deakin and G. R. Storry. Reprinted by permission of Harper & Row, Publishers, and Chatto & Windus, Ltd.

"The Red Orchestra," from *Soviet Espionage*, by David J. Dallin.

Copyright 1955 by Yale University Press. Reprinted by permission of the publisher.

"They Gave the Bomb Away," from *The Atom Spies*, by Oliver Pilat. Copyright © 1952 by Oliver Pilat. Copyright renewed © 1980 by Oliver Pilat. Reprinted by permission of McIntosh and Otis, Inc.

"The Capture of the Grand Chef," from *Soviet Espionage*, by David J. Dallin. Copyright 1955 by Yale University Press. Reprinted by permission of the publisher.

"The Naval Secrets Case," from *Spy Ring*, by John Bullock and Henry Miller. Copyright © 1961 by John Bullock and Henry Miller. Reprinted by permission of Martin Secker & Warburg Limited.

"The Agent the Soviets Wanted Caught," from *A Train of Powder*, by Rebecca West. Copyright 1953 by Rebecca West. Originally published in *The New Yorker*. Reprinted by permission of A. D. Peters & Co. Ltd.

"The Atom Spy Who Had to Confess," from "Klaus Fuchs" in *The Traitors*, Revised Edition, by Alan Moorehead. Copyright © 1952, 1957 by Alan Moorehead. Reprinted by permission of Harper & Row, Publishers, and Hamish Hamilton, Ltd.

"The Tell-Tale Air," from *Handbook for Spies*, by Alexander Foote. Copyright © 1964 by Museum Press Ltd. Reprinted by permission of the publisher.

"Crossing the Delaware," from *A Spy for Washington*, by Leonard Falkner. Copyright © 1957 by Reader's Digest Association, Inc. Reprinted from *American Heritage* (August, 1957) by permission of *The Reader's Digest*.

"To Kill a Czar," from *Aseff the Spy*, by Boris Nikolajewsky, published by Doubleday & Company, Inc., 1934, and Hurst and Blackett, Ltd.

"The Neutral Attaché," from *An Agent in Place*, by Thomas Whiteside. Copyright © 1966 by Thomas Whiteside. Reprinted by permission of Harold Ober Associates, Inc.

"The Clerk They Wouldn't Believe," from *The Iron Curtain*, by Igor Gouzenko. Copyright 1948 by Palm Publishers Press Services, Ltd. Reprinted by permission of E. P. Dutton & Co., Inc., and Palm Publishers Press Services, Ltd.

"Burma Farewell," from *Inside a Soviet Embassy*, by Aleksandr Kaznacheev. Copyright © 1962 by J. B. Lippincott Company. Reprinted by permission of the publisher.

"The Disappearing Fields," from *Red Pawn*, by Flora Lewis. Copyright © 1965 by Flora Gruson. Reprinted by permission of Doubleday & Company, Inc.

"Babylon Falls Again," from *Herodotus*, English translation by A. D. Godley. William Heinemann Ltd., London, 1963.

"The Man Who Never Was," by Ewen Montagu. Copyright 1953 by Walter Louis D'Arcy Hart and Oliver Harry Frost. Reprinted by permission of J. B. Lippincott Company and Evans Brothers, London.

"Overlord Goes Underground," from *The Tangled Web*. Copyright © 1963 by The Editors of the *Army Times*. Reprinted by permission of Robert B. Luce, Inc., Washington, D.C.

"A German Blunder," from *The Zimmermann Telegram*, by Bar-

Contents

FOREWORD   xiii

I PENETRATION: *The Spy Gets Inside*   1

1. Stealing the Plans   3
   from *Ten Thousand Eyes* by RICHARD COLLIER

2. The Spy the Nazis Missed   18
   by EDWARD P. MORGAN

3. Cicero—The Case of the Ambassador's Valet   37
   from *Operation Cicero* by L. C. MOYZISCH

4. The Rise and Fall of a Soviet Agent   60
   by EDWARD R. F. SHEEHAN

5. The Playboy Sergeant   80
   by DON OBERDORFER

6. The Colonel Turns West   90
   from *The Penkovskiy Papers* by OLEG PENKOVSKIY

7. Casanova's Journey to Dunkirk   117
   from *The Memoirs of Jacques Casanova*

II NETWORKS: *The Organization of Espionage*   123

1. Spymaster George Washington   125
      from *A Peculiar Service* by COREY FORD

2. The Spy on the Postage Stamp   138
      from *The Case of Richard Sorge* by F. W. DEAKIN and
      G. R. STORRY

3. The Red Orchestra   147
      from *Soviet Espionage* by DAVID J. DALLIN

4. They Gave the Bomb Away   153
      from *The Atom Spies* by OLIVER PILAT

III COUNTERESPIONAGE: *Spy to Catch a Spy*   161

1. Behind the Line   165
      from *A Letter from Alexander Hamilton to John Laurens*

2. The Capture of the Grand Chef   170
      from *Soviet Espionage* by DAVID J. DALLIN

3. The Naval Secrets Case   173
      from *Spy Ring* by JOHN BULLOCK and HENRY MILLER

4. The Agent the Soviets Wanted Caught   181
      from *A Train of Powder* by REBECCA WEST

5. The Atom Spy Who Had to Confess   197
      from *The Traitors* by ALAN MOOREHEAD

6. The Tell-Tale Air   216
      from *Handbook for Spies* by ALEXANDER FOOTE

IV DOUBLE AGENTS: *Working Both Sides
      of the Street*   227

1. Crossing the Delaware   231
      from *A Spy for Washington* by LEONARD FALKNER

2. To Kill a Czar   240
      from *Aseff the Spy* by BORIS NIKOLAJEWSKY

3. The Neutral Attaché   257
      from *An Agent in Place* by THOMAS WHITESIDE

v DEFECTION: *Changing Sides*   271

1. The Clerk They Wouldn't Believe   273
   from *The Iron Curtain* by IGOR GOUZENKO

2. Burma Farewell   291
   from *Inside a Soviet Embassy* by ALEKSANDR
   KAZNACHEEV

3. The Disappearing Fields   300
   from *Red Pawn* by FLORA LEWIS

vi DECEPTION: *Confusing the Adversary*   313

1. Babylon Falls Again   315
   from *Herodotus*

2. The Man Who Never Was   319
   by EWEN MONTAGU

3. Overlord Goes Underground   328
   from *The Tangled Web* by The Editors of the
   Army Times

4. News Made to Order   341
   from *Communist Forgeries,* U.S. Senate Hearings

vii CODES AND CIPHERS: *Secrets to Unravel*   345

1. A German Blunder   347
   from *The Zimmermann Telegram* by BARBARA W.
   TUCHMAN

2. Keeping a Secret   355
   from *Marshall-Dewey Letters* (Life Magazine)

viii SCIENTIFIC INTELLIGENCE: *The Technology
   of Espionage*   361

1. Eyes from the Sky   363
   from *Air Spy* by CONSTANCE BABINGTON-SMITH

2. The Case of the Wayward Missile   366
   from *Crossbow and Overcast* by JAMES McGOVERN

3. Spying on the Winds   372
   from *Men and Decisions* by LEWIS L. STRAUSS

IX EVALUATION: *Sifting the Evidence*   381

1. Last-Minute MAGIC   383
   from *Pearl Harbor: Warning and Decision* by ROBERTA
   WOHLSTETTER

2. The Dark December   390
   from *Battles Lost and Won* by HANSON W. BALDWIN

   A Review of Battles Lost and Won   396

X ACTION: *The Dagger Beneath the Cloak*   399

1. The Venlo Incident   401
   from *The Labyrinth* by WALTER SCHELLENBERG

2. Assassin Disarmed by Love   419
   by JOHN L. STEELE

X CLASSIC INSTANCES OF ESPIONAGE   437

1. The Archtraitor   439
   from *The Story of the Secret Service* by RICHARD
   WILMER ROWAN

2. London Calling North Pole   453
   by H. J. GISKES

3. Prelude to Invasion   473
   from *Sub Rosa* by STEWART ALSOP and THOMAS BRADEN

Foreword

ANYONE WHO EDITS a collection of Great True Spy Stories should be ready to say what makes a spy great. I would differentiate between two types of qualities in a spy. The spy can achieve something great by acquiring some vital information that may change the course of a battle, or even the history of a nation. He may succeed in doing this without having been involved in any hair-raising adventures, or he may have risked his life in the doing. And he may be great as a spy and yet be the kind of man who does not exactly arouse one's enthusiasm. For example, it is hard to find anything great or admirable in the person of Klaus Fuchs, but the results of his betrayal of our nuclear secrets to the Soviets may have changed the course of history.

The other quality of greatness in a spy concerns the person himself. The spy's conduct may have something of the heroic or some tremendously exciting quality about it, whether or not he succeeds, and whether or not his information proves to be vital. Many a man has been sent on a fool's errand and has acted nobly. Our spy hero of the American Revolution, Nathan Hale, was certainly great in his patriotic fervor and in his courage as he faced execution, and it is for this he is remembered. The sad fact remains, however, that he acccomplished no intelligence objective on his ill-fated mission, that he was, in all likelihood, ill-prepared for it and quite possibly the wrong sort of man to carry it out.

When these two qualities do come together in the person of a secret agent, that is, greatness as a human being and greatness in the accomplishment of his mission, then we have the ideal spy.

If the spy, however notorious, distinguishes himself in neither of the two ways I have indicated, I have omitted his story, unless it illustrates some intelligence technique of interest for its own sake.

In our own time certain spies have achieved great notoriety, although it remains uncertain whether the spy really accomplished much or not. The case of the Soviet spy master, Colonel Rudolf Abel, is a good example. He was apprehended by the FBI in New York in 1957 on the basis of information given to American authorities by one of his subordinates who defected. When he was caught, the paraphernalia in his possession—codes, radios, concealment devices—pointed to clandestine activities of a very extensive sort. Since Abel never talked about his spying, we do not actually know to this day the full nature of his activities. His trial and his eventual exchange in 1962 for the U-2 pilot, Francis Gary Powers, made him front-page news on several different occasions. He has been the subject of a number of articles and books, but try as you may, you will find hardly a word in these accounts about what Abel actually accomplished as a spy, and most of what you will find is pure surmise.

Do I hear complaints because one of the most notorious spies of them all, Mata Hari, does not dance across our page? I find greatness neither in her motives nor her methods, nor, as far as history records, in her achievements. It is doubtful that the information she elicited from her admirers was worth the paper it was written on. I do not doubt what she might have achieved under able guidance. She was, after all, primarily a free-lancer. The drama of her execution is chiefly responsible for her being remembered. She became a victim of wartime spy hysteria, and the pressure on the French authorities in 1917 to set an example. If I have left out Mata Hari because she was not much of a spy, I have partially made up for it by including someone whom the reader probably did not expect in the company of spies: Casanova, whose successful mission contains some lessons as to how a spy should conduct himself.

Greatness in a spy will thus have to remain a matter of judgment, personal judgment rather than any impartial judgment of history. But the authenticity of a spy story is another matter. Here the historian can apply the same yardstick as he does to other sectors of history. How reliable are the sources?

Recently the British Government brought out a volume describing the work of the SOE (Special Operations Executive) in France during World War II.* This was the organization behind the brave men and women who infiltrated enemy-occupied territory by air or by sea in order to bolster operatives of the underground—"setting Europe ablaze," as Churchill called it. A great hue and cry was raised after the publication of the book, even in Parliament itself, by former members of SOE and their friends and supporters, because much of what had been published about them and their exploits previously in magazines and books now appeared lurid and exaggerated in the light of the staid and sober official account. We can assume that the government account was as candid as it was possible to be under the security restrictions which had to be observed. But truth has a hard time once legends are established which appease our thirst for heroes and heroics.

When it comes to the problem of reliability, there is hardly a better example of what the collector of "true" spy stories may encounter than that afforded by our own Civil War. I initially intended to include in this collection a sampling of Civil War tales, certainly as many as I have assembled about the American Revolution. There was, after all, Pinkerton, founder of the world-renowned detective agency and intelligence chief of McClellan, and Lafayette Baker, who took much of the credit for tracking

---

* *SOE in France,* by M. R. D. Foot, Her Majesty's Stationery Office, London, 1966.

down Lincoln's assassins. And the ladies: Belle Boyd, spy
for Stonewall Jackson; Elizabeth van Lew, spy for Grant;
the romance of gallant officers misled; pretty women crossing the lines with vital intelligence concealed close to their
palpitating bosoms. To my dismay I discovered that very
few of these well-known and oft-repeated tales are verifi-
ably true, most of them having been foisted on a romance-
hungry reading public after the war was over, either by the
doers of the alleged deeds themselves or persons who found
their stories intriguing enough to write.*

Of all that may be held secret in the field of intelligence,
nothing is preserved more carefully than the identity of the
spy. Forty years after the Revolutionary War, John Jay
refused to reveal to James Fenimore Cooper the name of
a revolutionary spy whose exploits he had, however, described to Cooper in sufficient detail to inspire the latter to
write his novel *The Spy*. Tallmadge, Washington's chief of
intelligence, made reference only in a few brief lines in his
memoirs to the all-important Culper Ring, and the identity
of Samuel Culper, Jr., as Robert Townsend was ascertained
by historians only in 1939 on the basis of handwriting
specimens. From Washington's accountings to the Continental Congress we know how much he spent on secret
intelligence, $17,000, but little else except what historians
pieced together more than a century later.

One of the unusual ways in which "true" spy stories
buried in government archives have come to light is
through a claim for reimbursement for "services rendered"
made by the former spy or by his heirs. Governments are
often forgetful, or even ungrateful, when it comes to re-
warding spies. We might never have chanced on the per-
fidious and many-sided Edward Bancroft, one of Benjamin
Franklin's secretaries in Paris, who was in the pay of
George III, if Bancroft had not had cause to remind the
British Exchequer, in 1784, that they were in arrears to
him and was indiscreet enough to describe, on paper, for

---

* See "The Mythology of Civil War Intelligence," by Edwin C.
Fischel, in *Civil War History*, University of Iowa at Ames, December,
1964. Vol. X (IV), Also, the article by Curtis Carrol Davis in the
same issue.

what sort of services he was owed. His letter, long buried in British archives, came to light in 1889.*

Some of the tradition of governmental secrecy has, however, for many different reasons, recently been broken, and it is in some measure thanks to this change—to the fact that so much espionage material has recently been aired in public—that a volume like the present one is possible.

In the West three different sources of generally reliable information about contemporary espionage have developed as a result of the "cold war": the public trials of captured enemy agents, governmental investigations of the illegal clandestine undertakings of hostile powers, and the published revelations of defectors. It should be noted, of course, that what is brought out by all these means is not primarily the espionage efforts of one's own side, but those of its opponents. Thus, we sometimes reveal what the Soviets and their allies are up to in order to enlighten and warn our own public and, to some extent, to frustrate the Soviets and to deter them from continuing the practice. They do the same to us. Either way, the interested reader can pick up information on the espionage of our time here and there.

The White Book of the Royal Canadian Commission, which reported in 1945 on the investigation of Soviet atomic espionage in Canada during World War II, was one of the most revealing and politically explosive documents of the immediate postwar years. In the tradition established

---

* It is possible that Franklin knew what Bancroft was up to and let him continue while keeping an eye on him. In 1777 Franklin wrote to an American lady living in France, Juliana Ritchie, who had warned him that he was surrounded with spies:

"I am much oblig'd to you for your kind Attention to my Welfare in the Information you give me. I have no doubt of its being well founded. But as it is impossible to . . . prevent being watch'd by Spies, when interested People may think proper to place them for that purpose; I have long observ'd one Rule which prevents any Inconvenience from such Practices. It is simply this, to be concern'd into no Affairs that I should blush to have made publick; and to do nothing but what Spies may see and welcome. When a Man's Actions are just and honourable, the more they are known, the more his Reputation is increas'd and establish'd. If I was sure therefore that my Valet de Place was a Spy, as probably he is, I think I should not discharge him for that, if in other Respects I lik'd him. B.F."

by this commission there followed reports of the various special tribunals in England which looked into the Vassall and other cases, the report of the Royal Commission on Espionage of the Government of Australia in the case of the Soviet intelligence officer Petrov (August, 1955), the Swedish Commission which examined the Wennerstrom case, and our own congressional committees which have investigated security matters, large and small, during the last twenty years, and have published their results in government documents.

When knowledgeable and imaginative reporters such as Rebecca West or Alan Moorehead, versed in the lore of espionage, have examined the work of such commissions and the persons of the culprits on trial and the powers behind them, they can bring today's reader close to the heart of the matter.

As regards Soviet revelations about their spies, one is on uncertain ground. Here an astute analyst is needed to separate the propaganda from the truth. The very fact that the Soviets have recently taken to making revelations, giving up the total secrecy in espionage matters which they maintained in the past, is surprising and was hardly expected in the West. An unusual case that illustrates this change is that of the Soviet master spy, Richard Sorge.

When Sorge was caught and jailed by the Japanese in 1941, the Soviets did not raise a finger to help him, though he was credited with getting to Stalin the most vital information affecting the strategy of Soviet Russia at that time: the news that the Japanese were not then planning to attack the Russians.

Then, in 1964, more than twenty years after his execution—years of absolute silence about him on the part of the Soviets—Sorge was "rehabilitated." The Soviets found it useful, in 1964, to glorify Sorge and his exploits to the extent of publishing an official state biography of him and issuing a memorial postage stamp on which his likeness appeared. With this, Sorge was not only officially recognized as a hero, but the profession of spying, for the Soviets at least, was officially hailed.

One reason that has been suggested for this changed attitude on their part is that they felt some need—in the face of the many cases of Soviet agents captured and un-masked during the postwar decades—to bolster and glam-orize the profession, possibly because in Russia it had fallen into disrepute and the Soviets were finding it more difficult to recruit people to work clandestinely for the U.S.S.R.

Apparently, the Soviets had become concerned with the "image" of espionage itself. Whether or not they really cared about the memory of Sorge, he was clearly a con-venient peg on which to hang certain sentiments about a field of activity which, for five decades, has been a main-stay of Soviet policy.

In our time we have seen a great proliferation of intelli-gence services and of the uses and methods of intelligence. This has been, in part, a result of the aggressive behavior of totalitarian states and the need of the democracies to defend themselves against such aggression, in part a result of revolutionary scientific and technical discoveries. Three-quarters of the items in this collection are taken either from World War II or the "cold war," in both of which the intelligence services played such a major role. The Iron Curtain, though not always mentioned, becomes a major character in some of these stories. It had a triple impact on intelligence collection. It made intelligence difficult to get to, and difficult to get out once obtained; it made it difficult to keep contact with the agent who remained in hostile territory.

I have put the broadest possible interpretation on the words "spy story," not confining myself to espionage and the collection of intelligence, but including almost anything within the scope of "secret intelligence operations"—any-thing, that is, that a modern intelligence organization might be called upon to do. Some stories have even been included which are often, and sometimes wrongly, referred to as intelligence failures. There is only one constant in all these tales, one old-fashioned irreplaceable element that remains essential to the pursuit of our vital intelligence objectives in the nuclear-missile age—the skill of the human being himself. Despite the new tools which science is now putting into the hands of the intelligence collector, it is still the human competence to operate the tools and to interpret the product which remains the decisive element in the intelligence equation today.

I cannot, of course, vouch for the accuracy of all the statements in these stories. They have been taken on the authority of the authors who wrote and published them; I considered the authors worthy of being quoted because in their various ways they were in excellent positions to be acquainted with the facts, either as participants, observers or researchers. In many cases, for reasons of space, I have excerpted and condensed the authors' material.

I have not intended this volume merely as a collection of entertaining spy stories. My aim has been rather to present a comprehensive view of the business of clandestine intelligence as it has been practiced during the present historical era and to do so by drawing on available published materials. For this reason, I have arranged the selections throughout in categories used in professional intelligence rather than in random fashion. Each story has been chosen as an illustration of some specific and significant facet of intelligence work, and my comments on them appear in italics.

If I were to state my motive in editing this collection it would be that of wanting to throw more light on the real role of intelligence in our national life, and its contribution to our defense.

I wish to thank the various publishers and authors whose productions appear in this volume for their kind permission to make use of their material, and friends and colleagues who have given of their time and good advice in the compilation and editing of this anthology. Especially, I wish to thank Walter Pforzheimer, whose wide knowledge of the literature and history of intelligence led me to many of the less well-known items which appear in this collection; Howard Roman, for his collaboration and advice in the planning and writing of this volume; and Mrs. Margaret Butterfield of Harper & Row, for her excellent editorial suggestions. I am also deeply indebted to both publishers, Cass Canfield of Harper & Row and Kenneth Giniger of K. S. Giniger & Company, for the interest they have shown in *Great True Spy Stories*.

ALLEN DULLES

I

Penetration:

The Spy Gets Inside

IF AN INTELLIGENCE service wants to do more than count the number of the enemy and his cannon—if it wants to find out what enemy commanders are planning—it must do more than hide in the bushes and look over the fence, or even look down from high-flying planes or satellites. It has to get inside the enemy's headquarters and listen to his conversations. It must steal important plans or documents. Hence, the term "penetration" has been given to those espionage operations whose aim is to place, plant, or acquire an agent inside the target. This is a difficult achievement. In significant penetration cases an agent remains "in place," providing information over a long period of time whenever he can safely manage to do so.

Today, security precautions around any important target are such that an outsider is not likely to pass the scrutiny of guards even if he has a good story, speaks the local language, and can pass as a native. It is much more likely that the penetration agent will be someone who is actually a native and is already employed inside the target. In most of the accounts that follow, the agent was already "in place" when recruited.

I have often found that the best of such agents are the ones who volunteer, those who come forward on their own and make contact with representatives of another country because of their dislike of the conditions or the system under which they are forced to live and work, although some do it for financial gain. One of the problems for a man who is "in place" and wishes to volunteer "out" is to make contact with the intelligence service to which he is offering himself. Beyond that, once he has made the contact, he must prove to his new bosses that he is acting in good faith.

One of my best agents in World War II, whose exploits in the German Foreign Office are recounted in one of the selections which follows, was viewed with a great deal of suspicion by Washington when he first turned up as a volunteer. It was well-known that the Germans were most anxious to place an agent in my headquarters, and the best way for them to do this was to send me someone who claimed he hated the Nazis and offered to work for me. However, once I saw that the information he had lifted from Foreign Office files and had risked his life to carry over the border was of great strategic and political value to the West, I was morally certain of his bona fides. The Germans would never have gambled away anything that so greatly affected their own security merely in the hope of building up an agent.

1

Stealing the Plans

Richard Collier

*In 1943, expecting that sooner or later the Allies
would attempt to invade Europe, the Nazis were
feverishly engaged in building the system of coastal
defenses along the Atlantic seaboard of France
known as the Atlantic Wall. For heavy construction jobs of this sort the Nazis had created an
essentially civilian engineering outfit called the
Todt Organization, which had to rely largely on
local labor in occupied areas. The French Underground naturally took advantage wherever possible
of this situation. Its members found jobs working
on the "Wall" and in other construction projects in
order to get a good look at the German defenses.
For the most part the information acquired this
way was local and piecemeal, but in some notable
instances, such as the one recounted in the story
which follows, there were windfalls of extensive
vital intelligence. Once the report was obtained, it
had to be communicated to Allied headquarters in
England, a task as difficult and dangerous as the
acquisition of it.*

FROM the book *Ten Thousand Eyes.*

EARLY IN MAY a black-lettered notice printed on coarse buff paper was pinned to the official announcements board outside the *mairie* in Caen. It was about mid-morning on May 7th, a Thursday, that Duchez drew his battered gray *camionette* to a halt beside the board and read it.

The text of the notice, which was in French, asked for decorators to submit estimates to the *mairie* in connection with minor repairs to be carried out at the headquarters of the Todt Organization. The final date for submissions had been at 5 P.M. the previous day.

Duchez sat and thought about it. The deadline suggested that he had missed his chance, but Duchez was never a man to underestimate the value of *monnaie de singe*—an extremely French phrase, roughly translatable as blarney. Beneath his bland spoofing exterior was a clever, cold brain, which told him he could be of more value to the network inside the Todt Organization than any of his colleagues. The painter could recall vividly the long hot summers of his childhood in occupied Lorraine, playing on the stoop of his father's, the architect's, house in Nancy. The tall blond German soldiers would stop to banter with the boy, and his brain had retained much of the patois. The Todt Organization were building the Wall, and if they were to let drop any crumb of information on that score, Duchez stood more chance than most of understanding and retaining it.

And then, was he not Duchez? Later Arsène said this of him: "His greatest pride was that he could make fun of the Germans without their knowing it"; and it is likely that this motive influenced him as much as any. To beard the Germans in their own territory could, with luck, emerge as a really gorgeous hoax, a good tale to tell over a calvados— at any rate, it could do no harm to try.

In the gloomy tiled lobby of the *mairie* he made inquiries and was finally directed to the Bureau Civil, run by a man named Postel. Postel, however, pursed his lips dubiously. "I think you're too late," he said. "All the estimates were in twenty-four hours ago." Then, since he liked Duchez, he added, "On the other hand, they haven't told us yet that they've accepted any tenders. You could always try direct."

This was Duchez's version of what happened after that.

No one seemed too certain whom to approach, so the painter went back to his *camionette* and turned left across the first intersection into the Avenue Bagatelle. The Todt Organization in Caen was not of first importance, being what the Germans called a *Bauleitung* (works subsector) of the main headquarters at St. Malo, but they had taken over three buildings in the city: one for camouflage, one for administering forward area personnel and one for the *Abteilung Technik*, which dealt with mapping and works contracts. Duchez had no clue that he was driving toward the most important of the three buildings at that moment, a four-story stone mansion faced in brick with stone-sashed windows, fronting directly on the street.

Fifty yards from the main entrance this street was blocked by a picket fence barrier wound with a cat's cradle of barbed wire. Duchez brought the *camionette* to a shuddering halt within a few feet of it, then dismounted, grinning amiably. A sentry came out of the black-and-white-striped control box on the left and brought his rifle to the ready: *"Halten!"*

Duchez beamed at him in a fuddled way and kept going. The rifle barrel came hard against his ribs. *"Halten!* Your *Ausweis."*

Duchez explained that he had come to apply for the painting estimate, but the sentry did not follow his schoolboy German and was all the time motioning him backwards. Mystified by the rumpus, another sentry, guarding the main entrance, came forward to investigate. Then, so they say, there followed several indescribable moments of pure low comedy, as Duchez tried in desperation to bridge the language barrier by mimicking the actions of a man painting the side of a house, using the side of the sentry box by way of demonstration. The reaction was brisker than he had anticipated. A savage blow with the flat of the hand almost knocked him senseless, and to a running accompaniment of cuffs and kicks he was hustled along the street through a molded stone doorway into a ground-floor office.

A torrent of German followed, too fast for him to understand, and at last a monocled *Hauptbauführer* (Todt captain) with some knowledge of French asked icily whether he was aware of the penalties meted out to wretched Frenchmen who dared to poke fun at the Fuehrer. Duchez stared at him for a moment before the full savor of the jest hit him, then, controlling himself with difficulty, explained that he had cast no aspersions on the Fuehrer, nor indeed on house painters in general; he himself was a house painter in search of work. The man began to chuckle dryly, dismissed the sentries and sent an orderly for a junior officer in charge of the painting estimates.

A young officer led him up two flights of uncarpeted stairs; in peacetime these had been solid merchants' houses, and the steel filing cabinets, the jackboots, the whiplash precision of the "Heil Hitlers" seemed in bleak contrast to the molded pillars and the ornate plaster friezes. The *Oberbauführer* (Todt lieutenant) was explaining that it was merely a simple papering job, involving two offices on the second floor. Would Duchez submit an estimate?

The painter thought fast. He could gauge pretty accurately what his competitors would be charging. They would take only a small margin of profit, because work was scarce and anyone who did a good job for the Todt Organization might expect to be called on again. But a margin, just the same.

Duchez breathed a silent apology to his competitors and decided that for the sake of the network this was one job that would have to be done at a loss. "Twelve thousand francs," he said, conscious that this was at least one-third below anyone else's estimate, and before the officer even opened his mouth to speak he knew that the job was his.

"You will report in person," the *Oberbauführer* told him, "to Bauleiter (Todt major) Schnedderer."

Duchez could never understand, even afterward, why Schnedderer, whose office was not involved, should take a personal interest in the decoration of other offices. Possibly as *Gebietsingenieur* (engineer officer) he had a personal interest in the costing but from subsequent events Duchez thought it likely that the *Bauleiter* had a streak of frustrated interior decorator in his make-up. A bald, powerfully-built man with a thick crease of dueling scar on his right cheek, wearing the silver-lined Todt uniform collar and swastika brassard, Schnedderer received the painter jovially in his second-floor office. Then he began to expound at length on the patterns he had envisaged. Blue horsemen carrying flags on a light yellow background might look good. Or silver cannons against a background of navy blue.

Wallpaper, like most other items, was in short supply, but Duchez promised to return next day with some likely samples. He spent the rest of the day in his atelier near the Rue Grusse, hunting through pattern books, and that evening, at the Café des Touristes, he did not hesitate to tell little Dumis, the courteous ex-garage proprietor, and Deschambres, the redhaired plumber, that he had got a job with the Todt Organization and that much might come of it.

Dumis, who worshiped this reckless swashbuckler, remembers that he begged him to be careful, but Duchez, his eyes gleaming with mischief, replied, "No, look, mon ami, I am Duchez. I can do things with the Germans that others cannot do. Why? Simply because they think I am all sorts of a crétin, and they don't care what they say in front of me. C'est le sang-froid, my friend—c'est toujours le sang-froid."

Then, seeing "Albert" sitting in one corner, lost in thought over a cognac, he did not neglect to nod to him politely. "Albert" was an elderly German *Hauptmann*, whose real name they never knew; the only German who ever used the Café des Touristes, he had frequented it long before the network was formed. At first the agents had mistrusted him profoundly, giving the café a wide berth, but carefully laid traps had revealed that the man neither spoke nor understood a word of French.

And in a strange irrational way Duchez and the rest now welcomed "Albert's" visits; his presence was soothing rather than otherwise and he was such a good front that the network's business could be discussed freely before him. In turn, the shy elderly man seemed to derive comfort from watching what he evidently believed were the little traders of a French town, gossiping about life over a glass of *ordinaire*.

It was on Friday, May 8th, that things started to happen. Soon after ten o'clock Duchez presented himself at the Todt building. This time he had no trouble in gaining access to Schnedderer, and the liaison officer began to pore over the pattern books, sometimes grunting as one caught his fancy. Duchez was standing facing him, on the other side of his wide paper-littered desk. Schnedderer was debating between two particular patterns, when a knock sounded at the door. Still turning the pages, he called, "Come in."

A junior officer whom the painter had not seen before entered carrying a thick pile of what looked like papers. A "Heil Hitler" and a click of heels. Still browsing, Schnedderer said absently, "Put them down there," and then, a minute later, "Danke schön, Oberbauführer. I was waiting for these." As he put the pattern book aside and began to unfold the pile of papers lengthwise, Duchez saw from the corner of his eyes that they were not papers but maps.

Duchez stood quite still, watching, but after a moment it was obvious that Schnedderer, studying the maps intently, had temporarily forgotten his existence. Ostensibly the painter went on staring at the cypress trees outside the window, with the expression of amiable idiocy that he always wore when dealing with the Germans, but all the time his heart was going hard. The liaison officer had now thrown back his bald bullet-head to study a section of the map (it was too long to unfold in its entirety) at arm's length, and Duchez could see some of the details outlined plainly in reverse through the back. That was the narrow bottle-neck mouth of the Seine at Quillebeuf in the far corner and, beyond it, the Risle, winding down to Pont-Audemer; the coastline, smooth and rounded as far as Honfleur, then plunging abruptly downward to the smart watering places, Trouville and Deauville, and the cliffs north of Houlgate and Cabourg.

With an odd sense of hysteria, Duchez realized he was looking at a Todt Organization map of the coastline of Normandy.

From that moment he always had the confused impression that everything happened at once. Still dazed with the possible implications, he saw Schnedderer replace the top map from the pile, push the maps to the left-hand corner of his desk nearest Duchez, and return to the pattern book. But it seemed to be a busy morning on the Avenue Bagatelle. Another knock sounded, and this time it was a *Truppführer* (Todt sergeant) who entered, repeating something that sounded like a message, which Duchez could not catch. Whatever it was it made Schnedderer get up, turn his back on the painter and open the door leading to an inner office immediately behind his desk. The *Truppführer* withdrew, and Schnedderer, looming in the doorway with his back to the room, one hand propped on the jamb, seemed to be dictating to a clerk.

Duchez was left alone with the maps.

They were still lying on the table where the Germans had left them. Cautiously, as if it had been a red-hot stove lid, Duchez lifted the top one. It was printed, by the Ozalide system of mimeograph, on deep blue cartographic paper, the great red letter, SONDERZEICHNUNGEN—STRENG GEHEIM—meaning "Special Blueprint—Top Secret"— prominent in one corner. Duchez thought for a moment that he was going to be ill; although the map was too bulky to risk opening out in full, it seemed to be a blueprint for defense, right enough, though of what order he had no time to find out. Chance phrases like "Blockhaus" caught his eyes and "Sofort-program" (highest priority construction).

He cast a scared glance toward the door, but Schnedderer was still dictating. All the time a nagging irresistible voice inside his brain was saying, take it, you fool, take it. There may never be a chance like this, now, while he's not looking. . . .

He took three steps backward across the room, still holding the map, and there was the fireplace; that was no good, but above it was a heavy mirror, perhaps two feet square, with a chased gilt frame, like an oil painting. With his right hand Duchez slid the map behind the mirror lengthways so that the inward cant of the frame prevented it from falling. Then, treading lightly, he went back and took up his old innocent stand by the desk. Afterward he said that he was wet through with sweat and that there was a sick dead feeling in his throat and down to his stomach, because if Schnedderer found out what he had done, whether the map was important or not, it would be the last foolish and gallant *beau geste* that he would ever make.

Then he just waited for Schnedderer to stop dictating, which was the worst time of all, because he could not, in the few brief minutes remaining, collect his thoughts sufficiently to go over what he had done, looking for loopholes.

It had not even occurred to him to check whether the maps differed; if they did then the loss might be discovered before he was even out of the building. In the back of his mind was the idea that somehow, at some future date, he could abstract the map without anyone knowing, but beyond a fervent prayer that he might leave the building alive he had no other plans.

Almost before he realized it, Schnedderer had closed the inner door and was back at the desk again, selecting two patterns and making it plain that the interview was over. "Monday then," said the *Bauleiter,* and Duchez thought guiltily that Schnedderer gave him a suspicious glance, but later he told himself it was only imagination, for the officer turned to his papers without even glancing at the maps again, apparently suspecting nothing.

Duchez walked two flights of stairs to street level, quivering and rigid with fear, waiting for something to hit him. Nothing did. Then, feeling a lot older than his forty years, he went to the Café des Touristes and had a drink. He felt he had earned it.

By afternoon the paralyzing sense of dread had worn off, and he was almost his old self again. Before he went back to the café that evening, when his children, Jacques, aged eleven, and Monique, aged three, were safely tucked up in bed, he told Odette what he had done, and the good placid woman, who had come to accept her husband's pranks the way a mother indulges a mischievous youngster, said, "That's very good," and meant it. Thinking about it afterward she had to confess that the news didn't surprise her. In her own words, "He was always doing funny things like that."

At the time she was more concerned with persuading René to eat regular meals; the war was taking more toll of him than people realized, and unless she offered him cold chicken for almost every meal, the chances were he would push his plate away after a few mouthfuls. "Sorry, chérie . . . just not hungry." From the windows of their old-fashioned house she watched him lope off across the courtyard toward the café, with his peculiar shambling gait, and thought, with the blessed treason of her sex, He's never really grown up at all.

And she was not far wrong. At the café that evening

Duchez was in great form, treating everyone. "No, no, mon ami, this is with me. . . . Do you know, a most extraordinary thing happened to me today? Yes, this very morning, while I was with an officer at the Todt Organization . . ."

Duchez was lucky in his loyalties. No one talked. Yet, by curfew time that night half a dozen of the network had heard his story and perhaps it was lucky too that not everyone believed him; Duchez was a famous man for crying, "Wolf." Arsène, the argumentative one-eyed plumber, did not believe it for one, and never did, and another disbeliever was the shy fair-haired young Robert Thomas. "He's full of such stupidities," Thomas grumbled when he heard the story. There was no denying the truth of that. Without such indiscretions, Dewavrin* himself once said, his networks would have functioned more smoothly, admitting the wry paradox that without such bravery they would not have functioned at all.

Duchez, of course, slept soundly that night. He had already decided that on the Monday, when he started work, he could make an excuse to see Schnedderer and a way would present itself to him to remove the map. It had to, for he was Duchez. Only Odette lay still, and awake, remembering the Gestapo officers billeted only two doors up the street, wondering each time a car's headlamps swept a white windmill of light across the bedroom, Is it for us? Or the wheels of a car, cornering with a faint thin scream on the wet tarmac. Is it for us? Then the engine cutting out, a door slamming, feet scrunching on wet gravel, a second of eternity, of whispering a prayer, Please, God, dear God, not for us, not for our children. Then the feet dying away, the thick silence like a curtain, and the numb sick feeling of having lived all the fears and anguish of your life in the space of this minute.

Sleepless by her husband's side, Odette fought her war.

On the Monday, Duchez reported at the Todt Organization at half-past eight, armed with buckets, cans of size and rolls of wallpaper; it was his habit to start work early in

---

* Nom de guerre of Colonel Passy, chief of the underground intelligence service of the Free French.

order to knock off at four, leaving good time for meetings at the Touristes. At that hour the building was cold and silent, only the clerks and orderlies had arrived, and for about two hours he worked, washing the walls down to the plaster and sizing them, singing abominably through his nose, until an outraged orderly came and told him to cease.

The painter apologized profusely, saying, "When it is convenient, please, I would like to see Bauleiter Schnedderer."

The orderly said unsympathetically, "Well, you'd better take the train to St. Malo then, if you do."

Duchez saw the green light. If Schnedderer's office was unoccupied . . . "Any time will do," he said pacifically. "When will he be back?"

"Back?" The orderly stared. "Never here. He's been transferred to another unit. Bauleiter Keller is the new liaison officer."

Duchez was electrified.

The orderly stared at him curiously for a moment, then walked away. The painter spent the rest of the day in silence and misery, too depressed even to sing, and he said later that for a moment the idea crossed his mind that Schnedderer's abrupt departure had something to do with the missing map. Yet if it had he would surely have been rounded up for questioning. He could make nothing of it. Hadn't they even missed the map? And if they hadn't how could he get it out of the building before they did?

Sometime during the next twenty-four hours he did a lot of thinking, though as was usual when he really had a plan brewing he said nothing, not even to Odette. He began his campaign about ten on the Tuesday morning by asking the young *Oberbauführer* in charge of the painting. When the officer appeared, Duchez asked, with great deference, when Bauleiter Keller would be ready for him to begin. Begin what? the young man wanted to know. Why, the papering, of course, said Duchez innocently. The arrangement had been that sometime on the Tuesday he would also paper Schnedderer's room. Bauleiter Keller would know all about it.

He waited almost half an hour while the young officer made inquiries, before the man came back and said curtly that Duchez was mistaken: the requisition showed nothing but the papering of two offices on the second floor. "It wouldn't be on the requisition," Duchez pointed out. "It was a last-minute decision of Bauleiter Schnedderer's but he certainly wrote down some details on a scrap pad."

Anxious to settle it one way or the other, the *Oberbauführer* beckoned Duchez upstairs, and within a few minutes, his heart pounding beneath his ribs, the painter was ushered back into the office where it had all started. Everything looked much the same. . . . An uncomprehending N.C.O., apparently Schnedderer's chief clerk, was brought into the argument. Soon he heard a voice asking irritably, "What is all this nonsense about wallpaper?" And Bauleiter Adalbert Keller came out of the inner office to investigate the fuss.

More explanations. More mutual incomprehension. Keller said tersely—perhaps, Duchez wondered, rather wistfully—that the budget did not permit this extra expense at the present time. But surely, Duchez said, there had been some misapprehension. He had offered to paper the room free, as a gesture of good will. Bauleiter Schnedderer had done him the honor of accepting. If his successor would be similarly gracious . . . Both the *Oberbauführer* and *Truppführer* now looked a little put out, in the manner of men who had too hastily misjudged another's motives.

Bauleiter Keller, his face wreathed in smiles, slapped the painter on the back and said in measured but execrable French, "Vous êtes un bon français."

Unfortunately, Keller said, the papering could not begin that day. He also asked how long the job would be likely to take, and Duchez, reckoning quickly, said two days. Arrangements were made for the room to be cleared of furniture when work was finished for the day, but Duchez said hastily that there was no need for that. If the furniture was just moved to the center of the room, he could cover it with his own dust sheets and work perfectly well.

At 8 A.M. on the morning of Wednesday, May 13th, Duchez moved in and started work.

At 5:30 P.M. on May 13th, Girard arrived in Caen from Le Mans. On this day, by previous arrangement, he was to contact Duchez on his way through, but on the train journey that afternoon he had no knowledge of Duchez's map or that the painter had secured a temporary job with the

Todt Organization. Nor was he aware of the complications that had arisen at the Café des Touristes in the hour before his arrival.

One or two others had drifted in that afternoon to take a hand at dominoes: Deschambres, the ginger-haired plumber, little Léon Dumis, the ex-garage proprietor, and the insurance agent, Harivel. There was no sign of Duchez. The main subject under discussion was the map that Duchez claimed to have secreted somewhere inside the building on the Avenue Bagatelle, and how to retrieve it—if it existed. In view of Duchez's talent for tall stories, the melancholy Deschambres was inclined to doubt the whole yarn. Only Léon Dumis, staunchly loyal to his friend, had implicit faith.

The quiet authoritative Harivel drummed his fingers on the tabletop as various suggestions were talked over; none of them, it seemed to him, stood much chance of working. One idea, an agent dressed as a German officer walking in to retrieve the map, seemed feasible, but only just. A shadow fell across their table and instinctively they froze, lowering their voices, but it was only "Albert," the elderly German captain. Stripping off his heavy greatcoat, the German hung it on a coat stand, ordered a cognac and sat down a few tables away.

These three were not anticipating Girard, and toward five they were on the point of adjourning the meeting when Duchez ambled in.

Harivel was intrigued by the persistent buzz of rumors about Duchez's map, but he had heard the painter's gay fabrications before. He thought that they had better hear what Duchez had to say, and sat down again. "We might as well play another hand," he said. "Deschambres, I'll take you on." They nodded amiably to the painter, but, perhaps because of "Albert's" presence, Duchez seemed in no hurry to join them. He ordered a calvados from Paul's wife behind the zinc, hung his heavy paint-streaked topcoat on the coat stand, then came over to join them.

"Double-six," Deschambres said. "How is it, René, mon ami? Ça va?"

Duchez nodded amiably, said, "Ça va bien," and then, almost at once, got up again and wandered to the door. Silently the three others exchanged glances. They could not see what the painter was doing, but each man, without knowing why, could feel the tension mounting.

In the doorway Duchez was watching the Boulevard des Alliés. Across the roughly paved street, beneath the Eglise St. Pierre, the flower market spread its multicolored profusion: old peasant women, as brown as berries, were hawking wicker baskets of Easter anemones, crimson, purple and white. Duchez stayed in the doorway, like a man savoring the afternoon sun, long enough to see the black Citroën with police markings nose its way into the square, two men in raincoats and gray felt hats sitting silently in the back.

He came back into the café, humming, as he often did, loudly and discordantly. "With you in a moment, my friends," he said. "I need my cigarettes." And for a moment that awful discordant hum droned on before he joined them with a crumpled blue packet of Gauloises.

"You appear to have done a good job," Harivel said in low, conversational tones. "We have been an hour discussing how to get this German map out of that hornet's nest. Always supposing of course, that there is a map. Your move, Deschambres."

"Pass," said Deschambres.

Duchez said, almost mildly, "I have the map."

No one spoke. Deschambres's fingers remained glued to the domino board. Almost instinctively they glanced quickly at "Albert," but the *Hauptmann* had not moved. Then Harivel said in a cracked voice, "Not here, for heaven's sake? But you must get outside . . ."

"No time," said Duchez evenly. "The Gestapo are outside. There's no time to do anything now but sit tight. And play dominoes."

Harivel said carefully, "Why are they outside? Do they suspect you?"

"I don't think so. They may have followed me in a routine way, but no one seems to have missed the map yet. That's what seems so queer. Prenez garde, mes amis—here they come."

They bent diligently to their dominoes. No one could summon the courage to look up, yet Dumis swore later that he almost felt the physical presence of the car pass the door, and could distinguish the faint hiss of the tires on the paving from all the other street sounds filtering in. A voice in everyone's head was saying, "They're coming, they're coming, now, now, now . . ."

The minute crawled. It was Duchez who got up finally. He walked to the zinc, ordering another calvados. He leaned at such an angle against the bar that he could survey the whole street. At last an imperceptible nod of his head told them the Gestapo car had gone. And they relaxed, drawing a deep breath.

"Now then," Harivel said, when the painter had returned to the table, "be good enough to tell us . . ."

But this seemed to be one of Duchez's restless days. "Albert," the *Hauptmann*, having finished his drink, had risen to go. Duchez also got up, and the two men almost collided by the coat stand. Bewildered, the others saw Duchez stiffly beg "Albert's" pardon, relieve him of the Army greatcoat, which the German had lifted from the coat stand, and help him into it. Gratified, "Albert" inclined slightly from the waist, wished Paul's wife good afternoon and left the café.

Almost at once more Germans marched stolidly in to form a thick phalanx of field gray at the bar, and about five minutes later came the chunky figure of Girard, weaving among the tables. Duchez hailed him noisily: "Ça va, vieux? Que prenez-vous?" Girard accepted a cognac, sitting well forward on his chair, anxious to be gone. One more train was due to leave for Paris that day. He asked Duchez, "What have you got for me?"

Duchez beamed, enjoying the suspense. "A nice pile of dispatches from the P-1's. Things are not coming along to badly there. . . ."

Girard nodded imperturbably. These he had contracted to collect, since Himbert, the courier, was not due to visit Paris for another ten days, and Meslin had reported a backlog even of dispatches.

"And," Duchez recounted smugly, "a map of what I think are German defenses that I took from the Todt Organization."

Girard was aghast. "In the name of God, how did you get that?" Break into the place?"

Grinning, Duchez recounted the story of his coup, explaining that once Bauleiter Keller had accepted his story on the second visit, the rest had been easy. The mirror had not been moved, and the map was still in the same position as he had put it. He had worked in Keller's office all that day, and until finishing work he had not even touched the map. He concluded innocently, "Then I just put it in the cylinder that holds my paint brushes and walked out."

There was a shocked silence. Then Girard said harshly, "And you brought it here, instead of putting it in the boiler? You must be mad, raving mad. F'God's sake give it to me quickly with the other reports while there's still time."

The others had a fleeting glimpse of the thick envelope that Duchez, ignoring the Germans at the bar, passed over before Girard, not with difficulty, stuffed its bulk into his breast pocket. "The sooner I get this to Paris," he said, "the better I shall like it. And next time, for God's sake, use your head a little. If the Gestapo had come into the café and found that on you, we should have been finished."

Duchez was bland. "The Gestapo would have searched in vain, mon vieux."

"But how—?"

"The Gestapo were around a while back, so when I went to get my cigarettes, I put it in 'Albert's' pocket. I thought it would be safer in case they came in. Then, when he rose to go I played the gentleman, helped him on with his coat, and removed it again. After all, we do not want 'Albert' to get the firing squad."

He beamed at all of them with cheerful rascality. "C'est le sang-froid, my friends—c'est toujours le sang-froid."

"Your insanity is unquestionable," said Girard with a flash of anger, then grinned broadly and added, "But so also is your courage."

2

The Spy the Nazis Missed

Edward P. Morgan

*The Office of Strategic Services (OSS) was the
American intelligence organization founded shortly
after Pearl Harbor in 1942, under the direction of
General William J. Donovan. Besides its work in
collecting and evaluating intelligence, the OSS also
engaged in clandestine activities, espionage, counterespionage, paramilitary and guerrilla operations,
and political and psychological warfare. Its representatives were stationed in many of the neutral
and friendly capitals, under various covers, some
serving as diplomats. I was the OSS representative
in Switzerland and in charge of this particular
operation. The story which follows is an account
of one of our most important cases, as told by the
hero of the story, whose cover name was George
Wood, to the American newspaperman Edward P.
Morgan.*

GERALD MAYER HAD been sent to Bern from Washington in
1942 with the elastic title of "Special Assistant" to the
American Minister. He was given two assignments. The
first was to run a psychological warfare branch of the

FROM *True Magazine*, July, 1950.

Office of War Information, cooking up such projects as leaflet raids on the German lines and advising on propaganda broadcasts beamed to the Third Reich from countries other than Switzerland. In his other role Mayer worked closely with Allen Dulles, then chief of the Office of Strategic Services operations in Switzerland.

On the morning of August 23, 1943, Mayer was riffling through a stack of official mail in his office in the Legation annex in Bern when his secretary came in and said that a certain Dr. Brown was outside asking to see him. Bern at that time, like Lisbon, Madrid and other neutral capitals, was a nest of agents, counteragents and secret operatives, some as phony as rubber checks. One of Mayer's jobs was to try to sort them out. Technically, in the eyes of the neutral Swiss, both he and Dulles were potential spies themselves, breaking the law twenty-four hours a day. Tacitly, the Swiss had to turn their backs on a good deal of sleuthing by both sides. The American Legation had already given these OSS men the routine warning that if an emergency arose they should not rely on any claim to diplomatic immunity. Mayer had never heard of any Dr. Brown but he asked the secretary to show him in. "Tell him I can spare only a couple of minutes," he added.

Ceremoniously the doctor introduced himself as a friend of a banker from Basel whom Mayer remembered having met casually some months before. "It is he who has sent me to you," he said.

Then he launched into an involved explanation of his own identity. He was a German but he had long since broken with the Hitler regime and now carried citizenship papers of a certain Latin nation. "For a long time," he said, "I have been cautiously seeking a reliable contact with the Allies. I have faith in their ultimate triumph, and I should like to do what I can to hasten the victory. My motives are not entirely unselfish. I am anxious to renew the peaceful pursuits to which my prewar life was devoted."

Mayer sized his visitor up as at best a blacklisted businessman who had cultivated an approach to the Allied cause to get some funds unblocked. Switzerland swarmed with such types. Mayer was anxious to get rid of him and asked him, quite bluntly, to come to the point.

With that the doctor drew a long envelope from his inside coat pocket. He extracted several typewritten sheets from the envelope, unfolded them slowly and spread them out before Mayer on his desk. They were all in German and headed "Geheime Reichssache"—secret state document—addressed to the German Foreign Office in Berlin, and signed von Papen, Abetz and Neurath, respectively. They were copies of cables sent by these three Nazi ambassadors in Ankara, Paris and Prague to their chief in Berlin, Foreign Minister Ribbentrop.

From Paris, Abetz was relaying certain plans from the French Vichyites which might permit German agents to penetrate American and British lines in North Africa, via Algiers. Neurath was reporting on Czech morale. Despite the barbaric liquidation of the town of Lidice as a reprisal for the murder of Reinhardt Heidrich, the Nazi "hangman" of Prague, more than a year before, the Germans feared Czech resistance had not been crushed; the capital was restive again. Von Papen, from his strategic bailiwick in Turkey, was alerting Berlin on British attempts to sneak operatives into the Balkans via Istanbul.

If authentic, this information was obviously red hot. Trying to keep his voice casual, Mayer asked Dr. Brown where he had got the messages.

The doctor fixed him with a steady gaze. "There is more from the same source," he replied in a low voice. "I am merely acting as an emissary for a friend who works in the Auswaertige Amt [Foreign Office]. This man is here now in Bern. He arrived yesterday as a special diplomatic courier. That was the 'cover' which he used for travel. Actually he came with the avowed intention of effecting a liaison with the Allies. I have known him for years. I can assure you he is one hundred percent anti-Nazi and is determined to work actively against Hitler, at his own peril. He wants to meet you, personally. As proof of his good will he sends you this data. He has much more information he wishes to give you."

Mayer asked Dr. Brown to wait in the anteroom, and excused himself. He bolted upstairs to Dulles' office. Quickly he told Dulles what had happened and showed him the documents. The prospect of establishing a contact in the heart of Berlin, right in the Foreign Office, finding, as it were, a key to the top drawer of Nazi secrets, was too preposterous. This must be a trap.

"There are three possibilities," Dulles said. "This could be an attempt to break our code. The Germans figure we'll bite, cipher this stuff and radio it to Washington. They monitor everything, including Swiss commercial wireless channels. They'll be listening for these dispatches, in hope that a foreknowledge of the contents will give them the clue they need to decipher it. Or perhaps our friend is an *agent provocateur*. He plants the information with us and then tips off the Swiss police that we are spying. His rendezvous with us is proof and we are kicked out of the country. Still, there is just the glimmer of a chance that this man is on the square."

Mayer said he was keen to follow the glimmer, despite the odds. There was something about the doctor that had impressed him. Despite his overly consequential manner, he seemed to be genuine. So Dulles agreed that they should pursue the game at least until they could see the courier and size him up firsthand.

Mayer hurried down and told Dr. Brown that he was ready to meet the courier that evening. "Make it my house at midnight," Mayer found himself saying, as if he were arranging a rendezvous with Dr. Fu Manchu. As it happened, the courier was to dine that evening with a colleague at the German Legation. He and Dr. Brown could meet afterward and go to Mayer's apartment together. Dulles was to join them, incognito, at 12:30. Mayer lived in an apartment house on the River Aare in the Kirchenfeld district, the middle of the diplomatic colony. He drew the doctor a map so he could find his way without having to inquire and arouse unnecessary suspicion. Then the doctor left.

At that stage of the war, Switzerland was an isolated island in a belligerent sea. The country was completely surrounded by Nazi-or-Fascist-occupied territory. In some respects the Legation in Bern was more out of touch with home than troops in the field were. The only regular contact the Legation had with Washington was via the Swiss radio. Through a phenomenal gentleman of Moorish extraction nicknamed "The Spider" it was possible occasionally to pass something out to Lisbon, but this was a sporadic and unreliable route. And, as it became progressively harder to move around and gather information, the need for new sources became more urgent. There were unceasing queries from Washington. With Mussolini toppled from his Roman pedestal, the Italian situation was what the experts loved to call "fluid"—and the south Italy landings (which naturally, for security reasons, Bern knew nothing about in advance) were in the final planning stage. The tempo of bomb strikes on the Reich—RAF by night, USAAF by day—was just quickening to a sustained rhythm of destruction. An opportunity to get even a keyhole view of what was going on in Berlin could hardly have materialized at a more fortuitous time.

Mayer reflected on these matters as the day dragged on, and he found it difficult to address his mind to problems of psychological warfare. He dined alone that evening and then went home to the orderly loneliness of his bachelor apartment, on the floor above the suite of an assistant U.S. military attaché. He left the door of his flat ajar so his visitors would not have to ring the bell. Then he mixed himself a highball and sat down with a magazine to wait.

Punctually at midnight the door opened softly. Dr. Brown entered the room, followed by a short, stocky man in a leather jacket. He was hatless and his bald head glistened in the soft light of the room. With the doctor towering beside them, Mayer and the stranger stood there face to face, eying each other. There was no introduction. They did not shake hands. For a moment they just stood there, in silence.

Then Mayer invited him to take off his jacket. Before the man did so he reached swiftly into his pocket. Mayer was unarmed and for a dizzy instant he wondered if he could rouse the Army officer below him if his visitor pulled a gun. But the German brought out a large brown envelope, its flap open. There was the stamp of a swastika on the dark red wax which had sealed it.

"Dr. Brown has told you that I had more material," he said, in Berlin German, without preliminaries. "You will find here, if I remember rightly, one hundred eighty-six separate items of information." And he laid the bundle on a low table in front of a divan.

Mayer examined the packet. It contained reports of German troop morale on the Russian front, an inventory of damage inflicted by underground saboteurs in France, memoirs of visits by the Japanese ambassador and other miscellaneous officials to Ribbentrop. Most of the papers appeared to be verbatim copies of decoded telegrams sent to the German Foreign Office. Some were notes in meticulous German script; some were filled with hastily scrawled shorthand notes. Each fragment of information would fit neatly somewhere in the vast, never finished mosaic of strategic and tactical intelligence we were collecting on Hitler's dwindling Reich.

As Mayer was scanning this material, Dulles came in, and was introduced as Mr. Douglas, Mayer's associate. Mayer poured highballs for the four of them. But nobody relaxed. The suspicion which had invaded the room seemed to emit waves of tension from the shadows, charging their conversation with rigid formality: the two Germans endeavoring with a kind of desperate dignity to dissolve their identity as enemies; the two Americans incredulous, challenging. They talked in German.

"You gentlemen will ask whether these dispatches are authentic and if so how I was able to get them," the courier said. "They came from material which crossed my own desk in the Foreign Office."

He explained that he worked as an assistant to a Dr. Karl Ritter, who was the Auswaertige Amt liaison officer with all the German armed services. Ritter dealt not only with cables and documents arriving by pouch from German missions abroad, but with war plans, secrets of submarine warfare, moves of the Army, including military government in occupied territories, and the activities of Goering's Luftwaffe.

"My job," the courier went on, "is to sift this information to arrange its priority of importance before it reaches Ritter's desk for action."

Mayer and Dulles exchanged glances. Ritter was well known to them. As German Ambassador in Rio de Janeiro he had once been one of the most active and dangerous principals in the huge Nazi spy network in Latin America. He was a cold, shrewd and ruthless operator. His own defection or the spectacle of his having anybody but the most loyal Nazi fanatic as an aide seemed equally unthinkable.

"How long have you had this position?" Mayer asked.

"Three years," came the crisp reply. "I tried long ago to get out of Germany on a mission such as this but one has to be patient. However, I have been in the Foreign Service nearly twenty years, long before the Nazis ever came to power, and I have acquired a certain experience." He squared his shoulders as he said this and there was a defiant ring of pride in his voice.

"From the first day I found myself in touch with Nazi secrets, I knew I would have to find a way, somehow, to get them out," he said. "I tried, before Pearl Harbor, to reach certain Americans in Berlin through church sources, but this failed. One had to move like a snail. Months went by without my being able to do a thing. It became obvious that the only way to make a satisfactory contact would be on neutral territory. Switzerland seemed the best place. I knew the country. I had friends there, foremost among them Dr. Brown. It would be a short trip. But I would have to furnish a valid reason for an exit permit."

He decided to attempt the most innocent gesture first. Nazis not infrequently managed excursions to certain spots outside the Reich for a rest. He was not a party member; but a tired government official was entitled to a little relaxation too. He applied to his superiors for permission, explaining that he would like to take a brief vacation skiing in the Swiss Alps, or Italy, it didn't really matter. He was refused. Nearly a year elapsed before he dared make another approach. (It wouldn't do to get some party underling curious about his anxiety to travel.) This time he explained it had become necessary for him to divorce his second wife, who was Swiss, and he must go to Zurich to engage an attorney for proceedings. That could wait, he was told. When eventually he volunteered as a special diplomatic courier, he was informed there were others available.

Months later, a solution materialized in the form of Fräulein Maria, a strong, acutely perceptive young woman who was assistant chief of the courier section of the Foreign Office. Her father was a Prussian nobleman. One day

Wood went to her and said quite openly, "I find I must go to Switzerland to check on certain business interests of some friends. Would it be possible for me to take the next special courier's assignment?"

"There is a pouch to be ready for Bern in about a week's time," she replied quickly, "and I think it can be arranged to have you carry it." That was the third week of August, 1943.

The exit visa came through and he made the trip to Switzerland without event. As a diplomat he was not searched; he had strapped his secrets to his leg, under his trousers. But, in a way, Bern was more dangerous than Berlin. Dark, unholy realm that it was, he knew every side street in Berlin. He had not been in the Swiss capital for years. It seemed new and strange. He had to be careful not only of camouflaged Gestapo agents but of the Swiss secret police, constantly sniffing for the odors of espionage. His movements were inhibited. He should stay only two days in Bern, three at the most. He could not seclude himself in a back-street hotel. He was obliged to stay in the Terminus on the Bahnhofplatz, where the Foreign Office ran an account, and where a room had already been booked for him. And where, certainly his movements would be watched, the people he spoke to checked, his phone calls recorded. It took hours before he was able to slip out to a public telephone, in one of those sidewalk booths that looks like a clothes closet with windows in it, and made a call to Dr. Brown which led to the rendezvous in Mayer's flat.

The Americans already knew that a tenuous German underground existed, a ghostlike web consisting of certain Army officers and civilians, divided over the crucial issue of whether they should assassinate Hitler or kidnap him and form an anti-Nazi government to sue for peace. Among the plotters were members of the old German nobility, labor leaders and politicians. This extraordinary stranger might be one of them, but to probe the possibility now would risk betrayal of information.

"We have no way of knowing," Dulles put in, "that you are not an *agent provocateur*."

"You would be naïve," the courier confessed, "if you did not suspect that. I cannot prove at this moment that I am not. If I were, however, I would hardly have been so extravagant as to bring you the contents of so many documents. Two or three would have sufficed."

He paused and cleared his throat. Dr. Brown leaned forward in his chair. "If my friend will permit me," he said, "I should like to repeat a phrase he used when he came to my hotel yesterday. He said, 'It is not enough to clench one's fist and hide it in one's pocket. The fist must be used to strike.' We drank a toast to that."

Dulles and Mayer, in spite of themselves, were becoming genuinely impressed. Still . . . Damn it, even if he were on the level, there had to be a catch. Perhaps a bargain for the release of some captured German on the grounds that he was part of the conspiracy. At least the asking price for the courier's services would be something more than carfare.

Dr. Brown smiled, as if he had been able to read their minds. "I must confess," he said, "that our first approach was to the British Legation. I am better acquainted there. But when they asked what would be involved in a financial way and I told them 'nothing,' they refused to take me seriously. They laughed and said it was a joke and not a very good one."

"What are the conditions?" Mayer asked.

The courier turned first to him and then to Dulles. "Gentlemen," he said slowly, "I hate the Nazis. To me they are the enemy. I have a similar feeling about the Bolsheviks. They both menace the world. But we are in the middle of a war and this is no time to bargain. Try to believe that I am a patriotic German with a human conscience and that there are others. All we ask as payment for our services is help and encouragement and support after the war."

"We can hardly divine now what will happen after the war," Dulles said. "It must be won first." And he reached over and knocked on the table in front of him with his knuckles.

It was past 3 A.M. The two Germans could safely stay no longer. The courier had to catch the next train back to Berlin. He explained that his second trip might have to be to Sweden. They would want time, of course, to check on his story, but then if they desired him to get in touch with the legation in Stockholm he would need an alias for identification. Nobody remembered later just how the name George Wood was invented. Perhaps it came from Dulles' symbolic drumming of the table top. Anyway, Wood it was; somehow it sounded like a good omen. This time the men shook hands, all around, and George Wood and Dr. Brown went quietly down the stairs.

Dulles and Mayer sat up till sunrise that morning poring over the data and sorting out the most urgent information. They decided to gamble, to scramble it up and code it up for a wireless to Washington. They got this message off during the day, along with a lengthy dispatch to OSS headquarters reciting the details of personal history which Wood had given them, and asking for speedy checking.

Wood himself, meanwhile, was on the train on his way back to Berlin. The ordeal of the rendezvous was over now and he settled back comfortably in a corner seat of his compartment. Although he had had only snatches of sleep since setting out from the German capital more than four days before—he'd scarcely rumpled the sheets of his bed in the Terminus—he was not tired. He felt the same exhilarating sensation he remembered having when he made his first successful ski jump after long and careful practice. To be sure, the Americans had given him no guarantee of their cooperation (actually, the OSS in Washington was to reply within a week confirming the salient facts of his history, but he was not to know of this until his next trip to Bern). And the risks ahead were even greater. But he had made the first fearsome leap after waiting for such an interminable time.

When a shudder of the train roused him hours later he saw they were pulling into Berlin. Even though it was late afternoon, he went straight to his office in the Wilhelmstrasse. He had to be back at his desk as usual if he was going to get on with his own most unusual business. He would have to be more careful than ever to protect himself now. He would have to buckle on the armor of silence even more tightly and seem to lose himself in the duties of his office. That was one of the most maddening things about the whole operation, to have to lock it all within himself and not be able to confide fully in anyone the details of his secret task. He had acquaintances and friends who, he knew, were resisting the Nazis in their own way, but rarely did they dare invade one another's field to coordinate their conspiracies.

While the bombings of Berlin had been getting sharper, the city was still quite normal. Yet, as he crossed town this afternoon, Wood observed a spectral grayness about it he hadn't noticed before.

There was a message on his desk, marked urgent. "Report to the security officer at once," it said. Needles of apprehension stabbed at the back of his neck. Discovered already?

The security officer was a large pallid-faced man with deep-set eyes which seemed always to smoulder with suspicion, a suspicion which he could drill into a victim with a single look. When Wood entered his office, he was sitting stiffly at his desk, holding a telegram between his fingers as delicately as if it had been a tea wafer.

"You have been to Bern on a courier's mission?" he asked. His voice was cavernous.

"*Jawohl!*"

"It has come to our attention that you were absent from the Terminus Hotel virtually the entire night of August 23–24."

"That is quite correct," Wood replied with a cold smile. "One needs a little relaxation at times. You know how often one drifts around a strange city. A few drinks at a bar, a young woman . . ."

"Most indiscreet," the official cut in, "and not necessarily true."

"I confess I thought afterward I had been a little careless," Wood returned, calmly, "so I took precautions."

He extracted a slip of paper from his wallet and handed it across the desk. The security officer scanned it hastily. It was a certificate from a doctor's office in Bern stating that Wood had been given a prophylactic and a blood test on the morning of August 24.

"Very well," his inquisitor said grudgingly. "But take care how you waste your time in the future."

For several weeks Wood worked furiously at the Foreign Office. Time after time he had to watch vital but perishable information rustle through his office which he was helpless to divert to the Allies. An order for reinforcements to

Kesselring in Italy, for instance, would be known to the Fifth Army front before he could arrange another journey and get the news into the hands of Dulles and Mayer.

Despite his painstaking precautions, there was the constant danger of some unexpected event threatening to upset all his plans. One night one of his schoolday chums, heir of a wealthy family and now a lieutenant in the Army, burst into Wood's flat. He was in civilian clothes.

"Where is your uniform?" George asked him in alarm.

"I left it in the barracks," the officer replied. "I have deserted." Then he broke down and wept and implored Wood to escape with him to Switzerland. "Look," he continued pathetically, pulling a gold watch from his pocket, "this will bring enough money to get us there."

"You fool!" Wood exploded. "Don't you realize that guards and dogs patrol every foot of the frontier? It would be suicide."

He hustled the distraught lieutenant back to his quarters before he was missed, trying not to speculate on what would have happened if the police had pulled one of their frequent surprise house checks for passes and identity cards while they were in the apartment.

He spent long hours at the office. Surreptitiously while he worked he would dash off a shorthand memo about a certain document and stuff it in his pocket. Occasionally it would be his responsibility to destroy top secrets; some of these he kept until he could transcribe their contents. He never could risk leaving such evidence at home or secluded in his desk. He had to carry it with him; often he would be going about with dynamite on the papers in his pockets.

By late October he had learned of certain developments in Spain and Ireland which he thought made it imperative for him to attempt another journey. He was in luck. Another pouch was being readied and it would be for Bern again, not Stockholm. Fraülein Maria put him down for it.

The night before he left Berlin on his second trip to Bern, he was almost killed. He hated air raid shelters. Inside them he felt trapped. As a ministry official he was able to get a pass permitting him to move about during alerts. This night he had gone to say good-by to a lady friend. Then the sirens raised their hellish wail and the thunder of a heavy RAF attack shook the city as it lay starkly under the white light of the magnesium flares. The all-clear had not yet sounded when Wood walked down Unter den Linden.

He was just turning into Wilhelmstrasse when a warden ordered him to halt. "Get off the street," he said curtly. Wood produced his pass. As the warden examined it under his torch, a delayed-action bomb blew up directly in front of them, not fifty yards away, knocking them both violently to the ground. After some seconds they staggered to their feet, stunned, drenched with particles of debris, but unhurt. Wood politely expressed his gratitude to the warden for having stopped him, gave him one of the few Havana cigars he happened to have left from his previous trip to Switzerland, and walked on past the crater to the Foreign Office to finish some work.

In his preparations for the journey, Wood had followed the same careful routine that he had worked out in August, adding one ingenious variation. He didn't like the idea of strapping his own secrets to his leg. It was both dangerous and undignified. He knew that special courier pouches were not weighed. They were usually no more than a single large envelope with documents sealed inside. The morning after the raid, when Maria handed him the envelope, he took it back to his office and placed it in a wide shallow drawer in his desk. Using the drawer as a shield he slipped the packet into a larger official envelope. Then he quickly drew from his pocket the secret material he had gathered for his mission and enclosed that with the legation packet in the larger envelope. Now he sealed it, in the same way the other had been sealed, with wax and the official steel stamp bearing the swastika. Instead of a trunk with a false bottom, he had an envelope pouch with a false top.

He left Berlin from the Anhalter Bahnhof in the early evening. Ordinarily the train trip to Bern took eighteen hours but now air raids sometimes made it a nightmare that dragged on for days. As soon as he could, he drew the attendant of his car aside and, handing him a handsome tip, requested to be among the first warned if there was an alert. He was terrified of raids, he explained apologetically, and the attendant's courtesy would reassure him. Actually, the warning would give him time to dispose of his incriminating enclosures if danger seemed criticial.

It must have been about four in the morning when the porter rapped sharply on the door of his compartment. "Blue alert, sir," he said and hurried on. That meant an attack was imminent. The train had stopped. Wood had kept his clothes on; now he grabbed the pouch and his small handbag and darted out the vestibule door down to the graveled fairway edging the tracks. They were in a wooded section, somewhere, he guessed, between Frankfurt and Karlsruhe. A remnant chip of moon made the rails shine. Other passengers began scrambling out of the coaches. A baby cried. A man's voice cursed harshly; he couldn't find his suitcase in the darkness. Wood slipped down into a ditch behind the train, beside the right-of-way.

From far off he heard a rising hum. It blossomed into a roar of engines and abruptly the raider was upon the train, a maverick Mosquito bomber, swooping low and lacing tracer machine gun bullets at the locomotive. There was no answering ack-ack. (With rare exceptions, only the *Sonderzug*, Hitler's express train, was equipped with anti-aircraft guns.) The plane was gone. Suddenly around a curve of the track ahead there was a flash and the great enveloping thud of an explosion. The plane had planted a bomb on a trestle. It was not a square hit but daylight revealed a twisted, impassable track. It was late the next afternoon before another train chuffed up to the other side of the trestle and the stranded passengers could make their way to it through the gulch to resume their journey. There were no more attacks but this one had put Wood nearly a day behind schedule.

At Basel, both German and Swiss customs had to be cleared in the Badischer Bahnhof in the German enclave of the city. Despite his well-schooled courage, Wood invariably felt the cold hands of fear clutching his bowels as he crossed a frontier. His heart pounded, sometimes so hard he thought it would make his coat flutter. He felt the same flat panic today. A voice kept repeating inside him as he went through the barriers, "You have something here which if found could hang you." One customs man seemed to be regarding him oddly. Did he suspect? Outwardly, Wood was steady, his gaze as cold as a mackerel's. He kept the pouch in plain sight. The official glared at him, nodded and motioned him on. He was clear.

He hurried into the men's room of the station and locked himself in a toilet. He tore off the outer envelope of the pouch and tucked his own documents in his coat. He burned the extra envelope and flushed the ashes down the bowl. Then he took a taxi across the Rhine to the Schweizer Bundes Bahnhof, where he caught the train to Bern.

Wood delivered the legation envelope first and then telephoned Dr. Brown that he had arrived. Over a beer two hours later the doctor informed him that the Americans had been anxiously awaiting his return and wanted to see him that night. Mayer would pick him up on the Kirchenfeld bridge over the Aare at 11:30 P.M. in his car, a British Triumph.

The signal arranged for identification in the blackout was the pair of blue running lights on the Triumph's fenders. When he reached the middle of the bridge, Mayer switched them on. Wood darted out of a shadow along the railing and hopped in.

"It's mighty good to see that you've made it again," Mayer said. "We are going to Dulles' house but we must go separately." He drove to a footpath along the river bank where he let Wood out after directing him how to reach the house through the garden. Then he drove off and returned to the house from another direction. A few minutes later in the seclusion of Dulles' study, Wood was displaying the fruits of his second mission.

The German Legation in Dublin had been operating a secret radio station, menacing Allied shipping. After sharp State Department protests the Irish Government silenced it by taking custody of a vital piece of the equipment. Now Wood produced a cable showing the minister was attempting to smuggle in a duplicate part.

In a new move to combat French resistance, Ambassador Abetz had forwarded a plan invented by Laval calling for the arrest and possible execution of relatives of soldiers in the de Gaulle forces.

There was a cable from the German Embassy in Madrid stating in effect that "shipments of oranges will continue to arrive on schedule." Wood had discovered that Franco was cunningly breaking a pledge to the Allies, by smuggling tungsten—for tempering steel—into Germany in orange crates.

The most alarming item was a message from the German Embassy in Buenos Aires which had arrived in Berlin just before Wood left. It reported the impending departure of a large convoy from a U.S. Atlantic port.

The German and the two Americans were not to know until long afterward the effect of the intelligence they had dealt with behind drawn blinds in Bern that night, but it was little short of profound. Among other things, a convoy's schedule was altered in time to miss a submarine rendezvous, and an Anglo-American petroleum embargo was slapped on Spain as a reprisal for the tungsten smuggling.

Wood explained that to fill in the blank spaces between his visits he would occasionally try to get coded messages out via third parties, who would deliver them as innocent-looking family greetings to a brother-in-law of Dr. Brown in Zurich. He showed Mayer the key to an intricate cipher he had devised one evening while listening to Furtwaengler conduct a symphony in Berlin. "Sometimes I can think best when I am listening to music," he said.

He had also figured out how they could signal him to confirm receipt of information by this third-party circuit. "Through contacts of his own," he said, "Dr. Brown can arrange to have food parcels sent me, sardines, butter, coffee and the like. Have these mailed at regular intervals. But only include the coffee when you have received something; then I will know my message got through."

Before Wood departed he made two more requests: he wanted a small powerful camera capable of handling microfilm, and a gun. "Photographing documents will save a lot of time," he said. "I can send you or bring you the undeveloped rolls."

Mayer managed to get him the camera next day but he objected that a gun would only compound his jeopardy if he was caught. "Never mind," Wood laughed as they shook hands in farewell. "I will get one later in Germany. I won't shoot the Wehrmacht with it. I will use it only in an emergency—on myself."

As winter came, only a few of Dr. Brown's food packages had to be dispatched without the confirming consignment of coffee. Wood discovered an old colleague who had worked with him in the service in Spain and was now a regular courier. There were some people in the government whose sentiments were anti-Nazi but who were afraid to do anything; others dared participate in nothing more than vicarious opposition, a sort of keeping the right hand from knowing what the left hand was doing technique. Even they had their usefulness. The courier was willing to carry an occasional note of greeting to the Zurich "brother-in-law." Assistance also came from an eccentric in the Foreign Office named Werner, who after repeated difficulties with the Nazis managed through his seniority to get a semi-retirement status. He moved as far out of sight as possible, to a small mountain Hütte in the Bavarian Alps near the Swiss border above Lake Constance. Werner found a way to pass an occasional message along, taking care never to inquire about contents or destination. He was to provide a port in the storm for Wood, later on.

On one occasion, Wood succeeded in spiriting out a roll of microfilm in a watch case. It had become next to impossible for civilians to get things like watches repaired in Germany, so there was nothing particularly bizarre in Wood's request to his courier friend to leave the watch with the in-law in Zurich to be fixed.

The secret circuit from Berlin to Bern became heavily laden with important news. Washington and London were burning to get German war plant production figures in order to gauge the effectiveness of the air war. Wood was able, not once but several times, to transmit to Bern condensations of the latest surveys on industry, together with soundings on public morale under the bombings.

One day Bern got an urgent message from Washington ordering a concentration on intelligence about the Japanese. It was impossible to guess when Wood might show up again and it was folly to try to send him a coded message. Mayer hit upon an idea. He simply had a contact in Zurich mail Wood an open postal card. "Dear Friend," it read, "perhaps you remember my little son. His birthday is coming soon and I wanted to get him some of those clever Japanese toys with which the shops here used to be full, but I can find none. I wonder if there might be some left in Berlin. . . ."

Wood himself arrived in Bern shortly after that, bringing extensive data on the Japanese, including the battle order of the Imperial fleet, which, it turned out, the U.S. Navy was able to use in confirming that it had correctly broken the Jap code.

Long before the spring of 1944, evidence began reaching Bern from various sources in Germany making it appear that a real conspiracy to do away with Hitler was building up in the shadowy pockets of the German underground. Wood was not directly connected with the plot but a few of his friends were privy to some of the preparations, and one day in the spring of 1944 Wood came into possession of information giving a detailed description of the location and measurements of Hitler's main headquarters on the Eastern front which he was able to relay to Bern. This enlivened but did not decide the debate among Allied strategists on the possibilities and the wisdom of dropping a blockbuster on the Fuehrer's field stronghold.

Then, finally, on July 20, 1944, a one-armed colonel named von Stauffenberg planted a time bomb, concealed in a briefcase, under the map table in a flimsy wooden barracks where Hitler was holding a staff conference at this East Prussia HQ. The bomb exploded but Hitler miraculously escaped with minor wounds. The most important anti-Nazi conspiracy of the war was crushed.

Wood had not been heard from, directly or indirectly, since early June, and as the frenzied arrests and "trials" followed in the wake of the tragic failure of the bomb plot, Mayer became convinced that Wood had been caught and killed. They had no news of him actually until late September, when they received word via a traveler that he was alive. The flow of invaluable intelligence from the German Foreign Office direct to the Allies was resumed and continued till the war's end.

EDITOR'S NOTE: *I would like to add a personal reminiscence of George Wood which sheds some further light on his character, and also illustrates a rather special sort of difficulty which one can have with a highly motivated agent.*

Sometime late in 1943 or early in 1944—in any event, it was well before July 20, 1944, the date of the bomb plot against Hitler's life—George made one of his periodic visits to Switzerland. On this occasion he asked to have a private talk with me. What he proposed was both startling and disconcerting. He wanted to give up his work of snatching cables from inside the German Foreign Office so that he could secretly join the Underground as a member of the anti-Nazi resistance.

George felt that if he continued in his present work until Hitler's collapse he would be viewed as a "spy" by the new leadership which would take over in Germany. If, on the other hand, he were a recognized member of the resistance he would have political status in the new Germany.

If George carried out his plan he would have to abandon the work which had made him probably the most successful intelligence agent the Allies then had. Also, at that time, the security among the members of the resistance was at a low ebb. There was every reason to fear that Himmler and the Secret Police (SD) had already penetrated the plot against Hitler. If so, George would not only lose his special usefulness to the Allied cause, but would probably lose his life as well.

My duty in this situation was clear. I must use all my talents of persuasion to keep George on the job he was doing, where he was certainly performing the greatest service which he could render to the anti-Hitler causes. Here he was unique. There were plenty of other volunteers to join the underground resistance to Hitler, and intelligence work and this form of activist plotting do not mix.

It was not easy to persuade George, and we argued it back and forth for many hours. Finally, he agreed to stay on the job, and I breathed a sigh of relief. I promised to do everything in my power to arrange for him to join his friends in the resistance before Germany's final collapse.

3

Cicero—The Case of the Ambassador's Valet

L. C. Moyzisch

In the selection which follows, the former German intelligence officer L. C. Moyzisch, who was stationed at the German Embassy at Ankara, Turkey, during World War II, describes how the Albanian valet of the British Ambassador made contact with him in late 1943 and eventually persuaded him to purchase at a high price the papers which the valet had purloined from the Ambassador's safe and then photographed. Later in the book from which this selection has been taken, Moyzisch relates that "Cicero," as the German Intelligence Service called the Albanian, was after a while no longer able to bring the Germans high-level documents, although he was not above trying to foist off on them, still at a high price, various lesser items.

What Moyzisch did not know at the time he wrote his book, and certainly not at the time of the Cicero operation, was that the sudden inability of Cicero to lay his hands on the Ambassador's top-level dispatches resulted from the fact that Cicero's existence and activities had been revealed in the

---

FROM the book *Operation Cicero*.

German Foreign Office telegrams which George Wood, the hero of the previous piece, brought me one day early in 1944. The telegram which uncovered the German penetration to me had been sent by the German Ambassador in Turkey, Franz von Papen, to the Foreign Office in Berlin. Since both the level of the information Cicero had turned in and the amounts of cash he demanded required attention at a higher level than that of Moyzisch's intelligence bosses, none other than Ribbentrop himself, Nazi Foreign Minister, was the recipient of the von Papen telegram. It was owing to George Wood's perspicacity that, in his rapid scanning of the tremendous mass of Foreign Office material made for my benefit, he spotted this telegram as being of significance to the Allies and brought it to me in Bern.

I was startled when this particular piece popped out among the many papers Wood had delivered. Since a leak in British diplomatic security could have sorely hurt the Allied cause, I passed a copy of the telegram to my British colleague in Bern, who immediately cabled the contents to his office in London. Naturally I had warned the British that the information could be acted upon only in such a way as to protect my source. Soon afterward what appeared to be a routine inspection of the British Embassy in Ankara by British security officers resulted in some suggestions regarding the safekeeping of papers within that installation, and Cicero was suddenly cut off from his source of supply.

A further twist to the story: the Nazis paid Cicero in counterfeit pound notes, and Cicero later tried and failed to get compensation from the German Government.

THE 26TH OF October, 1943, was in appearance no different from any other day. I [Moyzisch] dealt with various routine matters. I left the office early and, as I drove home, I certainly had no suspicion that before this day was over my whole life would be changed.

I decided to go to bed early. I read for a while but soon switched off the light and was fast asleep when the telephone rang. Now it happened that my telephone had been out of order for a few days, which had been a considerable nuisance. Just before turning in, my wife and I had been grumbling because it still was not working. So when I was awakened by its insistent ringing I was not so annoyed as I might otherwise have been.

I have often wondered if, and how, Operation Cicero might have developed supposing the Ankara telephone service had taken a few more hours to repair my line and I had not been obtainable that night. I was still half asleep as I reached for the receiver. It was Frau Jenke, the wife of the First Secretary. There was a note of anxiety and urgency in her voice.

"Would you please come round to our flat at once? My husband wants to see you."

I said that I was already in bed and asked what it was all about, but was cut short by Frau Jenke.

"It's urgent. Please come immediately."

My wife had woken up too, and as I dressed we wondered what sort of a fool's errand this would turn out to be. It was probably some ridiculous signal from Berlin. That sort of thing had happened before. As I left the house I glanced at my watch. It was half past ten.

A few minutes' drive took me to the Embassy, which, on account of its German style and also because it contained several buildings, was called Alman Koy, or German village, by the Turks. The sleepy Turkish porter opened the big iron gate. A short walk brought me to where the Jenkes lived and I rang the bell. Frau Jenke opened the door herself, apologizing in a few words for having disturbed my sleep.

"My husband's gone to bed, but he would like to see you first thing in the morning." Then she pointed to the door of the drawing room. "There's a strange sort of character in there. He has something he wants to sell us. You're to talk to him and find out what it's all about. And when you go, do please remember to shut the front door after you. I've sent the servants to bed."

She disappeared, and as I stood alone in the hall I wondered whether it was really part of an attaché's duties to have conversations in the dead of night with strange characters. At any rate I was determined to make this one as brief as possible.

I went into the drawing room. The heavy curtains were drawn and the only light came from two table lamps, which made the large, well-furnished room appear more comfortable than it actually was.

In a deep armchair next to one of the table lamps a man was seated, in such a way that his face was in shadow. He sat so still that he might have been sleeping. But he was not. He got up and addressed me in French.

"Who are you?" he asked, with what seemed to me to be an anxious expression.

I told him that Jenke had instructed me to talk to him. He nodded and, judging by his expression, now fully visible in the light of the table lamp, seemed much relieved.

I guessed that he was in his early fifties. He had thick black hair, brushed straight back from his forehead, which was fairly high. His dark eyes kept darting nervously from me to the door and back again. His chin was firm, his nose small and shapeless. Not an attractive face on the whole. Later, after I'd seen a great deal of him, it occurred to me to compare his face to that of a clown without his make-up on—the face of a man accustomed to disguising his true feelings.

There was a moment's silence, probably not so long as it seemed to me, while we eyed one another. "Who on earth can he be?" I thought. "He's certainly not a member of the diplomatic corps."

I sat down and motioned him to do the same. Instead he tiptoed to the door, jerked it open, shut it silently again, and came back to resume his seat in the armchair with evident relief. At that moment he really did seem a strange sort of character.

Then, haltingly at first, and in his poor French, he began to speak: "I have an offer to make you, a proposition or whatever you call it, a proposition for the Germans. But before I tell you what it is I ask your word that whether you accept it or not you won't ever mention it to anyone except your chief. Any indiscretion on your part would make your life as worthless as mine. I'd see to that if it was the last thing I did."

As he said this he made an unpleasant but unmistakable gesture, passing his hand across his throat.

"Do you give me your word?"

"Of course I do. If I didn't know how to keep a secret I wouldn't be here now. Please be so good as to tell me what it is you want."

I made a show of looking at my wrist watch with some ostentation. He reacted at once.

"You'll have plenty of time for me once you know why I'm here. My proposition is of the utmost importance to your government. I am . . ." He hesitated, and I wondered if it was due to his difficulty in expressing himself in French or whether he wished to test my reaction. ". . . I can give you extremely secret papers, the most secret that exist."

He paused again for a moment, and then added: "They come straight from the British Embassy. Well? That would interest you, wouldn't it?"

I did my best to keep my poker face. My first thought was that he was a petty crook out for some easy money. I would have to be careful. He seemed to have guessed what I was thinking, for he said, "But I'll want money for them, a lot of money. My work, you know, is dangerous, and if I were caught . . ." He repeated the unpleasant gesture with his hand across his throat, though this time, at any rate, it was not meant for me.

"You've got funds for that sort of thing, haven't you? Or your Ambassador has? Your government would provide it. I want twenty thousand pounds, English pounds sterling."

"Nonsense," I said. "Quite out of the question. We don't dispose of such sums here. Certainly not in sterling. It would have to be something extraordinarily important to be worth anything near that price. Besides, first I'd have to see these papers of yours. Have you got them with you?"

He leaned back, so that his face was out of the light again. My eyes by now were accustomed to the dimness and I could see his expression. There was rather a superior smile on his unattractive face. I was not quite sure what to say. After all, I knew absolutely nothing about the fellow, save that he wanted an extremely large sum of money for documents which purported to come from the British Embassy. I said nothing, and he soon began to speak again.

"I'm not a fool. I've spent years preparing for this day. I've worked out all the details. Now the time has come to act. I'll tell you my terms. If you agree, very well. If you don't . . ."

He leaned forward, out into the full glare of the lamp, and with the thumb of his left hand pointed in the direction of the heavily curtained window.

". . . if you don't, then I'll see if they'd like to have my documents over there."

His thumb was pointing in the direction of the Soviet Embassy. There was a moment's silence, and then he added, hissing the words: "You see, I hate the British."

I cannot recall what exactly I said in answer to the proposition, but I do remember that at this moment, for the first time, it occurred to me that the man might not be a crook after all. A fanatic perhaps? Yet he was asking for a very great deal of money.

I offered him a cigarette, which he accepted gratefully, taking a few deep pulls and then stubbing it out. He rose and went to the door once again to make sure that there was no one listening. Then he turned back and planted himself squarely in front of me. I got up too.

"You'd like to know who I am, wouldn't you? My name is quite unimportant and has no bearing. Perhaps I'll tell you what I do, but first listen to me. I'll give you three days to consider my proposition. You'll have to see your chief, and he'll probably have to get in touch with Berlin. On the 30th of October, at three in the afternoon, I'll telephone you at your office and ask you if you've received a letter for me. I'll call myself Pierre. If you say no, you'll never see me again. If you say yes, it'll mean that you've accepted my offer. In that case I'll come to see you again at ten o'clock on the evening of the same day. Not here though. We'll have to arrange some other meeting place. You'll then receive from me two rolls of film, containing photographs of British secret documents. I'll receive from you the sum of twenty thousand pounds in bank notes. You'll be risking twenty thousand pounds, but I'll have risked my life. Should you approve of my first delivery you can have more. For each subsequent roll of film I'll want fifteen thousand pounds. Well?"

I was inclined to think that the offer might be genuine, but I was convinced that, in view of the exorbitant price he was asking, nothing could come of it, particularly since he seemed to expect us to buy the papers sight unseen. I made a mental note to stress the inordinate risk in the memo that I would have to write about all this. I was certain the offer would be turned down.

Nevertheless we agreed that he should telephone me at my office on the 30th day of October at three o'clock. We also agreed that in the event of his offer being accepted we would meet near the tool shed at the end of the embassy garden.

After these details had been arranged he asked me to switch out all the lights in the hall and on the stairs. He wished to leave the house in complete darkness. I complied with his request. When I came back to the drawing room he had put on his overcoat and his hat, which was pulled down low over his eyes. It was past midnight by now.

I stood at the door to let him pass. He suddenly gripped my arm, and whispered in my ear: "You'd like to know who I am? I'm the British Ambassador's valet."

Without awaiting my reaction to this he stepped out into the darkness.

Thus ended my first meeting with the man, who, a few days later, was given the code name of Cicero.

I switched out the lights in the drawing room and left the Jenkes' house. Walking through the Embassy garden I couldn't help wondering how the man whom Frau Jenke had called a strange sort of character had managed to find his way out in a pitch-dark and unfamiliar place. I left my car where I had parked it and walked home through the cool, starlit night.

At home I found everybody fast asleep but try as I might I could not get to sleep again myself.

The next morning I had a slight headache and that dry feeling that comes after a sleepless night. By daylight and in the slightly jaundiced frame of mind in which I found myself, the business of the night before seemed grotesque. I was inclined to revert to my original impression that the man was nothing but a trickster out to put one over on the gullible Germans.

Taken at its face value the offer was, of course, quite fantastic. On the other hand it was just possible that this might after all be the "hot stuff" that they were so imperiously demanding in Berlin.

After a long soak in my tub and some strong coffee I began to feel better. Besides, I told myself, there was really no need for me to worry about it at all. I wouldn't have to make any decision; that was a matter for the Ambassador or, more probably, for Berlin. My job was merely to report what had taken place.

I reached my office very early that morning. My secretary had not yet arrived and I was glad of the opportunity to draft my memo for the Ambassador completely undisturbed.

As I signed it I began to wonder why the mysterious visitor, who claimed to be the British Ambassador's valet, had gone to Jenke. But then, of course, all Ankara knew that Jenke was Ribbentrop's brother-in-law. That might explain it. I did not have to wait long, though, to discover the real reason, which was to go a long way toward dispersing my doubts about the genuineness of the man's offer. While I waited for the Ambassador to arrive Herr Jenke telephoned and asked me to come over. Unlike me, both Herr and Frau Jenke had passed a very good night.

I sat down at table with them. I could see that Jenke was consumed with curiosity about the events of the night before, though of course he could say nothing while the servant was in the room. She seemed to take forever, passing around coffee and rolls, while we did our best to make casual conversation. Jenke's evident impatience amused me. I felt that it was a slight revenge for my sleepless night. When at long last the servant had gone out I turned to Frau Jenke.

"That strange sort of character of yours—he had a most remarkable offer to make."

"I know," Jenke interrupted. "I had a few words with him before you arrived. I thought you were the best man to deal with him. In my position I have to be careful about getting involved in anything of that sort. His offer seemed, to put it mildly, somewhat unusual; just the sort of thing for which efficient young attachés are employed. In the diplomatic service, as you know, there are only two perfect jobs, that of attaché and that of being the First Secretary's wife. They can do things we others can't. Provided, of course, they don't get caught."

We all laughed, and the First Secretary's wife and I clinked our coffee cups together. Then I said to Jenke, "So you met the man. Why do you think he picked on you?"

"I've met the man all right, and he knows me too," said Jenke. "Some six or seven years ago, that was before I joined the diplomatic service, he worked for a while in our house. I haven't seen him since. I can't remember his name, but I did recognize his face when he came here last night. What's he after? I suppose he wants money?"

"He most certainly does," I said. "To be exact he wants twenty thousand pounds sterling."

"What!" Herr and Frau Jenke exclaimed together. "Twenty thousand pounds!"

I nodded, but before I could tell them more the telephone rang. I had asked for an appointment with the Ambassador as soon as he came in. He would see me now. Jenke came along too.

We entered Herr von Papen's office together. It was a large room on the first floor, simply and tastefully furnished, with fine pictures on the walls. Behind his big desk sat the Ambassador, gray-haired but still very handsome. He gazed at me with his striking blue eyes.

"Well, gentlemen, what have you been up to?"

"Last night," I said, "in Herr Jenke's house, I had a most remarkable conversation with the British Ambassador's valet."

"With whom?" asked Herr von Papen.

I repeated what I had said and handed him my memo. He put on his spectacles and, as he read, glanced at me once or twice over the top of them, which gave his serious face a strangely puckish expression. When he had finished reading he pushed the paper to the far side of his desk, as if he wanted instinctively to have nothing to do with its contents. He got up, went to the window, opened it, and still without a word stood staring out over the open country to the line of mountains rising blue in the far distance. At last he turned toward us.

"What sort of valets do we employ in our Embassy?"

I looked at the Ambassador and then at Herr Jenke. No one said anything.

"What are we to do, sir?" I asked finally.

"I don't know. In any case the sum mentioned is far too large for us to be in a position to decide the matter here. Draft a signal for Berlin and bring it to me personally. I'll have another word with you then."

I went to my office, leaving Jenke with the Ambassador. When half an hour later I came back, Herr von Papen was alone. I held the draft of the signal in my hand.

"You realize what might be behind all this?" the Ambassador asked.

"Well, sir, I suppose it might be a trap. They could let us have some documents, even genuine ones, and then bluff us later on with a bogus one. Even at best, that is if the man is genuine and it's not a British trap, we'd be involved in a most unpleasant scandal if the story ever came out."

"What impression did the man make on you personally?"

"Not a particularly good one, sir, though by the end of the conversation I was inclined to believe his tale. He struck me as unscrupulous enough, and his hatred of the British, unless it's put on, would be an additional motive, quite apart from his obvious desire for money. On the whole he didn't strike me as an ordinary crook. Of course all this is mere conjecture on my part."

"What do you think the British would do if one of our people made them a comparable offer?"

"I think they'd undoubtedly accept it, sir. In time of war no nation could afford to turn down such a proposition. In peacetime it would probably be better diplomatic business to do the gentlemanly thing and inform the British Ambassador rather than get involved with stolen documents. But in time of war, sir . . ."

The Ambassador reached for my draft signal and read it carefully. Then he took his green pencil—green was the Ambassador's color, and no one else at the Embassy, when signing documents or initialing files, was allowed to use it—and made a few small amendments, reread the text, and finally signed it. Then he pushed it over to me. The piece of paper had now become an official document.

"Read it to me again," he said.
I did so:

> TO THE REICH FOREIGN MINISTER, PERSONAL.
> MOST SECRET.
> WE HAVE OFFER OF BRITISH EMBASSY EMPLOYEE ALLEGED TO
> BE BRITISH AMBASSADOR'S VALET TO PROCURE PHOTOGRAPHS
> OF TOP SECRET ORIGINAL DOCUMENTS. FOR FIRST DELIVERY
> ON OCTOBER 30TH TWENTY THOUSAND POUNDS STERLING IN
> BANK NOTES ARE DEMANDED. FIFTEEN THOUSAND POUNDS
> FOR ANY FURTHER ROLL OF FILMS. PLEASE ADVISE WHETHER
> OFFER CAN BE ACCEPTED. IF SO SUM REQUIRED MUST BE
> DISPATCHED BY SPECIAL COURIER TO ARRIVE HERE NOT LATER
> THAN OCTOBER 30. ALLEGED VALET WAS EMPLOYED SEVERAL
> YEARS AGO BY FIRST SECRETARY OTHERWISE NOTHING MUCH
> KNOWN HERE. PAPEN.

This signal was coded at once and dispatched by wireless
before noon on October 27. It was on Ribbentrop's desk
within the hour.

Nothing happened on October 27 or 28 and by the evening of that day I was convinced that the Foreign Minister,
if he deigned to answer at all, would decide in the negative.
It had happened more than once that the Ambassador's
suggestions had been turned down merely because they
came from him, including some that might have gone a
long way to help our country's cause. The animosity between the Reich Foreign Minister and the Chancellor of
pre-Hitler Germany was unbridgeable, and once Ribbentrop's enmity was aroused it was difficult enough, at the
best of times and in the most straightforward matters, to
get a clear-cut decision out of him. In these circumstances
we were all of us practically certain that Berlin would say no.

The twenty-eighth October was the eve of a great Turkish national festival and that night all Ankara was floodlit.

On the twenty-ninth I had almost forgotten about the
answer that we were still awaiting from Berlin. When we
did give it a thought we took it absolutely for granted that
the offer would be rejected. Besides, that day there was
little time to think about anything except the routine business on hand. Apart from the numerous functions connected with the Turkish national festival and the official

gatherings to be attended, it also happened to be von Papen's birthday, so we too had a reception at the Embassy in the morning and a dinner at night. All this meant much work for us.

After the morning reception at our Embassy, attended by all nonenemy envoys and numerous Turkish friends, the entire diplomatic corps had to go to a reception given by the Turkish President in the building of the National Assembly. These extremely official functions were attended by friend and foe alike, but our tactful hosts saw to it that opposite camps never met in the same anteroom. On this occasion, however, there must have been some hitch in the usual arrangements. Wearing diplomatic uniform with orders and decorations and with the Ambassador leading us we had all gone forward individually to meet the Turkish President. A few moments later as we left the reception room I almost collided with a distinguished-looking elderly gentleman in full-dress uniform. I did not recognize him immediately, but I soon realized that it was the British Ambassador, who, at the head of the British mission, was entering the hall while the tail of the German one was still leaving.

I stepped aside at once. But as I made my way to the door I had to pass a long row of British diplomats who, I felt, rightly or wrongly, looked at me in a somewhat hostile manner. This was the last big reception of the Turkish President's to be attended by diplomatic representatives of the Third Reich. By that time next year we had all been interned and Germans no longer stood in the way of the British in Turkey.

In the early afternoon there was a military parade on the race course. The diplomatic boxes were fully occupied, with friend and foe once again tactfully separated. Only the few remaining neutrals could move about at will.

It was a curious sort of existence, being a diplomat in wartime Ankara. On the one hand the pretense of peaceful trivialities and diplomatic courtesy had to be kept up in a world torn by war. On the other hand the correct appearance of enmity had also to be maintained. Yet at home I still drank good Scotch whisky, while my enemy colleagues enjoyed equally good German hock. Indian curry powder and Hungarian paprika were popular objects of international barter, all this of course being done through the Turkish servants. Being neutrals, they were in the enviable position of being able to keep up diplomatic and business relations with both sides.

I could not help thinking of these pleasing human touches, as I watched the magnificent military spectacle that had been arranged by our hosts for both our and our enemies' special benefit. Barely five yards away from where I sat the enemy camp began. There were many frank and agreeable faces to be seen among them. But it was better not to look at them. Apart from being incorrect, it could only lead to confusion in one's own mind. They were the enemy and that was that.

When, after the parade, I returned to the Embassy, I found a message that the Ambassador wished to see me at once. I went to his office, where, without a word, he handed me a decoded signal. I read:

> TO AMBASSADOR VON PAPEN, PERSONAL
> MOST SECRET.
> BRITISH VALET'S OFFER TO BE ACCEPTED TAKING EVERY PRE-
> CAUTION. SPECIAL COURIER ARRIVING ANKARA 30TH BEFORE
> NOON. EXPECT IMMEDIATE REPORT AFTER DELIVERY OF DOCU-
> MENTS. RIBBENTROP.

The matter had been decided for us.

On October 30, at 3 P.M. sharp, the telephone rang in my office. I think my heart skipped a beat as I snatched for the receiver. The voice at the other end sounded faint and far away.

"Pierre here. Bonjour, monsieur. Have you got my letters?"

"Yes."

"I'll see you tonight. Au revoir!"

He hung up. I could distinctly hear the click at his end. My secretary was looking at me with surprise. I had grabbed the receiver from her hand when she was about to answer the call. There was an unspoken reproach in her eyes. She guessed that there was some sort of secret in which she was not allowed to share.

I asked to see the Ambassador. After a minute or two Fräulein Rose, his secretary, rang through to say he was awaiting me. I went in at once.

"The valet's just telephoned, sir. I'm meeting him at ten tonight."

"Take care, my boy, not to let him fool you. Between you and me I don't care for this business at all. Above all we can't afford any sort of scandal here. You have my instructions to go ahead, of course. But you must realize that if anything should go wrong, for example if there should be any scandal, I'm afraid I shan't be able to protect you, and in fact I'd probably have to disclaim all knowledge of what you were doing. Let me warn you to be particularly careful about not mentioning this to anyone, *anyone*. No one must know anything about it who doesn't absolutely have to. Remember, on n'est trahi que par les siens."

"I've thought a great deal about it, sir, including the actual manner of handing over the money. I won't give it to him before I've had a chance of making sure that the stuff's genuine. Frankly, sir, I don't care for this sort of thing any more than you do. I'll do my best and I fully realize that if anything goes wrong it'll be my responsibility and mine alone. But I'm sure that we'd have been wrong if we'd turned the offer down. No one could, in wartime. The other side wouldn't. Besides, it's not as though we were dipping into the British safe. The stuff's being brought to us. Anyway, we don't even know if it'll amount to anything. It may still turn out to be a trick."

"Perhaps," said the Ambassador. "Frankly I'm not quite sure whether I'd be altogether sorry if it were. Anyway, here's the money. You'd better count it."

Herr von Papen pulled out of his middle drawer an enormous bundle of banknotes, which he pushed across the desk to me. So the Berlin courier had arrived in time. I was astonished by that mass of banknotes, consisting as it did entirely of ten, twenty- and fifty-pound notes, wrapped up in bundles. Could they not have found some of larger denomination in Berlin? To carry all this paper one would have to cram one's pockets to bursting point. Furthermore, they all seemed to be suspiciously new. Only a small proportion of them seemed ever to have been in circulation. Somehow I felt vaguely suspicious about this.

The Ambassador seemed to have guessed my thoughts. "Look altogether too new, these notes."

I shrugged my shoulders and began to count. It was twenty thousand all right. I wrapped the whole lot up in the large front page of *La République*, which was lying on the Ambassador's desk. As I was leaving, Herr von Papen accompanied me as far as the door.

"Remember, don't get me into trouble—or yourself either."

Admirable wish, I thought. Unfortunately it was not to be fulfilled.

Hugging my expensive parcel I went downstairs and across the Embassy gardens to my office. There I locked up the money in my safe.

Later that afternoon I sent for my secretary. I knew I would have to hurt her feelings, but I had no choice in the matter. I didn't intend to take even the shadow of a risk.

"By the way, would you mind letting me have the other key to the safe? I'll take care of it from now on."

She gave me an astonished look. I could see that she resented this. "Don't you trust me any more?"

"This, my dear Schnurchen, isn't a question of trusting or not trusting. It's just that events could take place which would make it necessary for me to have both keys. Believe me, the last thing I want is to hurt your feelings."

She gave me the key at once, but there was still some resentment in her expression and I felt sorry for what I had done. But I remembered von Papen's words, *on n'est trahi que par les siens*. I was not going to risk that. As a matter of fact Schnurchen got the key back a week later, when I had to go to Berlin—and after that she kept it. For technical reasons this was unavoidable. Nor did she ever, at any time or in any way, betray the great trust I placed in her.

At ten minutes to ten that evening I was back in the Embassy. I drew the curtains in my office and put out the lights in the hall, so that there was no chance of my visitor being seen from outside.

In the Embassy cellar, where we had our darkroom, the

photographer was ready. The man was an entirely trust-worthy code clerk who, in civilian life, had been a profes-sional photographer. If the valet really brought a roll of film it was to be developed at once. As it happens, I am myself an amateur photographer, but I knew little about developing. That is why in the early stages of Operation Cicero I could not avoid employing the professional, but I think I managed to keep him from knowing what it was all about. I suppose he guessed that important documents were being handled, but where they came from and what they amounted to he never learned, at least not from me.

At two minutes to ten I was standing at the end of the Embassy garden, at the appointed meeting place near the tool shed. It was a dark night though the stars were out, and it seemed to me very suitable for the purpose in hand.

It was rather cold and absolutely still. I could almost hear the beating of my own heart. I had hardly waited a minute before I saw a person approaching me. My eyes tried to pierce the darkness. Then I heard his voice, speak-ing softly: "It's me, Pierre. Tout va bien?"

We walked together from the tool shed to the Embassy in silence. At the speed I was going he must have had ex-traordinarily good eyesight to find his way without stum-bling, for there were a number of small steps, and the ground was quite unfamiliar to him. Or was it? I won-dered. Neither of us spoke a word.

We crossed the darkened hall and went into my room. When I switched on the light we were both, for the mo-ment, dazzled by the glare.

He showed no trace of nervousness now, as he had done at our first meeting a few days before. He was apparently in the best of spirits and full of confidence. As for myself, I must admit that I was a little nervous. I was by no means sure what the end of all this would be.

He spoke first: "Have you the money?"

I nodded.

He reached into his overcoat pocket and took out two rolls of film which, I could see at a glance, were 36-mm films. They lay in his open hand, but he withdrew it when I reached for them.

"First the money," he said calmly.

I went to my safe and opened it. I recall that I had a

little trouble with the combination, probably on account of my nervousness. My back was turned to him, and this added to my discomfort. It occurred to me that there was nothing to stop his knocking me on the head from behind as I was opening the safe, taking the money and vanishing. After all, there were twenty thousand pounds in the safe, besides one or two other things that would have been of considerable value to other people. When at last I had got the safe open and reached for the bundle, my hands were trembling slightly. I shut the heavy door at once, and in my hurry nearly repeated Schnurchen's mistake of catching my thumb in it.

I turned around. He stood in the same spot, his eyes fixed on the newspaper package I held, an expression of mingled curiosity and greed on his face.

This was a critical moment. I had to remain firm now in my decision not to pay him the money before I had made sure what it was I was buying. As I unwrapped the bank notes I walked over to my desk. There I counted them, aloud and very slowly. Coming a little closer he counted them with me, for I could see his lips moving when I glanced up at him.

". . . fifteen thousand . . . two-fifty . . . five hundred . . . seven-fifty . . . sixteen thousand . . ."

And so until it was done. When I had finished I rewrapped the whole lot in the sheet of newspaper. This was the decisive point.

"Give me the films," I said, putting my left hand on the money and holding out my right. He gave me both rolls, at the same time reaching out toward the bundle of notes.

"Not yet," I said. "You can have it as soon as I know what the films are like. You'll have to wait for about a quarter of an hour while I develop them. Everything's ready. The money's all here, you've seen it and counted it yourself. If you won't agree to this you can have your film back at once. Well?"

"You're very suspicious. You should have more trust in me. But all right. I'll wait here."

I felt extremely relieved. Apparently it wasn't a trick after all. For the first time I felt that maybe the whole business would turn out all right. The sight of the money and my deliberately slow counting of it had had the effect I intended. He saw himself already in possession of a fortune, and he was not going to risk it all by being stubborn. Furthermore, I realized that through the money I had a certain power over him. He seemed to have considerably more confidence in me than I had in him.

He stood there quite calmly while I locked the money back in the safe. I too had fully recovered my composure by this time. The critical moment was past.

"Cigarette?" I held out my case and he helped himself to several.

"They'll last me till you get back," he said quite coolly. He sat down and began to smoke. I locked the door from the outside, because I didn't want the night watchman coming into the room on his round. The valet must have heard the key turn but, somewhat to my surprise, he made no protest at being locked in like a prisoner. Then, with the two rolls of film in my pocket, I hurried to the darkroom where the photographer was waiting.

He had made all the necessary preparations. The developer was ready and brought to the correct temperature. He put both the films into the developing tanks. I asked him to explain all his actions to me in detail, because in future I intended to do all this myself. It took much longer than I expected.

"Is it all right to smoke?" I asked.

"Certainly, sir, so long as the films are in the developing tanks."

The photographer was busy under his safe lights. Some ten minutes later the first tank was opened. I took out the spool myself and put it in the rinsing bath and immediately afterward into the fixing bath. The second film followed.

Again some minutes passed, very slowly it seemed to me. At last the photographer said, "The first one should be ready by now."

He held one end of the film up against the viewing box.

In spite of the small size of the negatives I could clearly see the typescript. The photographs of both rolls seemed to be technically perfect. Then the two precious strips were dipped into the washing tank. I stood there watching it all impatiently. Another few minutes and we would know what it was that we were buying at such a high price.

I pegged the wet films onto a line. Now the little room was brightly lit by a hundred-watt bulb. Taking a strong magnifying glass I bent over the wet strip. I could read the writing quite clearly:

MOST SECRET.
FROM FOREIGN OFFICE TO BRITISH EMBASSY, ANGORA [*Ankara*].

That, and the fact that the document bore a very recent date, were quite enough for me.

I hurried the photographer out, locked the door carefully, and asked him to meet me there again in about fifteen minutes' time. Then I went up to my office.

When I came in Cicero was still sitting exactly as I had left him. Only the full ashtray indicated that he had been waiting for quite some time. He seemed neither impatient nor irritated. All he said was: "Well?"

Instead of answering I opened my safe, took out the bundle of notes, and handed it over to him. I also presented him with a previously prepared receipt for the amount of twenty thousand pounds sterling but this he shoved aside with an arrogant gesture. I must say that at that moment I felt slightly ridiculous.

Then he stuffed the big bundle under his coat, which he had not taken off at any time. He pulled his hat down over his eyes and turned up the collar of his overcoat. In the darkness even a close friend might have failed to recognize him.

"Au revoir, monsieur," he said. "Same time tomorrow." He gave me a curt nod and vanished into the night.

As I wrote these lines I can recall the events of that night with the greatest distinctness. Phrases come back to me that I had thought I had forgotten, but above all I can see, as clearly as if he stood before me now, the man's hunched-up figure and queer face—a study in ambition, long frustrated and now about to be realized, the face of a slave who has long dreamed of power and who at last has it in his grasp. Barely an hour before, he had entered my office a simple domestic servant; he was leaving it a wealthy man. I can still hear the curiously sneering and triumphant tone of voice in which he spoke as he left me, clutching his previous package beneath his coat.

"A demain, monsieur. A la même heure."

Looking back on it all is like remembering scenes from another life. Yet my emotions during the next few hours remain absolutely clear to me. I did not go to bed. Hour after hour, behind the locked door of my office, I read, sifted, made notes, read again. Gradually as the night wore on much that, for me, had been confused and ill-understood in international affairs was thrown into harsh light by those coldly written, secret documents. Finally, exhausted by emotion as much as by anything else, I fell asleep over my desk, where my secretary's knock at the door next morning awakened me.

First I had gone down the narrow staircase once again to the darkroom. I waited in the little room, where the narrow strips of film were still in the washing tank, until the photographer came back. He put the films into a drying cabinet. I hated being dependent on help at such a time. Yet I do not think I need have worried. I doubt very much whether the photographer had any inkling of what was going on.

The first enlargements were made. I sat in front of the apparatus, while our man explained to me about focusing, duration of exposure and the preparation of the developing and fixing solutions. With his help I managed to make quite adequate enlargements. Once I was sure I could carry on on my own I thanked him and sent him off to bed. I was glad to be alone.

The two rolls consisted of fifty-two negatives which I now proceeded to enlarge. I did the work mechanically, fairly fast. For the time being I restrained myself from studying the contents of the documents. I could see that the prints were quite clear, perfectly exposed and easily legible when enlarged.

Hours passed. It was nearly 4 A.M. by the time I had finished the job. Fifty-two enlargements lay before me, perfectly dry and glazed. I didn't feel at all tired.

Next I gave the room a thorough inspection to make sure I had not left anything lying about. Some of my first enlargements had been spoiled and there were one or two duplicates. I would have liked to burn them, but there was no fireplace, as the whole building was centrally heated and I didn't want to risk an open fire. So I tore all the duplicates up into very small pieces and flushed them down the lavatory. Then, carefully carrying the two rolls of film and the fifty-two enlargements, I went back to my room, where I locked the door behind me. I remember how much I enjoyed the first cigarette after all those hours of concentrated work. The fifty-two glossy documents lay on my desk, still unread. Now, at last, I could settle down to study them.

My astonishment grew. It seemed almost beyond the realm of possibility. Here, on my desk, were most carefully guarded secrets of the enemy, both political and military, and of incalculable value. There was nothing suspect about these documents. These were no plant. There could be no shadow of a doubt that these were the real thing. Out of the blue there had dropped into our laps the sort of papers a secret service agent might dream about for a lifetime without believing that he could ever get hold of them. Even at a glance I could see that the valet's service to the Third Reich was unbelievably important. His price had not been exorbitant.

Being accustomed to working methodically, I tried at first to arrange the photographs in order of importance. Since every one of them was so vital, it was almost impossible to give them any sort of priority and I finally decided simply to arrange them by their dates.

None of these documents was older than a fortnight at most, and the majority bore a date of the last few days. They were all signals passed between the Foreign Office in London and the British Embassy in Ankara. They included instructions, queries and answers to queries. Many of them were reports concerning political and military matters of the utmost importance. All of them bore in the top left-hand corner the imprint: TOP SECRET or MOST SECRET. Apart from the date they also showed the time at which they had been sent and received by the wireless operators. This was an important technical point, which Berlin alleged was of material help to their experts in breaking the British diplomatic cipher.

Of particular value for us were signals from the Foreign Office concerning relations and exchanges of opinion between London, Washington and Moscow. It was doubtless the extremely important position that Sir Hugh occupied, no less than the personal respect and confidence that he enjoyed in London, that led to his being so well-informed about political and military affairs. I had clear proof of this in the batch of glossy photographs on my desk.

Yet for a German those documents had a far more important and upsetting message to reveal. They clearly showed the determination, as well as the ability, of the Allies utterly to destroy the Third Reich. And that in the comparatively near future. Chance, combined with the obscure motives of Cicero, had presented us with evidence which made it perfectly clear that Nazi Germany and its leaders were heading for absolute destruction. Here, in these shiny pieces of paper, lay the writing on the wall. As I sat, hunched over my desk for hour after hour of that sleepless night, I saw the facts and the figures. This was not propaganda. The grim future that lay ahead of us was there for all to see. The power of the Allies was so enormous that more than miracles would be needed if Germany was to win the war.

Dawn had long ago broken over the solemn Anatolian plain, and still, behind my heavily curtained windows, I sat hunched over the documents. I remember wondering whether the leaders of Germany, far away in Berlin or at the Fuehrer's headquarters, would grasp the full significance of what was here revealed. If they did then there was obviously only one course left open to them.

But I was wrong. When those people finally decided that the documents were genuine, when it was finally proved to them conclusively that it wasn't a trap, they refused to see what was there so plainly shown. Our bosses used Cicero's material as a subject about which to quarrel among themselves. All they cared for was to claim the credit for what the wretched valet had done.

Otherwise Berlin remained satisfied until the end with the cheap triumph of having stolen British secret documents. Strategically, and this was strategic material, they were never used. The only practical use to which they were put was by the cipher specialists. The leaders of the Reich made no attempt to apply their extraordinary knowledge of the enemy's capabilities and intentions. It is galling to think that all the hard work we did, and the enormous strain through which we went, was ultimately quite pointless.

Technically speaking, this feat of a mere servant who had no pretensions to being an expert photographer was a superb job. His only equipment was an ordinary Leica camera, which he handled with supreme skill. In the course of his story no shot was fired, no poison administered; no human life endangered by Cicero save, of course, his own; no one was bribed, blackmailed or otherwise victimized by him, as was the case in most other great spy stories of the two world wars. Looked at dispassionately, one might say that Operation Cicero was technically almost a perfect job. Politically, in the final analysis, the British lost little through it, mainly owing to the inability of the German leaders to do anything with the vital knowledge about the enemy that was presented to them.

4

The Rise and Fall of a Soviet Agent

Edward R. F. Sheehan

*Recent newspaper accounts portrayed this as
one of the most appalling spy cases of modern
times. They point out that during the years Kim
Philby was an officer of British intelligence, from
the early days of World War II until he was fired
in 1951, he was a Soviet agent. It is to be presumed that he informed the Soviets of everything
that he could lay his hands on which was of interest to them. This would have included, among
other things, such military and political secrets of
Great Britain as he had access to as a high intelligence official, as well as the operations of the
British Intelligence Service, certain sectors of which
were under his direct personal supervision. In the
case of British operations directed against Soviet
Russia itself, at one time Philby's main responsibility, he was obviously in a position to help the
Soviets to annul or neutralize such operations and
to apprehend the agents involved in them. This
meant in practice that he could have delivered into
enemy hands people in his own employ. Any re-
straint the Soviets may have shown in this regard*

FROM *The Saturday Evening Post*, February 15, 1964.

would only have been the result of a certain care that must be taken not to drive the opponent's losses too high lest he begin to suspect that there was a leak in his own operation.

As I wrote in The Craft of Intelligence *(Harper & Row, 1963), "The Burgess-Maclean case, which broke in 1951 with the sudden flight of the two British officials to Soviet Russia, has perhaps been given too much the coloration of a defection. Also, its lurid angles have beclouded the real issues. This was no ordinary defection. The two men fled because they had timely warning from the "third man," Harold (Kim) Philby, that British security was hot on their trail. These three men in positions of trust in the British foreign service had been working for Soviet intelligence for years. All three were Communist sympathizers while students at Cambridge in the 1930s. Their value to the Soviets was increased as each served a tour of duty in the British Embassy in Washington in early 1950s. Philby's espionage activities were disclosed in 1963, shortly after he had followed the other two behind the Iron Curtain."*

Over and above the tragic consequences of his treason, it is to be noted that Philby was no homeless alien, no outsider whose roots were elsewhere, as in the case of so many spies; nor was he blackmailed, trapped, or enticed by prospects of financial gain. He belonged to the privileged and educated class of his own country. All doors were open to him. For reasons which are easy enough to state but still immensely difficult to understand, he chose treason as a way of life. It apparently satisfied his need for adventure, for self-importance beyond the normal. To what extent he was really motivated by ideological convictions after the time of his undergraduate political enthusiasms remains open to question. I would think not so much as is generally imagined. What seems to prevail in the man's make-up is a grudge against his own background, a feeling which he shared with his fellow traitors, Burgess and Maclean; a deepseated and

*twisted hostility directed against all those things
toward which ordinary people feel natural loyalties.*

HE WAS A shy man, even when he was drinking, and he
spoke with a stutter, even when he was not. He was handsome, in a sort of melancholy way, and he had charm to
burn. Men liked him. Women wanted to mother him. His
name was Harold Adrian Russell Philby, but everybody
called him "Kim"—a nickname which evoked his Kip-
lingesque boyhood in the India of the British Raj.

Kim was the Middle East correspondent for two English
weeklies, *The Observer* and *The Economist*, and I first met
him in 1958, in Beirut, shortly after I had assumed my
duties as the American press attaché. I used to enjoy
watching his entrance at cocktail parties. Into a room
crammed with chattering diplomats, foreign correspondents and Arab intellectuals he would appear hesitantly,
tentatively, looking like a letter delivered to the wrong
address. As he squeezed past me mumbling, "Ch-cheers,
old b-boy," I could catch the clove and peppermint on
his breath, and wonder at what hour of the day he had
mixed his first highball.

On the evening of January 23, 1963, Kim Philby and his
wife, Eleanor, were invited to the convivial dinner party
which Mr. Hugh Glencairn Balfour-Paul, First Secretary
of the British Embassy in Beirut, gave for a few English
and American friends interested in archaeology. Eleanor
arrived alone, explaining that her husband had telephoned
to tell her he'd "be along a little later."

She hardly tasted her food and, as the evening progressed, became visibly concerned over Kim's failure to
show up. Finally she left the party in a distraught state,
much to the puzzlement of the other guests—after all, Kim
was a working newsman, and his wife was presumably
conditioned to sudden absences. She went home to her fifth-
floor apartment on the Rue Kantari and waited up until
well after midnight. She dozed off once or twice and woke
"with a dreadful feeling I couldn't explain"—as she said
later—"that something had happened to Kim."

Was he off on a story? Kim had always been circumspect about his work—even to her. He had become quite
preoccupied in recent weeks. His moods had seemed to

alternate between sullenness and an almost hysterical gaiety, and he had been drinking more than usual.

The morning after the dinner party she called a close friend, a prominent American businessman with high government connections in Beirut. "You've got to help me find Kim," she said. The businessman immediately telephoned Colonel Tewfik Jalbout, the chief of the Lebanese secret police. Philby's name was already familiar to Colonel Jalbout for a variety of reasons.

The next day, less than forty-eight hours after the Balfour-Paul dinner party, Eleanor telephoned the American businessman and the British Embassy and called off the search. She had, she said, gone to the Normandy Hotel —her mailing address—and found a farewell letter from Kim. He was off on a news assignment and "a quick tour of the Middle East." Everything, she insisted, was all right.

Was it? Eleanor had already confided to friends that Kim's toothbrush, razor and other personal effects were untouched. Although his hasty departure was premeditated to the extent that he had had time to type out the farewell letter, he had taken nothing with him but the clothes on his back. Furthermore, Colonel Jalbout had already established that Philby had not left Lebanon by any legal route, as he would on a normal reporting assignment. Eleanor's volte-face convinced no one; indeed, it aroused even greater curiosity.

On March 3, more than a month after Philby's disappearance, *The Observer* finally announced that it had requested the Foreign Office to help track him down. By this time rumors had begun to abound. Philby was in Cairo. Philby was with the Saudi Arabians fighting the republican revolutionaries in Yemen. Philby had been abducted by British Intelligence. Philby had been kidnaped by the CIA. Philby had killed himself.

The most persistent rumor was that Philby had fled to the Soviet Union, and that a major new security scandal was in the making. For Philby was no ordinary foreign correspondent. He had been a high official of British Intelligence and had once served as First Secretary at the British Embassy in Washington. In 1955 a member of Parliament had publicly accused him of being the "third man" in the Burgess-and-Maclean case—the man who had tipped off Guy Burgess and Donald Maclean and enabled the two diplomats to flee behind the Iron Curtain before they could be arrested for spying.

In early March a pack of reporters from Britain's popular press—prying, relentless, pitiless men—descended on Eleanor Philby. She responded with a series of misleading statements.

"Kim is touring the Middle East on a news assignment," she declared.

"Why don't his newspapers know anything about it?"

"Please leave me alone."

She was acting on instructions from Kim. Already she had received a series of messages—often in his handwriting —ostensibly sent from various Middle Eastern cities and promising that they would soon be reunited. But, if she was mystified by her husband's behavior, she was horrified by the suggestion of the British that the messages had originated from behind the Iron Curtain. "I can't believe it," she said. "It isn't true. Kim is on a trip."

Then, in April, another message came in from Kim. For the first time it gave Eleanor a specific "operational plan":

1. She should purchase for herself and the two young Philby children a BOAC ticket for London for a certain date, making no attempt to hide it.

2. Next she should go inconspicuously to the Beirut office of the Czech airline, where a ticket would be waiting for her.

3. The Czech plane—bound for Prague with prior stops in Western Europe—was to leave Beirut at approximately the same time as the BOAC aircraft. She should ignore the BOAC departure announcement and join the passengers for the Czech flight. After boarding the plane with the children, she would be informed of her destination. (In other words, not until she was airborne would she know whether she would debark on the east or west side of the Iron Curtain.)

4. She was at last given a means of contacting Kim "in case of emergency." She was to place a certain flowerpot in her kitchen window and a "trusted intermediary" would contact her at once.

Kim was obviously obsessed by the desire to be with Eleanor again; Eleanor's wish for the reunion was no less ardent, but the new message conveyed the first tangible indication that Kim might be behind the Iron Curtain, and she refused to go ahead with the scheme. Torn between her love for her husband and her suspicion that he might indeed have defected, she found the next week nightmarish.

Finally, in desperation, she decided to send Kim's emergency signal. She placed the flowerpot in the kitchen window. She mixed herself a double Scotch, and lit a cigarette. She hoped that the "trusted intermediary" would come quickly. It was just beginning to get dark.

Less than an hour later the doorbell rang. She opened it to find a thickset young man with thinning blond hair. He leaned casually against the door frame and asked, in a heavy Slavic accent, "You want to see me, Mrs. Philby?"

He was an official of the Soviet Embassy.

From that moment Eleanor Philby was forced to face the fact that her husband was in the Soviet Union. How had it happened? How had Kim Philby—the son of a famous father, the beneficiary of a Westminster and Cambridge education, the recipient of a wartime decoration from the hands of King George VI—ever come to cast his lot with the enemies of his country? The answers, as assembled from the most authoritative sources—including officials in Western intelligence—abound in paradox. Kim Philby typifies the confusions and cruelties of a whole generation who grew up during an era of revolution and war. Kim was an essentially decent person who during a more compassionate period of history might have become what he most wanted to be: a hero.

He was born on New Year's Day, 1912, in Ambala, India, the only son of the late Harry St. John Bridger Philby, at that time a civil servant in the government of India and destined to become, second only to T. E. Lawrence, the most famous Arabist of this century. Within little more than a decade of Kim's birth his father had already been interior minister of Mesopotamia (now Iraq), an adviser to Winston Churchill, and chief British representative in Trans-Jordan (now Jordan); he went on to become a powerful adviser to King ibn-Saud and the explorer of the immense Empty Quarter of Arabia. He went everywhere in flowing Arab costume and in due course became a Moslem, assuming the name "Haj Abdullah."

But if St. John Philby was an intrepid pioneer, he was also an imperious egoist. He terrified Kim, whose lifelong stutter can plausibly be attributed to fear of his father. Superimposed on this childhood awe was the memory of his father's violent opinions—his contempt for the methods of British bureaucracy and his rampages against British policy in the Middle East. In 1940 he was actually imprisoned for his outspoken disapproval of the Allied war effort. From all of this emerges the first clue to Kim's subsequent behavior—he inherited his father's bitterness toward the British Establishment.

In 1931 Kim entered Cambridge's Trinity College. It is difficult for a contemporary American to grasp the depth of feeling against the Establishment which animated most of the British intellectuals of that day. Anti-patriotism was not only tolerated, it was fashionable; Marxism was not only respectable, membership in the Communist Party was considered a badge of valor.

Intelligence sources believe that Kim was recruited into the Communist Party while still at Trinity—and told to keep quiet about it. We do not know the precise details of his recruitment, but the broad outline is clear enough. Two of Kim's contemporaries at Cambridge where Donald Maclean and Guy Burgess, both convinced Marxists; he did not known Maclean well, but he became an eager disciple of Burgess. Burgess was already a historian of considerable promise, and more than one writer has described him as the most brilliant undergraduate of his generation. Moreover, he exerted an uncanny influence on practically everyone who came in contact with him; from his seemingly inexhaustible supply of acid metaphors and devastating epigrams he could effortlessly reduce his critics to ashes. In addition to his intellectual qualities Burgess was a drunk, a roustabout and an obsessed homosexual. He carried copious quantities of raw garlic around in his pockets, and munched continuously; in later life he was suspected of drug addiction.

This was the romantic "hero" who probably persuaded Kim Philby to join the party, and was, in later life, to become his nemesis.

Philby was graduated from Cambridge in 1933, traveled on the continent, became a journalist and got married.

None of his writing reflected any pro-Soviet bias—on the contrary—but his first wife, Liza, was a robust, high-spirited Polish girl and an avowed Communist. They were in Paris at the start of the Spanish Civil War in 1936, and they turned their apartment into a recruiting office for the Republican forces. Western intelligence officers believe that it was during his first marriage that Philby was drawn into the Communist espionage network, and that he spied for the Republicans while covering the Franco side for *The Times* of London. His dispatches betrayed no partisanship, however, except that he quite accurately predicted that Franco would win. In 1938 he and Liza were divorced; she is now behind the Iron Curtain and married to a Communist official.

Philby wanted to fight in World War II but his stutter precluded an officer's commission. Through friends he was appointed to a high post in Section 5 of M.I.6 (M.I.6, the military term for British Intelligence, conducts espionage and counterespionage, almost entirely overseas. M.I.5 is the domestic security service and deals with internal security and counterintelligence.) Before entering M.I.6, Philby made what was accepted as a clean breast of all his earlier Communist connections, including those of the Spanish Civil War. At a time when the Soviets were comrades-in-arms and any sort of anti-Fascism was considered patriotic, his past—what he revealed of it—was not held against him. In Section 5 of M.I.6 his particular task was to mastermind British double agents, to penetrate enemy intelligence and—ironically—to feed false information to the Soviets. He soon established a reputation for brilliance in his work.

The British Government now believes Philby had already been recruited into Soviet Intelligence and had been passing secret information to the Russians throughout the war; exactly what he told them cannot be disclosed. Since one of his official duties was maintaining liaison with Soviet Intelligence, his open and frequent contacts with them were above suspicion, and at the end of the war he received the Order of the British Empire.

Kim's star continued to rise. Indeed a number of knowledgeable people were already predicting that in due course he would become chief of British Intelligence. There is evidence that the Soviets had a long-range investment in Philby dating from his days at Cambridge—and also that they were hopefully awaiting the day when he would achieve the ultimate position in M.I.6. In 1947 he was sent to Istanbul as First Secretary of the British Embassy— ostensibly a Foreign Office official but actually engaged in intelligence work on Russia's southwestern flank. In 1949 he was transferred to Washington, where he assumed the duties of First Secretary in charge of liaison with the U.S. Government on security matters; his contacts with the State Department, the Defense Department and the CIA were frequent and close. Some U.S. officials suspect that Philby passed American secrets to the Russians when he was in Washington. Others familiar with the case consider this unlikely. They argue that, since the Soviets were now confident of Philby's rise to the highest eminence in British Intelligence, they did not want to jeopardize his chances by taking premature advantage of him; it was better to mark time, and then capitalize on his services when he could be of maximum usefulness.

At this point, in August of 1950, Guy Burgess re-entered Kim Philby's life. Burgess was dispatched to Washington as Second Secretary of the Embassy. His friendship with Kim was resumed in all its previous êlan, and soon they were a familiar pair at Georgetown cocktail parties, hob-nobbing with the famous and consuming prodigious quantities of Scotch whiskey. Burgess even moved into Philby's home, adding further confusion to a household already upset by evidence of mental instability in Philby's wife.

As time passed, Burgess's behavior, which had always been odd, became openly hysterical. He became convinced that the United States was about to embark on a third world war, and expounded this belief not only at cocktail parties but in his written reports. (Curiously, Burgess's anti-Americanism was a passion which Philby never seemed to share.) Among numerous other indiscretions, Burgess had a public row with a well-known columnist, was three times stopped for speeding, and on one occasion was involved in an automobile accident in the company of a homosexual hitchhiker with a police record. This was the last straw for Sir Oliver Franks, the British Ambassador, who forthwith implored Whitehall to take Burgess off his hands. Before this request could be acted upon, Philby found out through his liaison with the U.S. Government that the FBI suspected both Burgess and Maclean of spying for the Soviet Union. He hastened to inform his friend. Burgess left America in great haste, in April of 1951, without Embassy permission, and warned Maclean when he reached England. The understaffed British security services were watching a number of other important suspects at the time; their surveillance of Burgess and Maclean was insufficient, and within a few weeks of Burgess's return to Britain the two diplomats were able to escape to Russia.

After Burgess and Maclean had vanished, British Intelligence subjected Philby to intensive questioning about his role in the affair. He assured them that his action had amounted only to what any member of the "old boy" network of Establishment members would have done—he had passed on to Burgess the gist of a report, too ridiculous to be believed, entrusted to him by an agency—the FBI—which was known to make ludicrous allegations from time to time. Philby claimed that the FBI accusations against Burgess and Maclean were contained in a routine report reposing in a stack of other routine reports dealing in the most unsubstantiated rumors.

According to Philby, Burgess happened to come into his office just after he had read the report. Under the circumstances, Philby's explanation went, it was understandable that he blurted out to Burgess, "Can you imagine the bloody nonsense the FBI is peddling now? They're claiming you're a Soviet spy!" Philby claimed that Burgess received the news with complete calm, and joined him in incredulous laughter. But he left the Embassy early that day. When Philby returned home later he found that Burgess had cleared out, leaving the place in disarray. Philby stated he then realized that Burgess might indeed be an enemy agent, and that he immediately reported his friend's disappearance—and his own indiscretion—to the British Ambassador.

Why did Philby endanger his whole position in British Intelligence—and the possibility of one day becoming its head—by admitting that he had warned Burgess? He had no choice: he had been the only official in the Embassy to read the FBI report. He gambled that his explanation would be believed, and he was right. For when Burgess and Maclean defected, the British Embassy in Washington rallied around Philby, justifying themselves on the ground that any English gentleman would have done what he did for an old school chum. As youths, some of these men had flirted with Communism themselves; they understood Philby's background, made allowances for it, and believed its complexities were beyond American comprehension.

But the FBI and CIA were furious. "Get rid of Philby or we break off liaison on secret matters," General Walter Bedell Smith—then head of CIA—demanded. Since the Americans had the upper hand on many important secrets —nuclear research, for example—this was a threat which the British could not afford to take lightly. In June of 1951 they called Philby home and fired him.

For a year afterward he lived in near penury with his second wife and five children in his mother's house in Kensington. Handout jobs given him by old friends provided his only income. He tried his hands at hack journalism and at one point was reduced to ghostwriting a family genealogy.

Although the Americans had had their way in the Philby affair, many British officials felt that he had suffered a shocking injustice and had been crucified on the cross of McCarthyism. But, despite the complaints of McCarthyism, the inner circles of British Intelligence believed from the beginning not only that Philby was the "third man" but that he might be an outright Soviet agent. In their investigations into Philby's past they began to entertain grave misgivings about his relations with the Soviets during the war. Past intimacy with the Russians was often forgiven by British Intelligence—some of M.I.6's best officers are ex-Communists—but they realized that the circumstances surrounding Philby's indiscretion to Burgess were entirely too curious to be filed and forgotten.

While Philby wasted away several years in semi-seclusion, British Intelligence began to concoct a scheme to make the most of his case—and to use him for its own devious purposes.

Espionage is the most elusive of all criminal acts; it simply requires the culprit to collect information which he often has the legal right to possess in the first place. It is in communicating what he knows that the spy commits his crime and exposes himself to the danger of being discovered. Nevertheless, he has at his command all the subterfuges of mankind's most occult profession, and catching him is never easy. The suspect must be given every opportunity to operate in order to betray himself—and since his movements are usually inconspicuous and apparently harmless, they are often impossible to identify as espionage. Moreover, even after his movements have revealed him as a spy, it is essential to leave him alone so as to uncover the apparatus of which he is a part. After all, counterespionage services are not interested in spies; they are interested in spy networks.

The investigation of Philby, therefore, was not simply a matter of running down more evidence on the Burgess-and-Maclean case. It was necessary, British Intelligence argued, to put Philby back into action and to watch his movements. He was in no position to attempt espionage in England, so it was essential to get him to a place where the Soviets were active and where he could be of potential use to them. Why not in the Arab world? There Philby would enjoy all the prestige of his father, his own reputation as a Middle East expert, and adequate freedom of movement. In the neutralist atmosphere of the Arab countries he would be accepted socially and it would not be too difficult to find out what he was up to—if anything. In other words, British Intelligence decided to plant Philby in the Middle East—in the hope not only that he would expose himself but that he would lead them to key members of the Soviet espionage network in the Arab world.

How did M.I.6 stage-manage this obviously risky intrigue? It wasn't easy. The plan took a great deal of time to gestate—more than five years between the time Philby was dismissed from British Intelligence and the day he actually arrived in the Middle East; a premature move might have aroused his suspicion. The scheme was the subject of an intense dispute between M.I.6 and M.I.5, which wanted to keep Philby in England at all costs. There were all sorts of other problems: a private firm would have to offer Philby a job in the Middle East, and above all he must not discover that he was being used as a pawn.

M.I.6 was on the point of acting when Colonel Marcus

Lipton, a Labour Member of Parliament, rose in the Commons and accused Philby of being the "third man." On November 7, 1955, Harold Macmillan, then Foreign Secretary, replied, "No evidence has been found to show that Philby was responsible for warning Burgess or Maclean. While in government services he carried out his duties ably and conscientiously. I have no reason to conclude that Mr. Philby has at any time betrayed the interests of his country, or to identify him with the so-called 'third man,' if indeed, there was one."

When a case of suspected espionage is under investigation, candor is the last thing to expect of a government; on the contrary, evasion, if not outright mendacity, is more probable. Macmillan knew that Philby had been under grave suspicion for some time, but he exonerated him in Parliament at the specific request of British Intelligence— and at the price of great subsequent damage to his own prestige. He cleared the statement with the leaders of the Labour Opposition beforehand, however, and explained at least some of the reasons behind it. A few days later Colonel Lipton withdrew his charges against Philby, and M.I.6 was free to proceed with its plan.

The following spring a member of the Foreign Office— acting at the behest of M.I.6—approached the editors of *The Observer* and asked them to make Philby their Middle East correspondent. The highest executives of *The Observer* were made aware from the beginning that Philby was under suspicion, though nothing had been proved; they were persuaded to hire him on the grounds that they would be performing an act of patriotism in assisting British Intelligence, or at least an act of compassion in aiding a victim of McCarthyism, either way accomplishing a worthy end. (Whether the editors of *The Economist* were also taken into M.I.6's confidence is unclear; they seem to have based their willingness to hire Philby on the fact that *The Observer* had done so.) Fortunately—for the sake of the plan—Philby had already asked *The Observer* for a job, so he could hardly have considered it unusual that the editors should send him to an area where he was specially qualified. In September of 1956, in the middle of the Suez crisis, Philby embarked for Beirut.

Shortly after his arrival, a British official confided to

certain prominent British and American private citizens resident in Lebanon that Philby might have Communist connections and that any information bearing on this suspicion would be appreciated. Thus, almost from the moment that he set foot in the Middle East, Philby was under "quiet surveillance," as it was called. It actually amounted to little more than inviting Kim to cocktail parties occasionally, and in fact produced nothing. M.I.6's own spot checks also drew a blank.

One of the Americans who was asked to report on Philby was Sam Pope Brewer, then the Middle East correspondent for *The New York Times*. During 1957 and 1958 Brewer and his wife, Eleanor, saw Kim frequently. Like other members of the "quiet surveillance" team, they came to the conclusion that he was completely harmless. As a correspondent representing two highly respected journals, he had a certain justification, and plenty of opportunity, to inquire into semiconfidential British and American matters. But when he made his occasional embassy calls, he displayed no particular curiosity, and indeed never once nibbled at the pieces of bait which were discreetly dangled before him.

When he had first arrived in Beirut, Kim had made an effort to cut down on his drinking, but as time passed he reverted to his previous pattern, and he adopted a general manner of life which was the worst possible cover for a spy. "If he is a Russian spook, he can't be a very good one," one Western official remarked at the time. "If he's a Soviet agent, let's have more like him," said another. The latter sentiment was expressed after Kim had overindulged at a diplomatic dinner and pinched the bottom of the French Ambassador's wife. This is not to say that Philby was any sort of Lothario. In Beirut his only romance was with the wife of his friend Sam Pope Brewer. This was not simply a physical infatuation; Eleanor was no Aphrodite, and like Kim, she had already reached her middle forties. During the period of the romance, Kim, Eleanor and Brewer were often seen together in public. Kim was a frequent visitor at the Brewer household, and the two men went off on news assignments together. Their friendship was unceremoniously terminated on a spring morning in 1959, just before civil war exploded in Lebanon. According to close friends, the three had gathered for coffee on the terrace of the St. Georges Hotel. There, in the shadow of those splendid mountains, overlooking the velvet waters of the eastern Mediterranean, Kim made up his mind. Brewer and Eleanor were bickering. Kim, after increasing signs of nervousness, blurted out, "Eleanor, l-let's t-tell him."

"Tell me what?" Brewer asked.

"Elean-n-nor and I want to g-g-get m-married."

"You mean," Brewer exclaimed, "that you are asking for my wife's hand in marriage?"

"S-s-something l-like that."

Eleanor flew off to Mexico for a quick divorce. Philby remained in Lebanon to write about the civil war, and Brewer was soon transferred to New York.

Shortly after their wedding, Kim and Eleanor began to exchange invitations with the great and the near great of Beirut. Or rather, not so much the great as the significant —Arabists, foreign correspondents, university professors and diplomats. It was a rather glittering society they frequented, and the conversation—mostly in English, sometimes in French, and rarely in Arabic, even from the Arabs —was often as literate and amusing as any that might be heard in the salons of Paris or Mayfair. I met Kim often at these parties, and, like most of his friends, I remember him with a mixture of affection and sorrow. Once, at a party in my apartment, I tried to introduce him to two attachés from the Soviet Embassy. Kim made a horrified gesture of backing off, exclaiming, "Oh, no! I want n-nothing to do with R-Russians." This uncharacteristic outburst puzzled me and other people standing nearby, but I did not think much of it at the time. In retrospect it seems curious that Kim should have so dramatically called attention to his past. The more devious thing would have been to greet the Russians perfunctorily and then drift off.

By early autumn of 1962 virtually everyone concerned with the Philby case had decided that if he was a Soviet spy he was on the inactive list—or that, at most, he was simply having talks with the Soviets now and then on general information. At about this time, however, an incident occurred which brought the case back to life.

The incident was simply that Philby attempted to recruit

an agent into British Intelligence. He approached a prominent Arab politician, began to cultivate his friendship, and finally stuttered out the suggestion that the gentleman might be of value to Her Majesty's government "in certain ways." He was clearly making an intelligence proposition. The Arab couldn't believe his ears, but he led Philby on and got a definite offer of money out of him. It so happened that the Arab was *already* working for British Intelligence.

When the politician reported the conversation to his "case officer," M.I.6 tentatively reached a new conclusion: Philby might well be recruiting agents for the Soviet espionage network, while pretending to the recruits that they would be working for the British. Against this hypothesis many of Philby's past activities outside Lebanon—his frequent trips to Syria, Jordan and Arabia, his knowledgeability about oil-company matters and his curious mixed contacts with Saudi royalists and antiroyalists—suddenly began to add up into a malevolent pattern.

British Intelligence decided to place Philby under day-and-night surveillance. Since they were watching a dozen other people at the time, and since their own staff was small, they approached Colonel Jalbout, the chief of the Lebanese secret police, and asked his help.

They had come to the right person. Jalbout is a brilliant policeman and probably one of the world's most competent counterespionage officers. Beirut, like all the Arab capitals, literally reeks with intrigue; working without the modern equipment of the FBI and Scotland Yard, Jalbout nonetheless manages to keep himself informed on the most occult and tortured intelligence machinations of the great powers in Lebanon. In fact, the colonel already knew a great deal about Philby and had, the previous summer, inscribed him on his suspect list.

The Lebanese surveillance of Philby soon produced extraordinary results. Colonel Jalbout's forces discovered that Philby was leading a double life, moving furtively about the city to avoid surveillance, and turning up at inexplicable addresses for secret meetings with a number of suspicious personalities.

On two successive nights a member of the secret police observed Philby emerging onto the open terrace of his apartment. Kim glanced at his watch, stood there for a few minutes, glanced at his watch again, and then began waving some sort of dark object in the air.

On a hunch of his chief, the security man acquired a pair of Polaroid spectacles and returned to his post the next evening. At about midnight Philby reappeared on his veranda and commenced sending "black light" messages.

The next step was to find out who was receiving Philby's messages. His apartment building was situated on a hill, and his terrace could be seen from literally thousands of windows in Beirut, not to mention the ships at sea. Nevertheless, a sweeping search was conducted, and somehow the Lebanese apprehended a grubby little Armenian who admitted receiving Philby's messages and passing them on to another intermediary.

Unhappily, the Armenian, while he could repeat the cryptic content of Philby's messages, had no idea what they meant, nor could they be deciphered by the Lebanese secret police or the British Intelligence officers working with them. The British asked the Lebanese to imprison the Armenian for a few weeks, thereby severing Philby's line of communications and forcing him to make direct contact with his spymasters. This was tried and it worked. After nearly a month of getting no response to his messages, Philby violated the cardinal rule of espionage: He "broke security" and communicated directly with his superiors.

Late one night he left his apartment, hailed a taxi and drove to the traffic-choked night-club quarter of Beirut. He hopped out of the taxi, walked briskly to a one-way street running in the opposite direction, hailed another cab, and proceeded to a public telephone in a different section of the city. There was a brief conversation followed by additional taxi rides and highly professional attempts to thwart surveillance. His shadows persevered and pursued him to the shabby Furn-esh-Shebbak quarter of Beirut. Philby emerged from his taxi and mounted to a darkened apartment above an Armenian candy shop.

A few minutes later he was joined by an official of the Soviet Embassy—a thickset young man with thinning blond hair, the same man who later appeared at Mrs. Philby's doorstep in response to her flowerpot signal.

The details of the meeting above the Armenian candy

shop remain unknown, but the Lebanese decided not to pursue the matter any further. Colonel Jalbout concluded that Philby was engaged in an East-West intrigue that did not specifically involve Lebanon, and he needed his agents to concentrate on some twenty or thirty political suspects more directly entangled in Lebanese affairs. The British were in no mood to drop the case. Late in 1962 they decided to confront Philby with some of the suspicions against him. Philby may already have assumed he was being watched, of course, since Eleanor Philby was once a member of the "quiet surveillance" team. Now two high security officers flew in from London and questioned him in a manner which must have left him in little doubt that they knew a great deal about his clandestine life; his answers they found unconvincing, contradictory and, apparently, incriminating. The British could not arrest Philby on alien soil, however, nor could they assume that the Lebanese would extradite him; chasing around in taxis and entering Armenian candy shops at midnight did not violate any local law. Disloyalty to Great Britain is not a crime in Lebanon.

Nevertheless, Philby, by now a nervous wreck, must have realized that the game was up. What alternatives were open to him now? He was badly in need of money and had a wife and several young children to support. He was paralyzed in his writing and aware that the *Observer* and *Economist* would probably dismiss him. The choices were hardly cheerful: he could commit suicide—or run. On the evening of the Balfour-Paul dinner party he ran. His flight, though extremely hasty, was apparently voluntary. It took Colonel Jalbout some weeks to track down the witness who had observed a man answering Philby's description, in the company of two burly escorts, boarding the Russian ship *Dolmatova*. The vessel left Beirut on January 24, before dawn—destination Odessa.

After her husband had vanished, Eleanor Philby vacillated between extreme candor and secretiveness in her dealings with the British Embassy in Beirut. Not until April, when she received the "operational plan" to leave Lebanon aboard the Czech airliner, did she decide to seek British help and to keep the Embassy abreast of all her communications with Kim. In May the British and Lebanese au-

thorities arranged Eleanor's secret departure from Beirut
with the two young Philby children; Eleanor deposited the
children in England with relatives of Kim and then proceeded to New York to visit her daughter Anne, who had
returned to America to live with Brewer. When she later
returned to Britain, she was apparently on the verge of a
breakdown and went into seclusion.

On July 1, acting on the fear that the Soviets were about
to unveil Philby at a press conference in Moscow, the
British government publicly reversed its previous position
and disclosed that Philby had in truth been the "third man"
in the Burgess-Maclean affair, and that he had worked for
the Soviets "before 1946." The announcement, coming in
the wake of the Profumo scandal, sent tremors of shock
through the British Establishment. In Parliament, Prime
Minister Macmillan and Harold Wilson, leader of the Labour Party, quickly crossed swords; from the opposition
benches outraged demands for the full facts of the case
mingled with shouts that Macmillan was a rogue or a
fool or both. The Prime Minister—his lips sealed in loyalty
to his intelligence services—could only reply that "I hope
the House will realize the danger of answering these questions." Only when Macmillan briefed Wilson on the secret
background of the affair did the opposition leader agree to
end further public discussion of it in the national interest.
On July 30 *Izvestia* finally announced that the Soviet
Union had granted political asylum to Philby.

EDITOR'S NOTE: *When Edward Sheehan wrote the
above selection in 1964, he put forth tentatively
what has recently been accepted as fact in a series
of articles about Philby in two leading British
newspapers. These followed Philby's highly ad-
vertised reception into Soviet society.*

*It is now generally acknowledged that Philby,
up to the time of the defection of Burgess and
Maclean in 1951, was indeed the fair-haired boy
of the British intelligence service and in the normal
course of events might have become its chief. Had
the suspicions regarding Burgess and Maclean not
arisen, and had Philby not also been implicated in
the tipoff of the two men, thus eventually throwing*

suspicion upon himself, there seemingly would have been nothing to interfere with his further advancement.

The claim has also been made in these London articles that what put a sudden end to Philby's activities in Beirut was the discovery of new evidence during the early 1960's, which, after painstaking analysis by counterespionage experts, pointed to the fact that Philby had been a Soviet agent for years. Philby, it seems, when confronted by his colleagues with this new evidence for once was unable, despite his persuasive manner, to dispel it. This in turn triggered Philby's own defection to the Soviet Union. A picture was published in the fall of 1967 of Philby in Red Square in Moscow, taken by his son, who had come over from England to visit him. To his son Philby is reported to have said on this occasion: "I have come home. I have come home."

In the Philby case it has been obvious that once the jig was up and Philby's story was to some extent in the open, the Soviets pushed rather than suppressed publicity regarding him (such as allowing the visit of Philby's son to Moscow), in hopes, no doubt, that the more publicity that could be given to this affair the deeper the wedge could be driven into the Anglo-American cooperation which has been in operation for many years. Certainly it would only play into Soviet hands if we engaged in recriminations as a result of the Philby treason.

5

The Playboy Sergeant

Don Oberdorfer

*The moral of this unfortunate case of the treason-
able American sergeant Jack Dunlap is that it is
not necessary to penetrate an establishment at the
highest level in order to acquire high-level information. In a complex modern bureaucracy where
large numbers of documents circulate from office
to office, they must be sorted, distributed and
eventually filed by a variety of clerks and messengers who, in most cases, have no knowledge of
their contents. Even if they had reason to read
them, they would probably not understand them.
If Sergeant Dunlap, who in the early 1960's earned
a small fortune by photographing secret U.S. documents for the Soviets, had lived long enough to be
interrogated concerning the extent of his treasonable activities, it is highly unlikely that he could
have remembered more than a few of the documents he copied in sufficient detail to identify
them, much less describe their contents.*

RAMROD-STRAIGHT THE soldiers stood, and fired their
twenty-one shots into the summer air. The solitary bugler

FROM *The Saturday Evening Post*, March 7, 1964.

sounded taps, its notes echoing sweetly and sadly across the grassy knolls of Arlington National Cemetery. The Army pallbearers solemnly removed Old Glory from the casket, folded it precisely and presented the flag to the grieving widow. There, in a panoramic view of the Capital, just over a hillock from the site where John F. Kennedy sleeps, the United States of America last July 25 buried one of its most damaging spies.

For five years Sergeant Jack E. Dunlap—a name still unfamiliar to most Americans—worked as a functionary in the most secret of all official bureaucracies, the National Security Agency. For about half that time, according to the best evidence now available, he was feeding American secrets to agents of the Soviet Union for cash on the barrelhead.

Until he took his own life rather than face an official inquiry, Dunlap had been living high under the very noses of napping counter-espionage agents. During his last three years he frequented expensive resort hotels and yacht clubs from New Jersey to Florida, and acquired in rapid succession a cabin cruiser, a world's championship racing boat, a Jaguar, two late-model Cadillacs and a mistress.

Through it all the lanky sergeant was unobtrusively making his rounds as a $100-a-week messenger. Until it was too late, nobody seems to have wondered about his sudden affluence or thought it odd that he drove a Cadillac to work.

Since no official charges had been lodged against him, the Army was required by law to grant his widow's request and bury him in Arlington. But his story refused to be buried; high-level investigations continue. For Dunlap's suicide at the age of thirty-five left many questions still unanswered—questions like: Exactly what secrets did he betray? And how did he get away with it for so long?

The Department of Defense, though it has announced that it holds evidence the sergeant did spy for Russia for pay, refuses to estimate the damage. Not everyone is so reticent. "He stole us blind," moaned one Government official.

To appreciate the full import of the short, happy life of Jack E. Dunlap, it is best to begin where he worked—at the sprawling concrete-and-steel National Security Agency headquarters on the outskirts of Fort Meade, Maryland, just twenty-two miles north of the nation's capital. Except for the cavernous Pentagon and the huge new State Department Building, the enormous U-shaped NSA headquarters is the largest structure in the Washington area. Three football gridirons could easily be laid end-to-end in its main corridor; its walls are interlaced with more electric wiring than those of any other building in the world. Despite its many distinctions, few tourists have even heard of it, and none has ever been inside. The way is barred night and day by a detachment of heavily armed, hand-picked Marines who patrol the four gatehouses and the triple row of high barbed-wire and electrified fences between them.

Far more mysterious than the well-publicized CIA, it is—in the words of a congressional committee—"the most sensitive and secretive of all agencies." Its mission is to eavesdrop on every Communist communications message within the range of the most powerful electronic ears that can be made. Reports pour into NSA headquarters from undercover agents, wiretappers and literally thousands of radio intercept stations located in every corner of the globe —on land and aboard ships and planes—and in orbiting reconnaissance satellites. Whirring in the NSA basement are the world's fastest and most efficient computers, designed and employed to break the secret codes of Communist nations and of every government worth the trouble.

Because of its keystone position in the security structure, NSA is privy to many of the nation's closest-held secrets. It is reportedly part of the agency's job to pinpoint the exact location of every Communist military unit known to the West. Another job is devising and constantly updating the secret codes and ciphers of the United States—an area of secrecy which the Pentagon says was beyond the reach of Sergeant Dunlap.

Before a civilian can be employed by NSA, he must undergo rigorous investigation and indoctrination, precautions which have been made increasingly strict following a series of damaging lapses during the past decade. In 1954 an NSA cryptographic expert was indicted for passing secrets to the Dutch Government, including the embarrassing fact that NSA had broken the Dutch codes. He pleaded guilty to a lesser charge and served four and a half years in federal prison. From 1957 to 1959 the agency harbored at headquarters a psychotic expert on Arabic affairs, who later defected to the Soviet Union. And in the summer of 1960 two NSA mathematicians—William H. Martin and Bernon F. Mitchell—disappeared on vacation and made their way from Cuba by Russian trawler to the Soviet Union, where they denounced their country and their agency at an elaborate Moscow press conference.

Investigation revealed that both Martin and Mitchell were sexually abnormal, a situation which should have alerted security agents. But Maurice H. Klein, NSA's assistant director and personnel chief at the time, insisted the agency enjoyed "as tight a security program as there is in the whole Government." Unimpressed congressional probers discovered it was loose enough for Klein himself to have fabricated some of the records in his own personnel file. He was forced out, and NSA took twenty-two steps to tighten its vigilance. It fired twenty-six suspected sex deviants on its rolls and in mid-1962 told Congress it had rechecked the security file of every employee.

Still a strange double standard persisted in NSA's employment of thousands of military personnel such as Sergeant Jack E. Dunlap. In his case—typical under agency procedures—NSA routinely accepted the Army's word that Dunlap was trustworthy. Unlike civilian employees, he was not subjected to polygraph (lie detector) tests.

Initially there was no apparent reason to question his loyalty. By all the usual standards of postwar espionage, Dunlap looked like an exceptionally good risk. He was a family man with a wife and five children; he seemed a complete average Joe in an average bungalow in an average suburb. Born in Louisiana, Jack Dunlap had seen combat in Korea, been wounded and decorated for "coolness under fire and sincere devotion to duty." Perpetually eager for adventure—he had quit high school after three years to ship out on a merchant ship—he nonetheless earned the Good Conduct Medal three times for his unblemished Army record.

When he was assigned to NSA in April, 1958, as part of the Army's regular quota of support personnel, he served first as chauffeur for Major General Garrison B. Cloverdale, NSA's assistant director and chief of staff. Later he graduated to duties which the Pentagon describes officially only as "clerk-messenger." Some sources say he was the obscure fellow who gathered scrap paper to be incinerated at the end of the day. Others describe him as a "documents expediter," whose job it was to deliver highly classified data from one authorized official to another. Higher-ups in secret agencies are limited in their access to such papers by a strict requirement of "need to know," but it is difficult to circumscribe the faceless clerks and messengers who plod the treadmill of bureaucracy. Paradoxically, they often handle documents which some of their bosses are not authorized to see.

No one had any reason to suspect Dunlap's politics. He was so politically inert that he wasn't even registered to vote; and he was never heard to criticize his country. By all accounts he was less a conventional spy than an enterprising salesman of pilfered documents.

A Pentagon spokesman has quoted an estimate that Dunlap gave his wife, putting his extra income at between $30,000 and $40,000 "the first year," which is considerably more than the salary of the Secretary of Defense.

Not even the Pentagon can be certain how or when Dunlap began selling secrets. But it is clear that he had long found it difficult to pursue the American Dream on $100 a week. At one point he had resorted to moonlighting in a local service station, pumping gas at night for one dollar an hour. That did little to fulfill the alluring promise of his agency's recruiting brochure. "NSA workers," it announces, "are a vigorous lot, interested in exploiting to the fullest the recreational and cultural activities of their surroundings . . . Washington . . . the upper Chesapeake Bay, a famous water-sports playland . . . colonial Annapolis."

In mid-1960, after more than two years at NSA, Dunlap apparently took up a different sort of moonlighting, and his fortunes changed radically. In May he bought a second-hand station wagon, which he put in his wife's name, as he did most of the family's new purchases. In that car he began actively exploring the nearby "water-sports playland." The following month he was able to put down $3,400 for a thirty-foot cabin cruiser, complete with a galley and a bar.

This was the start of a dizzying round of acquisitions and adventures. Flashing $100 bills, Dunlap cashed large checks for total strangers on the spur of the moment. He spent $2,000 on boat repairs and presented workmen with large and unaccustomed tips. His impulsiveness was legendary, and when neighbors criticized the appearance of his back yard, he was quick to take offense. "I'll fix them," he boasted to friends. "I'll put up a wall they can't even see over." Within a few days he had a high cinder-block rampart erected around the Dunlap property. "The Wall" was the talk of suburban Glen Burnie, Maryland.

A little later Dunlap attended his first meeting of a fraternity of speedboat fanciers known as the Stoney Creek Racing Boat Club. The newcomer impetuously produced a wad of bills and announced with a wave of the hand that the drinks were on him. "Always before it had been Dutch," explains a local businessman in the group. "We were flabbergasted." Eager for his own speedboat, Dunlap located the owner of the *Bobo*, a sleek hydroplane skimmer which had previously set a new world's record for its class —107.7 miles an hour. The sergeant peeled off the $1,500 asking price from his bankroll, hitched boat and trailer to his light-blue Jaguar and roared away toward Chesapeake Bay.

Dunlap became a dashing figure on Maryland's frolicsome Eastern Shore. Tall, engaging, an enthusiastic plunger, he could usually be found in a colorful sport shirt and slacks in one of his high-powered boats or cars, frequently accompanied by flashy lady companions. Always friendly and accommodating, he nevertheless demanded the best. Once he sent two friends to New York, expenses paid, to examine a large stock of hand-made Italian speedboat propellers and select the very finest for his craft. He loved to play the role of mysterious big shot. Ironically, the deep secrecy of NSA protected the casual hints that his modest military rank was a cover story for a job of major importance.

To questions about his golden touch there was always a ready—and everchanging—answer. To one friend he confided that he owned land where a precious mineral powder, valuable in cosmetics, had been discovered. Neighbors heard he was heir to an extensive plantation in Louisiana, an account which would have surprised his father, a bridge-tender for the Alabama State Docks. To others the grinning Dunlap admitted modestly that "I came into a little inheritance."

Testing the vaunted advantages of "colonial Annapolis," Dunlap began dating a blonde who lived there. Like many who knew him, Sarah—as we shall call her—was charmed by the energetic playboy. "He was always on the go," she recalled. "Today it would be a boat race or a dance, tomorrow the auto races. He had to keep moving, he could never sit still. The poor guy must have known all along that someday it would end the way it did."

Dunlap told Sarah he owned gas stations—first two, then three, then five, then a whole string of them, she never saw the stations, but she was more than willing to believe they existed. "I knew he worked at NSA," she says, "and I figured they knew where he was getting the money, and it must be all right."

She became aware of a curious silhouette in her lover's life—"the bookkeeper." She recalled that "when I first knew Jack [in 1961] he would go to see 'the bookkeeper' once every week. Later it was once a month. He'd return with a roll of bills, but he never said much about the meetings." Once he allowed Sarah to accompany him to Washington on a trip to see some men at a large apartment house. Later the FBI spent night after night retracing these steps with Sarah, but she could never identify the spot.

All the while, the lowly messenger, his top-secret pass dangling from a chain around his neck, trooped blithely to work each day past the heavily armed Marine guards and through the triple strand of fence. It is now believed he was transporting highly classified documents back and forth under his shirt. Some of them were reportedly passed to Soviet contacts in the parking lot of a large shopping center several miles from NSA.

NSA's slumbering watchdogs never roused. For months Dunlap drove his Jaguar, or his Cadillac convertible, or his high-powered yellow Cadillac sedan to work each day without attracting the slightest notice. At one point the married sergeant began dating an NSA secretary—but word of this relationship never reached anybody who cared. He arranged time off from work to race his championship speedboat, but there is no sign anyone wondered how he could afford it. When he injured his back piloting his boat at a yacht club regatta, an Army ambulance was sent to return him to Fort Meade Army Hospital, because, Dunlap explained, "They were afraid sedatives might make me tell a lot of secrets I know." Still no one asked what a $100-a-week messenger with a wife and five kids was doing there in the first place.

He might be at it yet except for an act of his own initiative. Fearful that he might be transferred overseas at the end of his NSA tour of duty, Dunlap applied in March to leave the Army but retain his same job as an NSA civilian. His application, as he must have known, subjected him to the stricter security checks applied to civilians at NSA. For the first time he met the polygraph. The machine was his undoing. Two lie detector tests quickly disclosed instances of "petty thievery" and "immoral conduct" which raised serious questions about his trustworthiness. For a while nothing happened. Then two months later additional investigations—which need not have extended any further than the agency's parking lot—revealed he was living beyond his means. The Army hastily transferred him to a routine job in a Fort Meade orderly room, and severed his access to all secret information.

As the investigation dragged on, Dunlap became nervous and depressed. "Nothing seemed to suit him," says a friend. "If plans went the slightest bit awry, he'd blow up without warning." On June 14 he checked into a motel near Fort Meade and paid for four days, telling the owner he was preparing to retire from the Army after twenty years service (in fact, he served eleven). The second night he attended stockcar races with friends, and hinted he was preparing to kill himself.

"At first we didn't take him seriously," recalls one of his companions, "but when he didn't show up the next morning we hurried to the motel. Jack was lying across the bed unconscious and burning up with heat. There were some empty beer bottles around and several used containers of sleeping pills. I think we got there just in time." While Dunlap was rushed to the Army hospital, investigators collected two suicide notes, one to Sarah and the other to his wife, Diane. There was no reference to espionage, but

Dunlap instructed his wife to tell the reporters, when they came around, about his meritorious service in Korea.

Now sleuths from NSA, the U.S. Army Counter Intelligence Corps and the Army Military Police began collaborating on the case of the top-secret messenger. Dunlap was put under what one acquaintance called "a halfhearted surveillance." After recovering from his overdose of pills, the sergeant frankly informed his company commander, an Army Security Agency officer, that he would try again to kill himself. Still it seems that no official steps were taken to stop him.

But if the Army appeared to be unconcerned, friends were anxious to save him. On July 20 a buddy wrested a revolver from Dunlap just before he apparently planned to use it on himself. Soon afterward, however, Dunlap was observed removing a length of new radiator hose from a motor pool at Fort Meade. Late on July 22 he methodically filled his gasoline tank, purchased a fifth of the finest Scotch whiskey, drove to a deserted roadway on nearby Markey's Creek and strung up the radiator hose to bring the deadly exhaust fumes through the right front window of his sealed automobile. Fishermen found his body in the morning.

On August 20, nearly a month after his suicide, the leisurely investigators were jolted to discover that Diane Dunlap had found a sheaf of highly classified official papers among her husband's belongings. At long last NSA flashed word of the case to the FBI; and an army of investigators immediately set to work questioning everyone who seemed likely to know anything. Some agents concentrated on the difficult task of identifying Dunlap's outside contacts, reportedly including Soviet diplomatic personnel. A mysterious seven-digit number engraved on the underside of Dunlap's identification bracelet appeared to provide a hot lead—perhaps to a secret numbered account in a faraway Swiss bank. It turned out to be his sweetheart's phone number, which she had placed on the bracelet because her lover could not keep it in his head.

Inside NSA, worried officials tried to piece together a record of all the files which Dunlap might have borrowed. According to reports which the Pentagon refuses to confirm or deny, these included top-secret CIA estimates of

Soviet Army, Navy and nuclear capabilities along with comparable data on NATO countries. "The hell of it is," said one knowledgeable source, "we'll probably never know which papers he might have handled. To be safe, you have to proceed on the assumption that everything which passed through his section might be resting in a file in Moscow."

The Pentagon recently completed a lengthy inquiry into the Dunlap affair, personally ordered by Secretary of Defense Robert S. McNamara, but no details have so far been made public. If a similar series of tragic blunders occurred in any ordinary agency of government, an aroused public would insist that those responsible be officially censured, demoted or fired. But the supersecret NSA is standing pat behind its protective curtain, hinting obliquely at yet another series of security reforms.

It is, of course, the age-old practice of bureaucracies, especially secret ones, to entomb their errors in obscurity. That is not particularly suprising. But there is special irony in the fact that NSA's guardians blundered so long that a man who "stole us blind" could be buried in hallowed ground at Arlington.

6

The Colonel Turns West

Oleg Penkovskiy

The case of Oleg Penkovskiy, the Soviet colonel who spied for the West in the early 1960's, came to light because he was caught and tried. At his trial, the Soviets, by producing certain evidence against him, openly admitted that they had successfully been spied against by one of their own number—in fact, by a very high-ranking member of their own society. There have been numberless trials, of course, throughout Soviet history at which for political reasons Soviet, and other, citizens have been accused of such actions, but these were generally frameups. Penkovskiy's is the only case of such stature which has come to public knowledge as the result of a Soviet trial of a Soviet citizen who volunteered to spy against his motherland for the West and did so successfully for a relatively long period. Frank Gibney, who has helped earlier Soviet defectors relate their experiences (Petr Deriabin), reconstructs in this account the course of the Penkovskiy epic, basing it on the Soviet court record but placing this against his knowledge of how Western intelligence services operate.

FROM the book *The Penkovskiy Papers*.

THE MOUNT ROYAL Hotel in London is a squat, unprepossessing beehive of commercial travelers and middle-priced tourists, which occupies its own block on Oxford Street, within sight of Marble Arch. Traffic around it is generally busy and people rush in and out of its entrances with an air of serious if transient purpose. At 11 P.M. on the night of April 20, after a rather hectic bilingual dinner, a trimly dressed visitor, whose accented English marked him as probably a foreign businessman, left his own party, passed through the crowded lobby, and went upstairs to an inconspicuous suite. There his knock was answered by an Englishman of his acquaintance, who quickly opened the door and let him in. There were four other gentlemen in the room, two of them British and two American. It was Oleg Penkovskiy's first encounter with Western intelligence.

For hours he talked. He had first handed over two packets of closely handwritten notes and documents, materials which he had been preparing for some time on Soviet military missiles and other matters, by way of showing his credentials. They were eagerly scanned. There was understandably an air of intense interest in the room as he went through the facts of his background and position. For it must have been quickly apparent that Colonel Penkovskiy represented a major intelligence breakthrough, better even than his advance billing had suggested.

The meeting in the Mount Royal was the fruit of a contact which Penkovskiy had established with a visiting Englishman in Moscow, and sedulously cultivated. Greville Wynne was a sort of commercial traveler on an international scale, specializing in the import and export of heavy industrial equipment between Soviet-bloc countries and the West.

In 1960 Wynne had organized the visit to Moscow of a British trade delegation. He arrived there in December, almost a week ahead of the delegation, and perforce spent a great deal of time with Penkovskiy, who represented the Soviet authorities in this matter, arranging the delegation's meetings and itinerary. Penkovskiy had "studied" Wynne. His earlier efforts to establish contact with U.S. Intelligence having failed—intelligence agencies seem to display either excessive boldness or excessive caution when faced with the main chance—Penkovskiy now saw the opportunity to state his case to the British. As he said later during his questioning at the Moscow trial: "Having become acquainted with Mr. Wynne, I decided to try to make contact with British Intelligence through him, but I did not do this at once. I wanted to study him first in order to discuss this question at subsequent meetings."

In their talks during Wynne's December visit, he and Penkovskiy had arranged for a Soviet delegation to fly to London early in 1961, in order to visit various British firms interested in Soviet trade. When the promised delegation did not appear, Wynne went back to Moscow to find out what was wrong. Again, Penkovskiy was the man he had to see. By this time the two were on a first-name basis. Penkovskiy—quite unknown to Wynne—seized the opportunity of Wnne's second visit as his chance to make contact with the West. This happened in the first week of April, 1961.

To the Soviet mind, anyone in Wynne's position would have had to be some sort of intelligence agent. So to Penkovskiy, who despite his exposure to foreigners inevitably retained the tactical outlook and limitations of a Soviet educational product.

By this time Penkovskiy had made up his mind to go over to the Western side. The uncertainties of his life with the GRU* must have been a catalyzing factor, given the steady dissatisfaction which had been building up within him over the dangerous "adventurism" of the Soviet regime and the nostalgia he continued to feel for the freer life of Westerners, even the bit he had glimpsed in his year's service in Turkey. As he wrote later, in the *Papers*: "Years ago I began to feel disgusted with myself, not to mention with our 'beloved' leaders and guides. I felt before, as I feel now, that I must find some justification for my existence which would give me inner satisfaction." It is the voice of a man seeking new roots, of a soldier who was looking for a new flag.

Not the least of the factors spurring Penkovskiy's search was the State Security's discovery of his father's identity as a White officer. Twenty-three years of hard work and

---

* Soviet Military Intelligence.

initiative in the Soviet service were now clouded by another man's decision, taken in 1918, to fight the Bokshevik Revolution. Why, Penkovskiy might ask himself, had the ubiquitous KGB not known of his father before this? Why had the information suddenly been used as a club over him? He had secretly been proud of his father's memory, despite their difference of allegiance. More and more, his own experience now suggested to him that Vladimir Penkovskiy had made the right choice in 1918.

When Penkovskiy saw Wynne in his room at the Hotel National in Moscow, he was able to assure Wynne that the promised Soviet delegation was already selected. As he had before, he talked a great deal about himself, in the course of discussing plans for the delegation's visit. Wynne was quick to detect a certain agitation in the behavior of his official Soviet contact. As they walked through the Moscow streets, safe from the danger of being overheard, Penkovskiy's comments about the Soviet scene became less circumspect. The Russian began to deride the official explanations for Soviet economic shortages and he made some fairly critical remarks about the regime. The life of the ordinary Soviet citizen, Penkovskiy implied, was far from a happy one.

Things came to a head when Wynne finally saw a list of the Soviet delegates. He objected that the distinguished delegates, principally professors and technical research experts, were people who had little if anything to do with commercial negotiations. They hardly constituted the businesslike trade delegation that his companies expected. It was clear to Wynne that the Russians were interested in obtaining information, not in purchasing goods.

Penkovskiy admitted that Wynne's objections were sound. But he pleaded with Wynne to accept the delegation, as constituted. "Please don't object to the delegation, Grev," he said. "I must come to England. If you make trouble, I cannot come. For if you do not accept this delegation, there will be no chance of my going to London at all—since I am scheduled to lead these delegates."

With this, for the first time Penkovskiy told Wynne bluntly about his fears for the Russian people. The situation in the Soviet Union, he said, was intolerable and its leadership dangerously unstable. He possessed certain facts about Soviet conditions which he must convey to "interested parties" in the West. Above all, he must talk himself to people in the West, "to tell them what conditions in the Soviet Union are really like."

Wynne was aware that the Soviet regime specialized in having secret police provocateurs tell similar stories of disenchantment with their own government, in the hope of entrapping Western visitors. But he was a shrewd judge of character. He had never met anyone quite like Penkovskiy. Not only had he come to believe in the man's sincerity, but he was able to appreciate the value of a man like Penkovskiy to the Western intelligence contacts whom Penkovskiy was obviously seeking. From his extensive travels in Eastern Europe, Wynne knew the conditions which Penkovskiy was endeavoring to describe.

He agreed, therefore, not to question the suitability of the Soviet delegates to London, so that Penkovskiy might have his chance to go there himself and tell his story to the "interested parties" he sought. Before he left Moscow, on April 12, 1961, Wynne had been given a double-wrapped, double-sealed envelope containing a letter from Penkovskiy addressed to British Intelligence. Penkovskiy gave Wynne the further information that he planned to arrive in London in about a week's time.

It was a sign of the GRU's trust in Penkovskiy, and his value as an intelligence officer, that he was sent to London in charge of a delegation (with nothing more said in the Arbat* offices about his damaging ancestry). He was shepherding a large group of Soviet technical and trade experts, for the ostensible purpose of making contact with British firms and discussing certain trade prospects and technical exchanges. He did this in his official capacity as deputy head of the foreign department in the State Committee for the Co-ordination of Scientific Research Work. As a colonel in the GRU, his real mission was of course an intelligence one: to conduct what industrial and technical espionage he could, and if possible develop some British contacts in the companies visited—all the while keeping an eye on the members of his own Soviet delegation. The visit of the delegation had been arranged through the office of

---

* An area of Moscow.

Anatoliy Pavlov, counselor of the Soviet Embassy and the committee's representative in London—actually himself also a GRU colonel and deputy chief of GRU activities in the U.K. (If nothing else, both the Soviet delegation and the British firms it visited enjoyed more than their quota of security supervision.)

Penkovskiy's visit to London lasted until May 6. For those sixteen days he led an extraordinary triple life. His delegation from Moscow obediently respected him as a trusted state and party official. Less obviously, he was greeted by the GRU *rezidency* in London as a working senior intelligence officer, with good political connections. The brand-new third layer of his existence was happily unsuspected by either of his two sets of Soviet colleagues. He continued to hold night meetings with Western intelligence officers, after he had arranged the affairs of his delegation during the day, and with them planned the pattern of his future work in Moscow. Wynne continued to be useful here as an intermediary. Since he represented some of the firms the Russians contemplated doing business with, his presence was plausible.

Penkovskiy boldly ordered his official work to fit his new intelligence mission. When he was hard put to arrange enough secret meetings—because the delegation had to visit a succession of British factories outside of London— Penkovskiy asked the Soviet Ambassador for permission to stay an extra four days. He wished, he said, to show the delegation the British Industrial Fair then about to open in London. Permission was granted, and Penkovskiy was thus enabled to have two additional sessions with the four Western intelligence officers, known to him only, in the words of his 1963 Soviet trial, as "the British intelligence officers named Grille and Miles and the representatives of the American intelligence service, who called themselves Alexander and Oslaf." For the sake of convenience and to avoid suspicion, they continued to meet in the Mount Royal Hotel, where members of the visiting delegation were housed.

Penkovskiy's energy was prodigious. While continuing to do his duty by the Soviet technical delegation, politically and socially (Penkovskiy had charge of their money, in the best Soviet tradition, so he supervised their shopping trips in the London stores), he received an intensive short course in intelligence communications. As he later admitted at his 1963 trial, he was given a Minox miniature camera and instructed in its use, as well as a transistor radio receiver for keeping up one-way communications with the West. It was arranged to maintain contact with him through Wynne, or another Western emissary, if he proved unable to return to Western Europe in the near future. He drilled himself in radio procedures and all the technical but vital minutiae of the spy in action.

His Soviet trial soberly records: "The foreign intelligence officers recommended to Penkovskiy that he keep this spy equipment in a secret hiding place that was specially equipped in his apartment. Alexander and Oslaf warned Penkovskiy that Wynne would soon be arriving in Moscow and would bring him a letter from them, but if necessary appropriate instructions would be transmitted to him by radio.

"At the same time Penkovskiy . . . received the assignment to photograph secret documents for the foreign intelligence services."

Penkovskiy asked in return that he be granted U.S. or British citizenship and work commensurate with his experience, in case events ever forced him to flee the Soviet Union.

Having thus crossed his Rubicon, Penkovskiy returned to Moscow, laden with presents for some of his high-placed Soviet friends, a full report of the trade and technical mission (which Moscow judged a great success), and an unobtrusive Minox camera with a great quantity of film.

On May 6, 1961, Oleg Penkovskiy returned to Moscow with what was apparently a precise concept of his mission. He carefully stored his camera, film and radio instructions in a secret drawer of his desk in the apartment which he and his family still occupied on Maksim Gorkiy Embankment. Then he began work in earnest. With free access to the Ministry of Defense and the GRU, as well as his own committee, he photographed documents almost wholesale, most of them in the top-secret category. Some were technical papers or highly classified instructions and tactical manuals in use by the ground (tactical) missile force.

Others were less technological, dealing with intelligence procedures, Soviet personalities or the goals and operations of the committee.

On May 27 Wynne flew into Moscow, to resume some of his negotiations with the Soviets on behalf of the firms he represented. Colonel Penkovskiy met him at Sheremetyevo Airport and drove him back to the city. On the way he handed Wynne a packet of some twenty exposed films and other materials, which Wynne transmitted to a representative of British Intelligence later in the day.

That evening Penkovskiy visited Wynne in his room at the Metropol Hotel. As he later admitted in their Soviet trial, Wynne gave Penkovskiy a package containing thirty fresh rolls of film and further instructions from the intelligence officers who had met him in London. It is hard to believe, from such goings-on, that Wynne was not himself an intelligence officer. He was not, however. It had simply happened that Penkovskiy chose him for his contact; and when he reported this, British Intelligence inevitably asked him to keep up the connection and transmit certain packages, etc., to Penkovskiy. Wynne's position gave him a facility for meeting Penkovskiy that could not easily be duplicated—at least not without arousing Soviet suspicions. (Even at the well-supervised Soviet trial, Penkovskiy insisted that Wynne never actually saw the information he was passing.)

Far from suspecting anything strange in his behavior, however, Penkovskiy's superiors at the GRU and the committee were delighted by his British associations. People like Greville Wynne were just the sort of contacts any good Soviet intelligence officer in Penkovskiy's shoes might be expected to make. They arranged to send him to London with another delegation of Soviet technical experts, this time to attend the opening of the Soviet Industrial Exhibition there.

The delegation arrived in London on July 15, 1961, but Penkovskiy came alone three days later, since he was not required to travel with the delegation. Fortuitously, no one from the Soviet Embassy was on hand to meet him. This oversight allowed him to telephone Wynne from the airport, whereupon the Englishman drove out to meet him—a pleasant encounter which was later related in painful detail at the 1963 trial. Penkovskiy went along to Wynne's house, shaved, bathed and turned over another fat batch of films and documents which he had brought with him. Then Wynne dropped him off at the Kensington Close Hotel, where he had a reservation—conveniently close to the old mansions in Kensington Gardens which comprise the working quarters of the Soviet Embassy.

Because most of his official work this time was concentrated in London, Penkovskiy was able to spend a great deal more time than formerly with the four British and American operatives who were waiting for him in one of M.I.6's "safe houses." He would spend most of the day working at the Soviet Embassy or at the exhibition with his delegates; but even this did not make too great demands on his time because the delegation was subdivided by specialties. Each division had its own subleader. Penkovskiy handled only the over-all direction.

Evenings he reserved for the rendezvous with his new friends: "Alexander," "Miles," "Grille," and "Oslaf." They went over the material he had previously given them in some detail, it having been checked by experts meanwhile. They made further assignments.

By this time, presumably, the first fruits of Colonel Penkovskiy's photography work with his new Minox had been received and evaluated in London and Washington. It was a tense summer in Europe that year. The Continent still reverberated from Khrushchev's threats over Berlin and the East Germany treaty. If anything, the Vienna meeting of Khrushchev and President Kennedy had only intensified the political electricity in the air. Against the background of a possible military showdown, therefore, in which Marshal Varentsov's missiles would play a heavy role, the personal reports and observations of his former aide had even greater value. That July, Penkovskiy's sessions with the intelligence officers lasted as long as ten hours at a stretch. To provide for the day when face-to-face communications might not be so easy, he was given further training in the use of a long-distance radio receiver.

Throughout this necessarily concentrated, grueling indoctrination course in Western intelligence procedures, Penkovskiy managed to preserve his amazing *sang-froid*. Only a few mortals are gifted with a natural talent for leading a double life and Oleg Penkovskiy was evidently one of them. Thanks to his diligent escort duty with General Serov's wife and daughter on his first London trip, he had accumulated quite a reputation among Moscow's upper crust as a man who knew his way around the West. This time he had a heavy shopping list with him. In his notebook, along with various orders and gift specifications, he had taken the trouble to draw the foot contours of various influential Soviet ladies and gentlemen, so he would make no mistake in purchasing the right shoes for them. (Shoes from abroad are a popular Soviet gift item, and ever since Khrushchev's famous Italian suit purchase there had been much official leniency in the matter of foreign clothing articles.) The Colonel purchased as much as his official allowance would allow, more than enough to qualify him as a latter-day Grandfather Frost (the Russian Santa Claus) on the flight home. (It was fortunate that Soviet customs rarely touched his baggage.) With some of his purchases—a few shirts, a watch or two, and other oddments—Wynne helped him.

At the same time, Penkovskiy managed to keep up with his Soviet intelligence observations, which he forwarded in the normal way to GRU headquarters through Colonel Pavlov, the local deputy *rezident*. It can be assumed that his Western contacts gave him some "material" for forwarding to Moscow that was apparently valuable, if in fact relatively harmless. But such information was enough to continue his reputation as a hard-working "Chekist."

With what must have been a profound sense of irony, he also went on advancing his standing as a zealous party man. One morning he quietly took a trip to Karl Marx's grave in Highgate Cemetery and discovered that it was in a bad state of neglect. Through Communist Party channels, he wrote a letter of protest direct to the First Secretary of the Central Committee in Moscow. Comrade Penkovskiy told Comrade Khrushchev that as a "loyal Marxist" he found such neglect appalling, a reflection upon Communism, the Soviet Union and, specifically, the local Soviet Embassy officials whose job it was to take care of such things.

Moscow took swift action on receipt of the letter and Penkovskiy was commended for his "socialist vigilance."

The London Embassy was ordered to set things right immediately. Promptly the grave was cleaned up and decorated. Penkovskiy, although hardly popular in Soviet Embassy circles in London as a result of his letter, was treated with increased respect.

In two hasty visits to the open society, Penkovskiy had seen enough to confirm his admiration for the West and his wrath—the word is used advisedly—at the regime which kept his own people behind the walls and conventions of a garrison state. "Oh, my poor Russian people, my poor Russian people," he had exclaimed to Wynne, when looking through his first London department store in April. It was not the abundance which intrigued and amazed him so much as its obvious accessibility to people of all walks of life, in contrast to conditions back home.

He remained fascinated by London and enjoyed walking about the city, quietly observing its still stately manners. He dressed well, in conservative taste. Although a moderate drinker who generally contented himself with a few glasses of wine in the course of an evening, Penkovskiy was fond of socializing. In the midst of his other activities in London, he even managed to find time to take a few dancing lessons, in which he sampled the mysteries of the twist and the cha-cha.

He returned to Moscow on August 10, having already received commendations for his mission from his Soviet superiors. In an August letter to Gvishiani, at the committee, Colonel Pavlov wrote his own endorsement of Penkovskiy's good work in England. The Western operatives were even more pleased. As his Soviet prosecutor later reported: "The foreign intelligence officers gave new assignments to Penkovskiy in which special emphasis was put on the collection of intelligence information on the Soviet armed forces, missile troops, troops assigned to the German Democratic Republic, and the preparation for the signing of a peace treaty with the G.D.R."

Penkovskiy had investigated the documentation necessary for applying for both British and American citizenship and received assurances that he would receive responsible employment and a decent position in Western society, whenever he was prepared to leave the Soviet Union forever. Two years later, Soviet investigators found in his apartment two photographs of Penkovskiy, taken in London, wearing the full uniform and regalia of a British and an American Army colonel.

All of this was clearly part of a deeply thought-out transfer of allegiance, from a military man in whom the tradition of obedience and loyalty was ingrained. Penkovskiy was not merely interested in helping the West; he had to be part of the West himself. Moscow had never seemed to be so far away.

In Moscow, one bright September afternoon in 1961, three pleasant English children were playing by a sandbox along the boulevard, while their mother sat watching them on a bench nearby. A well-dressed Russian civilian stopped for a moment near the children, evidently in the course of a leisurely walk. He smiled, talked to them for a moment or two, and offered one child a box of candy which he had pulled out of his pocket. The child accepted the candy and the smiling stranger walked on. Then the child brought the candy box over to the mother, as children often do.

It was in this manner that Oleg Penkovskiy transmitted a highly important package of exposed film concealed in the package of Drazhe candy drops, to Mrs. Janet Anne Chisholm, the wife of an attaché in the British Embassy in Moscow.

Penkovskiy had met Mrs. Chisholm during his second trip to London and he had been drilled in this procedure by his Western intelligence contacts. A month before, Greville Wynne had arrived again in Moscow to attend the French industrial fair. Penkovskiy as usual had visited him at his hotel. In Wynne's room at the Metropol, Penkovskiy had turned over film and several packets of information, as well as a broken Minox camera (he had dropped it during one of his nocturnal photography sessions). Wynne gave him a replacement camera, as well as the little box of Drazhe lozenges to use in the contact with Mrs. Chisholm, along with detailed instructions for meeting the children. The box was just big enough for four rolls of film.

The meeting with Mrs. Chisholm was the first contact Penkovskiy made with a person other than Wynne. In a city where foreigners are as closely watched as they are in Moscow, the novelty of "the meeting" was understandable, to say nothing of their caution in arranging it. Wynne, however, Penkovskiy could meet without fear of suspicion, virtually as often as he wished. Not only was Penkovskiy Wynne's official contact on the committee, but Wynne represented a promising prospect for the GRU, which was anxious to recruit a British businessman for use as an agent. As far as his military intelligence superiors were concerned, Penkovskiy was "developing" him. When Penkovskiy saw Wynne in August, he told him that he was about to take a trip to Paris himself with another Soviet trade delegation for the purpose of attending the Soviet industrial fair there.

When Penkovskiy arrived at Le Bourget Airport, near Paris, on September 20, 1961, Wynne met him and drove him to his hotel. Not knowing the exact day of his arrival, Wynne had gone to the airport for two weeks, watching every Moscow flight. From the standpoint of Western intelligence, his vigil was well spent. Penkovskiy brought with him at least fifteen rolls of exposed film: photographs of documents, secret processes, missile designs, highly classified military memoranda, and other pieces of scientific and technical information which his Soviet accusers later nicely lumped together under the heading "espionage material."

Three days after Penkovskiy's arrival, Wynne drove him to one of the Seine bridges, where he was met, a few minutes later, by one of the Anglo-American intelligence officers. The four members of the Anglo-American intelligence team evidently saw a great deal of Penkovskiy during the next month, when he was not conferring at the Soviet Embassy or visiting the Soviet exhibition in Paris, which had been the pretext for this trip.

Penkovskiy worked hard with his intelligence contacts during this third visit to the West. He not only discussed his information at some length, but he laid the groundwork for a system of contacts in Moscow by which he could later transmit information and receive instructions with a minimal amount of risk. Here, ironically, the terse language of his Soviet trial provides a concise account of a most successful intelligence mission:

While in Paris, Penkovskiy repeatedly met representatives of the British and American intelligence services at secret apartments. At these meetings he reported about the official assignment which he had been given for his stay in France, discussed a number of workers at the Soviet Embassy in Paris in whom the intelligence officers were interested, identified those persons for them in photographs, gave them brief histories of these persons, and on a floor plan of the Soviet Embassy showed them the places where those persons worked. In addition, he recognized and identified for them, on the basis of photographs, several other Soviet citizens who were of interest to the intelligence services, he gave important information, underwent instruction in espionage work, and received this assignment: to continue to photograph secret materials; select in Moscow and describe in detail eight to ten dead drops for impersonal contact with the intelligence services; establish new friendships among officers and workers of the State Committee for the Co-ordination of Scientific Research Work; study the possibility of obtaining espionage information from them; and collect information concerning new Soviet military equipment by making use of his acquaintance with members of the rocket forces. In addition, in Paris, Penkovskiy continued to study espionage radio equipment which the foreign intelligence officers promised to send him in Moscow through Wynne or Janet Anne Chisholm.

During one of the meetings Janet Anne Chisholm was present and specific details were worked out for maintaining contact between her and Penkovskiy in Moscow. At the next meeting in Paris, Penkovskiy was introduced to a highly placed person in American Intelligence. . . .

Having received from the foreign intelligence services in Paris thirty rolls of film and new treated paper for the preparation of secret reports, Penkovskiy returned to Moscow on October 16, 1961. . . .

What the Soviet indictment naturally did *not* include was the fact that most of the "Soviet citizens" Penkovskiy discussed were themselves members of either the GRU or KGB. It is clear that Penkovskiy gave precise details of the large Soviet intelligence and subversive network operating out of the Paris Embassy. In intelligence terms, he "blew" a major segment of the Soviet spy network.

In this Paris visit Penkovskiy behaved with his customary energy. He continued to handle a multitude of varied tasks and interests conjointly—performing all with

Faustian zest. (This is probably one reason why his Soviet superiors took so long to credit the suspicion that he might be playing a double game.) We can only conclude that the Colonel took more than a little pleasure in playing his perilous double game. In Paris as in London he was an avid tourist. The paintings in the Louvre and the night-club extravaganzas at the Lido he absorbed with apparently equal interest. The experience of the West was still new, still strangely free.

In his own memoirs, published in London in September, 1964, Wynne recalled some of his companion's impressions. By now they had become good friends:

> He used to attend the Embassy or the exhibition during the day; go to some official dinners at the Embassy; but whenever he got away I was always waiting for him in a car at a prearranged rendezvous and in Paris you can easily lose yourself. So we had quite a lot of amusement there, doing the usual tourist things, and he seemed to enjoy it very much. But he said he preferred England.
>
> Later, when we were in Paris, we went to cabarets at the Lido and Moulin Rouge. It was the first time he had ever seen such spectacular shows, with the chorus girls in line: they don't have that in Moscow. "Why can't the Russians have this, too?" he said. "It is a lively and happy art, and not so serious as the ballet."

Yet Oleg Penkovskiy was hardly the Russian version of the stereotyped "How you going to keep 'em down on the farm" Parisian tourist. When he had time to himself in Paris, as in London, he would simply walk the streets, observing people and looking in shop windows. The differences between this open society and his own were borne in upon him in the smallest ways, e.g., rather vain about his looks and growing bald, he even reveled in the large available store of Western European hair tonics.

He was surer than ever that the course he had chosen was the correct one. The only remaining question in his mind was: should he escape now? He knew the risks he took by returning to Moscow. And the intelligence officers with whom he was in contact were, by Wynne's later testimony, perfectly willing to have him remain in the West. The information he had already given was so great that they were concerned about his future personal security and were thus extremely careful not to jeopardize his security in Moscow.

For days Oleg Penkovskiy debated with himself as he walked the streets of Paris. He had family considerations at home—a pregnant wife, a mother, and a daughter. Could he cut them off from his life forever? To leave his own familiar society, much as he hated the regime, meant a considerable wrench.

On the other hand, he was captivated by the bright new world in the West. There were the lights, the stores—and, it might be added, the girls. For Penkovskiy, who could not be accused of puritanism, had managed to make a few pleasant acquaintanceships in the course of this trip. Everything in his immediate surroundings argued that he stay.

He almost did. His plane back to Moscow had been delayed by fog and the omen did not escape him. He hesitated, literally at the customs barrier, but at the last second he turned, said good-bye to Wynne, and marched back into a world from which he had emigrated in spirit. He had a job to do in Moscow. He had said this many times to Wynne as he argued aloud the pros and cons of his departure. He felt himself a "soldier" of his new allegiance. He said as much in the *Papers*, shortly after his return to Moscow: "I feel that for another year or two I must continue in the General Staff of the U.S.S.R., in order to reveal all the villainous plans and plottings of our common enemy, i.e., I consider, as your soldier, that my place during these troubled times is on the *front line*. I must remain on this front line in order to be your eyes and ears, and my opportunities for this are great. God grant only that my modest efforts be useful in the fight for our high ideals for mankind." To have stayed in Paris seemed too easy, when there remained a force in Moscow which he wished to stop.

As a professional intelligence officer himself, Penkovskiy needed to be told little about this aspect of his craft. In his earliest conversations with British and American Intelligence, he took pains to specify exact locations and exact dimensions. In Paris that autumn he had painstakingly re-

searched every detail of the methods by which he would
transmit his information. He knew better than most the
degree of surveillance exercised on the streets of Moscow.
He knew the consequences of a careless act and the importance given by Soviet counterintelligence to the slightest
occurrence or meeting that seemed out of the ordinary.
Accordingly, he delivered his information to the West in
three ways: 1. by chance encounters which could take
place without exciting suspicion, yet were regulated in a
most precise manner by the participants; 2. by meetings at
the homes or offices of British or Americans whom he
would be normally expected to visit; and 3. by the safe but
often circuitous device of the dead drop, the inconspicuous
hiding place where a packet can be left for a later pickup.
Each contact, however, was prearranged to work in a
clear, specific manner.

On October 21, just two weeks after his return from
Paris, Penkovskiy had his first meeting with one of his
contacts. At 9 P.M. he was walking along the Sadovniche-
skaya Embankment near the Balchug Hotel, smoking a
cigarette and holding in his hand a package wrapped in
white paper. A man walked up to him, wearing an overcoat, unbuttoned, and also smoking a cigarette. "Mr.
Alex," he said in English, "I am from your two friends
who send you a big, big welcome." The package changed
hands and another hoard of documents and observations
on Soviet military preparations was on its way westward.

"Alex," for such was his code name, coolly kept on with
his work of collecting and transmitting information, without skimping on his normal daily rounds. More than ever,
he kept up contacts with his friends in the Army. He
showed himself at his favorite restaurants and cafés, the
Baku on Neglinnaya Street, the Peking on Bolshaya Sada-
ovaya, or the restaurant at the Gorkiy Park of Culture and
Rest, but no more than was expected of him. Because of
his work on the committee, he was expected to do a good
bit of entertaining. He exuded confidence. In mid-
November he took his wife off for a month-long vacation.
First they went to the quiet spa at Kislovodsk in the
Caucasus, where most of the Soviet ministries have rather
large rest houses. Then they traveled south, to the Black

Sea beach resort of Sochi to round out a lavish Soviet-style vacation. They returned to Moscow on December 18.

In December and January, Penkovskiy resumed meetings with his Western contacts, this time—according to the Moscow trial—with Mrs. Chisholm, the same lady to whom he had passed the candy on Tsvetnoy Boulevard. But he quickly alerted himself to possible surveillance. On January 5, after he had passed some more film to Mrs. Chisholm in an elaborately casual encounter, he noticed a less than casual third party hovering in the background. A small car, violating traffic regulations, had entered the short lane, then swung around, while its two occupants surveyed the scene, before moving off in the direction of Arbat Square.

On January 12, the date of the next meeting, nothing happened. But the week following the same car appeared again, a small brown sedan with the license plate SHA 61—45, driven by a man in a black overcoat—enough to warn anybody off. Penkovskiy wrote a letter to a prearranged address in London, advising that no further meetings with Mrs. Chisholm be attempted.

From that time on, Penkovskiy relied on the two remaining methods of communication. He either handed over material in the houses of Westerners, to which he was invited in the course of his duties, or relied on the relative anonymity of dead drops. Over the course of the next six months his intelligence contacts supplied him with some more ingenious methods of transmitting his film, including a can of Harpic disinfectant, with a removable bottom, in which film could be inserted. (The Harpic jar was to be found in the bathroom of a British attaché's house, where Penkovskiy would occasionally be invited for receptions. The occasion to use it never arose, however.) But he was able to pass on his packages at the few social occasions to which he might be invited, without causing undue suspicion. He was some times invited to formal parties or, on occasion, to informal British or American parties like the special Moscow showing of Shelagh Delaney's film *A Taste of Honey*.

The dead drops were, of course, the safest way to communicate. But they had their own peculiar suspenses and horrors. An agent must take the gamble that whatever he puts in a dead drop will not be disturbed and that neither he nor the receiver of the item will look suspicious in the transaction. In some ways, an agent working through dead drops finds himself playing a grown-up game of blind man's buff.

Through the spring of 1962 Penkovskiy's existence was bounded by a collection of these inconspicuous hiding places. Drop no. 1 was located in the doorway of No. 5/6 Pushkin Street. To the right of the doorway, as one entered, stood a radiator painted dark green and fastened with special hooks. Between the radiator and the wall was a gap about three inches wide. The message to be sent was placed in a matchbox wrapped in light blue paper, bound with cellophane tape and wire, and hung on a certain hook behind the radiator.

When Penkovskiy had something to leave there, he was to make a black mark on post no. 35 on the Kutuzov Prospect. He would then put the materials in the drop, and make two telephone calls to nos. G 3-26-87 and G 3-26-94, each with a set number of rings. When the person answered he would hang up. But the "interested parties" would then know to expect something.

Penkovskiy celebrated the Fourth of July, 1962, by attending a reception at the American Embassy in Moscow. There he apparently made contact with the U.S. intelligence officer to whom he later turned over a detailed plan of new Soviet missile construction. Two days before, Greville Wynne had arrived in Moscow. Penkovskiy met him at the airport in a borrowed car and drove him to the Ukraina Hotel. He was nervous. Wynne later observed that he had never seen Penkovskiy so agitated. "I am under observation," he said.

Wynne passed some materials to Penkovskiy and a letter from the West, which visibly improved his spirits. Western intelligence officers had apparently arranged a passport for Penkovskiy to use, under another name, within the Soviet Union, in case the surveillance on him intensified to the danger point. Penkovskiy was now actively considering methods of escape. At one point, in his European visit, the possibility of his leaving Moscow and making a rendezvous with a submarine in the Baltic had been at least scouted.

He had been thinking of this, how feasible it was, and whether it would be possible—by some means or other—to get his family out as well.

Through this period Penkovskiy continued to get out his information at an almost frantic pace. Although he was well aware of the dangers involved, he was equally well aware of the need to get his information to the West. Soviet military preparations which were to culminate in the Cuban missile crisis had already begun. So he was caught in the age-old vise of the spy who has been all too successful. A less bold character would have sharply curtailed his activities, but this was not Penkovskiy's way. Yet, while he continued to send out ever-increasing amounts of information, he worried about his predicament. He had never wholly faced up to the idea of the danger to his family. Now he did. And now that he had a skillfully forged domestic passport to use for an escape, he pondered over the best way to bring the family out with him.

He knew that the KGB was at least somewhere on his trail. As early as January he had written:

> Supposedly the "neighbors" have information that my father did not die and is located abroad. This information appeared at the end of 1961. An immediate search of the place where my father was buried did not produce anything —the grave was not found. Also, no document concerning the death of my father was found. My command does not give this special attention and believes that my father is deceased.

By early spring the degree of interest in his investigation had obviously grown strong enough to block any of his pending travel plans. For months he had counted on making a trip to the U.S. in April with a Soviet mobile book exhibition. This had not worked out. With some agitation he wrote in the *Papers*:

> "If all is well, I will take off for the U.S. on April 19. But at present things go badly. They are continually searching for my father's burial place. They cannot find it—and therefore they are conjecturing that my father is alive. And therefore in the future it would not be suitable to send me on overseas assignments. My command considers these fears

meaningless and they defend me from all these conjectures of the "neighbors"—everything must be decided soon.

He was relieved by the messages which Wynne brought from the outside. But he had grown progressively more nervous about his contacts with Wynne himself. Greville Wynne had taken a terrible risk in returning to Moscow at all, and he knew it. But in his own agitation Penkovskiy worried whether Wynne had kept up the high degree of caution necessary at this point in their relations. Wynne was a very circumspect man. Penkovskiy's fear was probably the result of his own jumpiness.

On July 5 he had a last meeting with Wynne at the Peking Restaurant, where it was obvious that they both were under heavy surveillance. Trying to sort out the events of this day in mind he wrote down this account in the *Papers*:

Up to his recent trip to Moscow everything went normally, there were no questions, and the embassy was given approval for his visa. The first days of his work passed normally, but a day before his departure Levin told me that his people (KGB) were interested in the aims of Wynne's visit. I told him that besides the Committee, Wynne must visit the Trade Council or the Ministry of Foreign Trade about the question of organizing the mobile exhibition. Levin said that he knew all this, but that for some reason they have become interested in Wynne. I learned all this in the afternoon—after I had given Wynne the second batch of material. I had made a date with him for 2100 hours that same day for a farewell supper. I was working officially with Wynne, and the organs (KGB) had been informed of this—in such cases the "neighbors" are not supposed to surveil us. On approaching the Peking I noticed surveillance of Wynne. I decided to go away without approaching him. Then I became afraid that he might have some return material for me before his departure from Moscow. I decided to enter the restaurant and to have dinner with Wynne in plain sight of everyone. Entering the vestibule I saw that Wynne was "surrounded" (and that surveillance was either a demonstrative or an inept one). Having noted that there were no free tables, I decided to leave, knowing that Wynne would follow me. I only wanted to find out if he had material for me and then to part with him until morning, having told him that I would see him off. Having gone 100–150 meters I entered a large through courtyard with a garden, Wynne followed me, and the two of us immediately saw the two detectives following us. Exchanging a few words, we separated.

I was very indignant about this insolence, and on the following day, after seeing Wynne off, I reported officially to my superiors that KGB workers had prevented me from dining with a foreigner whom we respect, have known for a long time, with whom we have relations of mutual trust, with whom I have been working for a long time, etc. I said that our guest felt uncomfortable when he saw that he was being tendered such "attention." My superiors agreed with me that this was a disgrace, and Levin (the KGB representative) was equally indignant about the surveillance. Levin said that the committee and I as its representative granted the necessary courtesies to Wynne and that "we" (KGB) do not have any claims on him. . . .

Wynne's own report of the meeting, as given in his memoirs, bears repeating:

I happened to get to this restaurant a little earlier than I should and I walked up and down the pavement. I saw some characters standing around, but they didn't pay too much attention, for the moment. But then, after about ten minutes, Penkovskiy came along with his briefcase on his arm. I crossed the road and went up to him, but instead of greeting me, he just put his hand to his nose, lowered his head, and went straight into the doorway.

I followed him into the hotel, where there were people coming and going. He went up to the entrance door, and looked into the restaurant, walked about and as he was passing me he said something that sounded like, "Follow *behind* me." I gathered there was something wrong and I took the hint.

Penkovskiy went out into the street and walked for a few hundred yards to where there was a gap in the buildings leading to a tenement area of wooden houses. He went in there. As I was coming by he spoke to me, "Grev, quick!" I went into the alleyway and he said, "You must go away now, quick. I might see you at the airport tomorrow, but you are being followed. Go." And he went the other way.

As I came out of the alley I saw two men standing there. And of course later in Lubianka I saw photographs. They had had cameras. . . .

Wynne had already booked passage to London on a flight which left Moscow the next afternoon. He decided to check out of his hotel as quickly as possible and go to the airport, before the KGB might make its own decision to apprehend him. (Despite the widely vaunted omniscience of Soviet security forces, they do not move without something of the same consultations, approvals, and counter-signatures which are necessary in any bureaucracy.) He reached Sheremetyevo Airport at five-thirty the next morning.

At the airport, Wynne at first made no move to change his ticket. He merely sat down on an outer bench in the waiting room, to see if Penkovskiy would come. Wisely, he set out to make himself as inconspicuous as possible.

Forty-five minutes later, after two taxis had rolled up to the airport entrance, Wynne saw a private car come up to the outer gates of the airport, then park outside. Penkovskiy quickly got out of the car and walked into the terminal. He first walked past Wynne—as was his custom—to check any possible surveillance. Then he turned and sat beside him. He told Wynne he must leave immediately.

Using his authority with customs officials and the airport staff, Penkovskiy personally changed Wynne's tickets, rushed him through customs, and booked him on the first available flight to the West, an S.A.S. flight to Copenhagen leaving about 9 A.M. Although Penkovskiy succeeded in overawing the airport guards, it was obvious that for the long term this precipitate action killed whatever chances remained to him of neutralizing the regime's suspicion, or at least explaining away his connection with Wynne. It was an act of self-sacrifice and Wynne never forgot it.

For the next two months, instead of lying low, Penkovskiy redoubled his intelligence activity. Perhaps he knew that the game was up. But it was more likely that he was driven by the importance of what he had to communicate. There is little doubt that at this time his main concern was with Khrushchev's nuclear preparations.

On October 22, according to Soviet sources, Oleg Penkovskiy was arrested by the KGB. On November 2, Greville Wynne was kidnaped by the KGB in Budapest, where he had gone with more plans for a mobile trade exhibition in Eastern Europe. He was taken to Moscow. He next saw Penkovskiy through a peephole in Lubianka Prison.

The inevitable question occurs: what betrayed them? It was probably not shrewd, farseeing detective work either on the part of the KGB or the GRU. That is where real life so often departs from the spy stories of fiction. According to the canons of espionage literature, there must have been a lynx-eyed KGB colonel somewhere who had been patiently accumulating a mosaic of fact and hypothesis in the "Penkovskiy case," each element of which was innocent in itself but damning as part of a totality. The Soviet authorities, in fact, finally produced this master sleuth, one Lieutenant Colonel A. V. Gvozdilin, although he was not unveiled until two years after the trial.

Yet the real-life KGB, with or without Colonel Gvozdilin, took twenty-three years to find out that Penkovskiy's father was a White officer, a fact which does not suggest the presence of any Soviet Arsène Lupins or even Sam Spades buried in its table of organization. There is no evidence available that the KGB acted with any greater speed or shrewdness in determining that the GRU colonel was betraying the Soviet regime.

Penkovskiy had detected signs of surveillance in 1962, but such KGB activity was hardly a rarity in the life of the most trusted Soviet official. Although his chance meetings with Mrs. Chisholm look suspicious in hindsight, actually none of Penkovskiy's associations with foreigners—not even the circumstances of his casual meetings—had been out of line with his normal duties on the committee and in GRU. Only by the summer were the signs of surveillance multiplying. Even then, Greville Wynne himself felt that, at worst, the KGB thought he and Penkovskiy might have been engaged in some black-market trading.

A cautious man would have run to cover at the first signs of continuing surveillance. In July, for example, Penkovskiy could have sent off a message to London that he was breaking off communication, eased off his Western contacts for some months, and—above all—destroyed the incriminating home-espionage kit in the hidden compartment of his desk drawer.

Penkovskiy was a cautious man by training, but not by nature. Every human has his own "hubris," as the Greek dramatists used to tell us, and Oleg Penkovskiy was no exception to the rule. In some lines of work pride goeth before a fall and rises again; the victim of hubris can recover and go on to great heights, if humbler and wiser for having had his overconfidence shaken. But a spy can make only one mistake. He receives no second chance.

The same private personal assurance which made Penkovskiy so successful was undoubtedly what brought him down. Ivan Berzin, who had commanded the GRU in 1934, once made the classic comment about his craft: "In our work boldness, daring, risk, and great audacity must be combined with great prudence. Dialectics!" Penkovskiy never lost his audacity or his sense of risk. He chose to sacrifice his prudence.

When in January, 1962, he suspected that he had been observed during at least one rendezvous with one of his contacts, he quickly called off further meetings at that time and resorted to the use of the dead drop. But he continued to pass on documents and write down his observations. His friends and superiors at the committee continued to trust him. He continued to feel secure in the GRU offices on the Arbat. He knew that the danger, if it came, would come from the KGB, which had presumably been tinkering with his dossier since the discovery of his father's allegiance to the White Army. As the *Papers* indicate, he was aware of the danger.

It is easy to explain, by hindsight, how the KGB could have worked up its case against Penkovskiy. KGB agents abroad as well as in Moscow were trained to report any Soviet official's contacts with foreigners, as a matter of routine. By the spring of 1962 Penkovskiy's frequent meetings with Wynne and other foreigners must have occasioned many individual routine notations in his KGB file. Although they could be explained by virtue of his position, the number of observations were probably enough to cause the faintest kind of question mark.

The mass of gifts and presents which Penkovskiy brought back from the West must also have aroused the suspicions of the KGB in Moscow—even if most of them were destined for his superiors or co-workers. The presents were obviously worth more than Penkovskiy, given his earnings and expense allowances, could have spent for them. This might add up to another question mark on his record—not enough evidence of any trouble, but enough to deepen suspicion a little, even if only suspicion of black-market dealings.

There is another important factor. Through the spring and summer of 1962, as tension with the West increased, the KGB was tightening its surveillance of all foreigners. Thus even the casual contacts which Penkovskiy had made in Moscow with British and American attachés were now noted with more care than they might have been—since the foreigners were under closer watch.

Penkovskiy continued to feel free in meeting Wynne because he knew Wynne was not himself an intelligence officer but a businessman who was exactly what his calling card stated. The KGB, however, obviously regarded Wynne as a suspicious character, if only for his repeated trips to Moscow—and despite the fact that the GRU looked on the Englishman as a possible recruit.

Penkovskiy kept up his visits to libraries in the Ministry of Defense, where he read classified literature on many areas obviously not in his immediate purview. Given the volume of information that he transmitted, it is reasonable to assume that someone must have seen him and, again, made some small notation.

Penkovskiy constantly relied on his well-placed connections with people like Marshal Varentsov and General Serov to divert suspicion. But to the KGB mind these connections could arouse suspicion, as well as respect.

At the first hint of suspicion, the KGB is apt to make its own secret search of a suspect's apartment. Someone must inevitably have taken a close look at his desk. Once the secret drawer was found, the jig was up. But when this happened no one here knows.

We do know that Penkovskiy's meeting with Wynne in July was recorded and photographed. Wynne notes this in his own recollections of his trial: "They would produce a tape recorder and there would be Penkovskiy's voice, and mine. That was sufficient to tell me they had been listening to conversations. . . . In the conversation I could be heard saying, 'I wish you well, Alex,' and, 'I have a letter for you from them,' and Penkovskiy's voice—'Yes, in the letter they say very good things. . . .' "

Either Wynne's room happened to be bugged, as the rooms of so many foreigners in Moscow are, and the transcript led to Penkovskiy's search—or Penkovskiy's apartment was searched, which led to the KGB's watch on Wynne's room. In any event, someone in the KGB finally put two and two together.

We still do not know when this moment of truth came to the KGB. It was probably not in July. We assume that Penkovskiy was still sending out information to the West late in August, at the time of the last notations in the *Papers*. And it is highly doubtful, given the tensions of the Cuban missile effort, then abuilding, that someone of Penkovskiy's station would be allowed to continue sending out information, even for the purpose of tracking his contacts. He was too big a fish for any counterintelligence agency to dangle on a line.

More probably, given the normal mill of Soviet bureaucracy—imagine the job of recording and processing thousands of taped conversations by foreigners each day—it took weeks before the evidence against Penkovskiy and Wynne was put together and brought to the proper authorities.

7

Casanova's Journey to Dunkirk

Jacques Casanova

*The reasons why Casanova, who was occasionally
employed as a spy, is better remembered as a great
lover than for his exploits in the role of spy are
made amply clear by this selection. Here we see
this famous adventurer in his own account of an
espionage mission. Among other things, he breaks
a cardinal rule about not being conspicuous when
he complains about the inspection of his baggage
as he passes through customs. On the other hand,
this may display the expert psychology to which
certain hardened types will resort in an emergency.
If an agent makes a loud fuss and seems to be
going out of his way to draw attention to himself,
then he could hardly be a spy because a spy would
never do that.*

*The events described took place in 1757, when
elements of the English fleet were anchored off
Dunkirk during the Seven Years' War. Casanova's
mission was to penetrate the area for the French
Admiralty and bring back a report on the disposition and strength of the English fleet.*

FROM the book *The Memoirs of Jacques Casanova.*

THE FIRST QUESTION the abbé asked me was whether I thought myself capable of paying a visit to eight or ten men-of-war in the roads at Dunkirk, of making the acquaintance of the officers, and of completing a minute and circumstantial report of the victualing, the number of seamen, the guns, ammunition, discipline, etc., etc.

"I will make the attempt," I said, "and will hand you in my report on my return, and it will be for you to say if I have succeeded or not."

"As this is a secret mission, I cannot give you a letter of commendation; I can only give you some money and wish you a pleasant journey."

"I do not wish to be paid in advance—on my return you can give me what you think fit. I shall want three or four days before setting out, as I must procure some letters of introduction."

"Very good. Try to come back before the end of the month. I have no further instructions to give you. You quite understand how discreet your behaviour must be. Above all, do not get into any trouble; for I suppose you know that, if anything happened to you, it would be of no use to talk of your mission. We should be obliged to know nothing about you, for ambassadors are the only avowed spies. Remember that you must be even more careful and reserved than they, and yet, if you wish to succeed, all this must be concealed, and you must have an air of freedom from constraint that you may inspire confidence."

(Casanova goes to Dunkirk)

After we had partaken of an excellent supper several persons arrived, and play commenced, in which I did not join, as I wished to study the society of the place, and above all certain officers of both services who were present. By means of speaking with an air of authority about naval matters, and by saying that I had served in the Navy of the Venetian Republic, in three days I not only knew but was intimate with all the captains of the Dunkirk fleet. I talked at random about naval architecture, on the Venetian system of maneuvers, and I noticed that the jolly sailors were better pleased at my blunders than at my sensible remarks.

Four days after I had been at Dunkirk, one of the captains asked me to dinner on his ship, and after that all the others did the same; and on every occasion I stayed in the ship for the rest of the day. I was curious about everything—and Jack is so trustful! I went into the hold, I asked questions innumerable, and I found plenty of young officers delighted to show their own importance, who gossiped without needing any encouragement from me. I took care, however, to learn everything which would be of service to me, and in the evenings I put down on paper all the mental notes I had made during the day. Four or five hours was all I allowed myself for sleep, and in fifteen days I found I had learnt enough.

(Casanova sets out on the return journey to Paris)

My task was done, and bidding good-bye to all my friends, I set out in my post-chaise for Paris, going by another way for the sake of a change. About midnight, on my asking for horses at some stage, the name of which I forget, they told me that the next stage was the fortified town of Aire, which we should not be allowed to pass through at nighttime.

"Get me the horses," said I, "I will make them open the gates."

I was obeyed, and in due time we reached the gates. The postillion cracked his whip and the sentry called out, "Who goes there?"

"Express messenger."

After making me wait for an hour the gate was opened, and I was told that I must go and speak to the Governor. I did so, fretting and fuming on my way as if I were some great person, and I was taken to a room where a man in an elegant nightcap was lying in bed.

"Whose messenger are you?"

"Nobody's, but as I am in a hurry . . ."

"That will do. We will talk the matter over tomorrow. In the meanwhile you will accept the hospitality of the guard-room."

"But, sir . . ."

"But me no buts, if you please; leave the room."

I was taken to the guard-room, where I spent the night

seated on the ground. The daylight appeared. I shouted, swore, made all the racket I could, said I wanted to go on, but nobody took any notice of me.

(After further complications and disputes Casanova gets away from Aire and continues his journey)

At five o'clock in the morning I was fast alseep in my carriage, when I was suddenly awakened. We were at the gate of Amiens. The fellow at the door was an exciseman —a race everywhere detested and with good cause, for besides the insolence of their manners nothing makes a man feel more like a slave than the inquisitorial search they are accustomed to make through one's clothes and most secret possessions. He asked me if I had anything contraband; and being in a bad temper at being deprived of my sleep to answer such a question I replied with an oath that I had nothing of the sort, and that he would have done better to let me sleep.

"As you talk in that style," said the creature, "we will see what we can see."

He ordered the postillion to pass on with the carriage. He had my luggage hauled down, and not being able to hinder him I fumed in silence.

I saw my mistake, but there was now nothing to be done; and having no contraband goods I had nothing to fear, but my bad temper cost me two weary hours of delay. The joys of vengeance were depicted on the features of the exciseman. At the time of which I am writing these gougers were the dregs of the people, but would become tractable on being treated with a little politeness. The sum of twenty-four sous given with good grace would make them as supple as a pair of gloves; they would bow to the travelers, wish them a pleasant journey, and give no trouble. I knew all this, but there are times when a man acts mechanically, as I had done, unfortunately.

The scoundrels emptied my boxes and unfolded everything, even to my shirts, between which they said I might have concealed English lace.

After searching everything they gave me back my keys, but they had not yet done with me; they began to search my carriage. The rascal who was at the head of them

began to shout "victory"; he had discovered the remainder
of a pound of snuff which I had bought at St. Omer on my
way to Dunkirk.

With a voice of triumph the chief exciseman gave orders
that my carriage should be seized, and warned me that I
would have to pay a fine of twelve hundred francs.

(Casanova finally gets to Paris)

I took my report to M. de Bernis, at the Hotel Bourdon,
and his excellence spent two hours over it, making me take
out all unnecessary matter. I spent the time in making a
fair copy, and the next day I took it to M. de la Ville, who
read it through in silence, and told me that he would let me
know the result. A month after I received five hundred
louis, and I had the pleasure of hearing that M. de
Cremille, the First Lord of the Admiralty, had pronounced
my report to be not only perfectly accurate but very sug-
gestive. When I told M. de Bernis my adventures on the
way back, he laughed, but said that the highest merit of a
secret agent was to keep out of difficulties; for though he
might have the tact to extricate himself from them, yet he
got talked of, which it should be his chief care to avoid.

This mission cost the admiralty twelve thousand francs,
and the Minister might easily have procured all the information I gave him without spending a penny. Any intelligent young naval officer would have done it just as well,
and would have acquitted himself with zeal and discretion,
to gain the good opinion of the ministers.

II

Networks:

The Organization of Espionage

"THEY COME NOT single spies, but in battalions," as Shakespeare wrote in *Hamlet*. Spies working in a group for one intelligence service in a single area usually have little or no knowledge of each other; they are likely to be organized under a head agent who gives them their instructions and receives their reports. The head agent culls and processes the information and then funnels it into a communications channel through which it is transmitted to intelligence headquarters. The channel is likely to be a radio, operated by a clandestine operator who works closely with the head agent. Usually, there are numerous go-betweens or cut-outs who serve as messengers between the head agent and his subordinates. A major purpose of the cut-outs is to preserve the security of the network. The subagents may not know the identity or whereabouts of the head agent. They may not even know the identity of the cut-out. If they are caught they cannot betray the others; only the extent of their own work is in danger of being revealed.

This is the ideal. In practice, and especially in wartime, the members of a network learn about each other when emergencies make some contact between them necessary. Thus, in the case of two of the great Soviet networks in enemy territory, described in the following selections (the

Sorge Ring and the Rote Kapelle), the apprehension of various subordinate members of the ring eventually led to the apprehension of other members, including the leaders, because the subordinates, in the course of their work, had managed to learn about their associates and gave them away under pressure.

The radio transmitting is, of course, the most vulnerable point in the network. Not only is it exposed to radio-locating (direction-finding) techniques during transmission time, which was how the Germans closed in on the Rote Kapelle network, but the capture of the radio operator, especially with some of his messages intact, may lead to the agents whether or not the radio operator knows their identity. The contents of the messages (if they can be deciphered or are not yet enciphered) will give the counterespionage specialist a pretty good idea of the area where the sources are located or employed.

1

Spymaster George Washington

Corey Ford

The Culper Ring, a network of Revolutionary spies in the New York area, was operated by Washington's intelligence chief, Colonel Benjamin Tallmadge, but was to a great extent under the personal direction of Washington himself. Its members were, according to Corey Ford, "amateurs untrained in the business of spying. Nathan Hale's capture and death had pointed the need for a more efficient undercover operation; their unit was the result of his sacrifice. It was America's first organized espionage service, the beginning of our modern intelligence."

The target, as we would call it today, was British military headquarters in New York. The Culper Ring probably had many sources among merchants and artisans in New York who had commerce with the British, but for high-level information the ring had two important sources: Robert Townsend, who used the name Samuel Culper Junior in his reports, and his mistress, the lady known as "355."

From his home town of Setauket on the north shore of Long Island, Tallmadge recruited a num-

FROM the book *A Peculiar Service*.

*ber of acquaintances for his network. Abraham
Woodhull (Samuel Culper Senior), using the top
floor of his brother-in-law's boardinghouse in New
York as a hideaway, prepared the messages intended for Washington which were picked up and
carried on horseback by a farmer from Setauket,
Austin Roe, who, in turn, handed them over to a
boatman, Caleb Brewster, who took them across
Long Island Sound at night and delivered them to
Tallmadge (John Bolton), who then relayed them
to General Washington.*

ABRAHAM WOODHULL'S APPEARANCE was his best protection. No one could have seemed more unlikely as a spy.
His ashen face and thin trembling hands, his frightened
voice which seldom rose above a whisper, were the very
opposite of the conventional cloak-and-dagger operator. He
lived in constant terror of discovery, his stomach knotting
whenever a stranger looked at him twice. Only by sheer
force of will could he bring himself to visit enemy encamp-
ments on the island and observe their strength and position.
A sharp glance, a routine challenge by a sentry was enough
to send him into a nervous decline and he would take to his
bed with a chill. The Culper correspondence with Tallmadge fairly shivered with anxiety. "I have to request that
you will destroy every letter instantly after reading," he
pleaded, "for fear of some unforeseen accident that may
befall you and the letters get into the enemies hands and
probably find me out and take me before I have any warning. I desire you to be particularly cairfull."

His apprehension that the letters might betray him was
relieved by a Sympathetic Stain developed in London by
Sir James Jay, brother of John Jay, according to a formula
of his own that has never been solved. The secret ink
consisted of a fluid which would disappear immediately
when applied to the whitest paper, and a counterpart which
could be brushed over the paper to make the writing visible
again.

Even the use of Jay's Sympathetic Stain did not wholly
allay Woodhull's jitters. The presence of British officers in
adjoining chambers at the Underhill boardinghouse kept
his nerves on edge, and his conversations with Austin Roe

were conducted in whispers lest the enemy should overhear him through the thin walls. On one occasion, while he was sitting alone in his attic bedroom preparing a dispatch in secret ink, the door burst open behind him. In panic he leapt to his feet, upsetting the table and spilling the precious bottle on the floor, only to find that the intruder was his sister Mary. Tallmadge reported the incident to Washington, explaining soberly that the temporary lapse in Woodhull's correspondence was because "an excessive fright and turbulence of passions so wrought on poor Culper that he has hardly been in tolerable health since."

Slowly and cautiously the Culper Ring expanded that fall. Woodhull confided his mission—though not his code name of Samuel Culper—to his brother-in-law Amos Underhill, who was in a good position to gather information from his British boarders. William T. Robinson, a prominent local merchant who was accepted as a Loyalist, passed bits of intelligence to him, and occasionally prepared a letter, written in Tory style, which contained news of military interest. Joseph Lawrence of Bayside, a friend of Robinson and also of Caleb Brewster, cooperated in sending him word of enemy movements on Long Island.

Woodhull realized that his prolonged absence from home might arouse enemy suspicion in Setauket, and he made every effort to enlist a trustworthy confederate who would gather information in New York while he returned to Long Island. He found his answer in a quiet and highly respected young Quaker merchant from Oyster Bay named Robert Townsend.

Since much of Robert Townsend's business was conducted along the waterfront, he was in a good position to observe British shipping activity.

He entered into partnership with Henry Oakman, and opened a dry-goods business at 18 Smith Street, a block from his boardinghouse. It was a good precaution. Austin Roe's frequent calls at the Underhill home were bound to provoke enemy questions in time; but the courier could visit the Oakman & Townsend store without arousing suspicion, on the pretext of purchasing goods for his Setauket neighbors, and deliver a message from Tallmadge or pick up a dispatch from Samuel Culper Junior.

Townsend had entered into his new role with reluctance,

torn between a deep sense of guilt and a deeper sense of duty. His upright Quaker conscience rebelled against his shameful occupation, but the same conscience would not let him go back on his promise to Woodhull. He was a grave and introspective young man, not yet twenty-five, simply dressed in Quaker style, his chestnut hair cut short and drawn back in a club. His features were rugged rather than handsome; he had the prominent Townsend nose and cleft chin, and there was a dark pigmentation around his eyes, the result of sleepless nights. They were soft brooding eyes, not coldly estimating like Major John André's or glazed with fanatic conviction like those of Nathan Hale. His rare smile was shy and sensitive, and women found it irresistible.

Austin Roe possessed a serene indifference to danger, and his lackadaisical drawl disarmed any sentry who challenged him. His feats of horsemanship outshone those of Paul Revere; on innumerable occasions he rode the 110-mile round trip between Setauket and New York, through a countryside infested with bandits and regularly patrolled by Royal dragoons. Once his wife, Catherine, asked him on his return if he had run into any trouble on the road. "Nothin' to speak of, dear," he replied casually. "Just these couple of little holes in my hat."

He would leave his horse at the hitching post in front of Oakman & Townsend's and saunter into the store, covered with dust from his long morning ride, and hand Robert Townsend a written order from John Bolton: "You will be pleased to send by bearer ½ ream letter paper, same as last shipment." Townsend would wrap and seal the ream, and Roe would pay for his purchase and leave the store. As soon as his partner's back was turned, Townsend would slip out a rear door and hurry to the boardinghouse where Roe would be waiting. They would climb the stairs to his chamber, and he would take a vial of Sympathetic Stain from his closet and brush John Bolton's order with the restorative fluid, bringing out the message from Tallmadge inscribed between the lines. Carefully unwrapping the ream of paper so it could be sealed again, Townsend would remove a single page and write in invisible ink his answers to General Washington's questions. He would count the sheets in the ream until he reached a number agreed upon with Roe, insert the apparently blank page, and replace the wrapping; and Roe would stow the package with the other purchases in his saddlebag and set out on his perilous ride back to Setauket.

Roe had arranged to pasture his cattle in Abraham Woodhull's rear meadow which sloped down to Conscience Bay. On his return to the tavern that evening, he would pull out the blank sheet from the ream, conceal it in his shirt, and stroll over to the woodhull farm to attend his cows. Since it might have attracted attention if they were seen to meet, a wooden box was buried in a corner of the meadow. Roe would drop the paper in his box, and shortly afterward Woodhull would go to the pasture and retrieve it.

Locking the door of his bedroom, Culper Senior would develop Townsend's reply with the restorative, and either transcribe it or enclose it in an added letter of his own. A black petticoat on Anna Strong's clothesline across the bay would tell him that Caleb Brewster had arrived, and the number of handkerchiefs hanging beside it would direct him to the particular cove where the whaleboat was hidden. Shortly after dark, Woodhull would follow the back lanes to the rendezvous point and deliver the message, and Brewster would row back across the Devil's Belt to Connecticut, fighting down the temptation to tackle an enemy merchant sloop on the way. In Fairfield he would hand the message to Tallmadge, and a series of mounted dragoons, posted every fifteen miles, would forward Culper's dispatch to Washington's headquarters over by the Hudson.

The circuitous route was necessarily slow, and sometimes the delay proved costly. On June 29th, Culper Junior wrote Tallmadge from New York: "I was this day informed that 2 British Regt. of Col. Fanning's Corps & the associated loyalists, is now at white Stone, where they arrived yesterday from Rhode Island—This I have no doubt of, as it was told me by a person who came passenger with them—He thinks they are to make excursions into Connecticut—and from what I can collect I believe they are, and very soon." Woodhull forwarded the message with a

warning of his own. "Enclosed you have Mr. Saml. Culper
Junr's letter. . . . He hath hinted to you the prospect of
their making excursions in to Connecticut soon. Very
probably the war will be carried on in that manner, as free
liberty is granted to the Refugees to plunder as much as
they can. You must keep a very good look out or your
shores will be destroyed."

The Culper warning arrived too late. Colonel Sheldon's
Second Regiment of Dragoons was stationed at Poundridge,
near Bedford, New York, and Major Tallmadge and some
ninety troops occupied an advance post near the Poundridge Church. In a dawn attack, Lord Rawdon's Light
Horse and a body of light infantry charged the forward
position. The outnumbered Americans fought with clash-
ing cavalry sabers until Tallmadge ordered a retreat. Much
of the regiment's equipment fell into the enemy's hands,
and Tallmadge lost not only a fine horse and most of his
field baggage, but, far more serious, some money and confidential papers which Washington had sent him to be delivered to the Culpers. One captured letter from the General mentioned S—— C—— and "his successor (whose
name I have no desire to be informed of)," and also "a
man on York Island living at or near the North River of
the name of George Higday, who I am told hath given
signal proof of his attachment to us . . . his name and
business should be kept profoundly secret, otherwise we
not only lose the benefits derived from it, but may subject
him to some unhappy fate." Washington promised that
"when I can procure some more of the Liquid C——r
writes for, it shall be sent."

Tallmadge reported the loss of his papers, and Washington rebuked him in exceedingly mild terms, pointing out
that the unlucky accident "shows how dangerous it is to
keep papers of any consequence at an advanced post," and
offering to replace the guineas and also Tallmadge's personal effects which had been abandoned in his hasty flight.
The General added: "The person who is most endangered
by the acquisition of your letters is Higday. . . . I wish you
could endeavor to give him the speediest notice of what has
happened. My anxiety on his account is great."

The raid had given British counterintelligence some valuable information. Now they knew the existence of a secret ink, the route of the messages by way of Connecticut, the initials of two spies, S———— C———— and C————r, and the name and location of another. Though George Higday was promptly seized, he had been alerted in time to destroy any incriminating evidence. He escaped being hanged, but his usefulness to the Culper Ring was ended.

Since British intelligence had learned that the Americans were using a Sympathetic Stain, Washington was fearful that they might intercept a secret letter and find a way to develop it. Late in July, as an added measure of security, Major Tallmadge was ordered to work out a cipher and numerical code to be used by the Culpers in future correspondence. Only four code books were prepared, for General Washington and Townsend and Woodhull and Tallmadge himself. These were zealously guarded by the Culpers, for their discovery would mean certain conviction and death on the gallows.

The code was simple enough. On a double sheet of foolscap, Tallmadge listed in alphabetical order the words most apt to be employed in the Culper messages, taken from a copy of Entick's Dictionary, and opposite each word he wrote a corresponding number. In addition to the standard vocabulary, certain important geographical names had special designations—New York was 727, Long Island 728, Setauket 729—and the key personnel were likewise assigned numbers. General Washington was 711, and the leading members of the espionage ring followed in sequence: 721 was John Bolton; 722 was Culper Saml.; 723 was Culper Junr.; 724 was Austin Roe; 725 was C. Brewster.

The Culpers had still another accomplice in New York. In a cipher letter, using the code book supplied by Tallmadge, Woodhull wrote on August 15th: "Every 356 [letter] is opened at the entrance of 727 (New York), and every one is searched. They have some 345 (knowledge) of the route our 354 [letter] takes. . . . I intended to visit 727 [New York] before long and think by the assistance of a 355 of my acquaintance, shall be able to out wit them all."

355 was the code number for "lady." Although she be-

came one of the most important agents of the American secret service, and the mother of Robert Townsend's child, 355 was never known by any other name.

Of all the secrets of the Culper Ring, the identity of 355 has been the most carefully preserved. Only a few random facts have emerged from the past to guide us. We know from Woodhull's early letter that she was "an acquaintance" who resided in the city, and who could "outwit them all." This would indicate that 355 was already involved in espionage work when Robert Townsend met her. We know that sometime in 1780—perhaps at the same moment that Townsend resigned—she became his common-law wife, and their son was christened Robert Townsend Junior. We know that shortly after Arnold defected to the British she was arrested as a spy, on or about October 20th; Woodhull's letter of that date mentions the imprisonment of "one that hath been ever serviceable to this correspondence."

And that is all we know. Her very name is lost to us. Robert Townsend never revealed it during his lifetime. If his strait-laced Quaker family knew of her existence, they kept it to themselves; to this day the Townsend records at Raynham Hall list Robert as a bachelor. No fragmentary phrase in a letter or diary offers a clue to her background. Was she related to a prominent Tory family? Did her social position enable her to gain access to highly classified British intelligence, some of it known only to the Commander-in-Chief and his aide? Evidently Arnold suspected her of revealing the West Point plot; she was the only active member of the Culper Ring to be taken up when he fled to New York. General Clinton was too cautious and tight-lipped to betray any confidences; but Major André's vanity might have led him to babble military secrets to a charming companion.

Suppose, then, that 355 was one of the decorative females with whom the dilettante Major André liked to surround himself. Her appeal was intellectual; she flattered him about his poetry, he talked to her unguardedly. Though she and Robert Townsend had fallen in love, she continued her flirtation with André, hoping to pry more information from him, and her meetings with Townsend took place at a hidden rendezvous, perhaps the Underhill house. I like to picture 355 as the opposite of the reserved and sober young Quaker: small, pert, vivacious, clever enough to outwit the enemy, but feminine enough to give Townsend a brief interlude of happiness that he would never know again. Her eyes would tease him out of his somber mood, her warm throaty laugh could bring an unaccustomed smile to his grave face. Their romance prospered over the winter, while Clinton was in Carolina with his aide. A legal marriage was impossible, since it was bound to be discovered when André returned, but in their own eyes they were already man and wife; and in April Townsend learned that she was carrying his child.

News from the South warned that the surrender of Charleston was imminent, and we can suppose that Townsend, in light of her condition, insisted that she quit the Culper Ring with him. They would be married, they would leave the city together. 355 refused; her liaison with the British secret service was too valuable a source of intelligence to abandon, she insisted, and her duty was to remain here. It was their first quarrel. Racked by his Quaker conscience, filled with guilt and self-blame, he notified Washington that he would serve no longer.

His resignation left the Manhattan unit without a head, and Woodhull was unable to suggest a successor. "If any person can be pointed out by 711 (Washington) at N.Y. who can be safely relied on to supply C. Junr's place," he wrote Tallmadge, "I will make myself known to him, and settle a plan for the purpose," but he made it clear that he would not resume residence in the city under any circumstances. Tallmadge forwarded the letter to Washington, and offered his personal opinion that "even C. Senior grows timid & think the intercourse had better be dropt for the present."

General Washington's reply was blunt, and betrayed the Commander-in-Chief's impatience with his temperamental agents: "As C. Junior has totally declined and C. Senior seems to wish to do it, I think the intercourse may be dropped, more especially as from our present position the intelligence is so long getting to hand that it is of no use by the time it reaches me. . . . I am endeavoring to open a communication with New York across Staten Island, but who are the agents in the City, I do not know. I am &c., Go. Washington."

Although Culper Senior was cut to the quick by the General's curt dismissal, he tried to conceal his feelings in a plaintive letter of farewell. "I am happy to find that 711 is about to establish a more advantageous channel of information than heretofore. I perceive that the former he intimates hath been but of little service. Sorry we have been at so much cost and trouble for so little or no purpose. He also mentions my backwardness to serve. He certainly hath been misinformed. You are sensible that I have been indefatigable, and have done it from a principal of duty rather than from any mercenary end—and as hinted heretofore, if at any time theres need you may rely on my faithful endeavors."

The Sympathetic Stain was put away, no more signals fluttered from Anna Strong's clothesline, and grass grew over the buried box in Woodhull's pasture beside Conscience Bay. The Culper Ring was suspended.

Robert Townsend resumed the role of Culper Junior as abruptly as he had quit it two months before. Again there is no explanation in the correspondence, and again we can only surmise. Perhaps his sense of duty overcame his scruples; perhaps he found it unbearable to be away from 355, and Washington's request furnished him with the excuse he needed. In any case, soon after, while Roe remained in concealment at the Underhill house, the Manhattan spies gathered facts and figures about British military plans, some of them seemingly from Clinton's own headquarters. The method of smuggling this vital intelligence out of the city presented a new problem to Townsend. The British had posted guards at all the exits from Manhattan, and were searching everyone who might carry information of their anticipated move. Fortunately he still had enough Sympathetic Stain on hand to write his dispatch in invisible ink; but to follow the usual procedure of hiding it in a ream of black paper, and adding other heavy parcels in order to avert suspicion, would encumber Roe and delay his return.

Townsend's solution was to write an ordinary business

letter, addressed to Colonel Benjamin Floyd in Brookhaven: "New York, July 20th, 1780. Sir, I recd your favor by [here "Mr. Roe" is crossed out, but is still legible] and note the contents. The articles you want cannot be procured, as soon as they can will send them. I am, Your humble servant, Samuel Culper." Colonel Floyd's home had recently been plundered by raiders, and it would be natural for him to make purchases in the city. Not only would the letter seem plausible, but it would explain why Roe was returning empty-handed. No one could see the message on the reverse side, written in secret Stain.

The letter was read and passed by the British sentry at the Brooklyn ferry, and Roe rode back safely to Setauket. He stabled his horse, and strolled over to the Woodhull farm, ostensibly to inquire about his neighbor's health. Closing and bolting the door of Woodhull's chamber, he gave him Townsend's message and reported what he had learned. Woodhull propped himself up in bed, and in a shaky hand added a postscript to Tallmadge: "Your letter came to hand and found me very ill with a fever, and still continues . . . 724 [Austin Roe] returned this day in great haste with the enclosed dispatch from Culper Junior. Also assures of the arrival of Admiral Graves with six ships of the line and is joined by three more out of New York, also one of 50 and two of 40 guns and has sailed for Rhode Island and is supposed they will be there before this can possibly reach you. Also 8000 troops are this day embarking at Whitestone for the above mentioned port. . . . You must excuse all imperfections at this time on the account of my before mentioned fever. Nevertheless you have perhaps all the needful—and pray for your success and exercions. And am yours sincerely, Saml. Culper."

Caleb Brewster had been waiting at the Strong Mansion for Roe's return, and Woodhull sent him a personal note: "Sir, The enclosed requires your immediate departure this day by all means let not an hour pass: for this day must not be lost. You have news of the greatest consequence perhaps that ever happened to your country. John Bolton must order your returne when he thinks proper. S.C."

Brewster could not locate Tallmadge immediately on his arrival in Fairfield, and he persuaded another officer in the dragoons to carry the dispatch to Washington's Preakness, New Jersey, headquarters, where it arrived shortly before 4 P.M. on the 21st. In Washington's temporary absence, it was received by his aide-de-camp, Colonel Alexander Hamilton, who knew about the Sympathetic Stain and developed the secret intelligence on the back of the Floyd letter. Hamilton rushed the information to General Lafayette, who had left Preakness a few days before and was on his way to Newport. "The Gen'l is absent and may not return before midnight." Hamilton wrote Lafayette. "Though this may be only a demonstration, yet as it may be serious, I think it best to forward it without waiting for the Generals return."

Washington studied the situation at his headquarters that evening. At this very moment, he realized, Clinton's troops might well be on their way to Newport. Only a swift counterattack on New York could force them to turn back; and he knew his army was too weak to mount an assault. He picked up a quill pen, and twirled it absently in his fingers. Was it necessary to make a real attack, he pondered. Could Sir Henry be deluded into thinking that an offensive movement against Manhattan was threatened? Might his pen accomplish what his sword was unable to do?

The British transports were heading eastward on the Sound when a Tory farmer, held to be above suspicion, delivered to a British outpost a packet of letters which he said he had discovered on the highway. They were found to contain the details of General Washington's plans for a full-scale invasion of New York with an army of twelve thousand. Signal fires were lighted hastily along the Long Island coast, the fleet was halted at Huntington, and Clinton ordered his forces back to defend New York. Rochambeau completed his landing at Newport unmolested. Several days later, Clinton explained his failure to attack the French in a letter to Lord George Germain in London: "During this time Washington, by a rapid movement, had, with an army increased to 12000 men, passed the North-river, and was moving towards King's-bridge, when he must have learned that my armament had not proceeded to Rhode-Island. He, I apprehend in consequence of this, recrossed the river, and is now near Orange Town (Tappan)."

The Commander-in-Chief, with his delight in subterfuge and intrigue, must have relished the success of his deception.

2

The Spy on the Postage Stamp

F. W. Deakin and G. R. Storry

*I made some mention of one of the most famous
and successful of Soviet spies, Richard Sorge, in
the Foreword to this book. In the selection which
follows we see his network operating, or preparing
to operate, with particular emphasis on its technical management. By way of explanation: Sorge
and his network were reporting to the Fourth
Bureau (intelligence headquarters) of the Red
Army in Moscow. Both Sorge and his main radio
operator, Max Klausen, had been trained for their
jobs by the Fourth Bureau during long visits to
Moscow. Vukelic, one of Sorge's assistants, was
the only other European in the network. All the
rest were Japanese.*

REPRESENTATIVES OF SOVIET special agencies working
abroad normally received strict routine instructions—to
have no contact with the diplomatic missions of the Soviet
government in the countries in which they were operating.
After the outbreak of the European war in September,
1939, however, and the attendant risks of travel to the
International Settlement in Shanghai and the British colony

FROM the book *The Case of Richard Sorge.*

of Hong Kong, Sorge was instructed to risk the establishment of contact with Soviet emissaries in Japan.

In January, 1940, the following instructions from Moscow were received, addressed to Klausen. "You will henceforth receive funds from, and maintain liaison with, a comrade in Tokyo. He will send you two tickets for the Imperial Theatre . . . the man seated next to you will be the comrade." The two tickets appeared shortly afterward in Klausen's post box at the Tokyo Central Post Office and, together with his wife, he kept the rendezvous. In the darkness of the theatre Klausen's neighbor passed him a white handkerchief containing banknotes, and left his seat.

A similar contact in another theatre enabled Klausen to hand over seventy rolls of film and receive further funds. On the next occasion, as Klausen was ill, Sorge himself kept the rendezvous. On radio instructions Klausen subsequently went to a restaurant, where two men were awaiting him, and he was told that one of them would henceforth be his contact.

Further meetings took place either at Klausen's house or at his office. The Russian identified himself as "Serge" and from his conversation Klausen deduced that he was a member of the Soviet Embassy in Tokyo. As the activities of the Sorge ring were intensified by the need for accurate and detailed information on Japanese policy toward the Soviet Union after the outbreak of the European war, the meetings between "Serge" and Klausen became more frequent.

On one occasion, on August 6, 1941, there was a meeting between "Serge" and Klausen, in the latter's office, at which Sorge was also present. "I seem to recall that Sorge and 'Serge' argued about the Russo-German war. The latter said that he knew Sorge from a photograph which he had seen in Moscow."

Klausen met "Serge" for the last time on October 10, 1941, and handed over a map of the Tokyo, Kawasaki and Yokohama areas, marked with the anti-aircraft and searchlight positions. This proved to be Klausen's last mission. The two men fixed a rendezvous for November 20 which Klausen never kept. He was arrested on October 18.

During his subsequent interrogation he was shown two photographs by the Japanese investigating officer. The first was of Klausen's original contact in the Imperial Theatre, who had been identified by the Japanese as a Consul at the Soviet Embassy named Vutkevitch. The second contact— "Serge" to Klausen—was the Soviet Second Secretary and Consul, Viktor Sergevitch Zaitsev, a member of the Russian Military Intelligence.*

After the arrest of the Sorge group, he quietly left Japan. In 1943 he appeared as "Second Secretary" in the Soviet Embassy in Canberra, where one of his colleagues, Petrov, later defected.† In 1947 he was accredited as press attaché to the Soviet Embassy in Washington. It is perhaps significant, however, that by that date American authorities were still in the early stages of investigating the Sorge Case, and it is doubtful whether any connection would have been apparent between the new Soviet press attaché in Washington and Richard Sorge.

"Before I left on my missions to China and Japan," Sorge confessed, "the codes which I was to use were explained to me at my hotel by a man from the Fourth Bureau. We spent a full day going over the instructions."

The work of ciphering and deciphering was the closely guarded secret and the responsibility of the head of each mission abroad. The system adopted by Soviet agents was based on a simple chart substituting single or double figures for the letters of the alphabet for a combination. It was one which could easily be memorized. In order to complicate the breaking of the code an arbitrary list of figures was added to the ciphers of the coded message. These were taken at random from the pages of the German Statistical Year Book, the exact passage being identified in the message.

The ingenuity of this system lay in the infinite variety of figures available in the year book, and also in the fact that this publication was to be found in almost every German household in Japan, so that, provided the copy in use bore

---

* Klausen's memory of his meetings with these Soviet officials was refreshed and clarified when he was confronted with two volumes of his 1941 diary which the Japanese police had confiscated in his house.

† In reality Zaitsev was the first known representative appointed to Australia of the GRU (Chief Intelligence Directorate of the Soviet Armed Forces, previously the Fourth Bureau).

no suspicious markings and all messages were burnt after transmission or receipt, a house search by the police would yield no clue of the operation.

As the work, and therefore traffic, of the ring increased, Sorge obtained exceptional permission from Moscow after 1938 to entrust the ciphering work to Klausen.

The system proved to be secure during the period of operations of the group, and there is no evidence to suggest that the Japanese succeeded in breaking the code of those messages at the time.

The Sorge group in Japan was financed from Moscow in the early stages by cash transmitted through Soviet couriers at prearranged meetings in Shanghai or Hong Kong, by drafts through the National City Bank of New York or the American Express to private accounts in Japanese banks,* and after 1940 through clandestine meetings with Soviet Embassy representatives in Tokyo. Klausen was in charge of the accounts, which were rendered once or twice a year to Moscow in photostat by courier. The total sums received between 1936 and 1941 totaled about $40,000.

Sorge had originally been told by the Fourth Bureau that he must not spend more than $1,000 a month on the expenses of the group. This niggardly sum was mainly spent on rents and current expenses for the main members. Ozaki Hotsumi drew no allowance except when traveling. Small sums were needed to meet repairs to the radio set, and occasional payments to minor informants of Ozaki and Miyagi Yotoku. Sorge, Vukelic and Ozaki lived on their salaries as journalists, Miyagi as an artist, and Klausen as a businessman.

Sorge was never in possession of sufficient current funds from Moscow to meet the smallest emergency. When it was decided to send Edith Vukelic to Australia after her divorce a special sum of $400 had to be authorized by Moscow and paid over by Zaitsev in Tokyo for this operation.

Even the original estimate of $1,000 a month was successively cut, and Sorge was told to make further economies. Klausen was ordered by cable at the end of 1940 to use the profits from his firm "as funds for the ring," and

---

* Japanese exchange control became more extensive early in 1940.

this action of the Fourth Bureau accelerated his ideological disenchantment. From this moment he became idle in making up the accounts and, worse still, dilatory in destroying messages already received and sent, and in sending material awaiting radio transmission. The financial meanness of the Soviet agency thus directly created a security risk, and provided key evidence to the Japanese police when Klausen's house was searched at the time of his arrest.

Only Sorge himself and Klausen, who had been recruited directly by the Fourth Bureau in Germany, were aware of the identity of their superiors. Miyagi had been active in the Japanese section of the American Communist Party and assigned "a brief mission" in Japan by an unidentified Comintern agent. He severed connections with the American party, and had strict instructions not to contact Japanese comrades in Tokyo.

At first Miyagi thought that Sorge and himself were the only members of the group, but as the months passed he identified Vukelic, Ozaki and Klausen as completing the ring.

Like Miyagi, Vukelic assumed that he had been recruited in Paris, into "an organization directly belonging to the Comintern" with no connections with any national Communist parties. "Sorge never revealed the inside story of the precise character of our organization."

Ozaki's impressions of the work of the group were more explicit. He had already learnt from Agnes Smedley in Shanghai that he had been registered under the code name "Otto" with the Soviet authorities in Moscow, and that he was working for some section of the Comintern.

For practical reasons of security, Sorge limited contacts between members of the group. Klausen as the radio-operator and treasurer was aware of at least the aliases and code names of each member, but even he did not know the real identity of Ozaki until the last days of the existence of the ring; and he learnt Miyagi's name only after his arrest. Ozaki only met Klausen once and was unaware of his name. He never saw Vukelic. Sorge's arrangements to meet his assistants were always elaborately planned. He alone was in direct touch with the main members of the group. With Klausen this presented the least difficulty. They were both members of the German Club in Tokyo: it was normal that they should meet as compatriots. The main meetings took place at Sorge's house. The only danger was the handing over of documentary material and the chance of a bureaucratic and routine check by the Japanese police of Klausen's car. Klausen was well trained in using different routes each time that he drove to Sorge's house, and a simple code was arranged for an emergency, which might also imply the presence of a mistress. As Sorge once told Klausen, "When I have my gate lamp lighted please don't come in because it means I have a visitor."

In principle, all rendezvous were fixed in advance, and often openly by telephone.

Sorge and Vukelic were fellow European journalists, and they met frequently and openly at the latter's house until his divorce from Edith Vukelic. Indeed, there seemed little point in maintaining strict security rules for routine contacts between the three European members of the group. As Sorge put it, "Strict adherence over a long period to this theoretical principle was difficult and a waste of time."

Meetings between the European and Japanese agents presented a more serious risk of detection merely because it was a routine habit of the police to discourage intercourse between foreigners and the local population.

Sorge deliberately kept routine contacts with Ozaki and Miyagi as far as practicably possible in his own hands, and elaborate arrangements were made to meet in discreet restaurants in Tokyo, frequently changing the rendezvous, "but as time passed it was not at all easy to find a new place on each occasion."

Sorge and Ozaki used to meet regularly once a month, but as the work increased under the pressure of international events they were obliged to contact each other more often. After the German attack on Russia they met every Monday. Ozaki usually booked a table in his own name, and occasionally they also met at the Asia Restaurant in the South Manchurian Railway building where Ozaki had an office.

After the outbreak of the European war the group decided that, owing to a stricter supervision of foreigners in Tokyo, it would be less risky to meet in Sorge's house. Although this was located almost next door to a police station and was clearly under constant routine surveillance, it was natural for Ozaki as a leading newspaperman to call on a distinguished German colleague, and the risk of conversations being overheard was much less in a private house than in a Japanese restaurant.

Ozaki and Miyagi continued to meet at frequent intervals in restaurants, and after a time invented a cover which enabled Miyagi to call at Ozaki's house to give painting lessons to his daughter.

During the nine years of the ring's operations—except possibly for the last months in the case of Sorge himself—there is no evidence to show that the movements of its chief individual members, and their meetings, were the subject of any special surveillance or suspicion on the part of the Japanese police.

The main and constant danger which overshadowed the daily activities of each member was the discovery of compromising material as the result of an accidental or routine check, either in a car or at one of the houses of the group.

Klausen was perhaps the most exposed. On his frequent journeys by car he carried his transmitter in a black bag to the various private houses from which he operated the set. He had several close shaves.

One such episode took place in the autumn of 1937.

"I had taken a taxi from my neighborhood as usual to radio some messages to Moscow, and upon my arrival at Vukelic's home around 1400 or 1500 hours, I discovered that a large wallet I had put in my left trouser pocket was gone. I darted outside but the taxi had already disappeared. The wallet contained 230 yen in Japanese currency, my driver's license with photo attached, and Sorge's English text of a financial report that we were to send to Moscow. It was to be photographed at Vukelic's house. The other code messages, fortunately, were safely tucked away in my old black bag. I must have forgotten my wallet in the car because I am certain that I took it out and opened it. Of course, I didn't know the license number of the car. I didn't know what to do, so I told Vukelic I had lost my wallet and a large sum of money, and asked his advice. He was talkative by nature, and I was afraid he would tell Sorge about the financial report, so I kept it secret. The following day, I had the audacity to report my loss to the Lost and Found Department of the Metropolitan Police. I said that I had lost some Japanese currency, my driver's license and a scrap of paper with English writing on it. The wallet was never recovered. I was in a state of constant anxiety for several days."

Ozaki was passing to Sorge highly sensitive information from Japanese Government circles, but insisted on doing so verbally; and the results would be drafted, after discussion between the two men, by Sorge as messages to be radioed direct by Klausen. Materials and documents obtained from time to time by Ozaki were handed by him to Miyagi for translation into English and then brought by the latter to Sorge.

Material obtained by Sorge from the German Embassy would be filmed either by himself in the building, or by Vukelic if the documents were temporarily in his house, and, together with other "borrowed" documentary material collected by the group, handed from time to time by arrangement to Soviet couriers.

There was no hitch in these arrangements until the arrest of the group, when compromising material was found in each of the houses of the main members. This formed the preliminary basis of the charges and interrogations.

A theoretical security risk to the ring also lay in the varying degrees of complicity in their work of their womenfolk. While in prison Sorge wrote smugly: "Women are absolutely unfit for espionage work. They have no understanding of political and other affairs, and I have never received satisfactory information from them. Since they were useless to me, I did not employ them in my group."

It seems true that in Sorge's own extensive relations with women during his stay in Tokyo there was no element of espionage, and his private affairs never touched upon this activity.

The Sorge ring was able to operate with impunity, with the sole exception of the intercepting by the Japanese communications experts of unidentified messages, over a period of eight years. The technical achievement of this ring was masterly. As Sorge wrote later: "I myself was surprised that I was able to do secret work in Japan for years without being caught by the authorities. I believe that my group (the foreign members) and I escaped because we had legitimate occupations which gave us good social standing and inspired confidence in us. I believe that all members of foreign spy rings should have occupations such as newspaper correspondents, missionaries, business representatives, etc. The police did not pay much attention to us beyond sending plain-clothes men to our houses to question the servants. I was never shadowed. I never feared that our secret work would be exposed by the foreign members in the group, but I worried a good deal over the possibility that we should be discovered through our Japanese agents, and just as I expected this was what happened."

3

The Red Orchestra

David J. Dallin

*Much more widely ramified than the Sorge net-
work, the so-called Rote Kapelle network of Soviet
agents in Western Europe during the early years
of World War II was for a long time the target of
extensive German investigation. Eventually, the
German's succeeded in neutralizing most of its
elements in Belgium and France and in Germany
itself. How the members, who had more knowledge
of each other than they should have had, broke
down under German pressure and betrayed their
colleagues and further cooperated with the Germans is the substance of this excerpt. As the
author, David J. Dallin, says in commenting on the
behavior of the captured Soviet agents: "The story
of Soviet agents working under German control
. . . is one of the most shocking chapters in the
three-decade history of Soviet intelligence. It was
as if these men and women who for their cause
had engaged in most dangerous ventures, endured
trials and imprisonment, and gambled with their
very lives, had suddenly lost their human counte-
nance and morality."*

FROM the book *Soviet Espionage*.

BOTH THE ABWEHR (German Military Intelligence) and the Gestapo were well aware of the existence of a Soviet espionage network in Western Europe, having intercepted, through their monitors, about five hundred coded messages in 1941. The codes were excellent and not even the best German experts were able to decipher the radiograms. German agents spoke with awe of the ingenuity, size, and technical equipment of the Soviet network. The Soviet cover name for a short-wave radio set is "music box," and a radio operator is a "musician"; hence the name given by the Abwehr to the whole machine—*Rote Kapelle* (Red Orchestra); indeed, to the German authorities the network was like a group of able instrumentalists led by a talented conductor.

In Berlin, police and military counterespionage chiefs were becoming nervous. The knowledge that radio was carrying German war secrets aboard, that in their midst were groups of foreign spies operating without hindrance, and that they were impotent to do anything about it was humiliating. For a long time efforts to locate the spy ring had been fruitless; direction-finding instruments were still imperfect and slow. In the meantime the undecoded messages recorded by the monitors piled up in the Funk-Abwehr and other departments.

In the fall of 1941, as the result of a long search and investigation, the Funk-Abwehr learned that the main transmitter was located in the West, somewhere in Belgium. A group of Abwehr officers was dispatched to Brussels.

"Berlin was angry," related Heinrich Hofmann, a former Abwehr man in Brussels.

Every week new officers arrived in Brussels to prod us; it was of no avail. We were foolish enough to seek the Soviet agents among Belgian Communists and for this purpose infiltrated Belgian Communist circles. Our agents reported that all was quiet, the Communists were frightened and passive. We continued to look around in other Belgian cities, but again to no avail. Then we sent our agents into cafés, not knowing that at that time the Soviet agents in Belgium were meeting in parks, in departments stores, in lavatories, but not in cafés. Meantime the systematic *Peilung* (direction-finder) was making progress; the Soviet transmitter was working for five hours every night (this was a grave mistake on their part), from midnight to 5 A.M. Five hours made our search easier, actually it meant our eventual success.

Then a great expert came over from Berlin; on the basis of our preparatory work, he had narrowed down to three houses on the Rue des Attrebats the possible location of the station.

On the night of December 13, 1941, a troop of soldiers and police officers, wearing socks over their boots, entered the three houses and found the Soviet short-wave station on the second floor of one of them. They arrested Mikhail Makarov, Rita Arnould and "Anna Verlinden." A quantity of false documents, invisible ink of high quality, rubber stamps and so on were found in an adjoining hideout; the code book, however, had been destroyed. This was the night the "Grand Chef," Trepper, entered the house during the searching operation, succeeded in passing for a rabbit peddler, and was let go. He immediately sent warnings to the other members of the Belgian *apparat*.

As a result, Sukulov, the "Petit Chef," a frequent guest at the Rue des Attrebats, had to flee. He explained to his Simexco* staff that since his "fatherland," Uruguay, was about to join the war against Germany (all this occurred a few days after Pearl Harbor) he could not remain in a German-occupied country. He left for the free territory of France.

Interrogated by the German agencies, Makarov refused to talk. "Anna Verlinden" committed suicide. The weak and unhappy Rita Arnould, in mortal fear for her life, consented to give information to the Abwehr. She betrayed Wenzel, "Kent," and others, and she turned over to the Germans a picture of the "Grand Chef." For a time Rita was permitted to live at a hotel instead of being kept in prison, but after a few months, when her usefulness was over, she was executed. Rita Arnould was the first in a long line of Soviet spies who served Germany against the Soviet Union.

What Rita betrayed, however, did not suffice to establish the details of the espionage machinery; the strict Soviet

---

* A cover company.

system of *conspiratsia*† in this instance bore fruit: Rita had had her own tasks and assignments and had known only the men and the few addresses directly connected with her work. The German agencies were still in the dark.

In the heap of refuse found in the Rue des Attrebats the Abwehr found a few small scraps of paper on which had been jotted some mysterious figures and letters; it became obvious that coding had been done in the house. For more than six weeks the best experts on Russian codes in Germany put their skill to work on these scraps, but their labor brought forth only one name, "Proctor," as a part of the code. Rita Arnould was again interrogated: What were the titles of the books on the desks and shelves in the apartment? Rita told what she could remember; the books were bought. One of them contained the name Proctor, and was obviously the code. This development occurred in the spring of 1942; in the meantime Moscow had changed the code, with the result that current communications were again a mystery to the German agencies.

The breach in the Soviet *apparat* was soon repaired. With both Trepper and Sukulov in flight, Konstantin Yefremov took over. Yefremov was a handsome, blond Russian officer, younger looking than his twenty-eight years, deeply devoted to Russia, where he had left his parents and young wife, who was a hard-working locomotive engineer. His new colleague in the network was Johann Wenzel, the "Professor," who was chief radio man in this second Belgian setup, although part of the abundant information was being diverted to France to be transmitted from there. The intelligence machine was again working, and German counterintelligence was again on its heels. Finally, in June, 1942, the Germans located Wenzel's station, and on June 30 Wenzel was arrested. In his room the police found a number of messages in code and two in clear German.

Johann Wenzel, veteran KPD man, refused to collaborate with the Abwehr; he "would not compromise under any conditions." When, however, he was shown the old file containing records of his former activities, including the "arms *apparat*" of the KPD, and was told to choose be-

---

† Secrecy among members of a network.

tween death and collaboration, he changed his mind and made a comprehensive statement involving his Soviet chiefs and colleagues, codes, regulations—the whole system of Soviet espionage. A Soviet agent of long and high standing, he had so extensive a knowledge of things that his usefulness to the Germans was great. Among other things, he revealed the Soviet code currently in use. The task of the Abwehr and Gestapo was made much easier.

The radio-monitoring units of the army and the police intercepted a great number of wireless messages which they succeeded in deciphering by means of the key revealed by Wenzel after an exhaustive interrogation by the police. From these messages important indications of the existence of a Soviet intelligence organization in Berlin were obtained. This made possible the arrest of the group headed by First Lieutenant Harro Schulze-Boysen of the Air Force Ministry and the *Oberregierungsrat* of the Ministry of Economy, Arvid Harnack.

Wenzel's betrayal opened the floodgates. From that time on blows rained on the Rote Kapelle everywhere from Berlin to Paris. Almost every arrest of a new group supplied the Germans with new traitors; every traitor revealed new names.

Abraham Raichman, the Brussels group's expert in false documents, was suspected by the police, though they had no real proof of his activities. To obtain Belgian passports Raichman, like Wenzel a Comintern man, established connections with a Brussels policeman, Inspector Mathieu, actually a German agent who pretended to be in sympathy with the resistance movement. Mathieu agreed to supply Raichman with real passports signed and sealed by the police. In July, 1942, Raichman brought Mathieu a photograph of Konstantin Yefremov, chief of the Belgian *apparat*, who was in need of a Belgian passport. Yefremov was arrested July 30, 1942, in the act of receiving the false document from Inspector Mathieu.

It took time for the Abwehr to "break" Yefremov; he refused to answer questions or give information. Having learned of his strong attachment to his family, the Abwehr officers threatened, if he remained "stubborn," to notify his parents in Russia that he had not only been arrested but had betrayed Johann Wenzel (Which was not true). Grad-

ually Yefremov's resistance weakened; he began to enlarge
on his statements; in the end this chief of the Soviet intelligence ring became a full-fledged collaborator. After a while
he began to take a fancy to this work and to exhibit interest in it: "You are wrong," he would tell the Abwehr men
when they were planning this or that action against a
Soviet network, "you must do it another way. . . ." His
help proved invaluable. Among his most important pieces
of information was the fact that Anton Danilov, his Russian colleague, was to take over the radio station after his
(Yefremov's) arrest.

4

They Gave the Bomb Away

Oliver Pilat

The most damaging espionage operation mounted by the Soviets against this country in World War II was their atomic spy ring. Harry Gold, a chemist from Philadelphia, was used by the Soviet intelligence officer, Yakovlev, working under cover of the Soviet Consulate in New York, as a courier to various scientists in the United States who had been recruited as Soviet agents. Of these, Klaus Fuchs, whose separate story the reader of this volume will encounter a little later, was by far the most important.

In the present episode Gold has been assigned two pickup jobs on one trip—a dangerous undertaking. Gold is well aware of it, but the Soviets have insisted because the two agents are both in the Los Alamos area, and the information from both is wanted urgently. The first contact is to Fuchs, the second to David Greenglass, an army technician who casts molds used in the interior design of the bomb. Greenglass was originally recruited by his brother-in-law, Julius Rosenberg, a "spotter" for Yakovlev, who was later executed

FROM the book *The Atom Spies*.

in the electric chair along with his wife, Ethel, for
their part in this immense and costly treason.

ON SUNDAY MORNING, June 3, 1945, about six weeks before a supersolar flash in the sky over Alamogordo ushered
in the Atomic Era, a fat little man with discouraged shoulders and a pouting face walked up a steep flight of stairs at
209 North High Street, Albuquerque, New Mexico, and
knocked at the first apartment. A young fellow wearing
bathrobe and slippers opened the door. "Mr. Greenglass?"
inquired the stranger, and as the other nodded, he slipped
inside, saying, "Julius sent me," rather breathlessly, with
all the emphasis on the first word. Greenglass said, "Oh."
After closing the door, he walked to a table containing his
wife's purse, opened it, and removed a piece of cardboard
two or three inches long, a jagged piece from the instruction side (not the side showing the picture of the little girl)
of a box of Jello, raspberry flavor. From a pocket, the
visitor produced a similar fragment. The two pieces, held
in air, so obviously belonged together that a careful match-
ing was unnecessary. David Greenglass smiled triumph-
antly; though he was a burly 190-pounder, with unruly
black eyebrows and black hair, he gave an impression of
good nature. "My wife, Ruth," he said with a wave of his
hand. The visitor nodded his head toward the red-cheeked,
blue-eyed girl, scarcely out of her teens, who was also
wearing a bathrobe and slippers. "I'm Dave from Pittsburgh," he said, in an unexpectedly round tone.

"What a coincidence," said Ruth Greenglass, tritely,
while her roving glance picked out each weekend disorder
in the combination living room and bedroom. "Your name
is David and so is David's."

"We weren't exactly expecting anybody today," David
Greenglass told Dave from Pittsburgh, who was really
Harry Gold from Philadelphia. "This is a surprise. Will
you have something to eat?" Gold said he had eaten breakfast. He kept his head slanted and his eyelids down as
though he were listening for something. "Do you have any
information for me?" he demanded. Greenglass replied, "I
have some, but it will have to be written out." Ruth Greenglass went into the cubbyhole of a kitchen to make some
fresh coffee, but by the time she returned the two men

were shaking hands, having agreed that Gold would come back at 3 P.M. for the information which he required about Los Alamos.

Harry Gold read a mystery story for a couple of hours in his room at the Hotel Hilton, and ate his lunch there. He had registered under his right name, without baggage, the previous evening, after a visit to the North High Street address around eight o'clock had aroused only a tall, stoop-shouldered man with white hair who said the Greenglasses were out somewhere but would surely be back in the morning. Precisely at three o'clock, Gold returned to the Greenglass apartment. David was wearing his army uniform, with T/5 insignia showing he was a corporal. Ruth had made tea, and laid out some little cookies. David had a report ready, consisting of several sheets of 8-by-10-inch ruled white paper showing various schematic, or unscaled, drawings of flat-lens mold experiments for detonating an atom bomb on which he had been working in the smallest of the three ultra-secret technical shops at Los Alamos.

A couple of pages of descriptive matter about the various letters and symbols on the sketches, as well as a sheet containing a list of possible recruits at Los Alamos, were included. "On this list," said Greenglass, "I want to explain about one man, why I put his name down. I talked to people about him a little bit. He might not seem to be good material, but there is a story—"

Harry Gold cut him short. "Such procedure is extremely hazardous, it's foolhardy!" he said, with intense irritation. "Why do you do things like that? Under no circumstances, ever, should you try to proposition anybody to help in the work. You ought to be more circumspect in your conduct. Never give anybody the slightest hint that you are furnishing information on the outside."

David Greenglass shifted his heavy shoulders, and frowned, but his words were mild. "Julius wanted a list of people who were sympathetic with Communism and who might help furnish information," he said. "You come from Julius, don't you?"

The inference was: Julius is your boss, isn't he? Harry Gold saw no reason to explain that he did not even know Julius Rosenberg. "I'll take the list," he said.

Rosenberg had originally cut the Jello box in two halves

as a recognition device during a January meeting in New York with the Greenglasses. He had given one part to Ruth, explaining that the courier would bring the other part. He had implied that the courier would be a woman they had met earlier that evening, but arrangements had been changed by Anatoli A. Yakovlev, Rosenberg's Soviet superior in New York.

Gold had objected as loudly as he dared when Yakovlev handed him the Jello box fragment. It was vital, it had to be done, insisted Yakovlev. Gold said he thought it inadvisable to endanger his very important trip to see Dr. Klaus Fuchs at Santa Fe by adding this extra task. Yakovlev said Gold did not apparently understand this was also an extremely important business; in short, he must go to Albuquerque as well as to Santa Fe. "This is an order," Yakovlev had hissed, when Gold remained unconvinced. As usual, the Soviet agent had planned everything. Gold must take a circuitous route, he said, going first to Phoenix, then to El Paso, and finally to Santa Fe. From Santa Fe he could travel by bus to Albuquerque in a couple of hours.

Because he was able to secure only a limited vacation from his job in Philadelphia, Gold omitted the indirect approach to New Mexico by way of Arizona and Texas. He went directly to Santa Fe, arriving around 2:30 P.M. on Saturday, June 2, an hour and a half before his rendezvous. Walking around town, he stepped into a museum and picked up a Chamber of Commerce map of Santa Fe, as a way to avoid asking directions from some stranger. He marked the Castillo Street Bridge on the map. Promptly at four o'clock, Klaus Fuchs came driving down Alameda Street to the bridge in his battered Chevrolet coupé. The British scientist picked up Gold, addressing him as Raymond. The two went for a short drive in the country, during which Fuchs spoke in some detail of the scheduled test at Alamogordo. He did not expect a successful explosion before 1946, he said, though recent progress had been impressive. Just before their parting in Santa Fe, Fuchs had turned over to Gold a sizable packet of typewritten notes. From there he went to visit the Greenglasses in Albuquerque.

Gold had been trained to leave as soon as he took documents, or, to put it the other way around, to take no documents until he was ready to leave. An informant might claim innocence if seized with information still in his possession; after the transfer, both were vulnerable. Therefore, on that Sunday afternoon in June, although safely indoors with the Greenglasses in Albuquerque, Gold got jumpy as soon as he accepted the corporal's report. "I've got to go," he said, getting up from the table. David Greenglass smiled. "Wait a second and we'll go with you," he said. Ruth Greenglass mentioned seeing Julius just before leaving New York in February, and followed that up with a reference to Julius' wife Ethel, without drawing any comment from Gold, who handed a sealed white envelope to David. Greenglass fingered the fatness of the envelope, but did not tear it open to see how much money it contained.

"Will it be enough?" said Gold, as though urging examination of the money.

"Well, it will be enough for the present," said Greenglass, dropping the unopened envelope into his pocket.

"You need it badly," said Gold, more as a statement than as a question.

"We've had expenses," conceded Greenglass. "You know, Ruth's miscarriage in April, there were doctor's bills, and she couldn't work, and there were other expenses."

Ruth bit her lip. "I'm ready to go," she announced.

Gold glanced hurriedly from husband to wife and back again in an uncertain fashion. "I'll see what I can do about getting some more money for you," he promised.

"That will be nice," David said, as they left.

Gold hinted he would prefer no escort beyond a certain point by remarking that he would know where he was when he reached the USO building. They walked along a slanting back street to the USO. Greenglass said he expected a real furlough, not a week-end pass like the present one, but twenty days or more, around Christmastime, and that he might return then to New York.

"If you want to get in touch with me there," he said, "phone my brother-in-law, Julius." He gave Julius' phone number at Knickerbocker Village in New York. Gold said it was just possible he might see the Greenglasses before

Christmas, since he was planning another visit to the Southwest in the early fall. The Greenglasses went tactfully into the USO after saying good-bye to Gold, who kept on walking. When they came out of the building again, Gold was gone. They returned in silence to the apartment, opened the envelope, and found $500 in bills.

David Greenglass turned over the money to his wife. "We can live on it," he said. "You can get along on it, can't you? What's the trouble then?"

Ruth spoke rapidly, "Julius said we were sharing information for scientific purposes. Now I see how it is: you turn over the information and you get paid. Why, it's just—it's just C.O.D.!" Her voice broke as she burst into tears. David shook his head slowly and took her in his arms, giving her what comfort he could. Before he caught his bus back to Los Alamos, she was cheerful again, having planned precisely how to divide the money: $400 as a deposit in the morning at the Albuquerque Trust and Savings Bank, $37.50 for a war bond, and the rest for household expenses.

Somewhere in Kansas, on the train riding to Chicago, Harry Gold examined his historic haul. Though he possessed some scientific qualifications as a chemist, Gold found Fuchs's theoretical discussions of the application of fission to the manufacture of a new weapon rather heavy reading. After glancing at a sentence here and a sentence there, he put away the pages in a manila envelope with a brass clasp, printing DOCTOR on the outside. The Greenglass material was simpler, and illustrated, but the corporal's spidery handwriting proved difficult to decipher. After a few minutes, Gold abandoned that also and put it in a second manila envelope marked OTHER.

Gazing through the imperfectly cleaned window at merging images of flat, fertile land, Gold congratulated himself on the economy and efficiency of his operations. Including twenty minutes with Fuchs, and two short encounters with the Greenglasses, the total time spent with informants on the trip scarcely exceeded an hour. No money had been spent besides the $500 to the Greenglasses, since Dr. Fuchs had waved aside $1,500 brought to him by Gold at a previous rendezvous and had not been tempted again. Characteristically, Gold excluded his own expenses, which were slight; as usual, he was traveling in an upper, and eating odds and ends from vendors rather than meals in the expensive diner. A pair of restless youngsters in a seat across the aisle attracted his attention. Gold gave them some of his candy, explaining to their parents, "I have a couple of my own at home." Then he returned to an unseeing stare at the Kansan countryside.

Gold reached New York on the evening of June 5, in time for his prearranged rendezvous with Yakovlev, a thin, nervous man in his thirties who was registered as a clerk at the Soviet Consulate for espionage purposes. The meeting place was way out in Brooklyn where Metropolitan Avenue runs into the borough of Queens. Gold took his customary circuitous route, trying familiar tricks to throw off possible surveillance, such as waiting on a subway platform or in a train, apparently engrossed in a newspaper, until the doors began to close, and then squeezing through at the last second. The appointment was for 10 P.M. and the neighborhood seemed lonely and frightening to Gold, as he slid into a deserted side street nearby as a final test. His greatest asset in these matters, a feeling as to when he was under observation, told him he was all right, but he had to make sure.

Almost on the stroke of ten, Gold and Yakovlev saw each other in the distance. They approached leisurely to afford each other an opportunity to decline the encounter, if necessary. After a quiet greeting, they walked together about a block, stopped to chat, exchanged newspapers, then separated hurriedly. The paper delivered by Yakovlev with his inevitable hand tremor was just a newspaper, but the one from Gold held in its folds two manila envelopes—marked DOCTOR and OTHER—containing sufficient data for any modern, industrial country with substantial funds, manpower, and scientific know-how to go far along the road toward producing an atom bomb of its own.

Keeping a schedule worked out by them in May, the pair met again two weeks later. This rendezvous was set for early evening, at the end of the Flushing elevated line, on Main Street, Flushing. Sitting in a convenient bar, Yakovlev had Gold elaborate on the details of his New Mexican trip. Toward the end of the two-and-a-half-hour meeting, Yakovlev revealed that the two envelopes had gone immediately to Moscow, causing a sensation. The information from Greenglass was "particularly excellent and very valuable," said Yakovlev, words which from him meant highest praise. Even so, he was guilty of understatement. Six years later, the eyes of John A. Derry, a production chief of the Atomic Energy Commission, widened with astonishment at sketches by David Greenglass duplicating those handed to Harry Gold in 1945. "Why, they show the atom bomb," said Derry, "substantially as perfected!" By this he meant, explained the AEC expert, not the test bomb of Alamogordo, not the maiden attempt at Hiroshima, but the implosion-type, the third and most important of the wartime series, the Nagasaki bomb.

III

Counterespionage:

Spy to Catch a Spy

THE WORK OF counterespionage which becomes known to the public is the capture and arrest of spies. Thus, most of our selections are stories of apprehension, arrest, interrogation, and the like. In actual practice, of course, a great deal of effort—which the public never knows about—goes into the locating and identifying of hostile espionage agents. Often, even after a spy has been identified, no arrest may take place because it may be more valuable to watch the spy operate, to let him lead to other spies and to his employers, than simply to put him out of business.

The reader may wonder how the job of identifying spies ever even gets off the ground. After all, aren't spies well camouflaged or concealed—the deadliest of them usually able to pass as quite ordinary citizens? The Soviet spy master, Colonel Abel, was a photographer in Brooklyn, and his neighbors had only good things to say of him. Lonsdale, of the Naval Secrets case in England, sold juke boxes and vending machines and did not do too well at that. His associate, Kroger, ran a rare-book establishment.

There are many answers to the question, but mostly they point to the fact that sooner or later something gives, somebody slips. A member of Lonsdale's ring working in a secret British naval installation began to drink too much

and was observed investing money in real-estate ventures
which he could not have managed on his modest salary.
Once the eyes of the counterespionage specialist focused on
him a number of peculiarities in his life came to light.
When he was followed once on a trip to London he was
seen making furtive contact with a stranger, which had,
to the trained eye, all the earmarks of a secret espionage
rendezvous.

Sometimes there may be a windfall in the shape of a
defector from a network who simply tells on his colleagues.
We were able to apprehend Abel because one of his subordinates was disaffected and one day, deciding he had had
a bellyful, told American authorities about the harmless
photographer in Brooklyn.

The defection of Igor Gouzenko, the Soviet code clerk in
Ottawa, at the end of the war, gave the Canadian police
the information which helped them round up a far-flung
atomic espionage network of whose existence they had
been unaware.

Otherwise, the work of counterespionage consists of
many painstaking and minute tasks ranging from the
screening of applicants for sensitive jobs to the monitoring
of radio waves for suspicious-sounding transmissions. The
essence of the work is a continuous vigilance and a knowledge of how hostile powers run their spies and what they
are after. In closed societies like those of the communist
states the entire police mechanism is, in a sense, devoted to
spy watching. Every foreigner is suspect. Hotels are laced
with police informants, and even the ordinary citizen is
never certain which of his neighbors or fellow employees is
in the pay of the police. In a free society counterespionage
is based on the practice most useful for hunting rabbits.
Rather than look for the rabbit one posts oneself in a spot
where the rabbit is likely to pass by.

While I was in Switzerland during World War II, in the
years 1942–45, I had plenty of opportunity to observe in
action the Swiss counterespionage and security services. I
came away with high admiration for the efficiency and skill
with which they carried out their functions, while at the
same time being scrupulous to safeguard the rights of the
people against any improper police measures. A couple of
instances serve to illustrate the type of measures which the

Swiss used to detect those who crossed their frontiers without the proper papers and permissions.

I had noted that the Swiss officials who examined travelers' papers as they inspected trains, particularly those leaving Swiss frontier stations for the interior of the country, seemed to pay extraordinary attention to the feet of the individuals whose papers they were examining. After some quiet investigation I ascertained the reason for this. The ordinary Swiss citizen is extremely careful of his appearance. He rarely travels in dirty or muddy shoes unless there is a good reason for this. Hence, if anyone in a train leaving the Swiss frontier station turned up with mud on his shoes, there was reason to believe that he had been doing some cross-country walking and had not had time to clean away the traces of it. To the Swiss police this was a tip that the person in question might very likely have come into Switzerland "black," that is to say, illegally, by traversing the frontier on foot, and it was a clue which led the inspector to ask the person with the dirty shoes to produce his papers. If the papers proved to be all in order that ended it. The dirty shoes were innocently acquired. But it often proved to be the case that the man had not had time to provide himself with papers and in his anxiety to get away from the frontier which he had just crossed he was taking a train into Switzerland, hoping to avoid inspection long enough to find time to acquire adequate documentation, or to make his way to some other country less well equipped with security police.

I came across a second instance of this kind as a result of the arrest of my most cherished agent, who had crossed into Switzerland "black" from Italy, over the Alps, and arrived safely at the border town of Chiasso, in the Italian-speaking sector of Switzerland. He was on the platform of the train station walking up and down awaiting his train when a pleasant-looking man with an unlighted cigarette in his mouth walked up to him and asked him whether he could spare a match. It was a modest request. My agent complied with alacrity and produced a box of wax matches of which great quantities are made in Italy. They are not the type of match that a Swiss would normally be carrying, and this was prima facie that the person carrying them had recently been in Italy. The pleasant-looking man who had asked for the match, after lighting his cigarette, quietly asked the giver for a look at his papers and showed his credentials as a member of the Swiss security police. Unfortunately, my friend had no credentials. He had just arrived in Switzerland, and I was sending him elsewhere very promptly. The match, however, made it too late. He spent several weeks under Swiss detention, and it was with some difficulty that I was able to arrange for his release.

1

Behind the Line

Alexander Hamilton

*The oft-told story of the treachery of Benedict
Arnold and the capture and execution of the British agent Major John André, while on a mission
to Arnold at West Point in 1780, is reported here
by a great American contemporary with the poig-
nant immediacy of an observer close to the scene
of events and deeply involved in them. Alexander
Hamilton was on Washington's staff and was one
of the few privy to the General's espionage operations. John Laurens to whom he wrote this letter,
was a former aide of Washington's.*

*André, as Corey Ford intimated in his references
to him in "Spymaster George Washington" (p.
101), was a dandy, an aesthete and a gentleman,
quite the wrong person to send on a secret mission
in disguise with false papers. When in a tight spot
he insisted he was a British officer, which was his
undoing.*

*There is a mystery about this tale that has never
been solved. Washington's intelligence chief, Tallmadge, seems to have had some advance warning*

THIS letter to John Laurens appeared in a private printing by Charles
Heartmann in 1916. The original is among the Hamilton papers in
the possession of the Columbia University Library.

of André's mission to Arnold. Corey Ford suggests
that the lady known as "355" might have learned
of the mission from André himself.

SINCE MY RETURN from Hartford, my dear Laurens, my
mind has been too little at ease to permit me to write to
you sooner. It has been wholly occupied by the affecting
and tragic consequences of Arnold's treason. My feelings
were never put to so severe a trial. You will no doubt have
heard the principal facts before this reaches you; but there
are particulars to which my situation gave me access, that
cannot have come to your knowledge from public report,
which I am persuaded you will find interesting.

From several circumstances, the project seems to have
originated with Arnold himself, and to have been long
premeditated. The first overture is traced back to some time
in June last. It was conveyed in a letter to Colonel Robinson, the substance of which was, that the ingratitude he
had experienced from his country, concurring with other
causes, had entirely changed his principles; that he now
only sought to restore himself to the favour of his king by
some signal proof of his repentance, and would be happy
to open a correspondence with Sir Henry Clinton for that
purpose. About this period he made a journey to Connecticut; on his return from which to Philadelphia, he solicited
the command of West Point, alleging that the effects of his
wound had disqualified him for the active duties of the
field. The sacrifice of this important post was the atone-
ment he intended to make. General Washington hesitated
the less to gratify an officer who had rendered such emi-
nent services, as he was convinced the post might be safely
entrusted to one who had given so many distinguished
proofs of his bravery. In the beginning of August he joined
the army, and renewed his application. The enemy at this
juncture had embarked the greatest part of their force on
an expedition to Rhode Island, and our army was in motion to compel them to relinquish the enterprise, or to
attack New York in its weakened state. The General
offered Arnold the left wing of the army, which he declined, on the pretext already mentioned, but not without
visible embarrassment. He certainly might have executed
the duties of such a temporary command, and it was ex-

pected from his enterprising temper, that he would gladly
have embraced so splendid an opportunity. But he did not
choose to be diverted a moment from his favourite object;
probably from an apprehension, that some different disposition might have taken place which would have excluded
him. The extreme solicitude he discovered to get possession
of the post, would have led to a suspicion of treachery, had
it been possible, from his past conduct, to have supposed
him capable of it.

The correspondence thus begun, was carried on between
Arnold and Major André, Adjutant General to the British
army, in behalf of Sir Henry Clinton, under feigned sig-
natures, and in a mercantile disguise. In an intercepted
letter of Arnold, which lately fell into our hands, he pro-
poses an interview "to settle the risks and profits of the
copartnership," and in the same style of metaphor intimates an expected augmentation of the garrison, and
speaks of it as the means of extending their traffic. It
appears by another letter, that André was to have met him
on the lines, under the sanction of a flag, in the character
of Mr. John Anderson. But some cause or other, not
known, prevented this interview.

The twentieth of last month, Robinson and André went
up the river in the Vulture sloop of war. Robinson sent a
flag to Arnold with two letters, one to General Putnam,
enclosed in another to himself, proposing an interview with
Putnam, or in his absence with Arnold, to adjust some
private concerns. The one to General Putnam was evidently meant as a cover to the other, in case, by accident,
the letters should have fallen under the inspection of a
third person.

General Washington crossed the river on his way to
Hartford, the day these despatches arrived. Arnold, con-
ceiving he must have heard of the flag, thought it necessary, for the sake of appearances, to submit the letters to
him, and ask his opinion of the propriety of complying
with the request. The General, with his usual caution,
though without the least surmise of the design, dissuaded
him from it, and advised him to reply to Robinson, that
whatever related to his private affairs must be of a civil
nature, and could only properly be addressed to the civil
authority. This reference fortunately deranged the plan,

and was the first link in the chain of events that led to the detection. The interview could no longer take place in the form of a flag, but was obliged to be managed in a secret manner.

Arnold employed one Smith to go on board the Vulture the night of the twenty-second, to bring André on shore with a pass for Mr. John Anderson. André came ashore accordingly, and was conducted within a picket of ours to the house of Smith, where Arnold and he remained together in close conference all that night and the day following. At daylight in the morning, the commanding officer at King's Ferry, without the privity of Arnold, moved a couple of pieces of cannon to a point opposite to where the Vulture lay, and obliged her to take a more remote station. This event, or some lurking distrust, made the boatmen refuse to convey the two passengers back, and disconcerted Arnold so much, that by one of those strokes of infatuation which often confound the schemes of men conscious of guilt, he insisted on André's exchanging his uniform for a disguise, and returning in a mode different from that in which he came. André, who had been undesignedly brought within our posts, in the first instance, remonstrated warmly against this new and dangerous expedient. But Arnold persisting in declaring it impossible for him to return as he came, he at length reluctantly yielded to his direction, and consented to change his dress, and take the route he recommended. Smith furnished the disguise, and in the evening passed King's Ferry with him, and proceeded to Crompond, where they stopped the remainder of the night (at the instance of a militia officer), to avoid being suspected by him. The next morning they resumed their journey, Smith accompanying André a little beyond Pine's Bridge, where he left him. He had reached Tarrytown, when he was taken up by three militia men, who rushed out of the woods, and seized his horse. At this critical moment, his presence of mind forsook him. Instead of producing his pass, which would have extricated him from our parties, and could have done him no harm with his own, he asked the militia men if they were of the upper or lower party, distinctive appellations known among the refugee corps. The militia men replied, they were of the lower party; upon which he told them he was a British officer, and pressed them not to detain him as he was upon urgent business. This confession removed all doubt; and it was in vain he afterwards produced his pass. He was instantly forced off to a place of greater security; where, after a careful search, there were found concealed in the feet of his stockings, several papers of importance delivered to him by Arnold. Among these there were a plan of the fortifications of West Point, a memorial from the engineer on the attack and defence of the place, returns of the garrison, cannon, and stores, copy of the minutes of a council of war held by General Washington a few weeks before.

André was, without loss of time, conducted to the headquarters of the army, where he was immediately brought before a board of general officers, to prevent all possibility of misrepresentation or cavil on the part of the enemy.

The board reported that he ought to be considered as a spy, and according to the laws and usages of nations, to suffer death, which was executed two days after.

2

The Capture of the Grand Chef

David J. Dallin

*In the selection on the Red Orchestra in the sec-
tion on Networks (p. 118) mention was made of
the head of the Soviet network in France and
Belgium, the elusive "Grand Chef," Trepper, also
known as "Gilbert." This astounding gentleman,
as David Dallin relates in this episode, was able, in
Occupied France, to avoid capture by the Germans for a long time. He assumed (correctly) that
his captured subordinates would betray him, and
he turned down all invitations to meet with them.*

THE MAIN TARGET of the German police was, of course, the
"Grand Chef" himself, who they knew must be working
somewhere in France; only his address remained a secret.
Johann Wenzel, arrested in Brussels, confirmed that he had
known "Gilbert"; he knew also that the "Grand Chef" was
in Paris. But he did not have his address and knew of no
way to ascertain it. Then Abraham Raichman, brought to
Paris under police escort, tried to get in touch with his
"Grand Chef" for the Abwehr. As a long-time member of
the *apparat*, he appeared the one most likely to be able to
discover Trepper's whereabouts. But the chief, obviously

FROM the book *Soviet Espionage*.

sensing danger, avoided contact. In the course of his search Raichman got in touch with a number of other Soviet agents and betrayed them to the Germans: for instance, the Griotto couple, his French colleagues in the manufacture of false passports; and Germaine Schneider, Wenzel's common-law wife and one of the most important couriers of the war years. (Germaine Schneider disappeared from Paris, however, and was not seized until later.) But Trepper was out of reach; more than once invited through chain contacts to appear at a meeting with Raichman, he never showed up.

Then Trepper's main cover, Simex, was betrayed to the German police. Maria Kalinina, a former "white" Russian, and later a pro-Communist, working at Simex as an interpreter, and her son Evgeni served there as a driver; they betrayed secrets of the "trading firm" so far as they knew them. The German police, surprised to learn that the assiduously sought "Gilbert" was the manager of this firm, looked for him in the Simex offices only to find that he was no longer there. When his *laissez-passer*, the highly valuable paper which permitted him to travel freely everywhere, expired, the German agency requested him to appear in person to renew the document. He failed to show up. The agency informed Simex that a German firm wanted to buy 1,500,000 marks' worth of industrial diamonds and wished to discuss the transaction with the manager himself. In vain. From the notebook of Trepper's desk at Simex, however, the Germans obtained an important item: the dates of Trepper's visits to a dentist. Here is a report of the Abwehr officer who conducted the operation, on November 16, 1942, that followed this discovery:

The dentist's office was situated in a large professional building near the Tuileries. A German officer was ordered to find out from the dentist whether he had a patient whose description corresponded to that contained in the warrant of arrest of the "Grand Chef." He went to the dentist and, imposing silence upon him, asked for his appointment book. The dentist admitted that he was expecting a visit from this patient the following day at 2 P.M.

Shortly before this time, German officers had taken up posts near the entrance to the building, on the staircases, at the elevator door and on the first floor, where the dentist's office was located. Although everything was carefully prepared, the back-door delivery entrance was overlooked and left unguarded. The officers became worried when the man they were looking for did not show up at the main entrance. To find out whether he might have canceled his appointment at the last moment, two policemen entered the apartment and heard voices in the dentist's office. Could the man have entered the house unnoticed? When they saw a man sitting in the chair in front of the drill they jumped to the right and to the left: yes, this was their man. "You are under arrest," they shouted. For a second he was disturbed, then he said, in perfect German, "You did a fine job."

EDITOR'S NOTE: *The French magazine* Paris-Match *recently reported that Trepper is now living in Warsaw. During the war he escaped German detention not long after he was captured; he is one of the few survivors of the Rote Kapelle network.*

3

The Naval Secrets Case

John Bullock and Henry Miller

Gordon Lonsdale and the Krogers, in this London episode, are what the Soviet intelligence service terms "illegals." They are people whose identities and past histories, as given out by them in the country where they reside, are false. They have been made over with new documents and new biographies, so that it is difficult for any prying third party to determine who they really are or where they came from. Illegals are playing an increasingly important part in Soviet penetration operations, as the recent defection of Colonel Yevgeny Runge in West Germany amply illustrated.

The police apprehension in England of a group of five spies in 1961 in the case which follows is a good example of what can be accomplished by the counterespionage technique of "surveillance," which in simple parlance means tailing or following people. In the Naval Secrets case Scotland Yard began with a lead to the government employee Houghton, who was under suspicion. His trail led to an unknown man in London whom Houghton (accompanied by his girl friend, Ethel

FROM the book *Spy Ring*.

*Gee) was seen to meet furtively on the street,
clearly by prearrangement, for the quick turnover
of a package. The unknown man, in turn, who was
eventually identified as a small-time businessman,
made frequent visits to a house in suburban Ruislip.
These visits, as observed, were obviously for a
clandestine purpose. The police closed in on a day
when they knew Houghton and Gee were coming
to London. They usually came to deliver packages
to the stranger, but disguised their trips as shopping
sprees. The job of the police was to catch the three
network members before any of them could be
warned by the arrest of either of the others.*

THE MAN IN the cloth cap joined the group standing
around the massive indicator board in Waterloo Station.
As he scanned the catalogue of train arrivals, a crackling
loudspeaker gave him the information he wanted: "The
12:32 from Salisbury is running thirty minutes late and
will arrive at 2:45."

"Unhurriedly, he turned to walk toward a bowler-hatted
man leaning on an umbrella near platform 14, to start a
chain of communication involving fifteen alert figures
among the crowds of travelers on the dull Saturday afternoon of January 7th, 1961.

The announcement drew sighs of resignation from
friends waiting to meet passengers from the train. But, to
the fifteen men, it meant a postponement of half an hour
of an operation which was to lead to the sensational exposure of a highly-organized and dangerous spy ring.

For each of the fifteen was a special agent to whom the
wait at this busy London terminus was the climax to a ten-
month-long investigation. Each of the agents was posi-
tioned strategically around the station and its precincts to
await the arrival of two particular passengers among the
five hundred heading for London.

The news of the delay was passed from man to man;
from the man in the cloth cap to his bowler-hatted colleague. On to "a newspaper seller" at the main exit to
Waterloo Road; and finally, to the gray-haired pipe-smok-
ing Scotland Yard Superintendent directing the operation

from a car parked near the Old Vic, the famous London Shakespearian theatre.

He was prepared for the erratic running of the train; but neither he, nor any of his men, could predict the strange behavior in which their two suspects were to indulge.

The 12:32 from Salisbury should have arrived at 2:15 P.M. with the wanted couple and two more agents who had shadowed them from the time they began their journey. Although the train did not pull in until 2:45 P.M., still the plan was intact.

Harry Houghton and Ethel Gee, two respectable civil servants from the secret Admiralty base at Portland, Dorset, in town for a discreet weekend, whose activities had been the cause of this elaborate, well-organized reception, stepped off the train unaware of the trap awaiting them.

They behaved like any other couple at the end of a tiring journey. Miss Gee went to the ladies' room while Houghton bought a newspaper and glanced at the headlines. On her return, they walked down the steps to Waterloo Road, still with the patient and unobtrusive escorts who had been with them since early morning.

The "newspaper seller" suddenly lost interest in his customers; the bowler-hatted man hooked his umbrella onto his arm; the cloth-capped man walked slowly ahead of the suspects, and around the station all the agents, waiting so patiently, prepared for the final phase.

Suddenly came the moment of surprise. Houghton and Gee's behavior, which had followed a consistent pattern during the long months of observation, changed dramatically. Perhaps they sensed trouble. Perhaps it was an unrehearsed act of caution. It might well have been only a means of killing time before their appointment with treachery.

Whatever the reason, they dashed for a Number 68 bus which was pulling slowly away from a stop outside the station. It was a moment for swift action. Only one of the fifteen agents was close enough to keep in touch. He, too, had to board the bus if failure was to be averted.

Sprinting to match the bus's gathering speed, he clambered on, and the suspects were still in sight.

Only Houghton and Gee knew their destination. It proved to be a noisy street market off the Walworth Road, a twenty-minute journey from Waterloo.

At the market, they wandered aimlessly among the stalls, still accompanied by the only agent who had, at this stage, any hope of completing the operation successfully.

Back at Waterloo Road, his fourteen colleagues, now joined by the two from the train, waited helplessly. They could not move or assist him because they knew that Waterloo was to be the scene of a meeting which would provide them with the final evidence of complicity that they needed.

For twenty-five minutes, the wanted couple mingled with South London housewives in idle study of the bargains on sale. They walked along one row of stalls in East Street, paused as they were attracted by some huckster's sales talk, then returned to the Walworth Road to catch another bus.

Casually, they boarded a bus to take them back to their starting point, and to the Special Branch reception awaiting them.

At Waterloo, Houghton and Gee got off and crossed the road toward the Old Vic. Miss Gee, carrying a straw basket, looked like any housewife on a shopping expedition. But this basket contained the incriminating evidence which was to link her and Houghton with a Russian spy.

Watching the couple from the opposite pavement, Superintendent George Smith, who had planned and was now directing this Special Branch operation, felt confident that success was in sight. For, standing outside the Old Vic, was the third character who would complete the cast of the drama.

A swarthy figure in a dark overcoat, who had arrived by car while Houghton and Gee were away, had also been under observation. As he waited, studying posters advertising that night's performance of *A Midsummer Night's Dream,* many pairs of hidden eyes had noted his every movement.

Houghton and Gee approached him, they exchanged glances, then he fell in a few paces behind them. Behind him came Superintendent Smith, and swiftly other unobtrusive characters closed in. The odd procession continued for fifty yards, then the man in the dark overcoat, later to be identified as a Russian spy calling himself Gordon Lonsdale, caught up with Houghton and Gee.

There were affectionate, apparently surprised greetings as he put his arms around their shoulders. Courteously, he took Miss Gee's basket, with its two parcels of Admiralty secrets, and moved to the inside.

For the head of the security team, this was enough. Superintendent Smith hurried ahead of them, turned and said: "Wait a minute—you're all under arrest."

As the first shock of the Superintendent's appearance made its impact on the trio, other Special Branch men moved in and one of the many cars waiting conveniently near drew alongside.

Houghton and Gee were clearly startled; but Lonsdale who had lived so long with the fear of exposure, reacted instinctively. From him there was no response. Superintendent Smith had waited many patient months for this moment and was in no doubt which of the three was to be his special responsibility. Taking Lonsdale by the arm, he bundled him into the waiting "Q" car and with an air of finality said: "Scotland Yard for you, boy."

Houghton and Gee, with just as little ceremony, found themselves in two other cars. And fifteen minutes later all three were in separate rooms at Scotland Yard.

In a room overlooking the Thames, Superintendent Smith had his first conversation with the man he knew so well but had never met.

It was a short and one-sided talk. After the formalities of cautioning and searching his prisoner, the Superintendent went through the routine of asking for his name and address. It was then that Lonsdale gave the reply to which he later stuck through long hours of interrogation, a reply of obvious significance.

Relaxed and cynical, he said: "To any question you might ask me, my answer is 'No,' so you need not trouble to ask."

Patiently pursuing the questioning, Superintendent Smith pointed to the possessions found in the pockets of the Russian facing him. "Why," he asked, "did you have £125 in £5 notes in a sealed, unaddressed envelope?"

There was no response.

"Why an envelope containing fifteen twenty-dollar bills?"

Still Lonsdale remained silent. And the Superintendent, with much to do, left the Russian agent alone while he went to another part of the building to question Houghton and Gee in turn.

Houghton, the ex-Naval Master-at-Arms, who was to have received his £125 "wages" from Lonsdale that day, made two immediate and damaging statements.

First, shocked by his arrest, he said: "I have been a bloody fool." Then, concerned to know if he had been seriously incriminated by Lonsdale, he said: "Tell me, Superintendent, did Alex have any money on him?"

By Alex, Houghton meant Gordon Lonsdale. For, in a later statement, he claimed that at their first meeting the Russian introduced himself as Commander Alexander Johnson of the United States Navy, serving as an assistant attaché at the American Embassy in London.

When Miss Gee's turn came for questioning, her immediate reply demonstrated her naïve character. "I have done nothing wrong," she said, a reply later to be described as "most astonishing."

With little added to his knowledge, Superintendent Smith, with Chief Inspector Ferguson Smith and Woman Police Sergeant Winterbottom, set off for Ruislip.

The Superintendent knew that Lonsdale, now safely in custody, had been a regular visitor to an address there, and he wanted to know the purpose of those calls.

An impatient hour through Notting Hill, Shepherds Bush and on to the Western Avenue, and the Superintendent and his colleagues arrived in respectable Cranley Drive.

But on this day the road's outward appearance was deceptive, because for many hours Superintendent Smith's officers had been hidden around the detached bungalow which was in a secluded position at the end of the street. As he knocked at the door of the bungalow, Number 45, the Superintendent had no idea of the fantastic contents of this apparently typical suburban home. All he knew was that Lonsdale, at that stage unidentified as a Russian, had frequently stayed there. Neither did he know that the couple he was about to meet had for years been running the communications center of a highly-organized spy ring, and had acted as the ring's bankers. To the Superintendent, as to his men scattered in nearby Willow Gardens, in adjoining houses, delivery vans and other vehicles parked at strategic points, the occupants of the bungalow, Peter and Helen Kroger, were no more than associates of Lonsdale who had to be investigated.

Peter Kroger, to his neighbors a respectable, well-to-do bookseller, answered the Superintendent's knock. But when the Special Branch chief asked who had stayed there at weekends, it was Helen Kroger who reeled off a list of names which, significantly, did not include that of Lonsdale. And it was Mrs. Kroger who provided the first real indication of the discoveries to be made in this seemingly normal home.

Her deliberate exclusion of Lonsdale's name convinced Superintendent Smith that she was lying and that there was good reason to make a further investigation.

Told that she and her husband would be arrested, Mrs. Kroger put on a coat and then, picking up a handbag, said: "As I am going out for some time, may I go and stoke the boiler?"

"Certainly," said the Superintendent obligingly. "But first let me see what you have got in that handbag." Mrs. Kroger refused to hand it over, and it took the combined efforts of the Superintendent and Woman Police Sergeant Winterbottom to force it from her.

"The evidence he wanted was found inside the flap of the brown leather bag. From a plain white envelope the Superintendent shook a six-page letter in Russian; a glass slide bearing three microdots; and a typed sheet of cipher.

From that moment, Mrs. Kroger lost all interest in the boiler. She and her husband were taken to Hayes police station, and as they left, a small army of Special Branch detectives began a long search which was to uncover an incredible collection of spy equipment which Ian Flemming would have blushed to describe.

The arrests of these five people, so carefully planned and so nearly frustrated, ended one phase of an investigation which exposed the most successful and extraordinary spy network ever known in Britain. It started an intensive inquiry, which continued long after the five spies had begun their sentences, into the unknown activities of the ring during the years it had escaped suspicion.

4

The Agent the Soviets Wanted Caught

Rebecca West

*Dame Rebecca West, one of the outstanding novel-
ists of our time, has long been deeply concerned
with the roots and the shape of treason, and has
written widely on this subject, drawing in large
measure on information revealed at the court trials
of arrested agents or traitors. One such case I have
included here because the purpose of the Soviet
Intelligence Service in this instance, as Dame
Rebecca interprets it—namely, to deliver one's
own agent into the hands of the police in order to
divert attention from another, more important
agent—involves an unusual reversal of the ordinary
aims of counterespionage.*

ON JUNE 13TH, 1952, in King George's Park, Wandsworth,
some officers of the Special Branch of the Metropolitan
Police surrounded two men who had been sitting for over
half an hour on a bench and were then on their way out to
the park gates, and they told them that they were suspected
of committing offenses against the Official Secrets Act, and
must come to the local police station. One of the pair was
a young man of twenty-four, William Martin Marshall, a

FROM the book *A Train of Powder.*

radio-telegraphist in the service of the Foreign Office, and a native of Wandsworth. Through the bare preliminary reports and the blurred press photographs the fact stuck out that William Marshall was gangling and vulnerable, over six feet, and plainly once the kind of child that climbs out of its perambulator and crawls onto the railway line. He made no reply to the police officers. The other man was a stocky, balding, impassive middle-aged Russian named Pavel Kuznetsov, who gave them the not-at-all disarming answer, "It is up to you to prove your suspicions," and at the police station claimed that he could be neither detained nor searched, and produced a certificate of diplomatic immunity showing that he was a Third Secretary at the Russian Embassy in London, but pointed out that it did not give him his proper rank. He had recently been promoted to Second Secretary.

With a blandness which later excited the Soviet Embassy to a protest, the police searched Kuznetsov, as they tersely put it, "before this information could be checked." Twenty-five pounds were found on him in pound notes, and some documents, which were interesting but not what the police had hoped for, since none of them led back to the man in Foreign Service employment with whom he had been arrested. Again, through the bare preliminary reports a fact stuck out. Kuznetsov was not behaving as a man of his position would have been expected to behave in this predicament. He was guilty of indecision and inconsistency. He complained to the police that he had been arrested when he was walking in a park, which is no offense against the law. Then he simplified his complaint; he had been arrested when he was walking in a park with a man whom he did not know. In Marshall's presence he persisted that they had been strangers till that day. But when his statement was read back to him he withdrew the amplification, and went back to his first complaint: he had been arrested when he was walking in a park. Then he returned home, to his apartment in a converted Victorian house in a fading part of West London, where he lived with his pretty wife and his little son.

With Marshall the matter was much more straightforward. In his wallet they found a copy, written in his handwriting, of a confidential document which he had been given for the purposes of his work, and in his diary they found Mr. Kuznetsov's telephone number, and two groups of initials which looked like notes of the appointment which he had been keeping when he was arrested, and of another which he had arranged to keep in the same park at a future date, July 8th. Both of these appointments were bracketed with the words, "Day off." Marshall was employed at Hanslope Park, the out-of-town establishment which the Foreign Office maintains fifty miles north of London in Buckinghamshire. The boy also made a long statement in which he named seven other occasions on which he had met Kuznetsov during the last six months, and claimed that these were merely incidents in an innocent friendship, in which no question of loyalty was involved. But the police charged him under the Official Secrets Act with having communicated to Mr. Kuznetsov information useful to an enemy, and of obtaining secret information.

The trial took place on July 9th and 10th. As soon as William Marshall had come into the dock it had seemed unlikely that any foreign power should have wished its agents to engage in activities which it desired to keep secret with this odd-looking boy, who was so pale and tall and thin, so easily identifiable by the most curious molding of his cheeks and the steep angle of his sloping shoulders. Every moment he spent in court made it appear less likely that the police had lied when they described him as showing signs of nervousness when he was being watched. They need not have been close to him to have made such a report. As he sat and listened to the evidence he continually pursed his lips, then pouted them, then abruptly compressed them and puffed out his cheeks, and finally tried to wipe out the grimace by stroking his mouth and chin with his very long fingers. Considering that strain had this manifest physical effect on him, it was against all probability that the Soviet espionage authorities should have chosen one of the Embassy staff to handle him.

It does not seem likely that Embassy officials often deal with such matters in these days. Very sensibly, the standard Communist routine provides that all espionage should be carried out by three persons. The first is the "source," usually a national of the country in which the espionage is carried on, and the second is "the contact," who takes it from him, who also is usually a native. The third is "the agent," who is often a Soviet national and employed in a Soviet organization and delivers it to the local Soviet espionage headquarters. This routine was varied in the case of the atomic spies, whose communications were regarded as so important that the contacts were cut out and they were handled directly by the agents, even though these were Soviet diplomats. This was not too rash a step, for it was during the war and the Russians knew that the Allies were treating them with complete confidence, and rightly divined that these diplomats were not shadowed. But it is now known that Nunn May handed over his information straight into the hands of Lieutenant Angelov, an assistant of the military attaché in Ottawa, and that Fuchs's first contact was Simon Kremer, secretary to the military attaché at the Soviet Embassy in London. There is therefore little doubt that the British authorities shadow Soviet diplomats, and the temperamental bias of the Soviet authorities must lead them to exaggerate rather than minimize the amount of shadowing that is done. It is therefore not to be understood why they sent a Second Secretary to deal with a source whose appearance was God's gift to any detective.

But even if it be granted that they had to take William Marshall as a source because for some reason they needed a radio-telegraphist in the British Foreign Office at this particular moment so badly that the certainty of early detection did not matter, and even if it be supposed that Marshall himself had somehow come to know Kuznetsov and insisted on dealing with him and nobody else, their choice of meeting place leaves the matter still enigmatic. Spies usually meet in private houses or in country lanes, if they think they are a long way from having excited any suspicion, or, if there is any doubt, in crowded streets or bus stops or subway stations, or in large saloons. If there are any documents to be passed the encounters will be very brief. Much of the information Marshall was accused of handing over, such as the code letters for the various stations, would have been written down on paper. But Marshall and Kuznetsov met for leisurely meals at restaurants, at eight different restaurants, of which six were exactly the places one would have thought spies in general, and these men in particular, would avoid.

On January 2nd, shortly after Marshall had returned from Moscow, they lunched at the Berkeley, which is the London equivalent of the Colony, and three days later they dined at the Pigalle, a fairly grand restaurant which puts on a floor show, not far from Piccadilly Circus. Sir David and Lady Kelly might have been lunching at the Berkeley almost any day; and the Pigalle is the sort of place that a young diplomat might easily go after the theatre. At neither would one expect to see a young radio-telegraphist. It might be thought that Kuznetsov was trying to soften Marshall by giving him luxurious tastes, but that was evidently not the plan. For nine days later they lunched at the more popular Criterion. After that there were longer intervals between their meetings, because Marshall had gone to work at Hanslope Park and got back to London only on his leaves. It was three weeks before they dined together again, this time at Chez Auguste, which is in the Soho area. After dinner they went to a hotel in the Bloomsbury area frequented largely by prosperous businessmen from the provinces. Three weeks after that they lunched at the quiet and conventional Royal Court Hotel.

Not one of these restaurants was a mere nosebag. All of them were in the metropolitan nexus. Later Marshall and Kuznetsov were to eat in Wimbledon and in Kingston; and in such places a restaurant draws on a small, enclosed, local world, which will often find no clue to a stranger. But at these first six appointments the two exposed themselves to the scrutiny of a sprawling and well-informed system. At any one of them it was possible that people at the next table might be diplomats, or embassy employees, and even probable that they might from time to time have attended a diplomatic reception. At any one of them the waiters belong to the upper circle of their profession, which has its own unwritten "Who's Who," far meatier than the printed version. At any one of them a table has to be booked. If Kuznetsov did the booking, it would be rash of him to give his own name, still more rash to give a false one; and if it were Marshall, the question might be asked at any moment, "Who is this young man who is going about with the Second Secretary of the Soviet Embassy?"

It was so little surprising that Marshall had landed in the dock that it was very surprising. It was comprehensible enough that when Inspector Hughes of the Special Branch told how he had arrested Marshall and found the copied document in his wallet and searched his room in his parents' home, there was no joy of the chase in his tone. Marshall's counsel put it to him that the young man had a blameless record and had been given an excellent character when he left the Forces, and the inspector drearily agreed. But he added with sudden and grim emphasis, "Better than normal." It was not clear what he meant. It might have been that he had been nauseated at having had to watch for months this pitiable young man shutting himself up in a mousetrap. It might also have been that that character was framed in such strong terms of recommendation that it appeared possible that at some point there had been fiddling with his papers by some unauthorized person. Perhaps without his knowledge, persons who wanted to plant him in the Diplomatic Wireless Service might have seen to it that he could produce character which would make him seem an exceptionally desirable candidate.

It was, after all, out in Egypt that it had first occurred to him to seek employment in that service.

But that was dissolved in the general doubt. This oddly reckless pair had behaved in a way bound to arouse in any reasonably cautious person the suspicion that Marshall was a criminal; but it seemed not at all certain that he was going to be convicted of any crime. There were two counts of the indictment which related to the copy of the document which was found in his wallet. One charged him with unlawfully obtaining the information in the document for the benefit of a foreign power; but the judge announced early in the trial that he was going to direct the jury to acquit Marshall on this charge, since it was information which had been given him in the course of his duties and he had made no effort whatsoever to obtain it. It was in fact the copy of a notice which was put up in each of the bays in which the radio-telegraphists worked. Another count charged him with recording the information for the benefit of a foreign power, and there seemed little doubt that he could be found guilty of this offense, since an expert graphologist had testified that the copy was written in his handwriting. But even this was not certain. Since it had been found in Marshall's wallet, and there was no evidence that he had ever taken it out since he originally put it in, it seemed possible that he would be acquitted of that charge with its imputation of a desire to help a potential enemy, and that he would be charged again with the very much lesser offense of wrongly retaining the information. But the gravity of the case, the element in it which made his parents' distress reasonable enough, lay in the three other counts, which charged him with having on three dates communicated information to Kuznetsov which could be useful to a foreign power. And there was not a particle of direct evidence that there had been any such communication at all.

On the first date, April 25th, Marshall had been seen to go to the Thameside town of Kingston. There he met Kuznetsov, lunched with him at the Normandie Restaurant, and went with him to a public garden by the river where they sat on a bench for an hour and twenty minutes. Marshall was seen to take some papers out of his pocket, and he appeared to be explaining them to his companion; and he sometimes made a drawing on some paper laid on his lap, as if he were illustrating his explanations. If anybody halted in the neighborhood of the bench, he put away the papers; and when he left his friend and went home he looked nervous and worried. That was all the detectives could say. Nobody had overheard what he said, or seen him give any papers to Kuznetsov.

On the second date, May 19th, Marshall met Kuznetsov in Wimbledon High Street, close enough to his home in Wandsworth, and spent two hours with him in a restaurant. But neither then nor on their last meeting in King George's Park on June 13th was a word of what they had said taken down by the detectives, nor did any papers pass between them.

It seemed quite likely that he would be acquitted on these major charges until he went into the witness box to give evidence on his own behalf. There he damned himself. He was in all things a contrast to his parents. His swaying, fidgeting height shot up out of the witness box, like the rootless saplings that grow out of the crevices of bombed buildings; it did not seem possible that he should have been the child of this amply made woman, this compact and vigorous father. The boy shifted from foot to foot as he testified in a high, weak voice, which the judge and the counsel found hard to hear. This reluctant trickle was different from the slow, full river of sighs and persuasive murmurs and passionate exclamations with which his mother had tried to suggest his innocence, or the cascade of words with which his father had tried to sweep away his guilt; and it was flowing in the opposite direction.

He told an incredible story of how he had come to know Kuznetsov. He said that when he had come back from Moscow he had found that he had failed to return a pass issued by the Soviet Government which all British Embassy personnel had to carry in case they were stopped in the city. Though it had been issued to him by the Embassy officials, he did not hand it back to the Foreign Office, and accounted for this absurdly by saying that he "did not want to involve the Foreign Office" if he should have handed it back before he left Moscow. He returned it to the Soviet Embassy in Kensington Palace Gardens, and not by post. He took it himself, and when he explained the purpose of his visit to the doorman, he was taken in to see Kuznetsov. He implied that this was the first time he had ever met him; but it is to be noted that Kuznetsov had been sent from London to Moscow the previous autumn and had been there during the last three months of Marshall's service in the British Embassy there. With him he had a conversation which immediately engendered a feeling of friendship. "We found," he said in his statement, "we had a good deal in common and we looked at life in the same way. I told him I was still working at the Foreign Office and we agreed to meet again." He gave the duration of this conversation as a quarter of an hour.

In his statement he also said, "I gave him my address and told him I could not possibly meet him at home as my parents would not agree to such a proposition." Since he had also asserted that this friendship with Kuznetsov was of a perfectly innocent and personal nature, unconnected with the passing of information, he was cross-examined as to his reason for making that remark. He answered, "I told him that because my people's political views are opposed to my own." Neither the prosecuting counsel nor his own counsel had asked him whether he was a Communist, and it had not appeared in his statement. His vague complaint of feeling a social misfit at the British Embassy had not been accompanied by any avowal of Communist sympathies, and most people who had seen a vision of him being snubbed by arrogant diplomats and had thought of him as spying out of resentment against his humiliating experience saw him as doing it impetuously, as a young clerk who has had a talking-to from the boss might buy the *Daily Worker*, for a few mornings. The authorities had in fact had no suspicions regarding him. But he had now made it quite plain to the jury that when he went to see Kuznetsov he had already championed the Communist cause so definitely that it had caused disputes at home. The voices of his parents, asserting that he took no interest in politics but was absorbed in his records and his film magazines and his silk mats, sounded through the memory and their error now seemed touching and sacred.

Marshall made two more serious slips. He claimed that he had talked with Kuznetsov for the most part on political subjects: on the Russian way of life, on the division of Germany, on the war in Korea, on the unrest in Malaya. He explained that when he was sitting with Kuznetsov on the bench in the public garden at Kingston, he had been showing him papers on which there were written "general summaries of the news" and that the drawing he had shown him was a "map of parts of Russia in connection with the division of Germany." This was, of course, heart-rending stuff. It would be unlikely that the Second Secretary of the Soviet Embassy, an able and experienced man of middle age, should have spent an hour and twenty minutes listening to "general summaries of the news" and looking at maps of Russia set before him by any radio-telegraphist of twenty-four; least of all by this radio-telegraphist, whose every word betrayed a simplicity of mind so great that its effect was as disconcerting as complexity; whatever he said he made the listener think back along winding routes in search of the naïve misapprehension on which his view was based. The Attorney General suggested to him that on the papers there had been written the call signs of a number of wireless stations, and that the map he had drawn showed wireless circuits. This he denied, and he was asked again if he maintained that all he and Kuznetsov had talked about was Germany, Korea and Malaya. Tossing his long head he answered in a tart and ready tone, "Yes, and we exchanged cultural information on Moscow."

This perfect specimen of *Daily Worker* English dashed and depressed the court. Such words would come naturally only to a young man who had taken a linguistic tan from exposure to the fierce rays of Communist prose; and it takes time to get a tan. This had, of course, no evidential value, and it should have had no effect on the jury, though God preserve any of us from saying sibboleth for shibboleth quite so clearly when we are on trial. But Marshall's third slip was something which the jury had properly to take into account. When he was asked about the copy of the secret document found in his wallet, he said, pouting, that he knew nothing about it. Peevishly he insisted on oath that he had not written it, that he had never transcribed the notice which was put up in his bay, and that he had no notion of how the copy came to be in his wallet.

He had asked the court to clear a high hurdle. To accept his story one would have had to believe the police had obtained this document and specimens of Marshall's handwriting, and given them to a reliable forger to make a copy which could be fathered on Marshall, and then, after taking all that trouble, had planted it on the wrong man. For they would have had a water-tight case had they found it on Kuznetsov, but instead they found it on Marshall. It might be argued that the police shrank from the delicate international situation which would have been created had they found evidence that a Soviet diplomat had been acting as a spy; but they had shown no signs of shrinking from that hazard; they had, on the contrary, been advancing toward it with every sign of delighted appetite. They had, after all, searched Kuznetsov, after he had announced that he was Second Secretary of the Soviet Embassy, as they blandly said, "before this information could be checked." It was quite impossible to swallow Marshall's story; and it was no surprise to anybody that the jury found him guilty of the charge of having copied the document.

Kuznetsov had done worse than merely fail to coach Marshall in what he ought to say. It had been in his power to get Marshall acquitted, and he had not done it. For if he had come forward as a witness and had assured the court that he had in fact found pleasure in young Marshall's company, and had been edified by his views on the division of Germany and Korea and Malaya, and had exchanged cultural information on Moscow with him on a park bench, it would have been difficult for a jury to convict Marshall, particularly if Kuznetsov had spoken with a certain warmth. But nothing had been heard of Kuznetsov since a couple of days after Marshall's arrest, when a Soviet Security officer had called at his apartment and driven him and his wife and his little boy to the Soviet Embassy, where he had remained ever since.

That was considered by many to absolve him from blame for his desertion of his friend. They went on to say, "Poor chap, he'll be sent home now, and then his days won't be long in the land, considering how he bungled the job." But that conclusion was perhaps not entirely correct. It is possible to regard the trial as the result of reckless incompetence, which ventured on a change of plan when it was too late; to suppose that the acquaintance began in honest friendship, at which time Kuznetsov saw no reason why he should not be seen with Marshall in London restaurants, and that the thought of espionage only developed later, and drove the two to suburban trysts which offered real cover and would have been safe enough if they had not already attracted the attention of the security organizations. But the trail they left round the suburbs leads away from that supposition.

On April 25th, when Marshall and Kuznetsov visited Kingston, it was Friday, a popular shopping day, and there were plenty of people on the pavements to give cover for detectives. The pair went into the Normandie at one o'clock. The sole entrance opens into a bar, from which a narrow staircase with a sharp turn leads into the restaurant itself. There is no other way of getting in or out of the room. Upstairs the men took a table facing the door, which was visible from every other part of the room, for it is not large. Marshall's party, though he did not know it, occupied a seventh of the available accommodations. For there were twenty-one tables, and he and Kuznetsov had one table, the officers from the Special Branch were sitting at another, and a third was taken by the party of police from the Soviet Embassy, who, though Marshall would have been surprised to learn it, always shadowed him and Kuznetsov on their meetings.

After having eaten their meal in this goldfish bowl, Marshall and Kuznetsov walked away down a narrow street known as Water Lane, in which no boy of ten playing at sleuthing could have lost his quarry. They had before them an unusually large choice of retreats where they could have talked quietly and kept at a distance from any eavesdropper. A short bus ride would have taken them to Richmond Park; and within walking distance, just over Kingston Bridge, on the other side of the Thames were Bushey Park and Hampton Court Park. Instead the two men went to Canbury Gardens. This is a riverside strip of greenery which solves a problem grave enough for a town which relies for much of its income on people who come to enjoy its prettiness, but also has its industries. Canbury Gardens masks the gasworks and electricity plants of the town, and distracts the attention of the pedestrian from the covered dock where the barges discharge their cargoes of coal into an elevator. The Gardens run along the river for less than a quarter of a mile, and the depth is never more than a hundred and fifty yards and is at some places as little as fifty. There is a line of plane trees on the garden side of the tow path, with benches between them where one can sit and look over the glassy Thames at the opposite bank, where the weeping willows droop to their reflections, and the Georgian mansions are mellow in the green shade of the tall wetrooted trees. But there are never at any time many people sitting about in Canbury Gardens. Mothers with babies and very young children find pleasure there, and so do the elderly. But it is the river that captures the fancy here, and most people follow the tow path, looking inland only occasionally to see the bright flowers and shrubs. There are tennis courts on the town edge of the gardens, but the players usually enter them by a special gate.

If the two men had taken a bus to Richmond Park, or had crossed the river to Hampton Court or Bushey, they could have found an open space and set down their coats on the grass and spread out maps as if they were hikers talking of routes, and it would have been hard for the detectives to find an excuse for getting near enough to see what they were doing. In Canbury Gardens they sat down on one of the benches between the plane trees. They were therefore silhouetted against the waters of the Thames, and, as the bank faces westward, against the afternoon light. Marshall's sloping shoulders and his long narrow head must have been crassly identifiable, and when he took papers out of his pockets and showed them to his companion, and when he drew maps for him, not a shade of the explanatory gestures could have been missed. It was ten days after Easter Monday, on which date Canbury Gardens goes into its summer routine, so there were piles of deck chairs set at various points from which visitors could pick up as many chairs as they needed and set them down where they pleased. The detectives following the pair could have stationed themselves on the lawns behind Marshall and Kuznetsov, at any distance from them which seemed most prudent, without doing anything which seemed remarkable. There were only two or three benches which could not have been covered by people sitting on deck chairs behind them, and these were overlooked by the windows of a tea house, which was open.

We know little about the next meeting of the two men, which took place on May 19th, not very far from Marshall's home, in Wimbledon. The evidence regarding it was given in closed court, and Marshall could not remember the name of the restaurant where they ate. But it appeared that they met in the open street in heavy rain. There comes to mind a note made by Ragov, the organizer of the Canadian spy ring, on the margin of a contact's report on a meeting with the scientist Durnford-Smith: "Was a torrential downpour; but he nevertheless came. Give instructions not come in the future in such weather, it is not natural." Marshall and Kuznetsov did not even behave as two men keeping an appointment in a storm would be expected to behave; they did not give each other a perfunctory greeting and then hurry off to shelter. It seemed to the watchers that they went through a curious conspiratorial ritual; that they met and passed without a sign of recognition, then turned back and went off together into a doorway. Marshall denied this, and indeed, from his demeanor in the witness box, it would be believed that at that moment, peevish under the pelting rain, tense in his knowledge that he was defying authority, he might have weaved and fluttered so that the watchers were perplexed into inventing interpretations of his conduct which had no real basis. As Mr. Kuznetsov must have noticed long before, Marshall was constitutionally unfitted for underground work. Yet on June 13th the two men met at a trysting place which was even more exposed than the Normandie and Canbury Gardens, which could have been chosen, surely, only by someone who was saying "Take him. Oh, will you never take him? Take him, take him now."

This place where William Martin Marshall and the Russian diplomat Pavel Kuznetsov met on June 13th was very close to Marshall's home. It would have been quite impossible for Marshall to shake off any detectives who might have been shadowing him (as indeed they were doing, and as Kuznetsov must have suspected them of doing) during the short and direct walk which took him to King George's Park. The particular section of the park he sought was not the one prudent men would have chosen. Originally the park was a strip of open land alongside the river Wandle, about three-quarters of a mile in legnth, and was between two and three-hundred yards in breadth, which was continuous grassland, though cut into sections by two roads and several fenced and asphalted footpaths. Since the war a colony of prefabricated houses has been planted on one of the interior sections, so that there are now two separate King George's Parks, one on the north side of this settlement and one on its south. Two men who desired to talk in secrecy might well have arranged to meet within this colony and walked along its winding roads, or in the northern park, where there is a children's playground, a swimming pool, and a restaurant to attract crowds, several entrances, and a good many seats along the path which runs right round the grassland. But Marshall and Mr. Kuznetsov chose to go to the southern park, which is quite simply a playing field and nothing else. It is a rectangle of flat ground, about eight acres in extent, and there is not a yard of it on which a man might find cover. It is grass, save for a cinder track which runs along the western edge from a gate in one of the transverse roads to a gate in one of the transverse footpaths. Ten trees are planted along this cinder track and they shadow three benches. On one of these William Marshall sat himself down with his friend Mr. Kuznetsov.

It was on the bench nearest the gate to the footpath that Marshall and Mr. Kuznetsov had seated themselves. Again the young man had been tempted into a small and exposed position, even smaller and more exposed than Canbury Gardens. The path was only about two hundred yards long, and he could not stray from it, for it was seven o'clock and the expanse of grass in front of him was covered with children having their last game before supper. All three benches could be watched from behind by anyone who cared to enter the vegetable gardens on the lip of the Wandle. These were not market gardens, but allotment; that is to say, they were rented out to enthusiastic amateur gardeners who would choose this very time of day to pick up fork and spade and get to work. A detective could loiter there, smoking a pipe and looking wisely down at the celery and up at the beans, or along the rows of outdoor tomatoes, and keep two men under his eye without doing anything out of the ordinary. But the pattern of the hunt had hardened into a simpler form. The detectives settled down on the bench that was farthest away from the one on which the two men were sitting, near the gate into the road. After ten minutes they decided they would like to be nearer and they moved to the middle bench. When the two men rose to leave, the detectives closed in on them. This must have been, in a sense, premature, for they had not seen Marshall pass any documents to Kuznetsov, which is what they must have wanted. But perhaps they moved in to prevent an open scandal, for it was obviously only a matter of time before the pair, in their dogged search for conspicuous meeting places, would arrive at the vestibule of Scotland Yard.

For there could be only one reason why Soviet Intelligence should have wished to seduce the awkward and inept child, William Martin Marshall, put him on a salver and serve him up to British Intelligence: to divert its attention from another and more valuable agent, possibly not British at all, who was working on so nearly the same field as Marshall that the British and American Intelligence authorities would think, having arrested him, that they had stopped the leak which had been troubling them and could relax their vigilance. So far so good for Mr. Kuznetsov. He could not have trussed Marshall up more competently had he been a professional poulterer and the lad a Christmas goose. Mr. Kuznetsov had even put in some fancy touches on which he was able to congratulate himself: prodigious cantrips on his way to his appointments which looked the very things a not-too-clever spy would do if he were trying to throw detectives off his trail. But the other agent, the agent who was not Marshall, must be very valuable. He must indeed be enormously valuable if to cover him Soviet Intelligence deemed it worth while to stage this prolonged and elaborate farce, which involved the withdrawal from his duties of such a responsible official as Mr. Kuznetsov, even though that were only for a time.

5

The Atom Spy Who Had to Confess

Alan Moorehead

*In an earlier selection on the atom spies (II, 4), we
have already encountered "the activities of the spy
of the century," as he has sometimes been called,
the scientist Klaus Fuchs. There we met the courier, Harry Gold, as he carried Fuchs's vital contribution on United States atomic research from
Santa Fe to New York to be handed over to the
Soviet Vice Consul Yakovlev. That was in 1945.
In the spring of 1946 the defection of Igor Gouzenko, Soviet code clerk at Ottawa, revealed to the
West the startling information about Soviet intelligence operations against the American-British-
Canadian atomic research effort. During the en-
suing years the security authorities of all three
countries were on the trail of the atom spies, following up leads from the Gouzenko revelations and
from other information they had assembled. By
late 1949 the British authorities had narrowed
their suspicions regarding leaks from British scientists down to very few persons, foremost among
whom was Fuchs, who by then had left the United
States and was employed as a top-ranking research*

FROM the book *The Traitors*.

physicist at the British atomic center at Harwell. The extent of Fuchs's betrayal was not yet known, but it was of the utmost urgency that the whole matter be clarified.

The official handling of the matter, as Alan Moorehead deftly reports in this excerpt, was both unusual and most successful. While the British realized that Fuchs, once he sensed that he was suspect, might disappear with Soviet help (as Greenglass, Sobel, Rosenberg and a host of others tried to do), they also know that there was something about the man's personal attachment to his friends and his work at Harwell that might make this unlikely, and that the curious mind and conscience of the man could just possibly be tipped in the direction of a confession if the right touch was applied. To this job the experienced British security officer, William Skardon,* was assigned. Not the least interesting in this account are the rationalizations and self-justifications on Fuchs's part. Of these certainly the most amazing is that in confessing he thought he would clear the atmosphere and then be allowed to keep the job at Harwell he loved so well.

IN THE SECOND half of December it was decided that Fuchs should be questioned outright, using as a pretext for the interrogation the fact that Fuchs himself had sought advice about his father's appointment to Leipzig (already in Communist control). The man chosen to carry out the investi-

---

* In an interview with a British newspaperman in Moscow in November, 1967, Kim Philby (see "The Rise and Fall of a Soviet Agent," p. 49) disclosed that this same William Skardon grilled Philby in July, 1952, at the time he was under suspicion, following the Burgess-Maclean defection. "Skardon was," said Philby, "unquestionably the trickiest cross-examiner I have met."

The very existence of a specialist in government employ like Skardon, who is called in to confront and "break" a special category of high-level traitors and turncoats, is a phenomenon of the times in which we live. Today the safety of nations can be threatened by treasons perpetrated by trusted persons in positions of great responsibility who are secretly motivated by the subtle influences of Communist ideology and, therefore, all the harder to detect.

gation was William James Skardon. Skardon was not a scientist, but he was one of the most able and experienced investigators in England. Since the war he had handled the cases of William Joyce and other traitors. He was a man with a quiet, self-effacing manner. It would not be difficult to imagine him as a character in one of H. G. Wells's urban stories—perhaps Mr. Kipps. He had patience and tact and considerable tenacity, and it was apparent that all these qualities were going to be needed in the handling of Klaus Fuchs before the truth came out.

On December 21 Skardon went down to Harwell, and by appointment met Fuchs in Henry Arnold's office. Outwardly the atmosphere was cordial and unexceptional—it was simply a routine meeting on a security problem between a senior Harwell executive and a security officer. After making the introduction, Arnold withdrew. Skardon opened by referring to the information Fuchs had given about his father. Was there something more that Fuchs could tell them?

For the next hour and a quarter Fuchs discussed his family background with great frankness. He confirmed that he had a sister living at 94 Lakeview Avenue, Cambridge, Massachusetts, and a brother at Davos in Switzerland. He revealed that in Kiel, in 1932, at the Social Democrat Party election for a vice-president, he had supported the Communist candidate in the absence of a Socialist. For that, Fuchs said, he was expelled from the party, and had drifted into the Communist camp. He remembered the name and address of the Quaker family who had befriended him when he first came to England in 1933; they were introduced to him through the fiancée of a cousin, and he had stayed with them at different addresses in southern England until 1937. He remembered, too, that in Bristol he had joined a committee for the defense of the Spanish democracy at the time of the Civil War.

Then there were his years with Professor Born in Edinburgh; his six months as an internee at Camp "L" and at Sherbrooke, Quebec, where he had met Hans Kahle—he had seen Kahle only once after that, at a Free German Youth Organization meeting in London. He spoke of his work for "Tube Alloys" in Birmingham, of his trip to the United States in 1943, and of how he had visited his sister in Massachusetts that Christmas and again the following spring.

All this was given by Fuchs quite calmly and readily. And then Skardon said to him: "Were you not in touch with a Soviet official or a Soviet representative while you were in New York? And did you not pass on information to that person about your work?"

Fuchs opened his mouth in surprise and then smiled slightly. "I don't think so," he said.

Skardon went on: "I am in possession of precise information which shows that you have been guilty of espionage on behalf of the Soviet Union; for example, during the time when you were in New York you passed to them information concerning your work."

When Fuchs again shook his head, saying that he did not think so, Skardon suggested that, in view of the seriousness of the matter, this was rather an ambiguous reply.

Fuchs answered: "I don't understand; perhaps you will tell me what the evidence is. I have not done any such thing." He continued then to deny any knowledge of the matter, and added that in his opinion it had been wise to exclude Soviet Russia from information about the atomic bomb. Skardon then went on to other questions. Had Fuchs ever heard of Professor Halperin? Yes; Halperin used to send him periodicals while he was interned in Canada, but he had never met him. Fuchs remembered, however, that he (Fuchs) had made one visit to Montreal during the time he was in New York.

At 1:30 P.M. there was a break in the interview. Fuchs went off and lunched alone. When they resumed a little after 2 P.M., Skardon again confronted Fuchs with the charge of espionage, and Fuchs again denied it, saying there was no evidence. But in view of the suspicions about him, he said he felt he ought to resign from Harwell. The meeting ended with another discussion about his father's movements in Germany. The two men had been together for four hours in all, and Fuchs had shown no signs of breaking. Skardon went back to London.

Something had been gained, but not much. There had been an admission of Fuchs's activities in his youth, and there had been that inadequate phrase, "I don't think so." He had given a few details of his movements and his acquaintances. But that was all, and it was not enough. On this evidence he could not be arrested. There was always the possibility of mistaken identity.

Meanwhile, now that Fuchs had been alerted, there was the question of what next to do. If he was guilty, it was quite possible that he would try to escape from England. It was even conceivable that he would commit suicide. There were those who favored the idea of getting him into custody on one pretext or another at once, before it was too late. But Skardon was for waiting and taking a chance; he was not yet persuaded that Fuchs was in fact the guilty man. On the other hand, he had come away from Harwell convinced that Fuchs was wrestling with a moral problem of his own. If he were given time, if he were handled carefully, there were very good hopes that in the end he would break down of his own free will. In any event, they were dependent upon getting his confession: without it they could not proceed against him. Nothing, in Skardon's opinion, should be done to antagonize Fuchs. He should be given a little more time over the Christmas holidays to think things over. Skardon did not believe that Fuchs would make any desperate move. This was not much more than a hunch—a feeling that he had established a kind of understanding with Fuchs—but in the end he had his way.

It was not until December 30, on the day after Fuchs's thirty-eighth birthday, that Skardon went down to Harwell again. He found Fuchs calm and unhurried. He again denied the charges, and said that he could not help. There was a detailed discussion of his movements in the United States in 1944, but this led to nothing new. At the end of the interview Skardon did notice that Fuchs's lips were parched, but presumably that could have happened whether Fuchs were guilty or not.

On January 10, 1950, Sir John Cockcroft sent for Fuchs and told him that in view of his father's departure for Leipzig it would be best for all concerned if Fuchs resigned from Harwell and went to some university post instead.

On January 13 Skardon came down to Harwell for a third meeting in Arnold's office. They were again left alone. Did Fuchs remember the exact address of his apartment in New York in 1944? Nearly six years had gone by, and he was not quite certain of it. However, with the aid of a map he identified the place as West 77th Street, near Central Park, in the middle of a block between Columbus Avenue and Amsterdam Avenue. When Skardon told him that security was pressing inquiries about this apartment and other matters in New York, Fuchs appeared unconcerned. He still denied all the charges. He said he knew now, however, that he would have to leave Harwell. It should not be difficult, he said, for him to find a university post. But first he would take a holiday.

This, then, was the impasse reached after three long meetings. All along Skardon had urged upon Fuchs that security was not trying to ruin him. If some slip had been made in New York during the war, then it was much better to have the thing out in the open. Fuchs was a valuable man at Harwell. It was always possible that once this business was thrashed out some arrangement could be made to enable him to continue with his work. But the present strain was intolerable for everybody.

Fuchs himself was very well aware that as yet security had no inkling of the real extent of his treason, nor of its long duration. Through this fortnight in January, then, he was asking himself: "Shall I admit the lesser crime if they will let me stay on at Harwell? But then, even if I remain at Harwell, can I trust myself not to turn traitor again?"

He revealed all this in his confession when he said:

"I was then confronted with the fact that there was evidence that I had given away information in New York. I was given the chance of admitting it and staying at Harwell or clearing out. I was not sure enough of myself to stay at Harwell, and therefore I denied the allegation and decided that I would have to leave Harwell.

"However, it became clear to me that in leaving Harwell in these circumstances I would do two things. I would deal a grave blow to Harwell, to all the work which I have loved; and furthermore that I would leave suspicions against people whom I had loved, who were my friends and who believed that I was their friend.

"I had to face the fact that it had been possible for me in one half of my mind to be friends with people, to be close friends, and at the same time to deceive them and to endanger them. I had to realize that the control mechanism had warned me of danger to myself, but that it had also prevented me from realizing what I was doing to people close to me.

"I then realized that the combination of the three ideas which had made me what I was, was wrong: in fact every single one of them was wrong: that there are certain standards of moral behavior which are in you and that you cannot disregard. That in your actions you must be clear in your own mind whether they are right or wrong. That you must be able, before accepting somebody else's authority, to state your doubts and try to resolve them. And I found that at least I myself was made by circumstances."

This is very complicated. But several clear things come out of it. He is not quite humble yet; he regards himself as quite essential to Harwell, and by leaving he perceived he would deal it a grave blow. But now at last he is aware of the feelings of his friends. They will be hurt. Suspicion might fall on them. He had never thought of this before because the "control mechanism" had prevented him from taking account of anything as minor as the human beings around him whom he had betrayed. They were the casual victims of his grand design for the perfection of the world. But now he realized he had no right to hurt them. This was a considerable advance but Fuchs was still a long way off from realizing the real enormity of what he had done; he still could not see that what mattered was not his friends' feelings, but the fact that they and everybody else on this earth might be blown to smithereens as a consequence of his treason. This point never seems to have entered his mind, then or since. He was obsessed throughout by his own personal moral position.

After the January 13 meeting, Skardon was on slightly firmer ground. Nothing definite had happened, but an atmosphere of confidence had been created, and he felt sure that Fuchs would make no move without consulting him. The two men, the hunter and the quarry, were entering now into that strange, intensely intimate world of criminal investigation where personal animosities cease to count any more, and where each man trusts the other, even though they know that before the end one of them has got to be destroyed. There is an insect quality about this business—the slow, inevitable waiting of the spider for the fly. The fly has to be caught, and the spider has to pounce, and there is nothing either of them can do about it.

Fuchs was not quite ready yet. Outwardly he remained perfectly calm. He went about his work in the normal way, and he confided in nobody. His friends at Harwell knew nothing of what was going on, and they noticed nothing peculiar about him. There was just one incident.

A scandal broke out among the members of Fuchs's own staff. It was nothing more than an untidy love affair gone wrong, an incident of 'the kind that happens in every garrison, but which at the time seems outrageous because of the special intimacy of garrison life. This matter affected Fuchs to some extent—he made a point of visiting the distracted woman in hospital—and it might have been that he felt that this was one more sign that the life at Harwell he knew and liked so well was breaking up around him. At all events, the incident seems to have brought him to a decision at last. On Sunday, January 22, Fuchs phoned Arnold and said he wanted a private talk. They arranged to lunch at the old Railway House Hotel at Steventon on the following day. At the luncheon there was some discussion of politics—Fuchs said he was opposed to Communism as practiced in Russia now—and he also said he should like to see Skardon again; he had something more to tell him. It was agreed that the meeting should take place at Fuchs's "prefab" at 11 A.M. next day, Tuesday, January 24.

Arnold met Skardon at Didcot railway station and drove him to Harwell. Skardon walked down to "prefab" No. 17 alone. It was ten days or more since the two men had met, and the change in Fuchs was remarkable. He looked unusually pale, and he seemed to Skardon to be in a state of some agitation. When Skardon said, "You asked to see me, and here I am," Fuchs answered at once, "Yes. It's rather up to me now."

But having made that half admission he stopped—as though overtaken by some sudden misgiving about what he had to say. While Skardon waited he went wandering off into a long dissertation about his life, going over and over again the details they had discussed so much before—his underground days in Berlin, his father (who by now had left for Leipzig), his friends at Harwell, the importance of his work at Harwell, the need for him at Harwell. He told the story of his career again, giving nothing new, but talking with his head in his hands and his face haggard.

After two hours of this, Skardon said; "You have told me a long story providing the motives for actions, but nothing about the actions themselves."

Why couldn't Klaus break down? Why not confess and have done with it? He was only torturing himself. If only he would give way, then Skardon might be able to help him.

Fuchs paused, and then answered steadily: "I will never be persuaded by you to talk."

"All right," Skardon said, "let's have some lunch."

There was a luncheon van that went round the Harwell compound selling fish and chips and other snacks. Skardon indicated this van which was passing the house just then, and said, "Will we have some fish and chips?"

Fuchs answered, "No. Let's go into Abingdon."

They got into Fuchs's gray saloon car, with Fuchs at the wheel, and on the five-mile run into Abingdon he drove with a reckless, breakneck speed that bordered on insanity. He cut corners on the wrong side of the road, he passed all other traffic with inches to spare; and they raced at last through the streets of Abingdon up to the door of the principal hotel.

An English pub on a wet winter's afternoon is not a place that lends itself easily to high drama. There were other guests in the dining room. Skardon and Fuchs ate their way through a prosaic meal, talking about the gossip of Harwell, about the different personalities there, about anything but treason. It was a strained and desultory conversation.

Then they went into the lounge for coffee. Skardon spoke of Professor Skinner's departure from Harwell and asked who was going to take his place. Fuchs said he did not know.

"You are number three, aren't you?" Skardon said. "Might you not have got the job?"

"Possible," Fuchs said, and Skardon slightly shook his head. There was no likelihood of that now—not at any rate until Fuchs had confessed. Suddenly Fuchs jumped up and said, "Let's go back."

They returned to Harwell with excruciating slowness. For a great part of the way they drove behind a lorry traveling at barely ten miles an hour, and Fuchs would not pass it. They got out in silence at the "prefab," and as soon as they were inside Fuchs made his announcement. He had decided to confess, he said. His conscience was clear, but he was worried about his friends in Harwell and what they might think.

"When did it start?" Skardon asked.

"About the middle of 1942," Fuchs answered, "and it had continued until about a year ago."

That was seven years. That covered the whole period of the bomb, its conception, its construction, and its explosion. It covered the years in England, as well as those in New York and Los Alamos. This was the first shock Skardon had that afternoon. It was the first intimation that he or anybody else had had that they were dealing here, not with the leakage of a few facts and figures, but with treason on an immense scale and for a very long time.

And now that he had started, now that he was beginning to feel the relief of confession, Fuchs ran on quickly, recounting unbelievable facts. There had been frequent but irregular meetings, he said. He had taken the initiative. He had spoken to an intermediary who had arranged the first interview, and after that, through all these seven years, each meeting had been arranged in advance with an alternative.

At first Fuchs had told the Russians merely the products of his own brain, but as time went on this had developed into something more, until he had given them everything he knew. His contacts were sometimes Russians, sometimes people of other nationalities. He realized that he was carrying his life in his hands, but he had learned to do that in his underground days in Germany. He went on to speak of his meetings in New York, at Los Alamos, and more recently in London, until he failed to go to his February rendezvous in 1949, and the Russians had not approached him since. All the meetings were short: he handed over documents, fixed the next rendezvous, and then departed, sometimes his contact asked him questions, but these questions were not the questions of the contact, but of someone else with technical knowledge.

All this came out in a rapid voice, and it was no moment for Skardon to take notes or to interrupt. As soon as he could, he asked: what had Fuchs actually given the Russians?—and he received then his second shock that afternoon.

He supposed, Fuchs said, that the worst thing he had done was to tell the Russians the method of making the atomic bomb.

Now finally the truth was out, and it could not have been worse. Any possibility of Fuchs remaining at Harwell or anywhere else except inside a prison was obviously out of the question. All that could be done now was to extract from him every last damning fact, and so manage him that he would continue to talk until he had nothing left to say. Now that the break had come, and he was sure that Fuchs was pinned at last, Skardon was only anxious to end the interview as soon as possible so that he could take advice and get the full confession down in writing.

But Fuchs wanted to go on. He explained carefully that it was impossible for him, of course, to do more than tell the Russians the principle on which the bomb was made. It was up to the Russians to produce their own industrial equipment, and he had been astonished when they had succeeded in making and detonating a bomb as soon as the previous August. He knew, Fuchs said, that scientifically they were sufficiently advanced, but he had not supposed that commercially and industrially they were so far developed.

As for his own information, he had been gradually diminishing it over the past two years. That was because he began to have doubts about what he was doing. He still believed in Communism, he said, but not as now practiced by Russia—that sort of Communism was something to fight against. He had decided that the only place for him to live was in England, and he returned again to the subject of his friends. What were they going to think about his behavior—especially Henry Arnold, whom he had deceived most of all?

He insisted that his sister Kristel in the United States knew nothing of his contact with the Russians; if she had noticed anything suspicious she would have thought it was part of his underground activities on behalf of the German Communist Party.

He added one or two more scraps of information before Skardon brought the interview to an end. A typical place of rendezvous in London was Mornington Crescent. He was never given an alias by the Russians—they knew him simply as Fuchs, and he could not remember what all the various signals of recognition were. Just once he had taken a gift of £100, as a symbol of his subservience to the cause.

Fuchs was now much calmer and more self-possessed. He agreed that, since they were both tired, it would be best to break off and meet another time. The afternoon meeting had lasted just an hour. When should they meet again? Skardon asked. Fuchs recalled that he had a committee meeting the following day, so that would not be a suitable time. But the day after that, January 26, he would be free.

On this, Skardon left Fuchs at his doorway and drove back to London with possibly the most sinister report any man has ever had to deliver. What gave the affair a special sense of unreality was that Fuchs, having unburdened himself, still believed that all would be well—they would still continue to employ him at Harwell. Indeed, in the course of the interview he had made it clear that this was the reason why he had invited Skardon to Harwell and had confessed. He had been a Russian agent. That was a mistake, and now he had admitted it. But he had ceased to be a Russian agent. Now it was up to Skardon to explain all this to the authorities and wind up any tiresome official formalities as quickly as possible so that Fuchs could get on with his work. He had resolved not to take a university post outside Harwell; it was no longer necessary. He had confessed, and that was that. It was all over and done with. And the price Skardon had to pay for the confession was that he had to ensure that Fuchs remained on at Harwell.

Fuchs, in other words, was still a thousand miles away from any understanding of the real issues at stake. Yet there were certain advantages for security in his absurd illusions. So long as he was thinking along these lines it was not likely that he would bolt, nor would he commit suicide. Moreover, he would help in every way he could. More than ever now, it was necessary not to alarm him, not to surround him with police, not to drag him down from the dream world in which he was still living.

The next meeting, on January 26, once again took place at Harwell. Fuchs seemed to have maintained his composure during the intervening two days, and he was ready with a mass of details about his meetings with his contacts in London, Boston, New York and Santa Fe. He had been to see Arnold in the interval, and at that painful meeting it was one more unreality to be added to all the rest that Fuchs should have said he was a little worried lest Skardon had not appreciated the significance and importance of the whole affair. In particular he was concerned about the forthcoming declassification meeting with the Americans at which Fuchs was to be one of the British representatives. Did Skardon appreciate that it was absolutely essential for Fuchs to be there? If he were not people would notice his absence. Suspicions would be aroused. And this would be a very bad thing for Harwell. Did Skardon understand that? Arnold had reassured Fuchs, and suggested he might raise the matter at his next meeting with Skardon.

And now, on January 26, Fuchs urged Skardon to move in the matter as quickly as possible, as he was anxious to have his position clarified.

Skardon put forward three choices: either Fuchs could write out a confession himself, he could dictate it to a secretary, or he could dictate it to Skardon himself. Fuchs at once chose the last course, and it was arranged that they should meet the following day in a room at the War Office in London. The understanding between the two men was now complete. The fly was in the web, but he was held there by nothing visible. They were on a Christian name basis, they had a certain respect for one another, and to Fuchs at least it seemed that they were acting out their parts merely as instruments of some sort of inevitable fate that was larger than themselves. After the drama was over they could go away and take up their normal lives again.

Certainly after nearly eight years of silence, of living the double life and never confiding in anybody, it must have been an immense relief for Fuchs at last to telescope his two lives into one, and for the first time tell the story—the whole story—to someone who would sympathize and understand. That was the important thing—to be understood. To make oneself perfectly and precisely clear. As soon as Skardon had left Fuchs had a talk with Arnold, and very readily answered questions on what kind of information he had passed on to the Russians.

The following day, January 27, still in this mood of confession, Fuchs came up to London without police supervision of any kind. Skardon met him at Paddington Station and drove him to the War Office in Whitehall. They sat down, and when Skardon gave him the usual official caution, and asked him if he were ready to make a statement, Fuchs answered, "Yes, I quite understand. I would like you to carry on."

Skardon took the confession down by hand.

"I am Deputy Chief Scientific Officer (acting rank) at Atomic Energy Research Establishment, Harwell [it began]. I was born in Russelsheim on December 29, 1911. My father was a parson and I had a very happy childhood. I think that the one thing that stands out is that my father always did what he believed to be the right thing to do, and he always told us that we had to go our own way even if he disagreed. He himself had many fights because he did what his conscience decreed, even if this meant that he was at variance with accepted conventions. For example, he was the first person to join the Social Democratic Party."

So it went on through the whole involved story. It was when they were drawing to the end of it that Fuchs for the first time had something to say of his contrition.

"I know that I cannot go back on that [on what had happened] and I know that all I can do now is to try and repair the damage I have done. The first thing is to make sure that Harwell will suffer as little as possible and that I have to save for my friends as much as possible of that part that was good in my relations with them. This thought is at present uppermost in my mind, and I find it difficult to concentrate on any other points.

"However, I realize that I will have to state the extent of the information I have given and that I shall have to help as far as my conscience allows me in stopping other people who are still doing what I have done. There is nobody I know by name who is concerned with collecting information for the Russian authorities. There are people whom I know by sight whom I trusted with my life and who trusted me with theirs, and I do not know that I shall be able to do anything that might in the end give them away. They are not inside the project, but they were intermediaries between myself and the Russian Government.

"At first I thought that all I would do would be to inform the Russian authorities that work on the atomic bomb was going on. I concentrated at first mainly on the product of my own work, but in particular at Los Alamos I did what I consider to be the worst I have done, namely to give information about the principle of the design of the plutonium bomb.

"Later on at Harwell I began to be concerned about the information I was giving, and I began to sift it, but it is difficult to say exactly when and how I did it because it was a process which went up and down with my inner struggles. The last time when I handed over information was in February or March, 1949.

"Before I joined the project most of the English people with whom I made personal contacts were left wing, and affected in some degree or other by the same kind of philosophy. Since coming to Harwell I have met English people of all kinds, and I have come to see in many of them a deep-rooted firmness which enables them to lead a decent way of life. I do not know where this springs from and I don't think they do, but it is there.

"I have read this statement and to the best of my knowledge it is true."

He signed then "Klaus Fuchs," and Skardon made a note at the bottom that Fuchs had read the statement through, made such alterations as he wished, and had initialed each and every page.

Fuchs had one more reservation, however, and that in itself was part of the moral wonderland in which he was still firmly drifting: he would not tell Skardon the technical details of the construction of the atomic bomb that he had passed on to the Russians, because Skardon had not been cleared for access to such information. He agreed to confide in a qualified person, Mr. Michael Perrin, whom he had known since 1942 as the assistant to Sir Wallace Akers at "Tube Alloys," and who had stayed on with the Atomic Energy Division in the Ministry of Supply. An appointment was fixed for January 30 in London; Fuchs said he would like a rest over the weekend to gather his thoughts. He again repeated that he was anxious about his future, and did not want to waste time in getting it settled. He then returned alone to Harwell by train.

That same night a strange thing happened. Arnold got word that there was a light burning in Fuchs's office. He went at once to the administrative block and quietly let himself in. A light was indeed burning in Fuchs's room, and there were sounds that indicated that there was someone inside.

Arnold used his pass key to get into a room which was directly opposite across a corridor. The partitions between these offices in the administrative block have glass panes let into them about eight feet from the floor, close to the ceiling. By getting up on a cupboard Arnold found he could look across the corridor into Fuchs's room. Fuchs was sitting there at his desk, going through his papers. His cabinet was open, and as he read he smoked. The rest of the building was in darkness and silence.

For a long time Arnold watched him. At that moment many things were still possible. It could still have been that Fuchs was intending to commit suicide after all. He might also have been planning to escape from England in the night, taking his papers with him. Again, he might merely have come here to destroy those papers.

Arnold watched and waited. But Fuchs continued quietly reading, pausing occasionally to take other documents from the cabinet and sort them out in piles on the desk. Then, toward eleven o'clock, he got up, left his papers on the desk and light burning, locked the door behind him, and went out. Arnold calculated that Fuchs was bound to come back, if only to put out the light, and remained standing on the cupboard in the darkness.

It was an hour, however, and close to midnight, before Fuchs returned. Then he sat down and began reading again as he had before. This continued for another half hour or more, while still Arnold watched and waited. Then at last, about 12:30 A.M., Fuchs got up, locked his office door, put out the light, got into his car, and drove home. Arnold then entered the room and found that the papers which Fuchs had been reading dealt only with routine matters and were not important. The room, with the papers still spread out on the desk, remained untouched until it was officially searched after Fuchs's arrest.

Fuchs took a morning train up to London on Monday, January 30. He arrived at Paddington at 10:45 A.M., and Skardon brought him to the War Office, where Perrin was waiting. As they went into the meeting Fuchs said he had remembered one or two other facts about his contacts that might be useful. He said he was certain that there were other scientists besides himself who had been working for the Russians. Also he recalled now the place of the last rendezvous which he had failed to attend. It was the Spotted Dog at Putney, or alternatively another pub near Wood Green underground station.

Skardon opened the proceedings with Perrin by saying that Fuchs had decided to reveal everything. Perrin replied that he had plenty of notepaper, and they set to work. They went through the seven years of meetings chronologically, noting just what Fuchs had given to the Russians at each time and place: at first, his monthly reports when he was working with "Tube Alloys" in Birmingham in 1942; then, in New York, the details of the gaseous diffusion process; then, at Santa Fe, the principles of the putonium bomb; and finally, at Harwell, the information about the progress of the postwar British project.

It was a long business and after an hour or two the three men broke off for lunch. They went to a hotel behind the War Office in Whitehall, close to Scotland Yard, and finding all the tables occupied perched themselves at the snack bar, as strange a luncheon party as any in London that day. Then they went back to work again.

Fuchs repeated to Perrin that he was convinced that other scientists were at work for the Russians and had been all along. As an example, he described how, very early in his espionage, while he was still in England, they had asked him for details of the electromagnetic isotope separation process in Berkeley, California, and that was a matter of which no British scientist had any knowledge at that time.

It was 4 P.M. when the statement was finished. Fuchs then went off alone to Harwell, while Perrin got his notes typed; it was a long document of many pages. Now at last the authorities had enough. There were still a number of details to be got from Fuchs, but now they knew the worst. It was time to make the arrest.

There was an election going on in England at the time—the election that brought Labour back with a small majority in 1950—and the legal formalities were complicated. First, the Prime Minister, Mr. Attlee, had to be acquainted with the confession. Then the Attorney General, Sir Hartley Shawcross, had to be found—he was somewhere in the north of England. Shawcross returned to London, reading through the case in the train, and in London the Special Branch at Scotland Yard and others worked on the precise wording of the charge. These matters occupied the whole of January 31 and February 1. By February 2 they were ready to move.

Security preferred not to make the arrest inside Harwell, where nothing was yet known of the investigation. Instead, they decided to get Fuchs quietly to London, and the best way of doing this was for Perrin to telephone Fuchs and ask him to come up for a further interview. The arrest would take place at Perrin's office at Shell-Mex House. Perrin agreed to do this—though as a layman he lacked some of security's enthusiasm for the idea. His only stipulation was that if Fuchs was going to be arrested in his office, he, Perrin, should not be present. He got through to Fuchs by phone on the morning of February 2, and said: "Can you come up again this afternoon?" Fuchs agreed, and suggested a train from Didcot which would get into Paddington around 2:30 PM; it was a journey of little more than an hour.

It was arranged then that Commander Leonard Burt of Scotland Yard should be present in Perrin's room at 2:30 P.M., with the charge and a warrant for Fuchs's arrest. Perrin, somewhat restlessly, took up position in his office at 2:30; and then for half an hour nothing whatever happened. Perrin telephoned security, and was assured that Burt was on his way. At three o'clock Perrin's secretary telephoned through to say that Fuchs had arrived. Perrin gave instructions that Fuchs should be kept in his outer office until Burt appeared, and in agitation he telephoned security once again.

Finally, at 3:20 P.M., Burt arrived with a police inspector, and they were shown at once into Perrin's room. The delay had been caused by last-minute arrangements over the wording of the charge. They then sent for Fuchs, who had been waiting all this time in the adjoining room. Perrin introduced him quickly to Burt, and then slipped away into another room. Burt read out the charge at once and told Fuchs he was under arrest. Fuchs made no comment. He sat down in Perrin's chair, and then asked if he could see Perrin himself.

Burt agreed and brought Perrin back into the room again. Fuchs's face had suddenly gone gray. Now at last the whole elaborate dream edifice had collapsed, and looking directly at Perrin, he made his final absurd and touching *cri de coeur*: "You realize what this will mean at Harwell?"

The officers noted that down and took him away to Bow Street Police Station.

At the conclusion of his trial before the Lord Chief Justice on March 1, 1950, Lord Goddard, in his summing up, stated, "The maximum sentence which Parliament has ordained for this crime is fourteen years' imprisonment, and that is the sentence I pass upon you."

In England the charge of high treason, for which the penalty is death, can be made only against a traitor who assists an enemy. Fuchs gave information to an ally.

6

The Tell-Tale Air

Alexander Foote

Alexander Foote was an Irishman who worked for Soviet Intelligence, but who quit after World War II and lived to tell the tale. Along with two other persons known as Hamel and Bolli, he was one of three radio operators located in Switzerland during World War II whose job was to transmit to Moscow information received from Soviet agents in Germany. Via this circuit the Russians reportedly received vital military intelligence concerning German battle plans on the Eastern front which appears originally to have leaked from the German High Comand and General Staff in Berlin. To this day it is not known who the actual sources of the information were, though in a recent book (A Man Called Lucy)* two French authors attempted to pinpoint these sources as to position and motive without, however, giving their names.

The information was passed from Germany to Switzerland and then radioed to Russia so promptly that the Soviets are said to have learned of high-level German military decisions twenty-four hours

---

FROM the book *Handbook for Spies*.

* By Pierre Accoce & Pierre Quet, Coward-McCann, New York, 1967.

after they had been taken. It has been claimed that
the outcome of the war on the Eastern front might
have been different had this intelligence operation
not existed during the critical period of 1942–43.

The recipient of the information in Switzerland
was a certain Rudolf Roessler (whose code name
was LUCY*). The network to which Roessler, Foote*
and his fellow radio operators, and numerous sup-
porting agents all belonged was under the direction
of a Hungarian named Alexander Rado. Foote
gives an amusing picture of the rather undignified
antics of this group as the network was collapsing.
His account begins at the time when the Swiss
counterespionage service by means of radio-loca-
tion techniques has begun to track down the three
Soviet transmitters. The initials D.F. (direction
finding) refer to this technique.

THE TWO MAIN antagonists to our organization were
naturally the (German) Abwehr and the Swiss "Bupo"
(Bundespolizei, Federal Police). The former because the
actions of the network were aimed directly at the Third
Reich, and the latter because these actions were a violation
of Swiss neutrality. The Abwehr were naturally the more
concerned and were more active in attempting to penetrate
and to liquidate the organization. The Swiss were prepared
to take action if evidence was brought to their notice, but
would not go out of their way to liquidate a spy network,
especially if they thought it was working for the democracies. I use the word "democracies" advisedly; they became
much more enthusiastic in their work when they realized it
was a Soviet network, little love being lost between the
bourgeois Swiss and the Soviet Union.

The Swiss had an efficient monitoring system, and it
subsequently transpired that they, like the Germans, had
been monitoring our traffic for some time. Their original
information, however, came from a casual source, or so I
was told by the Swiss police after my arrest.

Sometime—it must have been a year or so previously—
one of the wireless staff at the Geneva airport was casually
twiddling the tuning dial of his set. No planes were due in
and he had no signals to listen to, and was looking for

something on the short-wave with which to lighten his boredom. Suddenly he picked up a strong signal transmitting in Morse, but in code and using amateur procedure. This intrigued him, as all amateur radio transmissions had been forbidden in Switzerland since the outbreak of war, and anyway an amateur transmitting five-figure groups was somewhat more than unusual. He noted the call sign and frequency and reported the matter to his superiors, and the report finally filtered through to the Bupo and the Army.

The station was monitored, and in due course by D.F. they discovered that it was located in Geneva. In the course of their investigations they came across another set, also working from the town and using a similar procedure. These sets were, of course, those of Bolli and Hamel. At that time the Swiss police were under the impression that these were either British transmissions or possibly a local Communist network working into Germany. It seems likely that at the same time they also picked up my transmissions from Lausanne and monitored them as well.

Exactly why the Swiss took no action for a period of at least a year and only started offensive action against these sets in the autumn of 1943, I do not know. It is possible that they were hoping to get enough traffic to enable them to break the cipher, or it may be that they were unwilling to take action against sets which they thought were being worked by the Allies. Indeed, they might never have taken action against them unless pressure had been brought to bear by the Abwehr, who could and may have given them the facts. The only people who can answer that question are the Swiss police and the Swiss General Staff. The fact remains that it was not till the autumn that any serious action was taken, and was speedily proved successful.

Mobile D.F. vans were ordered into action, but it was not easy to locate the exact whereabouts of the two Geneva transmitters, as they were in a built-up area (which was the precise reason why they had been put there by us). When the vans had pinpointed the two transmitters to a comparatively small area, another technique was brought into play; one, I believe, which was originated by the Germans and used with much success to locate Allied transmitters working in occupied countries. During the time that the sets were on the air they cut off the current from each house in succession. When on pulling the switch the set went off the air, they were certain that they had identified the house in which it was located. This they did, in turn, with both Bolli's and Hamel's transmitters.

On October 9 I was sitting in a café drinking my morning cup of coffee when I saw the first edition of the *Tribune de Genève* a small announcement that a secret short-wave transmitter had been discovered in Geneva and its operators arrested. This item was removed from all subsequent editions of the paper, and it was mere chance that it caught my eye. That night I heard the Centre vainly calling the Hamel transmitter and feared the worst. The next morning my telephone rang and I heard Rado's voice at the other end. "You will be sorry to hear that Eduard is much worse and the doctor has been called in. He decided after consultation that the only thing to do was to take him to hospital." I made suitable sympathetic noises to keep up the pretense, but my mind was working furiously. This meant that the only firm link with the Centre was my transmitter, with the possible doubtful use to which we might put Bolli's (here I was overoptimistic). Rado's agitation, though suitable to the tenor of the conversation, was also perfectly genuine. With the "doctor" looking after Hamel, Rado felt the "hospital" looming unpleasantly near for him also.

A day or so later he telephoned to me again and said that he was coming over to see me in my flat under cover of darkness, a thing he had never done before and an action symptomatic of his agitation. He arrived and told me that not only had the Hamels been arrested, but the police had also simultaneously raided Margarete Bolli's flat and arrested her as well. Hamel had been caught *flagrante delicto*, sitting working the transmitter; Margarete had been caught equally in the act, but in rather a different sense, as she had been found in bed with Peters, the Abwehr agent, who had succeeded only too admirably in his task of getting the girl's confidence. A complication, slightly embarrassing to the Abwehr, was that Peters had been arrested also as an accomplice!

We never understood why the Swiss, having held their hands so long, acted in the end with such precipitancy. They had not kept the buildings under observation, but if they had they could have scooped the whole gang, including Rado. As it was, Rado had a narrow escape, as he went round to see Hamel a few hours after his arrest and while the police were still searching the flat. Luckily he happened to glance at a clock which Hamel kept in his shop window, and the hands showed danger. It had been agreed that the hands of the clock should show midday when all was clear. During transmission times or if danger threatened the hands were changed to some other time. As Hamel was transmitting at the time of his arrest, the signal showed danger, and Rado was warned before he knocked and fell into the hands of the police.

All this was reported to the Centre over my set, which was now the only link the network had with Moscow. The Director expressed concern, but stated that "Lucy's" information was so important that we must continue working despite the arrests, and he ordered Rado and me to make every effort, with the aid of the local party, to recruit new operators and construct new sets.

Rado was frantic with worry and anxiety—worry over the breakdown of the organization and anxiety, for he had broken practically every security precaution in the espionage code. Fearing that he might be being tailed, he had, some time previously, deposited all his records with Hamel, who had a secure hiding place built into his flat. These records contained not only all the financial details of the network, but also copies of telegrams which had been sent, often with the encoded version attached to them. As if this were not sufficient, he had also been idiotic enough to leave a copy of his code book there, and this, too, fell into the hands of the police. He feared, not without reason, that his code was compromised and that, with the material captured, the Swiss would be able to read all the back traffic that he had sent, which they had picked up through their monitoring of the sets. This meant that not only was I the only physical link with the Centre, but also that my code was the only one which could be used.

The police haul had been even better than this. Among the messages that they discovered was one giving the details of a new Swiss Oerlikon cannon which was still on the secret list, and from the messages the Swiss were able, after some study, to discover that the source of much of the military information was none other than their trusted military evaluator "Lucy" himself. Thus not only was Rado guilty of espionage against Swiss interests, which would make the Bupo doubly anxious to get to the bottom of the affair, but his ill-considered actions had imperiled our most valuable source as well. I also shrewdly suspected that, among the other miscellaneous financial papers, the police would find clear pointers toward me and the rest of the network. My fears were not ungrounded, as subsequent events showed.

A few days later Rado reported that the Geneva Communist Party had been able to make contact with the Hamels and Bolli through the agency of the prison warder, who was a secret member of the party. Hamel told us that he had been shown a photograph of myself and told that the original was the head of the entire network. The police did not know then of the existence of Rado or so it appeared. (The photograph, of course, was one supplied by the Abwehr.)

Rado had gone to ground in Bern, but soon after he plucked up courage and went back and lived openly at his flat. He noticed, however, that it was under observation, or he thought it was, and went to ground again in the flat of a couple of party sympathizers in Geneva.

All this was reported back to the Centre, who ordered me to take control of the entire group, and the Director stated that he had given orders to Rado to put me in touch with his two main cut-outs, "Pakbo" and "Cissie." Although Rado had now ceased to use his cipher, the Centre still sent occasional messages in it for him. They regarded their codes as unbreakable unless the key fell into the wrong hands, and could not believe that an old old hand like Rado had been so foolish as to hand the whole thing to the Swiss on a plate, as he had done.

Rado agreed to put me in touch with "Pakbo," but said that "Cissie" declined to have any contact with me. He said that, owing to the visit of the two presumed German agents to her flat a month or two back, she feared that she would be compromised if she was in direct touch with me. That was Rado's story, but I learned after my release that it bore little relation to the truth. In fact, "Cissie" had asked to be put in touch with me, but this Rado had refused to do. The reasons were not difficult to understand. Rado wished at all costs to keep control of the organization, and in order to do so was prepared to disobey the Director's orders. He also knew that it would be extremely embarrassing to him were I to meet "Cissie" and compare notes, especially on finance. Rado had been indenting on me for large sums of money to pay "Cissie" and her agents, but had been keeping a large proportion of this money for himself. This discrepancy would immediately come out when we met, as it did a year later.

As a result Rado stated that he would continue to receive the "Lucy" information through "Cissie" and pass it on to me through a cut-out. He also said that he would act as cut-out between Pierre Nicole and myself. Pierre was the son of Léon Nicole, the leader of the extreme left-wing Geneva party, and was busy recruiting wireless operators for the time when we could once again start up new sets. We also arranged for a "place of conspiracy" for Pierre and myself in case of emergency.

Rado therefore suggested that the best thing for the network and himself would be for him to take refuge in the British Legation (there was, of course, no Soviet representation in Switzerland, and the nearest Soviet official was in Ankara or London). Once there, and he safely inside the hedge of diplomatic immunity, the network would continue functioning as before, with the one difference that the British would have to be brought into the picture. Rado himself was not in touch with the British, but "Pakbo," through his cut-out "Salter," the Balkan service attaché, made the approach, and Rado received the reply that the British were prepared to harbor him if necessary. The Swiss end of the deal was therefore settled and he had only to square the Centre. I therefore passed on to the Centre Rado's request that he should be allowed to retire from the world and take refuge with the British. Almost by return transmission I received a most emphatic "No." The Centre added that they could not understand how such an old hand as Rado could even think of making such a suggestion, as "the British would track down his lines of communication and use them for themselves."

This idea of Allied cooperation rather shook Rado, but it was not in the least inconsistent with the attitude that the

Centre had adopted on previous occasions. Once, in 1942, Rado had had in his hands certain documents and plans which would have been of great value to the British as well as to the Russians, but the material was so bulky that it was impossible for us to pass it over the air. He therefore had suggested that it be handed over to the Allies—through a suitable and secure cut-out, or course. The Centre's reaction was immediate. Rado received instructions to burn the information at once. From the Director's point of view there was little difference between information falling into German or British hands. It was Russian information, and if it could not be passed to the Centre, then the right place for it was the waste-paper basket, however valuable it might be to Russia's allies.

In the meantime I received further news from Hamel through the "fellow-traveling" warder in the jail. Hamel had been told by his interrogators that there was another transmitter working in Lausanne and that a posse of Army technicians had been sent out to track it down.

I informed the Centre of this, and was told that "Lucy's" information was still so vital that I must risk everything and continue to transmit. In the meantime, until other transmitters were available and I was able to move my residence, I was to send no information at all save for "Lucy's" material.

At this time I was seeing Rado twice weekly, or as near as we could make it having regard to his fears and to my other appointments. The only point of these meetings was for Rado to pass on "Lucy's" material and any messages he might have about the reconstruction of the network. At our rendezvous we used to check up carefully to see whether we were being followed, and this paid good dividends. On one occasion toward the end of October we had arranged to meet just inside the Parc d'Eaux Vives in Geneva. Rado arrived by taxi and entered the park. I noticed that the driver of the cab, as soon as he had been paid, drove off, but stopped almost at once at a telephone kiosk, into which he hurriedly shut himself. I told Rado, and we decided at once that, trivial as the incident might be, we had better play for safety, and we left the park at once by separate gates. We went just in time. I learned later that the police had circulated a photograph of Rado to all cab drivers in Geneva. The driver in question had recognized his fare and rung up police headquarters. A hurry call had been sent out to the various squad cars prowling around the town, and they covered the exits. But they were too late, for Rado and I had left and arranged a somewhat less disturbed rendezvous elsewhere.

This little incident put the finishing touch to Rado's fears. From that time on it was impossible to lure him out of his hidey-hole with the local Communist Party. In fact, he remained underground until he left the country a year later, and virtually took no further part in the network. His nerve had been going for some time. Small blame to him, as he had been working under a strain for many years. This strain had been increased by the fortuitous addition, through the accident of war, of a number of other networks to his own. He had coped manfully with the dribs and drabs of heterogeneous networks thrown at his head and succeeded up to a point for some time. I prefer to remember him at the height of his power as the genial cartographer to the world at large, and the successful spymaster to the favored few, rather than as the hunted rat of his last Swiss days or the frightened broken man of Paris and Cairo. Only the Centre knows his fate. He certainly cheated many out of their just dues, but equally he drove them to obtain the best results. He had been faithful to his masters—after his fashion.

To make matters worse, at that time the network was very short of money. My dollar deal through the watch company was still incomplete and our cash reserves were down to $5,000. Rado himself was completely broke, and in addition had borrowed $5,000 from the local Communist Party and a further $5,000 from "Pakbo." At that time the network was costing some $10,000 a month in salaries and expenses alone, quite apart from extras such as bonuses. To make financial matters worse, the Director had authorized me to spend $10,000 to finance a plan for the escape of the Hamels and Bolli from prison. This sum was needed as a bribe to the "fellow traveler" warder and his colleagues. The Director set great store by this plan, as he was apprehensive lest Bolli, the least experienced of the three, should break down under interrogation. She knew "Pakbo's" and my real names, and, of course, a great deal about Rado. The Hamels were not so important, as they knew the names of none of the network save that of Pierre Nicole, who had recruited them, though they knew Rado and me by sight.

I need not have worried unduly about the financial side, as matters were swiftly taken out of my hands. On the night of November 19–20 I contacted Moscow at the scheduled time, which was then half-past midnight. I passed over a short message to them and then began taking down a long message which they had for me.

Three-quarters of an hour later there was a splintering crash and my room was filled with police. At 1:15 in the morning of November 20 the "doctors" took the matter into their own hands. I was arrested, and the last link between the Centre and Switzerland was broken.

IV

Double Agents:

Working Both Sides of the Street

THE DOUBLE AGENT is one of the most intriguing figures in the annals of espionage. He is in touch with two, usually opposing, intelligence services, and is spying for each against the other or against the other's territory. Yet he will, in most cases, at a given time, truly be working only in favor of one of his employers and deceiving the other. An excellent example of this classic kind of double agent was the Hollywood director Boris Morros, who in the 1950's was engaged by the Soviets to recruit American intellectuals and scientists in sensitive spots, but kept the FBI informed throughout of what the Russians had asked him to do and what he had done about it. When the time was ripe the FBI arrested and prosecuted many of the people Morros had brought into the Soviet net. The Soviets, of course, did not know until the day of reckoning had dawned that Mr. Morros had been deceiving them all along.

It is quite a different and more complex situation when each side knows that the agent is in touch with the other, but believes, for reasons that will vary from case to case, that the agent is primarily loyal only to it. Thus, Edward Bancroft, the famous double agent of the American Revolution, made himself useful to his employers precisely because he knew each of them well enough to be trusted by both. To Benjamin Franklin in Paris, Bancroft seemed a worth-while agent because he had such good connections in British Government circles and was able to bring Franklin information about British plans. To the British, Bancroft was valuable because he knew Franklin and could report on the latter's efforts to persuade the French to come to the aid of the Colonies. Both the British and Franklin were aware of Bancroft's associations with the other, but not, we may assume, of the true nature of these associations. This kind of arrangement frequently tempts the double agent to play the game as he pleases or, where possible, for his own benefit. Thus, Bancroft, while generally favoring the British, did not deliver to George III certain information which he picked up from Franklin's office in Paris concerning shipments of armaments to the Colonies, because he had invested money in these shipments and didn't want the British Navy to intercept them. As one historian said of him, he achieved the "astonishing feat of serving simultaneously as an intelligence agent for two nations at war [with each other] while serving himself first of all, and mastering the art of duplicity so consummately as to conceal his treasons from some of the most astute men of his time and from historians for six decades after his death."

The case of Ievno Aseff, the police spy, which is told in one of our selections and which, incidentally, inspired the plot of Rebecca West's recent book *The Birds Fall Down*, is one of the most unusual in all intelligence history. Here the double agent shuttling between the police, whose agent he was, and a revolutionary underground, whose assassination plots he masterminded, maneuvered himself into a position where he could if he wished, decide between life and death for the most exalted authorities in Czarist Russia, not excluding the Czar himself.

Double agents figured in one of the most unusual conversations I ever had, namely with Nikita Khrushchev at a White House reception in September, 1959. Although I had been presented to the Soviet Premier as he stood in the receiving line, Vice President Nixon took me over to have a personal chat with him a little later. He was standing at one side of the room surrounded by newspapermen and guests, among whom was J. Edgar Hoover, the Director of the FBI. When Vice President Nixon introduced me to Premier Khrushchev the latter immediately said to me, "Oh, yes, I know you. I read your reports." When I asked him how he got them he stated that we were no doubt paying the same agents, and then he went on to suggest, tongue in cheek, as one newspaper later reported it, "that the two countries save money by pooling their intelligence nets 'so we don't have to pay twice for the same information.' "

1

Crossing the Delaware

Leonard Falkner

In this account from the American Revolution, Sergeant Honeyman, living almost within hailing distance of both the American and British lines, has a much more difficult row to hoe than today's rather elegant brand of double agent, who very likely travels by jet between various world capitals in order to visit the different espionage organizations which employ him. To get into General Washington's camp without arousing suspicion Honeyman must be captured and dragged there and must later escape. To his neighbors he must play the Tory so that they do not suspect he is working for Washington. In doing so he incurs their enmity, making life extremely unpleasant for his family. If his contacts to the authorities on the other side of the Delaware are discovered before Washington can come to his aid, he could be hanged as a traitor.

This was one time in our history when the U.S. Intelligence Service encountered no difficulty whatsoever in getting its findings accepted, correctly interpreted, and given due weight by the govern-

FROM "A Spy for Washington," *American Heritage*, August 1957.

ment's Executive Branch. There is much to be said for an intelligence operation which is run by the commander-in-chief himself.

THE FINEST CHRISTMAS present, and the most unexpected, our country ever received was handed to us by George Washington in the dismal winter of 1776 when he crossed the Delaware and captured Trenton just as the faltering fires of the American Revolution seemed about to go out.

There were to be other hard winters before independence was won, Valley Forge among them, but none more critical than this one. Since adoption of the Declaration of Independence five months before, the bedraggled Continental Army's road had been rutted with disasters. It had barely escaped destruction on Long Island and at White Plains and had lost 2,800 men captured at Fort Washington. Chased across New Jersey by the British regulars and their German mercenaries, it had been thinned by casualties and desertions to a few thousand hungry, half-naked diehards. Only Washington's foresight in confiscating all the available boats before his army fled across the Delaware River at Trenton had staved off capture. At best, it seemed only a breathing spell.

The British army under Sir William Howe was safely based in New York, while Lord Cornwallis, commanding the triumphant British forces in New Jersey, had started packing to go back to England. He might return in the spring to mop up if Howe thought it necessary. But he felt confident that hunger and cold would put out the last sparks of rebellion before then in the starving camp across the river.

Even Washington appeared to agree. From his headquarters on the Pennsylvania side of the Delaware, he wrote one of his soul-unburdening letters to his brother John Augustine: "I think the game is pretty near up. . . . No man, I believe, ever had a greater choice of difficulties and less means to extricate himself from them."

That was on December 18.

Seven days later, Christmas night, Washington suddenly forded his troops back across the Delaware, stormed into Trenton with the dawn, and defeated the Hessian army there. The attack was flawlessly executed, timed perfectly. Without an American fatality, the town was taken!

It was America's first major victory of the war. The startled Cornwallis rushed to the rescue, but Washington slipped around his flank in the dark and audaciously smashed his rear guard in the Battle of Princeton, then scampered into the New Jersey hills at Morristown for the rest of the winter.

In one brilliant, totally unexpected stroke, Washington had changed the complexion of the War for Independence from a dying pallor to a ruddy glow. America was jubilant, its confidence magically reborn. England was grave with sudden concern.

Official documents of the war leave us in the dark. But in the records of a colonial village family and the finds of a New Jersey Supreme Court justice and a well-known historian of the Revolution, the mystery comes out of hiding. It is a strange story of a silent man who performed an important and dangerous mission and never asked the least acclaim for it, never seemed to want anything more than his own soul-deep satisfaction in a job superbly done.

It is the story of John Honeyman, a plain, close-mouthed weaver, "the spy of Washington" at Trenton. Only one person got the story in all its details directly from him: his wife, who alone of his family was in on the secret from the start. It remained for his grandson, Justice John Van Dyke of the New Jersey Supreme Court, to record and annotate it carefully, and William S. Stryker, the nineteenth-century historian and adjutant general of New Jersey, to investigate further and in essence confirm it.

We first meet John Honeyman, a Scotch-Irish giant of forty-six, on the Rover Road west of the Hessian-held village of Trenton. It was the afternoon of December 22, 1776. A crust of two-day-old snow covered the brown fields. Patches of ice glinted in the hollows. John Honeyman, known as an outspoken Tory serving the British as both a butcher and "spy," strolled past the Hessian outposts, a coil of rope in one hand, a long cart whip in the other, hunting cattle.

A few miles up the Delaware River, on the other side, Washington's rebel army, without tents or blankets, half of the men barefooted, huddled around open campfires in the lee of Bowman's Hill, keeping barely alive on their scant ration of raw flour baked into a semblance of bread on stones around the fires. Behind Honeyman, in the snug Trenton he had just left, the Hessians had all the bread they needed, and rum, but not enough meat for the *Fröhliche Weihnachten* so dear to their Teutonic hearts. Another cow or two!

John Honeyman was a big man, his grandson remembered, with a deep burr of Scotch in his voice—when he used it. He knew the rebel commander, Washington, was looking for him. With many farmers in the area still loyal to the British, news like that traveled fast. Eyes alert, he moved cautiously across the frozen fields. Under a clump of trees some distance away, he spotted two dismounted horsemen sitting on stumps. Nearby, a farmer's cow browsed in a fence corner.

Honeyman nudged the cow into the open. As she dodged away, he ran, shouting, after her and cracked his whip. Across the fields, he saw the two horsemen—in Continental uniforms—jump into their saddles and gallop toward him. He ran but they were soon on top of him. Slashing with his long whip he held them off for a while. Then he was down and one of them was on top of him. Before the other could dismount, he had slugged himself free and was running again.

He lost his balance on a patch of ice and fell hard. This time both horsemen were on him before he could get up. While one straddled him, the other aimed a pistol at his head.

Honeyman protested that he was only a poor cattle dealer hunting meat to sell to the Hessians, but when they got his name out of him they elatedly bound him with his own rope. Mounted behind the one rider, while the other followed closely with his pistol ready, he was carried off to Washington's headquarters.

As Honeyman's wife later got the tale from him and passed it along in the family, he was a disheveled, scared-looking figure as the two troopers pushed him into the room where the Commander-in-Chief stood waiting. Washington gravely thanked the troopers for their accomplishment, then gave an order. This man was to be left alone

with him and guards posted outside with instructions to
shoot to kill if the spy tried to escape.

The door closed and Honeyman saw a smile break
across Washington's face. With a grin he straightened up
and brushed the dirt off his shoulders.

This was the fourth time, according to the family accounts, that these two, the tall commander of the Continental Army and the brawny Scotch-Irish cattle dealer and
butcher—and "notorious British spy"—had met. The first
two times had been in Philadelphia a year and a half
earlier, shortly after the Continental Congress appointed
Washington to lead the colonial forces. Honeyman, a
weaver who a few years before had married an Irish-born
Philadelphia girl and settled there, brought two documents
with him. One was his honorable discharge from the British Army in 1763 after the French and Indian War, of
which Washington was a fellow veteran. The other was a
letter from General James Wolfe, the British hero of that
war, announcing Honeyman's appointment as his bodyguard.

The Irish predominating in Honeyman burned for independence from the British. He had been conscripted into
the French and Indian War against his will. On the boat
coming over he had saved Wolfe from a bad fall when the
young officer stumbled coming down a ladder. This letter
was Honeyman's reward.

With these two documents, the Scottish accent he could
turn on full spigot, and a pretense of fervent loyalty to the
Crown, Honeyman pointed out to Washington—earnest-
ness for once overcoming his shyness with words—that he
could get into the confidence of the British, act the part of
a spy for them, but in reality spy for Washington.

A plan was worked out. As a weaver, there wasn't much
Honeyman could offer the British. One of them, and the
accounts are not clear which it was, determined that it
would be better for him to become a cattle dealer and
butcher, at which he had had some experience as a young
man back in Ireland, so he could supply provisions to the
British. Whenever Honeyman thought he had important
information, he should let himself be captured by Washington's outposts, but not without a convincing struggle, so
his usefulness wouldn't end. If Washington had sudden

reason to want him, he would in some way spread the word. Afterward, Honeyman's escape would be contrived. He would be accountable only to Washington, and for his family's safety the only other person who would know about it would be Honeyman's wife, Mary.

Soon afterward, Honeyman moved his wife and children —three little ones and a crippled daughter, Jane, going on nine—into New Jersey, a hotbed of loyalists. They settled in the village of Griggstown, a few miles north of Princeton.

The third meeting with Washington as the Honeyman family heard it, was a hurried one at Hackensack in northern New Jersey in middle November. Washington, harried and weary, was desperately trying to save his dwindling army. Driven out of New York and with the British on his heels, he was starting the long race to temporary safety across the Delaware. His orders to Honeyman were crisp: fall in with the British army and stay with them until Washington needed him or he felt he had something to tell.

And now they were met for the fourth time in the big room at headquarters, very likely at Keith's farmhouse, a few miles south of the Delaware.

If Washington had had a reservation about trusting Honeyman, the meeting apparently dispelled it. The scant information his scouts had been able to bring him supported the spy's story. When Honeyman finished telling what he knew, Washington called the sentry and ordered him locked in the guardhouse for court-martial next morning.

Late that night a haystack near the farmhouse is said to have caught fire. As the guard before the log hut ran off to help put it out, the door was mysteriously unlocked, and Honeyman ran for it. A sentry fired at him as he vanished in the dark. He crossed the Delaware partly on the ice, waded the rest of the way, and ran until he fell, drenched and exhausted, before one of the Hessian outposts.

Taken to Colonel Rall's quarters, he told the story of his capture in convincing detail, saying he had escaped by breaking out the window. As a loyal British subject, of course, he assured Rall, he had told Washington nothing that the rebels didn't already know. But he had juicy information for the German commander: the army across the river was hopelessly disorganized, on the brink of mutiny. He had heard them muttering around their camp-fires as they tried to keep their bare feet from freezing. Rall was delighted. It confirmed everything he had thought. There was nothing to worry about from that quarter, he said, and so he went ahead with his plans for a big Christmas.

At the Keith house across the river next morning, Washington was said to have appeared furious when told of the prisoner's escape.

When his medical officer, Dr. Benjamin Rush, came in, he found the Commander-in-Chief curiously preoccupied, scribbling words on scraps of paper as he talked. One of them fell on the floor and Dr. Rush picked it up. "Victory or Death!" was written on it, the watchword for the still unannounced march on Trenton.

Later that same day Washington sent a message to his generals: "Christmas day at night, one hour before day, is the time fixed for our attempt on Trenton."

He sent a general order to the troops to prepare and keep on hand three days' rations of cooked food.

In Trenton Colonel Rall was not without warning. Tory farmers in the neighborhood quickly passed along the word that the rebel army was getting ready to move. As Rall sat playing cards and drinking in the home of a Trenton loyalist Christmas night, a Tory farmer from across the river pounded on the door. The servant wouldn't let him interrupt the game, so he wrote a note, warning Rall that the Continentals were coming. Rall stuffed it in his pocket, unread, and went on with his cards and wine.

He was sleeping off a monumental hangover next morning, as were most of the rest of the garrison, when Washington's troops, many of them barefooted, others with rags around their bleeding feet, marched through a sleet storm in two columns that converged with perfect precision and stormed down unprotected King and Queen streets into the village.

It was all over in less than an hour. Rall was mortally wounded, shot as he tried to organize his men in the center of the village. One hundred and six of the mercenaries had been killed or wounded. Some nine hundred captives were ferried across the river into Pennsylvania, many of them to be paraded through the streets of Philadelphia to show that metropolis of Colonial America that the Revolution was still very much alive. Of the patriots, only two officers and two enlisted men had been wounded.

Stryker, the historian of the American Revolution in New Jersey, said in his book *The Battles of Trenton and Princeton*: "It is a well-established tradition that the most reliable account of Colonel Rall's post at Trenton was given by Washington's spy, John Honeyman, of Griggstown, Somerset County. There appears to be no doubt that the information given by him that winter night was the direct cause of the movement on Trenton three days afterwards."

Honeyman was not among the prisoners taken at Trenton. He had discreetly slipped off to New Brunswick after his meeting with Rall. But word of his arrest and escape from Washington's encampment had reached his home village. A crowd of patriots surrounded the house when a rumor spread that he was hiding there. Honeyman's eldest daughter, Jane, then ten, remembered that night in vivid detail for the rest of her life. She heard the crowd threaten to burn the house unless her father came out. Mrs. Honeyman, her children huddled behind her, denied he was there or that she knew where he was. The crowd closed in. Mrs. Honeyman asked the name of the leader. A soldier came to the door. By the light of a candle Mrs. Honeyman let him read a letter she unfolded.

It was dated "American Camp, New Jersey, Nov. A.D. 1776" and ordered that "the wife and children of John Honeyman, the notorious Tory, now within the British lines, and probably acting the part of a spy" were to be protected from harm. But this protection did not extend to John Honeyman.

The soldier had seen Washington's signature on other papers. He decided it was authentic and persuaded the crowd to go home.

John Honeyman apparently played out his lonely and dangerous role of "Tory and British spy" to the end of the war, for his family saw little if anything of him. But no details are known of his activities after the Battle of Trenton.

John Honeyman lived to be ninety-three and became a prosperous farmer in the neighboring village of Lamington, where he moved from Griggstown ten years after the war. There were reports that the government rewarded him for his services, but the incomplete records of the time fail to support them.

There is a Revolutionary War veteran marker beside the eroded headstone on Honeyman's grave in the old village cemetery at Lamington. And on the New Jersey side of the Delaware River at Washington Crossing State Park, where Washington's army landed for its march on Trenton, stands a stone memorial fountain with a bronze plaque on it. It was erected by the Patriotic Order Sons of America, and high officials of the state of New Jersey attended the dedication on December 26, 1930. It reads:

DEDICATED IN MEMORY OF
JOHN HONEYMAN
WHO SERVED WASHINGTON AND
THE CONTINENTAL ARMY
AS A SPY
DRINK OF THE FOUNT OF LIBERTY
LET POSTERITY INHERIT FREEDOM

John Honeyman, who found inner satisfaction far more important than acclaim for his daring achievement, would have been embarrassed at even this simple tribute.

2

To Kill a Czar

Boris Nikolajewsky

Ievno Aseff's story is one of the most fantastic in the history of police and intelligence work. It would have been impossible anywhere except in the autocratic Russia of sixty years ago, with its underground revolutionary and anarchist organizations. The Ochrana, the Czar's secret police, was supposed to be entirely concerned with smoking out the enemies of the state and went about its work chiefly through its own agents and informants planted in underground groups. A very popular tactic was "provocation," which usually went like this: the police agent in the underground group, who more often than not posed as one of its leaders, would propose some extreme act, such as the assassination of a public figure. As the group was about to carry out the act the police would swoop down and arrest the lot. But it not infrequently happened that the public figure was blown to bits in the process, because the bomb went off before the police had intervened. Considering that the whole plot might originally have been secretly proposed by the police for the purpose of corner-

FROM the book *Aseff the Spy*.

ing the assassins in the act, it is clear that the police were often to blame for the assassination of highly placed personalities. In Aseff's case, as we shall see, such plots were even planned against the person of the Czar himself.

As a young student in a revolutionary group, Aseff had secretly offered his services as an agent to the police. Because of what appeared to be revolutionary ardor and courage, he soon became the leader of a secret unit of the Social Revolutionary Party, dedicated to assassination and sabotage, and known as the Battle Organization. Aseff kept betraying the plans of the Battle Organization to the police, while on the other hand it seems that he also sympathized, in some measure, with the general aims of the party and despised the police for their stupidity and their reactionary politics. The result was that, while foiling the plans of the Battle Organization, he often foiled the police also.

The selection contains a number of anecdotes taken from different periods in which Aseff was aligned with both police and revolutionaries. The first episode takes place in 1906 at a time when Aseff's services to both police and revolutionaries had placed him high in the esteem of each. The police evidently relied on Aseff's schemes and took his advice. Hard as it is to believe, Aseff's assassination plan, ostensibly to be carried out for the Battle Organization, was directed against the Minister of the Interior, Pëtr Stolypin, who supervised the Ochrana and was aware, therefore, of Aseff's plan. Aseff worked through a subordinate of Stolypin's, the chief of the Ochrana branch in St. Petersburg, Gerassimoff. Armed with these facts, I trust the reader will be able to follow this immensely complicated story.

THE CENTRAL COMMITTEE of the Social Revolutionary Party now judged that individual terrorist acts could only help the rising tide of revolution. It was, therefore, decided to renew the activity of the Battle Organization. The first and only task given it was that of killing Stolypin.

It was Aseff, needless to say, who assumed leadership of the Battle Organization. He found no difficulty in enrolling the old members, the majority of whom were living in St. Petersburg or Finland, waiting for the moment to resume their work. Nor was there any lack of new volunteers. The necessary detachment was quickly formed, and it soon set to work. Their temper was of the most sanguine. The general atmosphere at the time fired people and made them believe in the success of their undertakings. Only Aseff showed himself very reserved and did not hide that he was far from sharing the general confidence. This was part of his plan, since he was, of course, arranging for the failure of the undertaking.

From the beginning, Aseff kept Gerassimoff informed of all the particulars of the renewed activity of the Battle Organization. Where St. Petersburg was concerned, the Ochrana knew all the details of the Battle Organization's plan, the names of all its members, and all that happened inside it. Arrests could have been made at any moment, but these did not enter into Gerassimoff's calculations, for Aseff had insisted that the arrest of any terrorist working under him would bring about his own downfall. The loss of Aseff was not part of Gerassimoff's plan, and the suppression of merely one terrorist detachment was far too insignificant a result of the close cooperation now established between the chief of the Ochrana and the head of the Battle Organization. The possibilities of this alliance might be exploited in a more brilliant fashion.

It was difficult, however, to find the most profitable line of action. They followed at first the line of least resistance, making no arrests but nipping every plot in the bud. Aseff could do this very well himself, since he was able to direct the terrorists on false trails. The terrorists were now keeping a lookout for Stolypin whenever he drove to see the Czar or to the Duma. By agreement with Gerassimoff, Aseff so posted the terrorists that for a considerable time they did not once succeed in catching sight of the Minister. Becoming aware of the fruitlessness of their work, they soon began to get nervous.

Aseff, noting the first results of his methods, suggested a further plan, which was both daring and original. This was to systematize the policy of frustration and thus force the terrorists and the Central Committee to the conclusion that terror on a grand scale had become impossible. The Battle Organization was to be made to work like a machine that is running at full pressure yet producing nothing of any consequence; and the terrorists were to be made to feel that they were doing all in their power but that their attempts broke themselves against an impenetrable wall. All this was to convince them and the Central Committee that the terror could not be pursued by the old methods and that the Battle Organization had, for a time at least, to be dissolved. This plan was greatly to Gerassimoff's liking, and he helped to work it out in all its details. The result was a far-reaching plan of campaign, which was to combine Aseff's party experience and authority and all the machinery of the Ochrana.

The plan was submitted for Stolypin's approval. The Minister against whose life Aseff was to pretend to organize an attempt at first hesitated and went carefully into all the details. He was apparently afraid of some hitch in the working of the "machinery" and of losing his life in consequence. But Gerassimoff guaranteed that there would be no "unfortunate accidents," and he got a similar assurance from Aseff. The latter agreed to do so because he was perfectly well aware of the strictness of the Battle Organization discipline, and that none of its members would dare to act on their own initiative. Moreover, the terrorists carried no arms during their preparatory work in order to avoid imperiling themselves needlessly in case of chance arrest. Gerassimoff also guaranteed that every possible measure of precaution would be taken and that the terrorists would be kept under the closest observation. Thus, according to Gerassimoff, no real danger threatened Stolypin, while the result of the scheme would be to put the Battle Organization under sure and permanent control. In the end, Stolypin was even pleased with this plan and set the seal of his approval upon it.

Thus began the campaign of the Battle Organization against Stolypin—a campaign, really, of Aseff, Gerassimoff, and Stolypin against the Battle Organization.

If we were to look at the work of the Battle Organization through the eyes of its members, it would seem to be progressing normally. Secret meeting places were arranged, some of the terrorists disguised themselves as cabmen, others as messengers, hawkers, and so forth. The attempt was being prepared on a grand scale, and no expenses were spared. The treasury of the Battle Organization was at that time full: hundreds of thousands of rubles passed through it, and its treasurers followed the rule, now consecrated by tradition, of satisfying all the demands of the Battle Organization without question.

Once the initial steps had been taken, the terrorists began their watch on Stolypin. They worked with zeal and self-denial but without any tangible results. It was rarely that one of them succeeded in catching sight of the minister as he drove by, and more often they had to content themselves with seeing groups of Ochrana agents, who carefully scrutinized everybody who came their way. If they happened to get hold of some detail which, they hoped, might enable them to take more direct action, there invariably appeared on the horizon some alarming sign, which not only dashed their hopes of outwitting the police, but even made them feel anxious for their own safety. That was the doing of Aseff's secret ally, Gerassimoff.

Aseff relied as far as possible upon his own resources and frustrated the work of the terrorists by misdirecting them. There were obviously limits to this procedure, since he had to create the illusion that the organization was doing everything in its power to achieve positive results. The terrorists, too, seeing that continual failure attended their efforts, began to show initiative and suggested plans of their own. When their independence began to importune, Gerassimoff, with Aseff's consent, resorted to "frightening" them.

To this end, the terrorists were permitted to try to put their plans into execution. Aseff criticized them beforehand but agreed to the attempts being made. The first steps raised hopes; but as soon as the terrorists' nerves became strung to their utmost, Gerassimoff let loose his "branders," as those not very competent detectives were called in Ochrana slang, who could not keep anybody under observation without making the fact immediately obvious. "We had real specialists in this line," Gerassimoff relates. "When following anybody, they almost breathed down the back of his neck. Only a blind man could fail to notice them. No self-respecting detective would accept such a mission and, besides, it would have been most inadvisable to use him in that way, as it would either spoil his work or make him too well known."

The terrorists, of course, noticed the "branders." They would immediately inform Aseff of the fact; the latter would sometimes pretend to doubt them at first and wonder whether they had not become too nervous. But examination of the evidence soon showed that the police were really on their track. Then Aseff would take the decision, which had become a rule, to abandon the plans and think only of the safety of the terrorists. And he would give them detailed instructions as to how to effect their escape. The horses, cabs, apartments, and other weapons of conspiracy were naturally abandoned to their fate, but the terrorists safely eluded the spies.

Such "frightenings" were practiced comparatively rarely, and every time the details were slightly varied. But all this helped to convince the terrorists that the police had learned their methods so well that there was no possibility of getting near Stolypin. And each time that the terrorists came together again somewhere in Finland, after a successful escape, and reviewed the past events, they all came to the conclusion that the police had come upon their tracks absolutely by chance, and that they had not even had the time to find out who they were (that is how they explained the ease with which they made their escape). But the fact that this "chance" repeated itself as often as they got anywhere near the Minister forced them to conclude that the Minister was ringed by an impenetrable wall of police protection. But as Aseff had "foreseen" the weaknesses of the terrorists' plans and had so successfully organized their escape, his authority only tended to increase, while the legend of his "coolness" and "foresight" seemingly received every confirmation.

After every such failure Aseff insinuated with ever greater insistence that the terror could not be pursued any longer by the "old methods." "The police," he said, "have become too well acquainted with our old devices. And there is nothing surprising in this, for we have still the same cabmen, hawkers and so on, who figured in Plehve's assassination. We rely too much on the old technique to think of anything new. This is hard, but it must be admitted. . . ."

Weeks and months went by in this fashion. . . . The Duma had already been dissolved. Risings had already flared up and had been crushed in Kronstadt, Sveaborg and Reval. A wave of terror, of widespread and sporadic partisan attempts on governor generals, gendarmes, policemen and public buildings swept over the country. But there was no mass explosion such as had occurred in 1905. The workers, who had been the backbone of the 1905 movement, now remained silent, tired out by their defeats and worn out by unemployment and the industrial crisis. Under these circumstances the government soon overcame its temporary hesitation and set up courts-martial everywhere to cope rapidly with armed risings. Reaction grew stronger every day, and Stolypin, its chief inspirer, had already become the best-hated representative of authority.

The Battle Organization, at this moment, found itself up against a competitor. The "Maximalists," who had broken away from the Social Revolutionary Party and had decided to conduct a terrorist campaign of their own, were now planning an attempt on Stolypin. They organized their attempt very differently from the Battle Organization, relying on short, swift blows, without long preparatory work and observation. Thus three of its members, armed with bombs, called at Stolypin's villa at the hour of official reception. The guards suspected that all was not well and refused to let them pass. They threw their bombs in the hall. The explosion destroyed the greater part of the Minister's villa: several dozens of people lost their lives, including the guards, many callers, and, of course, the terrorists themselves. The Minister's small children were also severely injured, but Stolypin himself escaped almost without a scratch. The shock of the explosion was only slightly felt in his study.

The news of this attempt reached Aseff in Finland. It put him into a state bordering on panic. "In August, on the day that Stolypin's villa was blown up," Popova, a member of the Battle Organization working in its Finnish laboratory, writes in her memoirs, "Ivan Nicholaievitch [Aseff] unexpectedly called upon us. He was very agitated and also seemed depressed and distraught. He sat for a time in silence, nervously turning over the pages of a railway guide. At first he wanted to spend the night with us, but then thought better of it and went off to the station."

The reasons for Aseff's agitation are clear. He was afraid that Stolypin and Gerassimoff would hold the Battle Organization responsible for the attempt; and he knew that, since he had pledged the Minister's safety with his head, he would find it much more difficult to justify himself than after the Dubassoff affair. There was the danger, too, that the Ochrana would, for want of better information, arrest those members of the Battle Organization whom it had under observation and would thus disgrace him in the eyes of the revolutionaries. That was why Aseff hastened to St. Petersburg to explain things personally to Gerassimoff.

Fortunately, at this time he enjoyed Gerassimoff's complete confidence, and the latter took no action that would have compromised him. But, in order to whitewash the Battle Organization in Stolypin's eyes, Aseff was obliged to induce the Central Committee to publish an official manifesto, disclaiming all participation of the party and of the Battle Organization in the affair, and even containing a "moral and political" condemnation of the means employed in this attempt. Such declarations were hardly in keeping with the revolutionary movement; the Central Committee had doubted its necessity, but Aseff's insistence prevailed upon them. It fell to him to draw up the text of this manifesto, which is the only official party document of which Aseff is the direct author. This manifesto was obviously of paramount importance to him. Aseff also settled his score with the "Maximalists," The organizers of the attempt. From that time onward, he gathered all the information he could about them and brought this to the notice of his police chiefs.

Aseff was, at this time, preparing to enter on a new phase of his prolonged double game, and he was about to play his last card. . . . And as he never gambled unless he knew his opponent's cards before hand, he was now particularly careful in preparing the setting for his last game.

Very many of the members of the Central Committee agreed in principle with Aseff's plan for the assassination of the Czar. His views were very logical from the point of view of the terror, and it is not surprising that the Central

Committee continued to support the Battle Organization with every means in its power.

Aseff was also given a free hand in choosing recruits for the Battle Organization. Karpovitch, who had to his credit a number of terrorist acts, including the assassination of Bogolepoff, the Minister of Education, in February, 1901, now became his right-hand man. He had spent some years in prison after the assassination and had now just escaped and was anxious to resume terrorist work. Tchernavsky, another old revolutionary, who had first been sentenced to penal servitude some thirty years before, now also played a leading part in the Battle Organization.

All were convinced that Aseff was doing everything in his power to organize a successful attempt against the Czar. He was full of plans. According to him, watch was being kept on the Czar's comings and goings in St. Petersburg, and there was a project to attack him in the street. Argunoff also speaks of a plan to gain entry into the palace as members of one of the innumerable deputations staged by the reactionaries to demonstrate the "loyalty of the masses." Aseff also welcomed eagerly the suggestion of a young Social revolutionary, who had just taken orders and who hoped with his family influence to be appointed priest somewhere in the vicinity of Tsarskoye Selo. He thought that in this way he might have the opportunity to get within striking distance of the Czar and thus to execute the party's sentence. A priest assassinating the Czar—this was obviously a combination which appealed to Aseff, and he urged the youth to abandon all other revolutionary work and to devote himself entirely to this plan. There was also a whole series of other plans and projects.

But there were two plans to which Aseff gave really serious attention. The first was an attempt to be made on the Czar while he was hunting, and the second while he was on a journey to Reval. For the execution of the first, the terrorists opened a tea shop in one of the villages in the hunting district, near Tsarskoye Selo. Tchernavsky was to play the part of proprietor, representing himself to be an old monarchist and a member of the "Union of the Russian People." The second plan contemplated either blowing up the Czar's train or a bomb attack in the streets of Reval.

For all these plans Aseff was merely playing with both the revolutionaries and the police; he had no intention of allowing such an attempt to take place, as the police would never have forgiven him. He therefore readily informed the police of most of the details of the plots against the Czar, but, as we can establish, he did withhold a certain amount of information such as his connection with the young priest, reserving this for future use. He was still on the best of terms with Gerassimoff. Since their common object was the frustration of the Czar's assassination, Gerassimoff took every care to "safeguard Aseff." No attempt was made to arrest the members of either the Central Committee or the Battle Organization; and if any of them were arrested by chance without his knowledge, he took great pains to arrange for their escape without rousing their suspicions.

That Gerassimoff had unbounded confidence in him is shown by the fact that Aseff was aware of his private address. For Gerassimoff was at that time living like a conspirator, under an assumed name and concealed his place of residence even from the most responsible officials in the Ochrana. Aseff was the only "secret agent" who knew his address and who had the right, in case of necessity, to call there at any hour of the day or night, after previously telephoning.

There can be no doubt that Aseff also made use of Gerassimoff to find out the extent of the police knowledge as to what was taking place within the party. In this way he had opportunities for discovering the identity of other secret agents against whom he had to be on his guard when betraying the police.

Gerassimoff only made one stipulation—that Aseff should successfully frustrate the attempt against the Czar which was projected for that spring—and to this Aseff agreed.

At this time, too, there occurred an episode—the accidental arrest, upon a denunciation, of Karpovitch, Aseff's right-hand man in the Battle Organization—which had some influence on Aseff and caused him to hurry forward to the final dénouement. Argunoff, who saw Aseff the moment he heard the news of this arrest, says that Aseff called on him at once and made an almost hysterical scene. He said that this arrest would irrevocably compromise him in the eyes of the revolutionaries, and he threatened to throw up everything and go abroad. Gerassimoff was entirely of his opinion, for the arrest had been made without his knowledge. He was therefore ready to do everything in his power to appease Aseff, who demanded that Karpovitch should be immediately released without his suspicions being roused. Gerassimoff acceded to this, and Karpovitch made his "escape." Everything was thus satisfactorily arranged, although Karpovitch himself very nearly spoiled it.

While he was being taken in a cab, his guard went into a tobacconist's on the pretext of getting cigarettes. "I was sure," the latter told Gerassimoff afterward, "that the cab would be empty on my return, but to my surprise Karpovitch was quietly sitting there." The guard then suggested that they should go to a restaurant and have something to eat. Karpovitch consented, and they ordered dinner. The guard then excused himself again to wash his hands but watched Karpovitch through the door. For a long time Karpovitch hesitated, apparently fearing that a trap was being set for him. "I got tired of him," said the guard. "I thought he would never escape! What could I do if he simply did not want to take his chance?"

The Battle Organization had several schemes for attempts on the Czar's life, depending on what route he was to take and where he was to stay. The problem before Aseff and Gerassimoff was to arrange the Czar's itinerary in such a way as to thwart all these plans, and yet to leave the terrorists firmly convinced that their failure was due to accidental circumstances. This they succeeded in doing without great difficulty: thus on one occasion a prearranged telegram arrived late, and on another a terrorist missed his train. Furthermore, the Czar did not, as had been arranged, visit a certain Esthonian baron, and it was on this that the Battle Organization had placed their chief hopes. Thus the various schemes were thwarted one after another. . . .

Gerassimoff recalls that he was particularly struck at the time with the extraordinary fullness of Aseff's information as to all the Czar's intended movements.

Any proposed changes in the Czar's itinerary, however

secretly they were kept, were immediately known to him. He even boasted of this to Gerassimoff, who, in fact, usually got news of these changes later than Aseff. On one occasion they had a dispute over this: while discussing their plan of campaign, Aseff pointed to the necessity of attending to a small detail in the Czar's proposed itinerary. Gerassimoff objected that there was no such detail in the itinerary and referred to the official documents in support of his views. Aseff, however, stuck to his point.

"This new change has evidently not yet reached you," he declared authoritatively. "You will probably hear of it tomorrow or the day after."

And however much Gerassimoff tried to convince him of the improbability of such a change, Aseff remained unmoved.

"Our information is perfectly reliable!"

What was Gerassimoff's astonishment when, on the following day, he received a "strictly confidential" envelope, which informed him of the proposed change in the Czar's itinerary of which Aseff had spoken.

When they next met, Gerassimoff naturally enough tried to find out the source from which Aseff obtained such full and accurate information, but the latter definitely refused to satisfy the curiosity of his police chief.

"You know that I am taking every means to thwart this attempt and that I guarantee to be successful. But I am unable to give you the name of my informant because he is very highly placed, and only two or three people know of our relations. If he should notice that his role was becoming known, his suspicions would fall upon me, and I should be lost. . . . Please don't press it: I must have some regard for my own safety."

He did not fail, however, to emphasize the fact that he had been right.

"You see, I was right, after all. Where would you be if there was someone else at the head of the Battle Organization?"

Gerassimoff did not think it advisable to press this question. Aseff's right to "look after his safety" had long been recognized, and it was also clear that insistence would lead nowhere. But later, when the excitement of the Reval trip was over, Gerassimoff instituted a strictly secret investigation to find out Aseff's informant. As the number of those initiated into the details of the Czar's itinerary was very limited, and as Aseff had unwittingly let fall a few hints, there were some clues to work upon. The results of this investigation made Gerassimoff doubt his own senses: everything pointed to the fact that this informer was no minor official, as Gerassimoff had hoped would be the case, but a very highly placed personage. Gerassimoff was not in a position to take any measures against him on his own responsibility, and he therefore decided to make a confidential report on the matter to Stolypin. The latter for a long time refused to believe the facts put before him, and he insisted on further verification of them being made. This only confirmed the results of the first investigation. The highly placed personage, judging by all the evidence, would really seem to have been deliberately cooperating with the terrorists in their attempt against the Czar. . . . The government, it might seem, had no right to connive at such a state of affairs, but nevertheless, after long reflection, Stolypin decided that no further action was to be taken in the matter.

"The scandal would be too great; we cannot allow ourselves this luxury at the moment. . . . Later, perhaps.

". . . We would be obliged also to expose Aseff's role in the affair, and he is essential to us. . . . We had better leave the matter alone. . . . We must look after him. . . ."

Stolypin, as can be seen, was also very much concerned with "Aseff's safety," and the highly placed personage was left untouched. After Aseff's exposure, it became absolutely impossible to make public that a personage of almost Cabinet rank had actively helped in a plot organized against the Czar's life by the Battle Organization, whose very chief was a police agent acting under the orders of the president of the Cabinet himself. The name of this personage still remains a mystery, for Gerassimoff considers it impossible to publish it even now. This incident, however, gives us an idea of the connections now at the disposal of the Battle Organization, and which might, if necessary, have been put to serious use instead of being wasted in Aseff's game.

The Reval celebrations passed off without a hitch. All were content: the Czar and Stolypin with the political results of their interview with the King of England; Gerassimoff with his rewards; and Aseff chiefly with the one hundred thousand rubles which he had just lodged safely in the Battle Organization's treasury.

Reval was not Aseff's last card. Immediately after the "Reval campaign," Aseff again hastened to go abroad with Gerassimoff's permission, for he had news of another possibility of attempting the Czar's life with a greater chance of success. On hearing of this, Aseff sent his assistant, Karpovitch, to get full particulars. Karpovitch's reports were exceedingly hopeful, and Aseff now hastened to the spot himself.

Aseff took leave of Gerassimoff as if he was destined never to see him again. He said that he had grown weary and wished to retire and that he would soon give up any active participation in party affairs, but that he would like to be able to refute the accusations brought against him by Burtzeff* in order that he might be able to end his days in peace, without the fear of vengeance on the part of the revolutionaries. He was now finally giving up his work as a police agent, but he promised as a personal favor to Gerassimoff to inform him from time to time of the more important events taking place in the Central Committee, which would serve as material for reports to Stolypin, for whom Aseff felt something akin to personal sympathy. Gerassimoff promised that his salary would be paid as long as it was possible to do so, and he regarded this in the light of a pension for his past work. It is hardly necessary to add that Aseff did not even hint to Gerassimoff of the existence of a new plot against the Czar.

In June, 1908, Aseff left Russia with the idea of never returning (he returned only once for a short visit in November, 1908, to see Lopuhin). Leaving his mistress, Madame N——, who had of course accompanied him, in Germany, he himself hurried on to Paris, and then to Scotland, where in Glasgow an attempt was being prepared against the Czar.

The new plan was as follows: There was being built in Vickers' Glasgow shipyard a new Russian cruiser, *Rurik*,

---

* A member of the Social Revolutionary Party who first assembled the evidence pointing to Aseff's duplicity.

one of those intended to replace the old Russian fleet which had met with such a disastrous end in the Yellow Sea. A skeleton crew had been sent over to Glasgow to watch the work and to acquaint themselves with the ship. The revolutionaries had approached its members, and both the Social Democrats and Social Revolutionaries were conducting propaganda work among them. The work of the latter party was directed by Kostenko, a naval engineer, who was a member of the central group of the party's officer organization, and who was in direct touch with the Central Committee. It was his idea to have the Czar assassinated during the ceremonial review which would be held on the arrival of the cruiser in a Russian port.

Such an attempt might be successfully carried out in one of two ways: either by a member of the crew, who would shoot the Czar during the review or the inspection of the ship; or, if there was no volunteer from the crew, by a member of the Battle Organization who was to be smuggled aboard and hidden until the inspection took place.

As there was no volunteer from the crew at the beginning, all attention was concentrated on the second plan. There was no difficulty in smuggling a revolutionary on board the cruiser while she was in Glasgow. Kostenko helped to find a hiding place where a man might remain concealed without fear of discovery. The place was small and uncomfortable. The volunteer would have to remain in a cramped position, unable to stretch his limbs. It had, however, this advantage: from it one could get quite easily into the central ventilating shaft, and, by the ladder inside it, reach the admiral's quarters and blow them up while the Czar was breakfasting there.

This plan was open to several objections. It was not known in advance when the review would take place, and it might happen that the terrorist would have to spend not days but whole weeks in his hiding place (in fact, the review did not take place till two months after the cruiser had left Glasgow), and no man could hope to withstand such a trial. Still, it was thought worthwhile to take this risk.

Aseff arrived in Glasgow in the middle of July. Through Kostenko's influence he obtained permission, under an assumed name, of course, to look round the cruiser, and he explored it thoroughly, inspecting possible hiding places, the ventilation shaft, and so on. As a result, he reported unfavorably on the plan, considering it impracticable, and it was therefore abandoned. All hopes were now centered on finding a volunteer among the crew. After some time, two volunteers, the sailor Gerassim Avdeyeff and the signaler Kaptelovitch, were found. Particular hope was laid on the first, a very daring, energetic, and most revolutionary-minded man. Both Savinkoff and Karpovitch* knew him, and Aseff was to meet him later. They were provided with revolvers by the Battle Organization, and they wrote farewell letters in which they explained the motives for their action. These letters, together with photographs, were taken by Aseff, and they were to be published after the attempt had taken place.

In the middle of August, 1908, the cruiser sailed for Russia. On the way, Avdeyeff wrote in a personal letter to Savinkoff: "Only now do I begin to understand myself. I shall never be a propagandist. . . . After serious reflection I can now realize the significance of the task entrusted to me. . . . One minute will decide more than whole months."

The Czar's review took place on October 7th. "Both Avdeyeff and Kaptelovitch met the Czar face to face." According to Kostenko's account, Avdeyeff was even asked by the Czar to bring him a glass of champagne and was therefore as close as possible to him for a few moments. Although the attempt could easily have taken place, it was not made. Savinkoff explains this by the fact that both Avdeyeff and Kaptelovitch lost their nerve at the critical moment. But Kostenko, who was better informed, tells quite a different story. It would seem that the crew was plotting a mutiny: the number gained over by propaganda was large, and the plotters hoped for success. Avdeyeff and Kaptelovitch were members of the organization which was plotting this mutiny, but they had not informed it of their own plan. Its other members, however, guessed by their conduct that they had a plot of their own and insisted on an explanation. They confessed the truth, and it became clear that the plan to assassinate the Czar would upset the

---

* Two revolutionary activists who worked with Aseff.

plan for the mutiny; such an attempt would lead to arrests and inquiries on board and could not fail to put the police on the track of the plotters and of their plan to seize Kronstadt. The result was that the plotters forced Avdeyeff and Kaptelovitch to renounce their plan.

There are good reasons for believing that Kostenko's version is the correct one. If this is so, Aseff's last move, on which his safety depended, was thwarted by the supporters of the mass movement in which he never believed and against which he always struggled. One thing is clear, the attempt failed through no fault of Aseff's. He had done everything in his power to bring this attempt to a successful conclusion. Gerassimoff knew nothing of what was to take place on the *Rurik*. Avdeyeff's farewell letter, together with his photograph, which might have cost him his life, remained in Aseff's possession until his exposure. When leaving his Paris apartment on January 6, 1909, Aseff deliberately put this letter on his writing table for all the world to see, as a proof that he was no traitor, since he had not betrayed Avdeyeff when he could very well have done so. . . . In reality, the significance of this document was quite different; it merely showed that, at this stage of his game, Aseff thought it more profitable to betray not the revolutionaries, but rather the other side. . . .

3

The Neutral Attaché

Thomas Whiteside

Colonel Stig Wennerstrom of the Swedish Air Force was sentenced to life imprisonment in Sweden in May, 1964, for treason and espionage practiced against his own country in favor of Soviet Russia. He was—at least according to his own claim—at one period of his career a double agent of sorts. He claims he was employed by the United States to work against the Soviets at the same time as the Soviets thought he was working full time in their favor against the Americans. It seems likely that this account, which Wennerstrom gave in the course of his interrogation and trial in Sweden, was chiefly intended to mitigate his crime in the eyes of the Swedish tribunal. Certainly I can state that the extent to which he claims to have collaborated with the Americans is greatly exaggerated and in many cases false.

In any case, Thomas Whiteside, the author of an exhaustive book on the Wennerstrom affair, first gives us this story of Wennerstrom, the self-proclaimed double agent, and then proceeds to

FROM the book *An Agent in Place.*

raise important questions regarding the reliability of Wennerstrom's own story.

The "General" referred to in the text was a high-ranking Soviet intelligence officer who was "handling" Wennerstrom. As Whiteside relates elsewhere, the "General's" methods for winning Wennerstrom's deepest loyalties consisted of a series of ploys and bonuses calculated to appeal to Wennerstrom's vanity and pocketbook. Wennerstrom was told that he had been given the rank of major general in the Red Army Intelligence Service (he had been passed over for promotion in the Swedish Air Force). He was secretly given a high Soviet decoration, and large sums were reportedly deposited in his name to an account which was to be kept for him in the Soviet Union. He took all these blandishments quite seriously, and was immensely flattered by them.

UNDER THE GENERAL'S orders, Wennerstrom set about cultivating his acquaintances at the American Embassy so as to obtain information there that he could pass on. His respect for the General notwithstanding, it appears from his own testimony that he did not tell his Soviet contact man as much about his relations with the Americans as he might have. According to what he told his Swedish interrogators after his arrest, he began—at the very time he was pushing ahead with his work on behalf of Soviet Intelligence—to do what he could to fulfill the urge that had seized him in Stockholm, to "get myself a direct contact" with American military intelligence and "become my own master." Shortly after he returned to Moscow, he said, he was approached by an American air attaché, who said he had learned from Washington that Wennerstrom had managed to acquire valuable information in the Soviet Union from an unknown source, and that Washington was eager to know what that source was. Wennerstrom testified that while he still declined to reveal the source, he did establish further contacts with United States Air Force Intelligence. As a result, he has said, he obtained an agreement whereby he would supply the United States with additional military information about the Soviet Union through an American contact man in Moscow, in return for a certain sum of money, which he asked the Americans to pay him in Italian lire. According to Wennerstrom, "So far as I personally was concerned this meant that I had achieved my aim; namely, that of being an independent agent."

By his account, the tasks that he carried out on behalf of the Americans were supposed to fit into the framework of a vastly expanded intelligence network that the United States was building up around the Soviet Union. He had said that this network employed, among other things, United States aircraft equipped with special radio transmitters, which patrolled as close as possible to the borders of the Soviet Union in order to communicate with resident agents, some of whom had been parachuted into the country; illegal high-altitude reconnaissance flights by the RB-36, a predecessor of the U-2; camera-equipped balloons that were released in Western Europe to drift eastward with the prevailing winds, automatically taking high-altitude photographs until they came down in the Pacific, where many of them were picked up; and, finally, and most important, the collection of a great mass of information from miscellaneous sources inside and outside the Soviet Union. Wennerstrom says that his own efforts on behalf of American Intelligence were devoted to seeking out information about suitable bombing targets within the U.S.S.R., and that he was assigned this task because, as a neutral, he would presumably find it relatively easy to move about the country.

Moving about the Soviet Union was indeed relatively easy for Wennerstrom, for when he wanted to go somewhere, he had only to apply to Nikitushev, his former contact man, who was under orders to help him as much as possible in connection with his official Swedish work, so that he could get on all the faster with his spying for the Soviets. Ostensibly on Swedish business, Wennerstrom made trips to various parts of the Soviet Union, including Siberia, the Caucasus and the Ukraine, and in these places, he claimed, he obtained military information for the Americans. Thus, he has said, on a trip to Novosibirsk, in Siberia, the plane in which he was traveling did not land, as he had expected, at a commercial airfield in the town of Kazan, but instead made an unscheduled stop at a military air base east of there. The Americans, he continued, had been highly interested in this particular military field, because they suspected that it was a base for strategic bombers intended for use against American installations along the perimeter of the Soviet Union. When he landed, he said, he observed that the airplanes on the field were the latest type of Soviet strategic bomber. "I took photographs with a telescopic lens from a toilet window at the airport building," he testified. "I turned the film over later to my American contact man. Thanks to the telescopic lens, it was possible to discern all the details of the planes within its range." At the same time, he went on, he was able to pick up another piece of military information that the Americans did not possess. Inside the airport building, he glimpsed on a bulletin board a notice that jobs were available for meteorologists at an air base at Varlamovo Bay, near Murmansk, on the Arctic Ocean. The notice was marked as having emanated from the staff headquarters of the Soviet Strategic Air Command in Moscow, and Wennerstrom has said that by putting these facts together he gave the Americans their first intimation of the existence of a Soviet strategic air base at Varlamovo Bay—a point from which Russian bombers could take off on flights over the North Pole to Canada and the United States.

Just as Wennerstrom did not inform the Soviet Intelligence Service of whatever tasks he may have been carrying out for the Americans, he did not tell the Americans about the spying he was doing on behalf of the Soviets. And, of course, he told his Swedish superiors about neither of his extracurricular activities; in fact, it seems that he hardly let his Swedish colleagues in Moscow know what he was doing on behalf of Sweden. He later indicated that in no time he found that his surreptitious activities on behalf of Soviet Intelligence could be made to dovetail nicely with his activities on behalf of United States Intelligence. As an agent of the Soviets, he has said, his initial task, once he had passed through his probationary period, was to obtain information on American military planning against Russia.

His new Soviet contact, the General, began briefing him on this assignment by saying that he was highly pleased with Wennerstrom for establishing such good contacts within the embassies of the NATO powers in such short order. The General then mentioned that the Russians had been able to discover a great deal about the intelligence work that was being carried on in the Moscow embassies of the NATO powers under the guidance of the Americans, and he went on to say that the important thing was to obtain an evaluation of the aim of such intelligence work, because, together with other similar activities, it could probably provide an indication of NATO's basic war planning against the Soviet Union, and, in particular, could clarify the question of whether the United States planned to use only its air power and nuclear bombs against specific targets or was planning on a land invasion as well. He told Wennerstrom that, in view of the contacts he had made among the Americans, he seemed to be the person within the Western camp in Moscow most competent to obtain such information. The General needed a brief prepared in time for another Soviet conference on strategy, he said, and he urged Wennerstrom to concentrate on this task to the exclusion of everything else.

"The task was easier for me than [the General] could ever have thought," Wennerstrom recalled after his arrest. "Thanks to my role as an agent for both sides . . . it was almost comical. I would get a query from my Soviet contact man that, from his point of view, was fairly hard to answer. When, later on, I would meet my American contact man, I would get a direct reply to the question . . . as well as a task from him." Thus, Wennerstrom has remarked, while he was busy gathering information for the Americans on potential bombing targets within the Soviet Union, he was also able at the same time to carry out instructions from Soviet Intelligence to find out what those targets were. He has said that as he came to the Americans with what he called "bits of the jigsaw puzzle" concerning targets, he learned that this information was collated with other data and plotted on a situation map in the American Embassy—a map that he was not allowed to see. However, he told his interrogators, as he turned over to the Soviet Intelligence Service whatever he could about the Americans' interest in particular targets, the General set up a target map of his own, on which all the information that Wennerstrom brought in was marked, along with information from other sources.

According to Wennerstrom, some of the information relating to presumed targets was for a while quite puzzling to the Soviets. By way of illustration, he described a trip he made to Odessa with the ostensible purpose of visiting a scientific institute there but with the actual purpose of carrying out an American Intelligence assignment. "The task given me by the Americans seemed almost laughable at first glance," he said. "They wanted to know whether the roofs in a certain village were of thatch or of sheet metal." However, he said, he later learned that the assignment had to do with a particular type of American radar bombsight, in which a village with tin roofs would show up in a characteristic fashion. Wennerstrom has said that after carrying out this task he informed the General that the Americans were displaying curiosity about tin roofs, obviously as navigational aids. The General was deeply interested, and having ordered his people to collect data on the incidence of sheet metal roofs in the Ukraine, he began to plot them on his map in an attempt to determine just which targets the Americans might have in mind. Wennerstrom has said that, after studying the pattern of metal roofs, the General concluded that because they did not tend to lead to such things as factory sites, whatever targets the Americans were aiming at must be spread over the entire Ukraine and Kuban areas, so what the Americans had in mind was probably the chance of waging aerial biological warfare against the harvests in the breadbasket area of the Soviet Union, using the roofs as navigational markers.

"Taken together, everything began to show . . . that the essence of NATO's planning consisted of air strikes against the Soviet Union, but no invasion," Wennerstrom testified. The General suggested to him that the Soviet leaders might find it difficult to accept this conclusion, because they themselves had a natural leaning toward land-based strategy. As a result, the General told him, particularly clear proofs of the Americans' intentions would have to be provided at the forthcoming conference. As things turned out, Wennerstrom was instrumental in producing just such proofs. Soon after he had learned of the existence of the target map at the United States Embassy, he said, he had told the General about it, and also about his inability to get a look at it. But one day later on, he said, he happened to overhear a conversation in which it was revealed that a copy of this map was to be sent by courier to American Air Force Headquarters at Wiesbaden, Germany, and he so informed the General. The General displayed intense interest, asking for all sorts of details—who the courier would be, how he proposed to travel, the time of his departure, and so on. Wennerstrom has said that he was able to give the General all this information. One day about a week later, according to Wennerstrom, he was walking to the Swedish Embassy from his home when he saw the Soviet contact car pass him and draw up to the curb a short distance ahead. In accordance with the prescribed procedure in such circumstances, Wennerstrom ignored the car and walked on to the nearest telephone booth, from which he dialed the secret number. The voice at the other end told him that arrangements had been made for him to be taken to the headquarters villa outside Moscow. When Wennerstrom arrived there, he found the General, who produced a map and asked him if he believed it to be identical with the one at the American Embassy. Wennerstrom said, in the light of the target information he had collected, he thought it was, and when he asked the General how on earth he had managed to obtain it, the General told him that, thanks to his information about the dispatch of the map to Wiesbaden, Soviet agents had been able to track the courier and at some point along the route managed to obtain access to it long enough to photograph it.

According to Wennerstrom, the major Soviet strategic conference for which he had gathered information concerning NATO military planning and potential American bombing targets ended with a decision to give the highest priority to building up Soviet anti-aircraft defenses. The General told him that in the effort to strengthen Russia against aerial attack, there was just one model in the world that was worthy of being followed—the British air-defense system—and he urged Wennerstrom to obtain whatever information he could about it. He also asked Wennerstrom to seek information on the development of American strategic bombers, on the structure of the Strategic Air Command, on the planning of American air bases from which attacks could be aimed at the Soviet Union, and on American bombing tactics in general. For information on the British air-defense system, Wennerstrom sought out the British air attaché and the British Ambassador to Moscow, he has said, and obtained what he could from them, and supplemented this information with material taken from publications he consulted on visits to Stockholm. To obtain information on the Strategic Air Command and on American air bases, he further cultivated officials at the United States Embassy and the embassies of the other NATO countries. He has said that he found it fairly easy to provide his Soviet superiors with new material concerning SAC, because there were large gaps in Soviet Russia's knowledge of the subject.

Meanwhile, in his capacity as a self-styled "independent agent," Wennerstrom continued to deliver military information about the Soviet Union to the Americans—or so he told his interrogators—even though by now his schedule had grown so crowded that he was using his vacations for this purpose. In the early fifties, he said, he took a vacation with his wife in the Caucasus, staying at Tiflis, Georgia, for the purpose of confirming some information that had been passed to the Americans. The Americans, it seemed, had discovered "through some agent" that a factory between Tiflis and Baku had begun production of a new jet fighter plane, and they had also found out the routes and times of scheduled test flights of the plane. Wennerstrom's assignment was to travel on a certain day to a point west of Tiflis and observe the plane as it flew overhead, noting the exact time of its passage. Wennerstrom said he carried out this assignment satisfactorily, and that in return the Americans paid the entire cost of the vacation. He said that all his expenses were paid on a number of other excursions he undertook for the Americans, but apart from this money, and the earlier payment in lire, he received no compensation from the United States, though the transcript of his interrogation hazily describes his receipt of "certain *valuta*" in 1950 or 1951.

Whatever the quantity of military information about the Soviet Union allegedly passed on to the Americans by Wennerstrom, it was certainly exceeded by the amount of military information about United States military affairs and interests passed on by him to the Soviet Intelligence Service. In the course of time, Wennerstrom has said, there began to grow within him "a significant feeling of loyalty" toward both the General and the Soviet Intelligence Service as a whole. The General, for his part, continued his collaboration with Wennerstrom in a manner that conveyed an increasing confidence in the Swede's ability as a Soviet agent, and he went on with the painstaking briefings in which he filled in details of the strategic considerations related to Wennerstrom's clandestine activities. According to Wennerstrom, the Russians' decision to expand their nation's air defenses against nuclear and other bombers was followed by another Soviet strategic conference on air power. At this conference, he said, the Soviet Union's strategic air power was conceded to be far below that of the United States in both quality and quantity. On the one hand, Wennerstrom said, the American system of air bases clearly made it possible for the United States to launch toward the Soviet Union not only long-range aircraft from the United States but shortrange aircraft from forward bases; on the other hand, the Soviet Union, which had no chance of building up a ring of bases around the United States, could depend only on long-range aircraft, for which Russia had no significant construction program at the time. Competition against the United States in this area was therefore considered hopeless, and the Russians decided to give the highest priority to the development of intercontinental rockets with nuclear warheads, which they did not then have. It was also decided, Wennerstrom said, to develop Soviet strategic aircraft capable of reaching European and Asiatic targets—most notably, American bases on those continents.

At the conclusion of that conference, the General gave Wennerstrom new instructions for obtaining information that Soviet Intelligence needed in order to fill out its current picture of American air power. Wennerstrom said that he carried out those instructions as well as he could but that precise technical information was hard to come by. He continued to use his secret telephone number, and also to meet the General according to the prearranged routine. Sometimes, when he stepped into the car with a lengthy report to make, the General would flip a switch beside his seat, so that the dialogue could be recorded, and, when the information he had was very urgently needed, the General would have a stenographer in the car with him to take notes.

Wennerstrom still said nothing to the General about any activities, past or present, he might have been engaging in on behalf of the Americans. As a matter of fact, he later told his Swedish interrogators, he was finding it difficult, because of his increasing sympathy toward the Soviet side, to keep up such work. Thus, in 1951, he said, at the request of the American air attaché, he made a trip to the house of a foreign journalist who lived some six miles from a proving ground, outside Moscow, where jet and rocket engines were being tested, to listen to the noises of the tests and deduce what he could from them. He was able to conclude, he said, that one of the engines being tested was that of an ordinary German V-2 rocket, since it always ran for exactly fifty-five seconds, the normal burning time for a V-2. On the same occasion, he heard something else—the sound of a rocket far more powerful than a V-2, and capable of shaking windows for miles around. "I came to the conclusion that this was the first sample of the new Soviet . . . intercontinental rocket research," Wennerstrom has said. "I thought this was unusually interesting. [But] my change of sympathies had gone so far that I said nothing about it to my American contact man."

Whatever other activities Wennerstrom engaged in during his service in Moscow, he seems to have carried out his legitimate work as Swedish air attaché to the satisfaction of his superiors in Stockholm. During one of his trips home, he told Major General Gustaf Adolf Westring, Chief of the Swedish Air Force Staff, that he "was very happy with my Moscow assignment and was not at all averse to having it extended several years." At the same time, he let General Westring know that he would not be averse to a future assignment in London or Washington—preferably Washington. Some time after this conversation, the Swedish air attaché in Washington happened to become ill, and at the beginning of 1952 General Westring wrote to Wennerstrom formally offering him the assignment, beginning that April. Wennerstrom accepted, and informed his Soviet contact man of his impending transfer. "This came as a complete surprise to him and his superior, and their reaction was somewhat as though they had won the big prize in a lottery," Wennerstrom has remarked. In Washington, as an agent "in place"—that is, a qualified and cleared insider, rather than a clandestine operative, or "illegal"—his usefulness would presumably be even greater.

In Wennerstrom's remaining weeks in Moscow, he was given detailed briefings on the activities he was expected to carry out for the Russians in Washington. Midway through this series of briefings, however, he received a terrible shock: the Russians told him that they had discovered his connection with the Americans. According to his account, this had occurred not through any lack of caution on his part but because of carelessness on the American side. It had been impressed upon him, as it was on all Soviet Intelligence officers, that the real name of an agent was never to be used in a report, and it seemed that the Americans had broken this rule, using his name in a coded message sent out over the radio transmitter in the American Embassy in Moscow; Soviet Intelligence, which routinely monitored such transmissions, was able to decipher the broadcast. "The radio message in question referred to certain information I had furnished [the Americans] upon my return from certain trips. After the Soviets had made a check, they had no doubt at all about my being a double agent [for the Americans]," Wennerstrom has said.

Wennerstrom was told of this discovery at one of the meetings in the villa. "My first reaction was one of unspeakable bitterness against the Americans for not being able to protect themselves better," Wennerstrom recalled. He testified that he had no idea what to do or say when he was confronted with this information. He remembered that he had thought it strange, when the meeting began, that the General had four people with him, including a man who was introduced as the General's superior officer and another whom Wennerstrom recognized, from their previous encounter, as the man responsible for surveillance of foreign diplomats in Moscow. "The first thought that went through my mind was that it was very possible they were going to liquidate me with a shot in the nape of the neck. We were a long distance from Moscow, and nobody knew where I was," Wennerstrom said. But, he went on, it turned out that he was mistaken about the Soviet reaction. "I don't know what happened between the General and his superior before our meeting. One thing stood out clearly, however, and that was that my contact man was heart and soul on my side. There was not a single word from the Soviets of reproach. . . . The Soviet General had thought about my situation before, and he and several of his superiors had wondered many times how I could possibly obtain the information I did from the Americans. He said now, "Here is the explanation of your success."

According to his account of the meeting, Wennerstrom assured the General that by this time no one could have any doubt about where his, Wennerstrom's, true sympathies lay. The General then explained to him "that if the discovery had occurred at a considerably earlier stage, it could have had consequences that there was no use in even talking about now." But, the General said, as things stood, it was a tremendous advantage for the Soviets to have contacts in United States Intelligence circles, and it was the desire of the Soviets, looking toward Wennerstrom's appointment in Washington, that he continue his relations with the Americans as though no charge had taken place, and that, if possible, he made the contacts even more intimate. At the same time, Wennerstrom has said, the General obtained from him details of his work on behalf of the Americans in the Soviet Union, and they came to an understanding about the reporting of his future dealing with American Intelligence.

Understandably, Wennerstrom was enormously relieved at this outcome of the confrontation. At that point, he has said, "from my side the swing to the Soviet side was complete and definitive. . . . Instead of being a false agent inside of Soviet Intelligence, I was now this same thing within the American organization." As he later put it, "My truly great opportunities did not open up until I went to Washington."

Whatever double game Wennerstrom may have attempted to play during his period in Moscow, the GRU people must have had a pretty good idea of it, and they certainly made use of this information at a time of their own choosing. It can hardly have been mere coincidence that the dramatic confrontation between the General and

Wennerstrom occurred shortly before Wennerstrom's transfer to Washington. The General, necessarily recognizing that when the transfer took place the GRU would no longer be able to exert complete physical control over Wennerstrom's activities, chose a time just before his departure to impress upon him unforgettably the realization that Soviet Intelligence was no organization to be trifled with. When Wennerstrom was given the terrifying news that the Russians had broken the American code and had found his name mentioned as an informant on Soviet military matters, what was being put on for Wennerstrom was a play in which he was made the central character. The General's story about breaking the American code was almost certainly made up out of whole cloth. If such a code-breaking feat really had been achieved, the fact would have been concealed by the tightest security precautions possible, and if a Soviet Intelligence officer had ever gone as far as to reveal such a secret to a man accused of being a double agent, the officer would unquestionably have been shot. (So, in Stalinist times, would anybody associated with him in committing such an error; and his family would probably have been sent to Siberia.) Soviet Intelligence people have been known to be sentenced to terms in Siberia for such lapses as forgetting to lock a safe.

An American familiar with such matters said recently, "The story of the code's being broken is just the kind of thing you could expect from Wennerstrom's case officer. It's the kind of thing that happens constantly in this business. When you need to impress an agent with your omniscience, you go to elaborate lengths to do so. Of course, Wennerstrom had no way of knowing that the Russians *hadn't* broken the American code, or that his name *hadn't* been used in a radio message, but we've been unable to find the slightest evidence that his name ever was so used. Whatever real evidence the Russians might have had on hand about any tips given by Wennerstrom to the Americans in Moscow had probably been acquired through the usual GRU surveillance—conceivably through their routine bugging of the American offices and residential quarters in Moscow. The GRU people wouldn't necessarily use this kind of compromising material right away. One striking thing about the Soviet Intelligence system is its infinite patience. Wennerstrom's case officer doubtless waited for just the right moment to use the material on Wennerstrom. To build the agent up and cut him down so that he responds just as you want him to respond requires, among other things, a keen sense of timing."

The results of that dramatic confrontation were admirably successful, from the General's point of view. Wennerstrom later indicated that he was immensely grateful to the General at the time for being "heart and soul on my side." Thus, Wennerstrom was able to emerge from the confrontation feeling immense relief, extreme respect for the long arm of Soviet Intelligence, and increased devotion toward the General.

V

Defection:

Changing Sides

PERSONS WHO CHANGE sides during a time of war or cold war, generally for ideological reasons, are called defectors, particularly when they have something to offer to the other side, whether it be of informational or propaganda value. A man or woman who occupies a comfortable position in his country of origin and still risks the hazards both of escaping and of building a new life from scratch in a society whose language and customs are strange to him must have good reason to do so. Usually it is because he has suffered a very deep-set disillusionment with the system under which he has been living.

The most striking recent case of a defection was that of Stalin's daughter, Svetlana Alliluyeva, who sought freedom of religion and self-expression in the West. Aside from these spiritual needs, she was certainly well off and well cared for in her native land, and need not have left it for material reasons.

The propaganda value for the West of such cases is, of course, significant; it is no wonder that the Soviets and their satellites do everything possible to discourage and prevent defection and to punish defectors when they can get their hands on them. The Soviets have not been above kidnaping and doing away with defectors, either out of pure vengeance or because they simply wished to silence them. Once the defection is publicized, however, the defector has a measure of immunity, since then any act of violence—or even a mysterious disappearance—would bring a new surge of publicity about the defection, which is just what the Soviets desire to avoid.

There are many kinds of defectors, but none quite so welcome to an intelligence service as the kind who was himself a member of the intelligence service of the country from which he has defected. When an intelligence officer from a country which has been hostile to the West flees to a Western country and requests asylum, he usually makes certain of receiving a warm reception by bringing with him as much information as possible, if not in documents, then at least in his mind.

Defection is, of course, a two-way street. The West has had its Burgesses and Macleans.

Most of our selections describe the climactic moments just after a defector has made his decision to break away, and as he sets out to seek contact with those whom he hopes will welcome and protect him.

1

The Clerk They Wouldn't Believe

Igor Gouzenko

*I have already mentioned the code clerk of the
Soviet Embassy in Ottawa, Igor Gouzenko, in connection with the atom spy cases (II. 4, and III. 5).
He defected in September, 1945. At the time, his
defection and his subsequent revelations caused a
tremendous sensation. This was the signal for early
disillusionment about our wartime ally. In fact,
Gouzenko defected because, as a Russian, he was
ashamed of his country. He saw the cables coming
across his desk night after night which reported to
Moscow the subversion of Canadian citizens and
the stealing of Canadian secrets at a time when the
two countries were allies in the life-and-death
struggle against the Nazis. Ever since his defection,
over twenty years ago, Gouzenko's whereabouts
have remained a deep secret. As a result, he has
evaded any attempts of the long arm of Soviet
intelligence to avenge itself upon him.*

IT WAS AN unseasonably hot and sultry night as I walked
back to the military attaché's. But I knew the perspiration
trickling inside my shirt was caused by more than the

FROM the book *The Iron Curtain.*

weather. Tonight was to be the turning point of my life, and the lives of my family, from Soviet slavery to democratic freedom.

The deadline had been forced by Colonel Zabotin's abrupt decision for me to turn over my work to Lieutenant Koulakov in the very near future, and act henceforth as advisory onlooker. Zabotin felt this would assure him of a capable cipher clerk after I left.

I am no hero. Nature seems to allow very few to don the heroic mantle. I was born a very ordinary little man of Russia. I had never excelled in athletics. My triumphs seemed limited to the realm of studies. Dangerous living never had appealed to me, and adventure always associated itself with unromantic danger in my mind. But that night of September 5, 1945, during the long walk from Somerset Street to Range Road, I came as close to becoming a hero as I ever will.

This could be, I was fully aware, my last night on earth. One wrong move could mean the complete ruination of all our plans and, as far as I was aware, the NKVD* might have been watching me for some time. Perhaps Zabotin's sudden imposition of the deadline was actually the setting up of a trap into which I was now entering. My very roots had been injected with fearful respect for the omnipresence and vengeance of the NKVD.

There was an easier, a vastly safer, way out than by going back for those documents. Yet somehow I managed to freeze my mind into the course Anna and I had mapped out. Come what may, that would have to be the course.

So, it meant I had to remove the documents tonight or never.

Anna and I had decided long since that it would be necessary to make my escape during a weekday although a Saturday night would have been ideal, allowing me until Monday morning to make good my getaway. But the newspaper offices would not be open Saturday night and we had decided I should take the documents and my story to a newspaper.

---

* The initials of the whole Soviet police organization at the time of Gouzenko's defection.

There was no thought of going to the police. That was a natural result of our experience with the thoroughly corrupt NKVD police. I naturally thought the local police would sell out to the Soviet Embassy. At the same time, we had been impressed with the freedom and fearlessness of the Canadian press.

Other factors were involved in the Wednesday-night choice. I knew this was Koulakov's assigned night to sit up on watch at the military attaché's and, in consequence, he was permitted to sleep until noon next day. This would allow me more leeway because Koulakov would be the most likely one to first report me as missing. Since the cipher section work was so secret, the rest of the staff, with the exception of Colonel Zabotin, knew little of the hours I was supposed to be on or off duty. And I knew that Zabotin, who was scheduled to attend a moving-picture show at the National Film Board that night with Rogov, would hardly turn up before noon.

What made the forthcoming ordeal all the more hazardous was that I would have to go to the military attaché's ostensibly to complete some work and then go to the Embassy, where most of the really important documents were kept. As a trusted cipher clerk, I was admitted without question at any hour of the day or night.

Finally I turned into Range Road, and curiously, I felt a sensation of exhilaration. The suspense of recent weeks had put my nerves on edge, but now that the moment of action was upon me I felt strangely relieved.

As I entered the hall I noted Koulakov had already taken his place at the night-watch desk. That was good. A switch in Koulakov's plans would have hurt mine for the morning.

Captain Galkin, supposedly a door guard but in reality an extremely well-trained intelligence operator, appeared as I entered.

"How about coming to a movie with me?" he asked.

I tried to appear interested. "Which one are you going to?"

Galkin mentioned a neighborhood theatre. The thought occurred to me that this would provide an ideal opportunity to leave the military attaché's since I had really wanted only to see if Koulakov was on the job.

"That's a good idea," I said. "It's too hot to work anyway."

Galkin said some of the other members of the staff were coming and we waited outside until they joined us.

We walked to the theatre, where I pretended disappointment.

"Damn it, I've seen that show! You fellows go ahead because it's a good picture. I'll take a streetcar and go to another show downtown."

I walked in the direction of a car stop but veered when they vanished into the theatre. So far so good. I turned toward Charlotte Street, walked deliberately to the Soviet Embassy, mounted the steps and nodded to the guard, who nodded in return as I signed the book. As I was putting my fountain pen back in my pocket I glanced toward the reception room and my blood seemed to freeze

There sat Vitali Pavlov, chief of the NKVD in Canada!

Somehow I managed to act naturally and walked by the reception room seemingly concerned with the clip of my pen not fastening into my pocket the way it should. From the corner of my eye I noted that Pavlov had apparently failed to notice me. I pressed the secret bell under the banister, mounted the stairs leading to the secret cipher room, pulled aside the curtain and held my face in front of the small opening in the steel door.

The attendant inside unbarred the steel door. It was Ryazanov, commercial attaché cipher clerk and a friend of mine. I noted with relief that he was alone.

We exchanged a few remarks on the weather. Ryazanov asked if I was working late again.

"No," I replied, "there are just a couple of telegrams to do and then I'll catch an 8:30 show."

Ryazanov said I was being sensible and turned to his own work.

I entered my little office and closed the door carefully behind me. I went to my desk, opened it and removed Zabotin's cipher pouch, which I had left there that afternoon. Most of the documents I wanted were there. The others were in the files. All were marked by the turned-down corners.

Some of the documents were large sheets of paper,

Others were small scraps. Later, the police count showed 109 items.

I opened my shirt and carefully distributed the documents inside. Then I completed the telegrams which represented my reason for being there. They dealt with information supplied by Emma Woikin, an agent in the Canadian External Affairs Department.

Originally these "excuse" telegrams hadn't seemed very important, but on second thought I saw they fitted in with other data. It was too bad for Emma that I stopped to reconsider them. Those telegrams cost her a three-year prison sentence.

Once the ciphering task was finished I stood up and gingerly examined my shirt, which to me appeared to bulge suspiciously. However, the evening was so warm I felt a sloppy-looking shirt wouldn't arouse undue interest.

I walked across the corridor and handed the telegrams to Ryazanov for dispatching to Moscow. I also handed him Zabotin's sealed pouch to be placed in the safe.

I watched Ryazanov's face for any evidence that he noted anything unusual in my manner or appearance. Certainly, I felt conspicuous around the waist. But Ryazanov displayed no undue interest. Casually I stepped into the men's room and washed my hands.

While doing so I called out:

"It's too hot to stick around here. Why don't you skip out with me to the show?"

Ryazanov grunted.

"Fat chance of getting away with anything around here. Besides, Pavlov is downstairs. Thanks just the same, I'd better stick around."

Mention of Pavlov left me a little weak around the knees. I had momentarily forgotten him. But there was no turning back now. I adjusted my shirt again and stepped to the door. Ryazanov opened it and I bid him good night.

I was careful about walking down the steps, afraid that I might disturb the documents and cause an extra large bulge. There was also danger that a smaller document might slip through my belt and drop from a pant leg on the floor.

Sweat was standing out on my brow and I felt my chest

tightening as I approached the reception room. This will never do, I thought. I didn't even dare reach into a pocket for my handkerchief lest the movement might disturb something.

The street door seemed miles away. Gradually I neared the reception room. Then I was passing it. My heart leapt with joy. The room was empty. Pavlov had gone. A good omen. I was very much in luck. I signed myself out in the book, bid the attendant good night and walked out into the night. It was still humid but I sucked in the air gratefully.

I took a streetcar downtown and went quickly to the office of the *Ottawa Journal* newspaper.

I was trembling like a leaf. I couldn't figure just why, except that it must be due to nervous reaction. Outside the building I stopped to mop my brow and make sure nobody was following me. Finally, I entered and asked the elevator man where I could find the editor.

"Sixth floor," he said, and slammed the door shut behind me.

At the sixth floor I walked toward the door marked "Editor" but just as I was about to knock something happened inside me. Grim doubts filled my mind. Surely, I thought, every big newspaper must have an NKVD agent working in it. Was I doing the right thing? Hurriedly I decided to think it over and turned back to the elevator. The door opened to let somebody out and the operator yelled:

"Down!"

I stepped in. The elevator descended a few floors and stopped to pick up some people. Among them was a girl who looked at me and smiled.

"What are you doing here? Is there news breaking at the Embassy?"

I was panic-stricken. Her face was familiar. Where had I seen her before? What would I do?

The elevator reached the ground floor. As the door opened I muttered an apology to the girl, said something about being in a big hurry and walked quickly to the street. Outside I ran to the first corner and then slowed to a fast walk. This went on for blocks, as I tried to calm my burning mind. What would I do now? I boarded a streetcar and went home to Anna. We would talk it over.

Anna answered my code knock. Her face was drawn and white.

"Did something go wrong?" she whispered tensely.

I sat down heavily on the sofa. Anna came over and sat beside me. I told her the whole story, finishing up with the account of being spotted by the girl in the elevator.

Anna listed attentively. After I finished, her voice came absolutely unruffled:

"Don't worry about her, Igor. She must be a journalist or she would not have been in the office. Many journalists were entertained at the Embassy and that is where she probably met you. They have good memories. But even if there is an NKVD agent in the newspaper office, it needn't matter. What could he do in time to stop you?"

I took renewed strength from her confidence.

"What now?" I asked.

"Go right back to the newspaper office and see the editor. You still have several hours before the Embassy learns what has happened."

I opened my shirt and removed the documents. They were soaked with sweat. Anna tried to dry them a bit by waving them. Then she wrapped them in a paper.

Anna kissed me as she opened the door. I squeezed her arm and went out into the night again. At the *Ottawa Journal* the same elevator man took me up to the sixth floor. I stepped quickly to the editor's door and knocked. There was no answer. I knocked again. Still no answer. I tried the door. It was locked. I walked down to a door leading into a large room. It was the City Room and it was filled with busy people. Nobody paid any attention to me. I saw an office boy hurrying in my direction. I asked him where I could find the editor.

"Gone for the night," the office boy said and dashed past me.

I walked to the nearest desk and told a man working at a typewriter that I wished to see whoever was in charge.

"It is extremely important," I said.

He looked at me inquiringly, then took me over to a desk at the other side of the big room where an older man wearing a green eyeshade told me to sit down.

I took out the stolen documents and spread them on the desk. As I did so, I explained who I was and that these were proof that Soviet agents in Canda were seeking data on the atomic bomb.

The man with the eyeshade stared at me, then picked up several of the documents. But he looked at them only for a moment. They were written in Russian.

"I'm sorry," he said finally, "this is out of our field. I would suggest you go to the Royal Canadian Mounted Police or come back in the morning to see the editor."

I hastened to explain that by morning the NKVD might be on my trail and even kill me. But as I spoke my heart was failing. I could see from the man's expression that he thought I was crazy.

"Sorry," he said. "I'm busy."

He stood up and walked away, leaving me sitting there. I felt helpless and confused. Out on the street I leaned against the wall and tried to collect my thoughts. There was only one thing to do and that was to contact a high official. The Minister of Justice seemed the logical person. I walked to the Justice Building on Wellington Street, where a tall man in RCMP uniform stopped me at the door. I hesitated for a moment but realized things were getting desperate. I said it was most important that I see the Minister of Justice immediately.

The policeman replied politely but firmly:

"It's almost midnight. You can see nobody until morning. Sorry."

Sorry? That word was getting on my nerves. "But," I repeated, "it is desperately necessary that I reach the Minister right away—by telephone at least."

He shook his head. "It can't be done."

I returned home, thoroughly subdued and more than a little frightened. Anna, however, bolstered me again.

"Don't worry about it. You have the whole morning to reach the Minister. Have a good sleep and you will feel better."

She tucked the documents in her handbag and put it under her pillow. But neither of us slept that night. We just lay there thinking and talking until the first light of dawn was filtering through our bedroom window. I raised myself on one elbow and looked out. There was a tinge of red in the eastern sky. Somehow, it comforted me immensely to know there was a nice day coming.

"Anna," I said, "we will all go to the Minister of Justice's office as soon as it opens, around nine o'clock. I might be kept waiting and the suspense would be unbearable if I wasn't certain about your safety. I'll dress Andrei. Do you think you could stand the strain . . . even if you are ill when you get up?"

"I will be all right, Igor," she replied instantly. "We will all go together and you will have nothing to worry about once we are all in the Minister of Justice's office."

I lay back with a sigh of relief. Things were clearing somewhat. The next thing I knew, Anna was shaking me.

"It is seven o'clock, Igor."

I had dozed off into heavy slumber, but the sleep had done me a world of good. I shaved and put on my good brown suit. Anna was already feeding Andrei and had a pot of coffee boiling on the stove. It was a bright, sunshiny day without the clamminess of yesterday. I felt prepared for anything that lay ahead.

But even my immense optimism would have wilted if I had been able to foresee the staggering disappointments in store for us.

Before leaving the house we decided that Anna should carry the documents in her purse, because if the NKVD caught up with us they would go after me. I would try to create a diversion and Anna might have a chance to slip away. The documents would be a passport to protective custody with the Canadian Government, I thought.

At the Justice Building, I explained to the man at the reception desk that I had to see the Minister of Justice on a matter of absolute emergency. The man looked at me doubtfully, then spoke for some time into the telephone. We were escorted to the Minister's office, where a courteous secretary asked what was the nature of my business.

I did my best to tell him the matter was of such urgency and importance that I dared not speak to anybody but the Minister. The secretary glanced from me to Anna to the child. I could imagine what was running through his mind; this man may be off his head but if that is the case why would he bring along his wife and child? I had not thought of that angle in my planning but it seemed a fortunate one. The secretary went into the inside office and I could hear him telephoning somebody.

The secretary finally returned.

"The Minister is in his other office over in the Parliament Buildings," he said. "I will take you there."

We went over to Parliament Hill and through the picturesque halls to the Minister's office. But I had to see another secretary first. It was the same thing all over again. I had to speak to the Minister personally, nobody else would do. The secretary picked up his telephone and talked to somebody at length—in French. I knew it was about me because I heard my name mentioned, but I could not understand anything else. After some time he hung up the telephone and told the first secretary to take us back to the Justice Building and wait there for the Minister.

Back we went and sat there for two precious hours. Andrei was getting impatient and we had trouble keeping him from crying. The telephone rang. The secretary listened, and said: "Very well, sir," then turned to us:

"I am very sorry. The Minister is unable to see you."

Sorry? Again that word! I looked at Anna with a hint of panic. She was biting her lip. Poor Anna.

"Let us go to the newspaper office again," she said quietly.

The editor wasn't available, we were told on arrival at the *Ottawa Journal*. But a girl reporter was sent out to talk to us. She was a beautiful blonde girl, named Lesley Johnstone. She was kind and interested, patting Andrei on the head as she invited us to sit down.

I told her the whole story. She listened intently, looking at Anna repeatedly as if seeking confirmation. She studied the documents momentarily, then took them into the editor's office. Within a very short time she came out.

"I am terribly sorry," she said, handing me back the documents. "Your story just doesn't seem to register here. Nobody wants to say anything but nice things about Stalin these days."

It was Anna who spoke first. "What should we do now, miss?"

The girl reporter pondered. "Why not go to see the RCMP about taking out naturalization papers? That should prevent the Reds from taking you back."

In utter desperation we returned to the Justice Building. An officer at the police identification branch said the

RCMP had nothing to do with naturalization and told us to go to the Crown Attorney's office on Nicholas Street.

We had quite a distance to go and the day was getting hot. Andrei was whimpering so I carried him. Anna was obviously growing weary. But these things seemed minor. Through my actions we were all in an awful predicament and something had to be done.

At the Crown Attorney's office we were told the woman who handled naturalization applications had just gone out to lunch and would not be back for some time. It suddenly dawned on me that we hadn't eaten since early morning. I took Anna and Andrei to a little restaurant near the courthouse building where the Crown Attorney's office was located. As I ordered a light lunch, I noticed the clock. It was fifteen minutes to two. I could imagine what was happening at the Embassy. But perhaps they hadn't yet noticed the missing documents and were merely wondering why I hadn't shown up for work.

Andrei fell asleep at the table. Anna then decided we had better take the child to a friend of hers, a British woman in the next building to ours. It was risky, but we just couldn't get around with the tired child. We got on a streetcar and went back to Somerset Street. The neighbor was most kind when Anna stated she had to do some shopping before returning to Moscow. The child would be all right until we returned, she said.

Back we went to the Crown Attorney's Office. The girl gave us forms to fill out, then told us to return next day to arrange for photographs. I looked at her in alarm:

"How long will this naturalization take?"

"Oh," she replied, "I'm not sure. A few months, perhaps."

Anna burst into tears. It was the first time her courage had failed her. I put my arm around her and spoke in Russian. Miserably, I looked around the office. There, at another desk, was a woman in a red dress whom we had spoken to when we came before lunch. Just what I saw in her expression I don't know but, on sudden impulse, I moved quickly across the room and poured out my story to her.

She listened in obvious amazement, then stood up and brought over a couple of chairs. She brought Anna to her desk and signaled for us to be seated. I noted a name plate on her desk: Mrs. Fernande Joubarne.

"This is something the world should know," she said firmly. "I will try to help you."

I felt like crying. Anna grasped my hand as Mrs. Joubarne telephoned another newspaper. I heard her telling somebody there was a "story" in her office of "world importance" and suggested a reporter be sent immediately. The conversation seemed to run into difficulties. Everybody was busy, it appeared, and couldn't she explain what it was all about over the telephone? Mrs. Joubarne called somebody else.

In about half an hour a male reporter appeared. He knew Mrs. Joubarne and greeted her by name. She introduced us and, once again, I related my story. Anna handed me the documents and I translated them for him. He asked me to repeat the contents of the documents relating to the atomic bomb. Then I translated the dossier on Labor Progressive Party organizer, Sam Carr. This seemed to impress him, but he finally shook his head.

"It's too big for us to handle—much too big. It is a matter for the police or the government. I suggest you take it to them."

Mrs. Joubarne, Anna and I all started speaking at once, trying to enlist his active cooperation. But he merely voiced his regrets, and left. Mrs. Joubarne sighed:

"There is nothing more I can do. You had better follow his advice." Then, to Anna she said: "And good luck to you. Let me know if it is a boy or a girl."

We walked out into the blazing afternoon sun. I stopped at the foot of the stairs, not knowing which way to turn.

Anna took my arm.

"Let us go home, Igor," she said with immense weariness.

The danger of going home didn't mean anything to me any more. I was near total exhaustion and home, at least, meant rest; somewhere to think, somewhere to plan what to do next.

In the back of my mind was a pet belief that I had held since childhood—that many obstacles encountered on the road to an objective usually signify a good end.

As we neared Somerset Street I told Anna to go into the

next building for Andrei while I went up to our apartment, apartment No. 4. If all was well I would wave to her across the areaway.

I went up the stairs quietly and listened at our apartment door. Everything was quiet. I unlocked the door and looked inside. Everything seemed in order. I stepped out onto the rear balcony. All was clear. Anna was already looking from the friend's window and I waved for her to come home.

After she returned with Andrei I lay down across the bed, but sleep wouldn't come. Every noise was bothering me. After a short time I went to one of the windows. My heart skipped a beat!

Two men were seated on a bench in the park directly opposite, and both were looking up at my window!

I stepped back farther from the curtain so my shadow wouldn't be seen. Every little while they would look up at the apartment, and then resume conversation. My windows were the only ones in which they were interested. I studied them closely but, from that distance, could not see their faces. They appeared to be total strangers. As I turned to bring Anna from the kitchen, a knock sounded on the apartment door.

I froze in my steps. As Anna came from the kitchen, I signaled for her to remain quiet. There was another knock, louder and more insistent. This was repeated four times. The person outside had apparently decided to call it a day, but Andrei chose that moment to dash across the living room to Anna.

A fist banged harshly on the door. An even voice rasped: "Gouzenko!"

I recognized the voice. It belonged to Under-Lieutenant Lavrentiev, Zabotin's chauffeur and contact man!

He called my name several times. Then we heard his footsteps going down the steps. I returned to the front window. The men were still sitting on the bench, occasionally looking up.

Anna was sitting in the living room, holding Andrei. Her eyes were fastened on me. I knew that the time for positive action had arrived. The clock said 7:05. That meant Sergeant Harold Main of the Royal Canadian Air Force who lived next door would be at home. I hurried out to the rear balcony. Main and his wife were seated there seeking relief from the heat.

I asked Sergeant Main if I could speak to him. He said "Sure, go ahead!" I asked him if he and his wife would take care of little Andrei if something happened suddenly to Anna and me.

The sergeant showed surprise. Then he beckoned me to come over the railing and follow him inside. I felt there wasn't much time to talk so I boiled everything down to the fact that Anna and I expected an attempt to be made on our lives by the NKVD and we were worried about the boy. Sergeant Main looked at me doubtfully but his expression changed when I pointed out the men on the park bench. As he led the way back out onto the rear balcony, he stopped short. There was a man in the areaway looking up!

Sergeant Main made up his mind promptly.

"Get your wife and boy, Gouzenko, and bring them over here. I'm going to get the police."

The idea of consulting the police no longer alarmed me. I was between the devil and the deep blue sea and the capable, assured manner of my Air Force friend carried a confident impression that everything would soon be all right.

I climbed back onto our balcony and entered the house. The door was open—Anna and Andrei were gone!

Rushing through the doorway and into the hall, I stopped short, somewhat abashed on seeing them in the apartment directly across the way talking to a Mrs. Francis Elliott, who lived there.

After listening to our story, Mrs. Elliott suggested we stay with her for the night because her husband and son were away and there was a day-bed we could use. She would find a place for Andrei.

I accepted her kindness gratefully. While Anna and Mrs. Elliott were talking I sat down in the dining room, feeling rather spent. Before long, heavy footsteps sounded in the hall. It was Sergeant Main, with two Ottawa constables. I told them the story, concluding with our fears of being killed, the men in the park and at the rear, and the visit of Under-Lieutenant Lavrentiev.

They asked a number of questions, then spoke to Mrs. Elliott.

"We'll keep this building under observation all night. The light in your bathroom will show on the front street. Leave it turned on unless something happens, then turn it off. That will be our signal to come up."

Then he turned to me.

"Take it easy, Mr. Gouzenko—you've got nothing to worry about now. If we're needed we will be upstairs in a flash. O.K.?"

His smile was most comforting.

"O.K." I replied automatically.

"Attaboy!" With that the constables left.

Around ten o'clock Mrs. Elliott made up the day-bed and suggested we get some much-needed rest. Just before I lay down I turned out the light and pulled up the window blind. There was nobody below.

Sometime between 11:30 and midnight Anna and I woke up with a start. There was a sound of knocking on our apartment door across the hallway. I slipped out of bed and over to the door. Through the keyhole, I could see our door clearly. Knocking on it was Pavlov, the NKVD chief!

With Pavlov were Rogov, Angelov and Pavlov's cipher clerk, Farafontov. As I watched, I heard another door open. It was Sergeant Main's. I could hear him asking what they wanted. One of the four mentioned my name. The sergeant replied:

"The Gouzenkos are away."

Pavlov thanked him and the four went downstairs.

Anna squeezed my arm as I made a motion to move away. "Keep still," she whispered, "they're coming back!"

I looked through the keyhole once more and saw Pavlov working on our door with a jimmy. There was a rasping sound and the door opened. They entered and shut the door quietly behind them.

Mrs. Elliott tiptoed beside me.

"I've tried turning the light on and off but it doesn't get the policemen. What should I do?"

I told her to call them on the telephone. She dialed central and asked for the police. She reported somebody was trying to break into apartment 4, 511 Somerset Street.

In an unbelievably short space of time, the same two constables appeared at my apartment door. The one who had done the speaking, a Constable Thomas Walsh, didn't wait for any formality. He threw open the door. Together with the other policeman, Constable John McCulloch, they caught the four men in the act of rifling my desk and bureau drawers.

We opened Mrs Elliott's door a crack and listened to what was going on. Constable Walsh had apparently asked for an explanation and Pavlov said in crisp, official tones:

"This apartment belongs to a fellow member of the Soviet Embassy, a man named Gouzenko, who happens to be in Toronto tonight. He left some documents here and we have his permission to look for them."

Constable Walsh's tone was just as official.

"Did he also give you permission to break his lock or . . ." he pointed to the twisted lock, "was this done with your bare hands?"

Pavlov waxed indignant.

"How dare you talk to me like that? We had a key for this apartment, but lost it. Anyway, this lock is Soviet property and we can do what we like with it. I order you to leave this apartment!"

Walsh looked at McCulloch, then back to Pavlov. "Constable McCulloch," said Walsh, "insists we remain here until the Inspector arrives. I hope you don't mind. Meanwhile, let me see your identification!"

An Inspector Macdonald finally came and queried the four more extensively. Pavlov was fuming. He charged the constables had insulted them and that Soviet diplomatic immunity had been assailed. The Inspector told them to wait while he made some inquiries, but after he was gone Pavlov told the other three to leave with him. Walsh and McCulloch made no effort to stop them.

Shortly before four in the morning there was another knock, this one a low, careful one, on our apartment door across the hall. But whoever it was left before I could identify him.

In the morning another Ottawa city police inspector visited us. He said the Royal Canadian Mounted Police would like to have a talk with me at the Justice Building.

Anna gave a big, deep sigh of relief.

"At last, Igor, at last," she said. "They are going to listen to you. I am so glad!"

As I hurried into my coat, I looked at Anna. She appeared pale and nervous. "What are you going to do while I am at the Justice Building?" I asked. Anna's reply was typical.

"I have a big washing to do. Don't worry about me, Igor."

My reception at the Justice Building was a marked contrast with my two worried visits of the previous day. High-ranking Royal Canadian Mounted Police and civilian investigators were waiting. They treated me most courteously and, for almost five hours, I answered their questions. The documents aroused considerable interest and discussion after they had listened to my translation of them.

When I described my difficulty in trying to get somebody to listen to me, the RCMP officer in charge smiled.

"You weren't quite as neglected as you thought," he said.

One of the civilian investigators added: "That's a fine way to talk, after my partner and I spent so much time sitting in the park watching your apartment."

The two men had been policemen, and not NKVD men as I suspected. Actually, during the two hours Anna, Andrei and I had waited outside the Justice Minister's office, the Canadian Department of External Affairs and the RCMP had been pondering over what to do with me. Prime Minister Mackenzie King was consulted. It had been decided to "shadow" me for a few days to judge by developments whether I was what I claimed to be or just a mental case suffering from an anti-Red complex. It was realized, too, that if I was bona-fide the case would be an international hot coal to handle.

Since the anxious hours of those days there have been many periods of worry in my life of heavily guarded hiding. Anna's pregnancy called for intensive planning, since I knew Pavlov was aware of Anna's condition and would be watching the hospitals for miles around. So, one night in December, it was arranged that a Royal Canadian Mounted Police constable should take her to a hospital, where he posed as the father. By pretending to be an illiterate foreigner he managed to overcome much of the red tape demanded in making out official forms. He said, in broken English, that he was a Polish farmer and Anna also pretended to be Polish, with very little knowledge of the English language.

The baby was a girl, seven pounds and twelve ounces. Two days after it was born, a passing nurse stopped by Anna's bed and exclaimed: "Why, hello there, you! Don't you remember me! I took care of you in Ottawa when you had another baby."

Anna was petrified with fear but, somehow, managed to play her role. She was a Polish farmer's wife. She had never been to Ottawa. Then her "husband" appeared and apparently the nurse thought she had made a mistake. There was no sequel to the incident, but we were worried.

Life in hiding can never be ideal. I have emerged for the various espionage trials—some twenty of them, I believe—but only under heavy guard. The RCMP are taking no chances with Pavlov's long memory and the equally long memory of the NKVD. There might be a time when they can relax, and Anna and I can enter normal existence with our children.

2

Burma Farewell

Aleksandr Kaznacheev

In the late 1950's the Soviet diplomat Aleksandr Kaznacheev, who had been "co-opted" as an intelligence officer, was stationed in Burma, a country where he could not expect any very effective protection from native security forces. He was, however, not intending to defect to the Burmese (as Gouzenko defected to the Canadians on their own ground), but to the Americans, who were represented in Burma by the diplomatic officers in their Embassy. Kaznacheev had before him the very recent example of a colleague who had tried to defect, had fumbled, and had been picked up and finally sent home, most likely to a very unpleasant fate. Far from dissuading him from attempting the same thing himself, this not only prompted him all the more to break with the oppressive system of the Soviets, but gave him some useful guidelines in planning the tactics of his own defection.

MY MIND WAS now made up: I couldn't wait any longer; I couldn't go on working for criminals in the Kremlin and their henchmen in the Soviet Embassy; I must defect as

---

FROM the book *Inside a Soviet Embassy*.

soon as possible. But as clear as my decision was, just as clear was the realization that I could not remain in Burma, even though my greatest wish was to do just that. My presence in Burma after defection would be an impossible embarrassment to the Burmese government. I knew it myself, but it also was what my Burmese friends, who made some inquiries, finally told me. To defect to the United States—a recognized (at least by all Communists) leader of the Free World—seemed to be the most logical solution and the best way to give my modest service to the cause of Burma's freedom and happiness.

My plan was simple. I would wait for the first opportune moment, when my defection would be most harmful to the prestige of the Soviet Government in Burma, and then go to the Americans. I knew my Soviet masters would denounce me as a traitor, but my conscience would be clear, for I would be betraying "them," not my country. I would tell to all the world the truth about the dirty game of the Soviet government in Burma. This would be my contribution to the future of Russia and my Burmese friends. If my defection in Burma should turn out to be successful, it would be an additional blow to the position and stability of the Communist tyranny in Russia, and it would give moral support to all the forces of freedom and democracy in this world.

I told my closest Burmese friends about my final decision to defect to the United States. They were distressed at the prospect of our separation, but they promised to give whatever help was possible—even to conceal me if things went badly.

I did not have to wait long. In late April, 1959, two things happened in quick succession which set the time for my defection and smoothed the path. The first was the scandalous failure of the Soviet Intelligence's provocation against the major Burmese newspapers—the case of the TASS representative, Kovtunenko. His slanderous forgery was published in the local TASS bulletin on April 23 and raised a tremendous fuss in the Burmese press, which called the public's attention to this instance of Soviet interference in Burma's internal affairs.

An even bigger blow to Soviet prestige was struck about a week later—the unsuccessful attempt by the Soviet milirary attaché, Colonel Strygin, to defect and the notoriety which was attracted by the Embassy's handling of the affair. Just before this, on April 27, Strygin had been severely criticized in the Embassy's party organization for some unspecified shortcomings in his work (probably for being too "soft" toward the Burmese). Two hours later he tried to commit suicide by taking an overdose of sleeping pills, but was brought to a Rangoon hospital and revived. Two guards from the Soviet Embassy took their posts near Strygin's bed. When he woke and realized his terrible predicament Strygin apparently decided to defect. For several hours he kept shouting to the hospital's personnel in English pleading them to call for the Burmese police, Army, or Intelligence.

The Burmese attendants did not call anybody, for they thought the Soviet Colonel was undergoing a mental shock; in fact, they even helped the Russian guards to catch Strygin in the hospital yard when he jumped out of the window trying to escape. Reinforcements arrived from the Embassy, and poor Strygin was brought to his home, all the doors were locked, and guards were set to watch him twenty-four hours a day. The Embassy doctor visited the patient regularly to give him some mysterious shots. A few days later, on May 3, 1959, under a guard of forty bulky Russians, the doped Strygin was taken to Mingaladon Airport and put aboard a Chinese Communist plane bound for Peking. The Embassy had received orders from Moscow to make sure that Strygin got on the plane at all costs; if necessary, Strygin was to be killed. The Soviets could not afford to lose someone as much "in the know" in military intelligence as Strygin. At the airport the burly Russians guarding Strygin smashed the cameras of Burmese newsmen and roughed some of them. Angered at this treatment, a crowd of Burmese demonstrated in front of the Soviet Embassy, showering it with rotten tomatoes. There was again a scuffle between the Burmese and the Embassy guards.

All of this left a bad taste in the mouth of the Burmese and other Southeast Asians. I heard the Ambassador remark during the heat of these events that one more such incident and Soviet prestige would be shattered in that part of the world. I knew that this was an exaggeration, but I saw that my defection now would be in itself a strong blow to the Soviet government's position and an effective piece of anti-Communist propaganda. My only fear was that in such a tense situation the United States might be unwilling to accept me in Burma, or might even suspect that I was a provocateur.

Everything had to be prepared carefully; there had to be no mistake, for a mistake could mean death. I decided to ask for home leave in Moscow, hoping that I could travel via Rome and Vienna, where I might have a safer opportunity to defect, in case the Americans should refuse to accept me in Rangoon. No one in the Embassy thought my request out of the ordinary, since I had already been in Burma longer than usual without leave. The Ambassador agreed readily; I was finally promoted to attaché, he told me, and while in Moscow I would get the official documents of promotion. But I had to go right now in June, so that I could return to Burma in August when preparations for the Burmese general elections would begin.

To go right now! This was against all my plans; I had to establish first of all contact with the Americans in Rangoon and secure their help before acting. But fate struck another blow; the Foreign Office issued a new order, specifying that in the future we must return home via New Delhi and Soviet Central Asia, since the Soviet Airline Aeroflot was now operating jet flights over that route. To travel through Europe, special permission from Moscow was needed. I was panic-stricken. New Delhi was definitely a much less secure place than Rome for Soviet defectors. The Ambassador had already ordered the Consular Section to prepare my passport and plane ticket for a flight to New Delhi. I had less than a week left, and I had not yet arranged anything. What I needed most was an American acquaintance, but I had none, and I had no idea how to go about making contact with the Americans; it would be a risky business with so many Communist agents in Rangoon. I could have consulted the file of American names and addresses which were in Galashin's desk drawer, but I knew that there would probably be Communist surveillance of these; I did not dare use them.

Three days passed in an agony of indecision. In the mornings I was busy cleaning out my desk and winding up details of my work. At night I drove five or six times by the American Embassy, by the houses of the Americans, in the vague hope that maybe something would happen, maybe I might meet one of them on the street. Despair was getting hold of me; finally I decided to take the risky step of going directly to the United States Embassy.

On June 23, 1959, I got into my car in the afternoon, telling my Embassy colleagues that I was bound for downtown to arrange the details of my trip to Moscow, and I actually did visit the Indian Airlines office and various Burmese offices, getting police clearance, vaccination certificates, and similar travel papers. All the time I was thinking about only one thing—I can't delay a single day more! I have to make contact with the Americans! Suddenly . . . an inspiration. A Burmese customs officer looked surprised as I grabbed my papers and rushed from his office to my car. The traffic on the streets seemed to be heavy as never before. The cars didn't seem to move at all!

I drove to the large office building downtown which housed the Indian insurance company which had insured my car. But I was not really here to talk about insurance; on the street floor of this building was the United States Information Service Library. If my presence in this building was noticed, I could always claim that I was there on insurance business and had merely stopped in at the library to kill some time while waiting to see someone. My heart was ready to jump out as I stepped into a big quiet hall filled with bookshelves. Trying to look calm, I asked to see the director of the library. The only person there, a Burmese girl employee, told me that the director would be back in about an hour. I got back in my car and drove around the city, street after street, and around Royal Lake. When I returned to the USIS Library, there was a young Burmese man now on duty. The director was still out.

In near panic I got back in my car. I began to lose hope that I could get away with my plan. I drove out to Rangoon University, where I revealed my troubles to my friends. They offered to help me; if necessary they would conceal me in the teachers' hostel if the Soviets came after me. Many students would help, they assured me. An hour passed; it was now late afternoon. Soon I would have to return to the Embassy. People would become suspicious;

they knew I had many things to straighten out there before my supposed departure.

Once more I summoned up my courage and returned downtown to the USIS Library. This time I found the director in—a middle-aged woman, Mrs. Graham. She was busy in her office with some visitor. Three Burmese secretaries were sitting at the desks around the office.

"I am here on a serious matter, may we talk in some other place?" I asked her, when she turned to me. We went down the corridor and entered her private room.

"I'm from the Soviet Embassy. I want to speak with any officer from the American Embassy," I told her. She didn't seem very surprised at my request and went out to make a phone call. The United States Embassy was only three blocks away; an official from the Political Section arrived in ten minutes. We talked for more than an hour in Mrs. Graham's room. Stumblingly, I told the American diplomat that I wanted to leave the Soviet Foreign Service, that I was disillusioned with Communism and particularly with the Soviet government's foreign policy. I asked him to help me get a visa and a ticket from Calcutta to Karachi, or Bangkok. But he couldn't promise me this.

"You'd better think more about what you are doing," he advised me. My fears turned out to be well-founded; he obviously did not believe in my sincerity and probably suspected a frame-up. What could I do? I couldn't even show him any credentials or identity card, for I had none. However, I told him that I had my driver's license in my car outside the USIS Library. That seemed not to convince him either. Finally, without committing himself to anything, he agreed to meet me the following morning, June 24, at nine o'clock, for further discussion. That was the most terrible blow. I gave myself to the mercy of the Americans without even getting any promise from them to keep my approach in secrecy!

I couldn't return to the Embassy. All evening and the rest of the night I was with my friends. We went to a movie, ate in the restaurant, then in the half-darkness in their hostel room talked and listened to music. Long after midnight I drove to my house. Everything was calm. Probably I hadn't aroused anybody's suspicion yet. There was no sleep for me. The big fan above me was turning madly in ceaseless circles. Frogs croaked deafeningly outside in the monsoon rain. The wind flapped in the unlocked window in the hall.

At 8 A.M. as usual, I had breakfast with my Russian roommates. I told them I had some more business downtown. Slowly I drove through the Rangoon streets; there was plenty of time. I had to meet the United States official at 9 A.M. at the same USIS Library building. Fifteen minutes before the time, I parked my car two blocks away from the library on Bar Street, just opposite the police station. Two American diplomats from the Embassy were waiting for me in Mrs. Graham's room, one of them my acquaintance of the day before. With all my strength I tried to keep myself calm, and managed to smile at them. We shook hands.

"The United States Government agrees to give you political asylum, Mr. Kaznacheev. Are you ready to go?" A mountain seemed to fall off my shoulders upon meeting with such sympathetic friendliness so soon after my first approach.

"Yes, I'm ready. . . ."

"In this case we have to go right now."

"How? . . . Just like this! But . . . wait . . . my papers, documents, and the letters—I left them all in my room."

"We must go right now!"

An American car was waiting for us on the street near the entrance. We all got in and drove away.

I was taken to a house "under American Embassy control" in a residential section of Rangoon, where my new American friends began questioning me more closely about my background, my position in the Soviet Embassy, and about the possible consequences to my parents living in Moscow. They told me that I couldn't be taken to the American Embassy immediately because by a coincidence almost worthy of Hollywood, Soviet Ambassador Alexei Shiborin was due there at noon by much earlier prearrangement to pay a formal farewell call upon Ambassador Walter McConaughy. Shiborin was leaving his post for reassignment. Americans probably felt that it would be somewhat tasteless to have the Soviet Ambassador paying a social visit while one of his employees was in the building arranging his escape to freedom.

While Mr. McConaughy and the Soviet Ambassador were exchanging amiable pleasantries on the second floor of the United States Embassy, I and other American officials were lunching privately some distance away in "an American-controlled place" on crab meat, salad, and tea.

As soon as a telephone call was received to the effect that Shiborin had left the Embassy, I was brought to the building and whisked up to the top floor, where a temporary bedroom was rigged up for my use. Food, Chinese or Burmese style, was brought in, because the Embassy had no kitchen facilities. There I lived until my departure, on June 29, from Rangoon Airport in a United States Air Force C-130.

On the night of June 26 the American Embassy issued a formal announcement of my defection, having earlier notified the Burmese Government of the event. On the next day, June 27, there was a press conference attended by Burmese newspapermen, who tested my knowledge of Burmese, which I passed perfectly after a few direct questions, and then followed questions and answers in English.

During my five-day stay at the Embassy, I wrote out in longhand my personal statement and autobiography in English. I read magazines, and more avidly, news stories about my defection. I was also shown movies, USIS-type as well as Hollywood-made, and was given a change of clothes because I came to the American Embassy with only what I wore.

The only occasion during which I was out of American sight was June 29 when I was taken by Ambassador Mc-Conaughy in his limousine to the National Defense College to be questioned by Burmese Foreign Ministry officials. Mr. McConaughy left for the Embassy and after an interval went back to the college and waited for the Burmese Government to satisfy itself that I was leaving Soviet employ of my own accord.

Burmese Foreign Minister U Chan Htoon Aung offered the Soviet Ambassador an opportunity to meet and interrogate me, but Shiborin refused to avail himself of that offer. From the National Defense College I again entered the American Ambassador's limousine and was driven out to the airport under Burmese military escort. There I posed for farewell photos and said good-bye to American officials, while trying to find a familiar face in the big crowd of military and civilians that gathered near the airport. I hoped I would be able to see my Burmese friends whom I had not seen since my last night at Rangoon University. I didn't find them, but I saw a group of Soviet Embassy people who were filming the departure from a distance.

I entered the Air Force plane alone. An American Embassy official started up the steps with me but halted and turned away. The Americans, definitely, did not forget the forty Soviet guards who had dragged, pushed, and shoved Colonel Strygin into the Chinese plane less than two months before. They apparently decided that nothing was to be allowed to give the impression that I was leaving in any fashion except by my own decision—even at the last minute.

The two starboard engines of the C-130 were turning over even before I entered the plane, and as soon as I was in, the hatch closed, the port engines fired, and the plane taxied out to the runway and took off.

Farewell Burma!

3

The Disappearing Fields

Flora Lewis

*The case of the disappearing Fields is one still sur-
rounded by a good deal of mystery, and it is not
likely that we shall ever see it all clarified. The
central character in the story is Noel Field, an
American of distinguished background and excellent education who was at one time before World
War II with the U.S. State Department and later
with the League of Nations. During the war when
he was in Switzerland he made himself useful, for
a short period, to the OSS office in Berne. He knew
many Communist and left-wing exiles with whom
the Allies at that time had common cause against
the Nazis on the field of battle.*

*After his disappearance behind the Iron Curtain
in 1949 described in the following excerpt from
Flora Lewis' book, Field's name frequently figured
in the trials of prominent Communists in Czechoslovakia and Hungary whom Field had once known
and who were now accused of Titoism and other
"deviationist" crimes. In these trials Field was
depicted as an American agent, although I am sure
he had been a Soviet agent. It is likely that he was*

FROM the book *Red Pawn*.

chosen by the Stalinists as an available and convenient scapegoat. His connections to the OSS and to those Communists Stalin wished to remove from the scene could now be made the basis for trumped-up charges that they had been "tools of the Imperialists." Whether Field was enticed to Prague or went on his own is unknown. Once he was there it was certainly in line with Stalin's methods that he should disappear from sight. When his wife and his brother, Hermann, and his adopted daughter all went looking for him behind the Iron Curtain, it was also necessary for them to disappear. Stalin never liked witnesses.

We might never have heard of any of them again except for the defection of the Polish intelligence officer, Joseph Swiatlo, in 1954. He had been Hermann Field's interrogator and keeper in Warsaw. Swiatlo was able to tell American authorities where Hermann was imprisoned in Poland and that Noel and his wife had been jailed in Hungary. Prompt protests on the part of the U.S. Government brought about Hermann's release and would also have secured that of Noel and his wife, but this pair, although they had been incarcerated in separate cells in a Hungarian prison for five years, unknown to each other, chose to stay in Hungary. The daughter, Erika, was also eventually released from an East German prison.

THERE ARE PALACE Hotels and Palace Hotels around the world, some stretching to live up to their name and some frankly mocking it. The Palace Hotel in Prague probably meant to be in the first group, somber and imposing with a bleak, high-ceilinged lobby and a broad wood-paneled stairway to give a tinge of grandeur. But by 1949, or by another calendar reckoning the year 2 A.C. (after Communism came to Czechoslovakia), it was only dreary and depressing, the transient home of a dwindling group of foreigners who no longer cared to chat with strangers and avoided asking or telling each other the purpose of their visit. There was always a silent assortment of them in the lobby or in the gloomy café up the stairs, staring, leafing

through the multilingual collection of Communist newspapers that lay about on empty tables, waiting mutely
without explanation.

Foreigners with money to spend, or whom the government chose to pamper with deluxe treatment, stayed at the
Alcron, dingy too in 1949 but more alive with comings and
goings, brightened now and then with a diplomatic sari or
an easy burst of tourist laughter. There was something
about the atmosphere at the Palace that made people
glance swiftly around and lower their voices as they pushed
through the revolving door from the narrow, time-softened
Prague street. There was nothing apparently sinister, just a
lumpy inelegant reserve that was totally devoid of either
the palatial or the carefree air of travel.

A tall gaunt American checked into the Palace in the
spring of 1949. His name was Noel Haviland Field, and
with his soft voice, his stooped and shambling gait, his
thick but neatly combed gray hair, he had an air of gentle
culture and transparent goodness that usually brought him
trust and respect.

For two years he had been without a job. It was a
serious discomfort, although not a tragedy because there
was a steady if small income from his father's estate, and he
had trained himself to frugal living years before. Besides,
with his education and his immense experience of Europe,
all the racked and torn and bled-out parts of Europe,
he could always manage to pick up a bit by writing. To save
expenses, he and his wife Herta had closed their Geneva
apartment, stored their furniture, and moved into a family
hotel in Geneva until they could find another place to
settle. Noel told friends in Geneva and Paris that he was
going to make his headquarters in Prague for a while and
roam Eastern Europe to gather material for a book on the
stark new structures that were being hammered together as
Peoples' Democracies, the Communist empire between the
Soviet frontier and the high-tide mark of the Red Army at
the end of World War II. To others, Noel had said that he
wanted to study at Prague's ancient Charles University,
revered over centuries as a center of enlightenment. And to
others yet, he said he had hopes of finding a job as a
visiting professor, perhaps of languages or modern literature.

He had already collected two big suitcases of material on earlier trips to Prague and Warsaw, and had left them with friends to be sent on when he flew home to Geneva. The Prague suitcase had never arrived—lost, stolen, sequestered? There could be a dozen explantions, and there was none. It seemed somehow ominous. He wrote to his sister Elsie, in the United States, that he was getting extremely worried about the Prague suitcase, now more than two months overdue, because it contained "some material that could never be replaced," and suggested he was going to Prague to track it.

In April, Noel and Herta went to Paris for a few days. The first Partisans for Peace congress was being held, a forerunner of the pro-Communist Stockholm Appeal, and Noel told friends he was attending as an independent observer. A French newspaperman who recognized Noel, standing disconsolately in front of the Salle Pleyel where the congress was held, had to sneak him in past the guards, however, for Noel had no admission card.

With increasing excitement Noel talked to friends about his coming trip to Prague and his plans to work there. On May 5 he boarded an Air France plane and flew directly to Czechoslovakia. He left no address with acquaintances in Paris. But he said they could always reach him at the Journalists' Club, where he often dropped in for a meal and a sociable hour or two with the new elite, the party newspapermen whose gossip, seldom idle, echoed the cold, secret voices of the leaders in the gray concrete party building and sometimes carried a hint of things unheard. The girl who looked after the cloakroom at the club would take letters and messages for him, he said, and hold them in the drawer behind her counter where she kept cigarettes and matches to sell.

Herta went back to Geneva to pay off their bills, pack up, and get her own visa for Czechoslovakia. Five days later, on May 10, both of them wrote letters to Noel's sister Elsie. Noel wrote about how the looks of Prague had changed under the new regime. He said there was plenty of food, but prices were high. He was looking around for a place where Herta could do some light housekeeping, because he was having another bout of his old stomach trouble and didn't want to live on heavy Czech restaurant

food. Herta's letter to Elsie said she had spoken to Noel on
the telephone and that he was cheerful and eagerly awaiting her arrival. He told her that a friend she knew, but
whose name he did not want to mention on the phone, was
coming to see him.

Noel had several friends in Prague, people he had met in
wartime in the West and people he had come to know on a
series of visits to Czechoslovakia since the war. Some of
them were now very important, as important as a person
can be in a Peoples' Democracy. But Noel himself was not
a widely known figure. The people who watched him come
and go at the Palace, off for appointments or long lonely
walks through the beautiful stony city, saw nothing extraordinary in him. An odd American, perhaps, but there were
so many odd Americans, odd all sorts of people wandering
about Europe in those days.

Whomever he had seen, whomever he was trying to see,
Noel took it calmly when two men came to the Palace to
fetch him a day or two after the letters to Elsie had been
sent. He acted as though he had been waiting for someone
to take him to an important meeting, and strode off with
the men after they had spoken to him. But he said nothing
to anyone else; he took nothing with him. Noel and the
two men turned in the direction of Wenceslaus Square, and
he disappeared without a trace.

A few days later, the Czech friend whom Herta thought
he had referred to on the telephone went to call on Noel at
the Palace. The manager said Mr. Field had gone out
with two men and had still not returned. Several days later
the manager said again that the room was still paid for,
and he understood Noel had gone on a short trip to Hungary, leaving his things behind. Then he reported he had
had a telegram from Noel in Bratislava, near the Hungarian border. Finally, a few weeks later, there was another
telegram saying that a man named René Kimmel would
come from Bratislava to pick up Noel's things and pay the
mounting bill. Elsie learned later that the friend looked up
the wire in the Bratislava telegraph office and did not recognize the signature as anything like Noel's.

It was a month later when the manager of the Palace
told an inquirer that René Kimmel had turned up and
taken away all Noel's belongings, but no one else ever saw

Kimmel. There was nothing but the hotel manager's word to suggest that he existed at all. Nor, after he walked out of the door with the two strangers, was there another sign anywhere that Noel Field still existed.

The malicious *bise* that blows damp Alpine cold but none of the mountain freshness down on Geneva all winter dies in spring, leaving the city to sprawl in warm comfort around its end of a picture-postcard lake. Horse chestnuts bloom in the streets, lilacs bloom in the gardens, and minute sails bloom prettily on the water. There is a tenderness in the air to lift all but the heaviest spirits. But the spring of 1949 gave no solace to Herta Field.

Herta was not flighty or hysterical, far from it. If ever a woman was solid and sturdy of mind as well as body, it was Noel Field's German-born wife. Her determination, her energy, her courage had been tested before and not found wanting. But even the firmest people have a staff to hold them upright, although some keep it secret. The mainstay of Herta's life, no secret, was her adoration of her well-born, well-educated, well-mannered husband. Her character was in many ways stronger and more decisive than his, but all her strength and her decisions were concentrated on maintaining what she always considered her incomparably fortunate and honored place as Noel's wife. She shared his ideals and his secrets, guarding them with her life. She fussed about his medicine and his muffler. For Herta, Noel could do no wrong; without Noel nothing could be right.

And the weeks went by without news from Noel. In July, relatives invited Herta to join them for a seaside vacation. Herta did not answer the letter, so they telephoned her from Paris. She sounded strange on the phone, they said later, but when they asked about Noel she assured them he was all right, but that she had to stay in Geneva in case he should want to call her. It was not like Herta to be so illogical and distant, but insisting did no good and they gave up.

Herta had moved into the apartment of a friend who was away for a time in Rome, a roomy, pleasant place in one of the handsome modern buildings on a hill above the Old City. She puttered among the bibelots, wandered about the city, in growing despair.

When the friend, a widow, returned from her trip, she could not help notice that Herta was writhing with worry. The two had been friends for several years, and discreetly, sympathetically at first, the hostess offered to listen to Herta's troubles. Herta was fiercely secretive, evading all questions, shrugging aside as futile all the offers of help. Finally, a little impatient at Herta's strange behavior, the other insisted.

"If you're going to live with me as my guest, and friend," she told Herta one evening, "how can I help you if you refuse to tell me what's bothering you?"

At last, Herta blurted it out. "I have had no news from Noel," she said explosively. "I want to go to Prague. I'd much rather be in prison with Noel in Prague than be free here in Switzerland."

It was the first time she had spoken the dread word "prison" since Noel had disappeared. And she never explained what knowledge put the picture in her mind and made her feel it was the right one. She would say nothing more, but she decided to pack up and fly to Prague.

It was July by then, two months since Noel had taken off so jauntily from Paris. His younger brother Hermann, an architect, came to Europe to attend an architects' congress in Bergamo, Italy, and then to go on to Poland for a visit. Two years before, he had organized and led a tour of American architects around Eastern Europe to look at the rubble legacy of war being piled up again into new buildings, new cities, and he had friends in Warsaw.

Hermann stopped briefly to see Herta in Geneva. Then she took off for Prague. It was agreed that as soon as his congress in Bergamo had ended, he would come to Prague to help her in the search. When he arrived, toward the end of July, Herta had checked into the Palace Hotel, but she had got no farther. Together they went to the police.

"Noel Haviland Field?" the men behind all the desks would say, pronouncing the foreign name very carefully. And they would shuffle industriously through papers, looking at each as though they expected it to be the right one, giving a little grunt of sympathetic disappointment each time it was not. Politely, with kindly smiles, they would promise to look further, to check, to inquire, and just as politely they always finished with the same answer: "No, we know nothing about him."

Both Herta and Hermann stayed carefully away from the one place Americans in trouble would naturally seek help—the rabbit warren of an old palace sprawling up a hillside across the Vltava River and now, with the Stars and Stripes fluttering above its great arched gateway, the United States Embassy. Hermann explained later that they made their search so furtively and so alone because they believed there was a better chance of prying Noel loose from whoever clutched him if there were no official protests and no noise.

Eventually Hermann went on to Warsaw, promising to stop again in Prague on his way home to see what more could be done. It was nearly three months since Noel had disappeared. No one but his wife and brother even knew that he was missing.

Hermann wrote from Warsaw to his sister Elsie. On August 3, he said, Herta had telephoned from Prague, asking him to join her there. Her tone, he told Elsie, was urgent, but he said nothing more.

The streets had been cleared and most of the rubble piled up and carted away from Warsaw by midsummer 1949, but it was a bleak and broken city, still showing that it was there at all because one thing, and only one thing, had emerged unshattered from the wreckage of the war: will power. Now even the will power that had so bitterly preserved itself against the Nazi onslaught seemed about to crumble, like the few tottering buildings that had withstood the fury of destruction but had lost their healthy balance and were inching toward collapse. It was a gloomy, grim city, shivering with apprehension despite the summer skies because the shadows of a new round of purges, a new campaign of persecutions, were already clear on the horizon. Prague somehow drew itself in, closed and cold, at danger signs. Warsaw chattered nervously.

Hermann Haviland Field, tall like his older brother but more lithe and not so gangly, more elegant and not so tweedy, more confident and not so intense, went on endless rounds of sightseeing, gazing at the dirty open sites where he had seen famous buildings on his trip to Warsaw just before the war and at the cluttered sites of raw new building. His frequent companions were Simon and Helena Cyrkus, leading architects on the government Reconstruction Board. It was Helena, a plump, enthusiastic woman, who had arranged the visa for Hermann. But, for all their government contacts the Cyrkuses could give no help in tracking Noel. Wherever he tried, Hermann met only blank disbelief.

Hermann had left his English-born wife, Kate, and their two children, in London. He sent word to Kate that he would be flying to Prague to see Herta once more on August 22, and would fly to London the next day to pick up the family and sail home. On the morning of the twenty-second he went in the Cyrkuses' little car to Okecie, Warsaw's airport. There was the usual fluster in the waiting room as they exchanged warm farewells and promises to write, and Helena waved as Hermann joined the line for passport and customs inspection. The passengers filed through into the departure waiting room and boarded the rickety plane, a Soviet version of the famous American DC-3 workhorse, for the two-hour flight to Prague.

Herta went out to the Prague airport to meet the plane. She was seriously unnerved by now, for she had still heard nothing of Noel. It was three and a half months, and all she had gotten in Prague were such bland denials that they seemed to cast doubt on whether a man named Noel H. Field had ever existed at all. She took to strange habits. An American friend, knowing she was in Prague, went to ask for her at the Palace. Herta was out, but she had left a list of places where she intended to be each hour of the day. Wondering about this businesslike efficiency that was so out of character for Herta, the friend tracked her down and invited her to supper. Herta refused curtly and told the friend, a social worker named Dorothea Jones, "I can't talk to you, I've got to go to bed. It's all right though, I know Noel is all right. I know, I'll find him." But she gave no explanation.

When the plane from Warsaw came in, Herta posted herself at the opaque glass door leading from the immigration and customs room. Impatiently she scanned each face as it came through. Finally she asked a passing airlines employee if there were any more passengers from Warsaw. There was no one left. She persuaded the officials to show her the flight manifest. There was no Hermann Field on the list. Someone remembered the tall, slim American entering the waiting room in Warsaw. Others thought they remembered his coming out to board the plane, but no one was sure. Certainly there had been nothing untoward during the flight; no one had noticed anything unusual. Like his brother Noel, Hermann had vanished. This time it seemed literally into thin air.

There was little more Herta could do. There were no more planes from Warsaw. She probably telephoned Warsaw and was assured that Hermann had packed and left just as he had planned. Still, she waited a few more hours. The next day she sat down and wrote to Hermann's wife that Hermann had failed to reach Prague. She could have telephoned London, but she did not.

Kate Thorneycroft Field, an apple-cheeked, bright-humored, no-nonsense Englishwoman, was not the type who mulls over nightmares of catastrophe. On the same day that Herta mailed a letter saying Hermann had not arrived on the plane from Warsaw, Kate went out to meet the flight he was to have taken on from Prague. A quick check showed he had neither appeared nor canceled the reservation, and she was certain Hermann would have let her know if he had changed his plans. She marched directly to the American Embassy on Grosvenor Square and reported that Hermann Field was missing in a Communist land. The wires went out—the first in what was to become an enormous file of diplomatic messages on the Field case.

In Prague, Herta finally, although still guardedly, decided to speak to the embassy. She told them in precise detail about the plane that was to have brought Hermann. Asked why she stayed on in Prague, she told them for the first time that Noel too had disappeared. There was a long list of all the usual questions, and she answered them, but she volunteered no further information or suspicion.

It was sinister enough, two Americans vanishing without trace or explanation, but the diplomats in Prague had no reason to see any extraordinary significance in the mystery.

Checks were begun, and Herta was promised a report as soon as anything came in. She went back to the Palace Hotel. That was on the twenty-fifth of August.

The next day, August 26, the Embassy tried to reach Herta. She was no longer at the Palace. Herta Field had vanished.

"One little, two little, three little Indians . . ." The nursery rhyme was coming true. Three Americans, one after another, gone. There were headlines and head-shakings, diplomatic protests and finger-shakings, but no clues. The governments of Czechoslovakia and Poland formally and flatly denied that Noel, Hermann and Herta Field were in their countries or that they had any knowledge of where the Fields might be. There seemed nothing more to say, and no use saying it. After a time the fuss died down.

It was exactly a year later, on August 26, 1950, that Erika Glaser Wallach, foster daughter of Noel and Herta Field, stepped onto the covered apron of Berlin's Tempelhof airport after a flight from Frankfurt. Erika was a slim, headstrong, attractive young woman of impulse. The impulse had taken her to seek the trail of the missing Fields in the only city that is half free, half Communist. West Berlin was just beginning to recover after the long hunger siege of the blockade, lifted a few months earlier. But the East and the West were at war, a distant remote-control war that was Stalin's last vicious probe of Western resistance, and the rulers of East Berlin, like those of all Communist places, were more enemy-conscious than ever. Still, the war in Korea was very far away, and Erika was concentrating on immediate dangers. She was frightened, and she was determined to be brave, a combination that makes people foolhardy.

She checked in at a small hotel and began to telephone. She had already been warned against going to Berlin by an American consul who said bluntly, "Three Fields have disappeared already. We don't want anything to happen to you."

When she insisted she would go anyway, the consul offered to send someone along for protection—and probably for observation, since the United States Government was as unsure as the public whether the missing Fields had been kidnaped, lured, or had voluntarily arranged to melt into the Communist pot. Though her husband, Robert Wallach, was American, Erika had only the papers of a stateless refugee. She had adamantly turned down the idea of an American bodyguard, convinced that if the Communists found her in such company she would surely be shot as a spy. And then, telling no one but her husband, she had sneaked off quickly to Berlin before one bureaucrat could tell another bureaucrat and arrange to bar her flight, or have her followed.

After telephoning, she changed her clothes and locked her money and papers in the cupboard. Then, without leaving a word for anyone, she walked out on the streets of West Berlin, took a subway to the East sector, and vanished.

That made four.

Four people, three of them American citizens, with families and friends, with records, with pasts, had marched or stumbled or fallen into seeming nonexistence. There was nothing on the face of it to show why. The threads that led them were invisible, some hidden carefully in the past, and some still being woven for the future. But there were threads. There had to be.

By the end of 1955 Noel Field, his wife Herta, his brother Hermann, and his foster daughter Erika Wallach had reappeared. Noel and Herta, it turned out, had spent the years since 1949 unknown to each other in a Budapest prison; Hermann, in a prison cellar in Warsaw; Erika, in a torture cell in East Germany and then in the slave-labor camp at Vorkuta in the Soviet arctic. During the years they had been gone, almost all the powerful Communist leaders of Eastern Europe had been toppled, one after another, in purge waves that began with klieg-lit show trials and spread irresistibly wider. At the trials in Hungary and Czechoslovakia, Noel Field's name had been a key of the indictment. Noel Field, the prosecutor said, was a well-known American master spy, and therefore to have known him was proof of conspiracy in an American spy ring. The trials scheduled for Poland and East Germany were never held, but they were fully prepared, and again and again in the investigations Noel Field's name cropped up.

No one of the three Fields or Erika was ever produced in an open courtroom, but the name of Noel Field became a touchstone of treason, the very finger of pain and death.

One by one, the four of them were released. After them by the scores and the hundreds came others, dropped as flotsam by the receding purge tide. Slowly, as the prisons in five countries spewed forth what they had hidden in their depths, the scope of the maelstrom centering on Noel Field began to show. Hundreds had died or been executed. Many thousands had been jailed. The mighty had fallen, and so had the humble: the anonymous people who happened once to have received a parcel from Noel Field or to have met him at a dinner party. It came out that Field had been a kind of Typhoid Mary, unwitting carrier of some invisible and vicious germ that afflicted all who came near him. The stricken passed the disease along all unawares, and Field became a word of fear.

The riddle of the Fields' disappearance was solved. They had been arrested by Communist police. But it left a greater mystery.

An American, a man of quiet distinction but no personal fame or visible importance, had been a vortex for great swirling powers of evil. With no special power of his own, he had provided the pinpoint center of forces that reached out to make the unhappy history of our times. There had been all kinds of rumors. In the East, he was pronounced an American super spy. In the West, some people said he was a Soviet agent. And yet there was no real evidence of either. To listen to Jakub Berman, Stalin himself trembled—in fear or fury?—at the name of Noel Field, and personally supervised the cauterization of all that Field had touched. And when it was all over—when Stalin was dead, when the prisons were drained, when in America the name McCarthy was no longer a threat but a jeer—people who knew still hushed and shook their heads in worry at the mention of Noel Field.

What was so special about him? A man of the twentieth century, Field lived through all the turbulences of these extraordinary times. But he was singled out in a strange way, used differently from others by the awesome years. Why?

VI

Deception:

Confusing the Adversary

IN INTELLIGENCE PARLANCE, deception refers to the placing of misleading information in enemy hands, usually of a military nature—since it is primarily in wartime that deception is practiced. If the enemy believes the deception, he then makes preparations for something which does not happen and is caught off guard by what does. The planted information must, of course, not be so far off from the possible as to appear silly and hence suspect. Also, the means by which the false information is made to fall into enemy hands must seem normal, or at least credible, if the enemy is not to see through the stratagem.

In George Washington's day if a bag full of dispatches was found in the middle of the road by the enemy it could conceivably have come loose from the saddle of a courier riding at a fast gallop, and Washington was not above resorting to this means of placing false information in British hands from time to time.

The reader will see that one of the great deception operations of World War II, Operation Mincemeat, recounted in this section is really based on the same fundamental principle as the mislaid saddlebags. Some misfortune or accident, easily explained by the fortunes of war, is responsible for secret, enemy dispatches falling into hostile hands, except that the "secret enemy dispatches" were doctored before the accident—which was carefully planned.

1

Babylon Falls Again

Herodotus

*Deception of a rather intricate sort was a regular
practice in antiquity, if we can judge by the many
tales both in legend and in history itself in which
it is reported. The most frequent pattern involves
an ostensible deserter who goes over to the other
side because he is allegedly discontented with or
has been maltreated by the side to which he originally owed allegiance. He is supposed to be anxious
to take vengeance on those who mistreated him
and for this reason, out of pique, discloses to the
enemy the plans of the side from which he has just
defected. But these plans are, of course, designed
to throw the enemy off his guard.*

*Thus, Sinon, the defecting Greek captain in
Virgil's version of the Trojan horse story, misleads
the Trojans by telling them that the Greeks have
sailed away and have left the horse behind as an
offering to the gods. Zopyrus, in the tale which
follows from Herodotus, goes to ghastly lengths to
convince the Babylonians that the Persians have
mistreated him—in order to be believed.*

FROM *Herodotus*.

DARIUS MUSTERED ALL his power and led it against Babylon, and he marched to the town and laid siege to it; but the townsmen cared nothing for what he did. They came up onto the bastions of the wall, and mocked Darius and his army with gesture and word; and this saying came from one of them: "Why sit you there, Persians, instead of departing? You will take our city when mules bear offspring." This said the Babylonian, supposing that no mule would ever bear offspring.

A year and seven months passed and Darius and all his army were vexed by ever failing to take Babylon. Yet Darius had used every trick and every device against it. He essayed the stratagem whereby Cyrus took the city, and every other stratagem and device, yet with no success; for the Babylonians kept a marvelous strict watch and he could not take them.

But in the twentieth month of the siege a miraculous thing befell Zopyrus, son of that Megabyzus who was one of the seven destroyers of the Magian: one of his food-carrying mules bore offspring. Zopyrus would not believe the news; but when he saw the foal for himself, he bade those who had seen it to tell no one; then taking counsel he bethought him of the Babylonian's word at the beginning of the siege—that the city would be taken when mules bore offspring—and having this utterance in mind he conceived that Babylon might be taken; for the hand of heaven, he supposed, was in the man's word and the birth from his own mule.

Being then persuaded that Babylon was fated to fall, he came and inquired of Darius if he set great store by the taking of the city; and when he was assured that this was so, he next looked about for a plan whereby the city's fall should be wrought by himself alone; for good service among the Persians is much honored, and rewarded by high preferment. He could think of no way of mastering the city but to do violence to himself and then desert to the Babylonians; so he accounted it but a little thing to mishandle himself past cure; cutting off his nose and ears, shaving his head for a disfigurement, and scourging himself, he came in this guise before Darius.

The king was greatly moved at the sight of so notable a man thus mishandled. Leaping up with a cry from where he sat he asked Zopyrus who had done him this outrage and why. "There is no man," answered Zopyrus, "save yourself, who could bring me to this plight; this, O King! is the work of none other but myself; for I could not bear that Persians should be mocked by Assyrians."

Darius answered, "Hard-hearted man; if you say that it is to win the city that you have maltreated yourself past cure, you do but give a fair name to a foul deed. Foolish man! think you that our enemies will yield the sooner for this violence done to you? Nay, you were clean out of your wits to destroy yourself thus." "Had I told you," said Zopyrus, "what I was minded to do, you would have forbidden it; as it is, I have considered with myself alone and done it. Now, then, matters so stand that if you but play your part Babylon is ours. I will in my present plight desert into the city, pretending to them that you have done this violence upon me; and I think that I shall persuade them that this is so, and thus gain the command of an army. Now, for your part, on the tenth day from my entering the city do you take a thousand men from that part of your army whereof you will least rue the loss, and post them before the gate of Semiramis; on the seventh day after that, post me again two thousand before the gate called the gate of the Ninevites; and when twenty days are past after that seventh, lead out four thousand more and post them before the Chaldean gate, as they call it; suffering neither these, nor the others that have come before them, to carry any weapons of war save daggers; leave them these. But immediately after the twentieth day bid the rest of your army to assault the whole circuit of the walls, and, I pray you, post the Persians before the gate of Belus and the gate called Cissian. For I think that I shall have achieved such exploits that the Babylonians will give into my charge the keys of their gates, and all else besides; and it will thenceforward by my business and the Persians' to do what is needful."

With this charge, he went toward the city gate, turning and looking back as though he were in truth a deserter. When the watchers posted on the towers saw him, they ran down, and opening half the gate a little asked him who he was and for what purpose he was come; he told them that he was Zopyrus, come to them as a deserter. Hearing this the gate wardens brought him before the general assembly of the Babylonians, where he bade them see his lamentable plight, saying of his own work that it was Darius' doing, because that he had advised the king to lead his army away, seeing that they could find no way to take the city. "Now," said he in his speech to them, "I am come greatly to aid you, men of Babylon, and greatly to harm Darius and his army and the Persians; not unpunished shall he go for the outrage he has wrought upon me; and I know all the plan and order of his counsels." Thus he spoke.

When the Babylonians saw the most honored in Persia with his nose and ears cut off and all bedabbled with blood from the scourging, they were fully persuaded that he spoke truth and was come to be their ally, and were ready to grant him all that he asked, which was, that he might have an army; and having received this from them he did according to his agreement with Darius. On the tenth day he led out the Babylonian army, and surrounded and put to the sword the thousand whom he had charged Darius to set first in the field. Seeing that his deeds answered his words, the Babylonians were overjoyed and ready to serve him in every way. When the agreed number of days was past, he led out again a chosen body of Babylonians, and slew the two thousand men of Darius' army. When the Babylonians saw this second feat of arms, the praise of Zopyrus was in every man's mouth. The agreed number of days being again past, he led out his men to the place he had named, where he surrounded the four thousand and put them to the sword. After this his third exploit, Zopyrus was the one man for Babylon: he was made the captain of their armies and the warden of their walls.

So when Darius assaulted the whole circuit of the wall, according to the agreed plan, then Zopyrus' treason was fully revealed. For while the townsmen were on the wall defending it against Darius' assault, he opened the gates called Cissian and Belian, and let in the Persians within the walls. Those Babylonians who saw what he did fled to the temple of that Zeus whom they call Belus; those who had not seen it abode each in his place, till they too perceived how they had been betrayed. Thus was Babylon the second time taken.

2

The Man Who Never Was

Ewen Montagu

In this notable operation (known at the time as Operation Mincemeat) from World War II, the means of getting false information into the hands of the enemy in such a fashion that he will believe it is achieved by concocting an accident which seems natural to the enemy, a seemingly lucky chance which throws some important information his way.

In the spring of 1943 the body of a British courier, who was ostensibly drowned after his airplane was forced down in the Mediterranean, was washed up on the shores of Spain. The courier's briefcase contained important messages from the Imperial General Staff in London to Field Marshal Alexander, in Tunisia, which pointed to the "fact" that the Allies were planning to invade Southern Europe via Sardinia and Greece (instead of via Sicily). The body of Major Martin, the courier, was recovered by the Spaniards, as intended by the plotters of the deception, and the important papers in his briefcase were passed on to the German authorities,

FROM the book *The Man Who Never Was.*

*eventually reaching the German High Command.
The latter took the information as bona fide and
arranged its defenses accordingly, but not without
first carefully investigating everything that could
be found out about Major Martin from the personal papers he was carrying to make sure that
there was nothing phony about him. Our excerpt
has to do with the preparation of these personal
papers before Major Martin took his trip.*

*Major Martin was, in actual fact, the corpse of
a recently deceased civilian who was carried frozen
in a canister via British submarine to a point off
the Spanish shore and then floated in on the tide
so that he would be found. The military papers in
his briefcase, as well as all his personal papers,
were forged by British Intelligence experts, but the
actual "misinformation" which was placed in German hands by this method had, of course, to be
approved by the highest Allied authorities as appropriate to their actual strategy, which was to
invade via Sicily.*

FROM QUITE AN early stage Major Martin had become a
real person to us and it was obviously desirable that as
much of that feeling as possible should be shared by whoever investigated the body; the more real he appeared the
more convincing the whole affair would be. Besides, I was
quite sure that in a matter of this importance every little
detail would be studied by the Germans in an effort to find
a flaw in Major Martin's make-up, so as to be sure that the
whole thing was genuine and not a plant. That I was not
mistaken is evidenced by the fact that, as we learnt later,
the Germans even noticed the dates on the two theatre-
ticket stubs that we placed in Major Martin's pocket.

The method that we adopted in deciding on Major Martin's personality was to keep on discussing him—rather as
if we were pulling a friend to pieces behind his back. In
fact, we talked about him until we did feel that he was an
old friend whom we had known for years. I must, however,
admit that, although he became completely real to us, we

did tend to mold his character and history to suit our convenience.

We had decided that Major Martin was a rather brilliant officer and was trusted by his superiors; his only visible lapses were the all too common ones of having lost his identity card and having recently let his pass to Combined Operations H.Q. run out of date.

On that foundation we built a character which could be evidenced by documents in his pockets: that was the only means that we had whereby to convey his personality to the Germans.

We decided that he should be fond of a good time, so he could have an invitation to a night club; it was a probable result of a certain amount of extravagance that he would have a letter from his bank about his overdraft; he could have been staying at a Service club while in London, so he might have a receipted bill for the last part of his stay there. In this way he was developing from an abstraction into something rather more definite.

But how could we make him really "come to life"?

The only way to do it was by letting him carry in his pockets letters which would convey to the reader something really personal about him. On the other hand, if one were able to stop a passer-by in the street and search his pockets, it would be very seldom that one would hit on any occasion when he had letters about him which covered more than trivial details. When we approached our problem in that way, we came to the conclusion that the only times when a man is certain to be carrying "live" letters conveying a vivid picture of him and his life would be when he had recently become engaged and was carrying love letters on him and making arrangements for married life. We therefore decided that "a marriage should be arranged" between Bill Martin and some girl just before he was sent abroad.

So Major Martin "met" a charming girl called Pam early in April, became engaged to her almost at once (those wartime courtships!); she gave him a snap of herself and he gave her an engagement ring; he had a couple of ecstatic letters from her, one written when staying away the weekend and one written in the office (while her boss was out) in an agony of emotion, as he had hinted that he was being sent abroad somewhere. He would have with him the bill for the engagement ring—unpaid of course, as he had an overdraft to deal with. Lastly, he could have an old-fashioned father who disapproved of war weddings and who would insist on his son making a will if he persisted in so foolish and improvident a step.

We felt that we could not hope to build up a personality more definitely than that with only a pocketful of letters—but they had to sound genuine and they had to be written by someone. We could, of course, have written them ourselves—most of us knew only too well what a letter about an overdraft looked like, and some of us had made wills or received love letters, but I thought it best to rely on the expert hand so that there could be no possibility of any mistake.

Some of the items were easy. For instance, one of our number had an invitation to the Cabaret Club with no name on it, so the night club was easily provided for. The letter about the overdraft was only slightly more difficult. Through another of our number we got a letter from Lloyds Bank dated the 14th April calling on Major Martin to pay off an overdraft of some seventy-nine pounds. I was asked, later on, whether it was usual for a letter dealing with such a comparatively small sum to have been signed by the Joint General Manager at Head Office; I had already considered this, as I know from bitter experience that such letters are usually signed by the branch manager. When I raised this question at the time, I was assured that, although it was true that such letters were more usually signed by the manager of the appropriate branch, it did quite often happen that the letter would come from Head Office in certain circumstances. As the officer concerned in getting this letter had a "lead in" to the Head Office, it was decided to use that: I did not think that the Germans would have had the experience that we had had of over-drafts and, after all, even if the amount was small, Major Martin's father was clearly a man of some importance. This letter was drafted for us personally by Mr. Whitley Jones, the Joint General Manager of Lloyds Bank, typed in his office and signed by him. It read as follows:

LLOYDS BANK LIMITED
HEAD OFFICE
LONDON, E.C.3

14th April, 1943

Private
Major W. Martin, R.M.,
Army and Navy Club
Pall Mall,
London, S.W.1
DEAR SIR,

I am given to understand that in spite of repeated application your overdraft amounting to £79. 19s. 2d. still out-
stands.

In the circumstances, I am now writing to inform you
that unless this amount, plus interest at 4% to date of payment, is received forthwith we shall have no alternative but
to take the necessary steps to protect our interests.

Yours faithfully,
[Signed] E. WHITLEY JONES
Joint General Manager

It had been arranged that this letter from the bank
should be sent through the post to Major Martin at the
Naval and Military Club, but it was erroneously posted
addressed to him at the Army and Navy Club, Pall Mall;
there the hall porter marked the envelope "Not known at
this address" and added "Try Naval and Military Club, 94
Piccadilly." This seemed to us to be a most convincing
indication that the letter was real and not specially prepared, so we decided that Major Martin should keep this
letter in its envelope.

One of us had got the cooperation of the Naval and
Military Club; we had been given a bill dated the 24th
April which showed that Major Martin had been a temporary member of that club and had stayed there for the
nights of the 18th to 23rd April inclusive; apart from its
other purpose of general build-up of the Major's personality, it afforded a strong indication that he was still in London on the 24th.

Similarly, there was but little difficulty in getting the bill
for the engagement ring. I chose S. J. Phillips, the Bond
Street jewelers, as I knew that they had an international
trade, so that it was probable that there would be bill-heads

of theirs available in Germany to prove, if comparison were to be made, how genuine Major Martin's bill was. That bill was dated the 19th April, but showed that the ring had actually been bought on the 15th.

We were in some difficulty in getting these and the other documents. Obviously, the true story of why we wanted them could not be told, but I was convinced that just to ask for them and to give no reason, except that it was for something secret, was liable to cause talk; on the other hand, once a plausible reason was given we felt sure that we could rely on those whom we approached.

So my "cover story" was that there was someone who seemed suspiciously interested in officers who were temporarily hard up: we wanted to have some documents, building up toward a shortage of money, which a particular person could leave about his rooms where they would be seen by this individual. We could then observe what his conduct was. This seemed to be a satisfying story, and we received ready help—and no one ever let us down with the slightest leak.

What might be called the supporting cast among the documents having been provided for, we now had to obtain the "stars."

First of all we needed a suitable snapshot of Pam, Major Martin's fiancée. The scheme which we devised was to ask the more attractive girls in our various offices to lend us a snapshot of themselves for use in a photographic identity parade—the sort of thing where the photographs of one or two suspects are shuffled in among those of a number of perfectly innocent persons and the "witness" is asked to pick out the one of the person whom he had seen; we asked for a variegated lot, and got quite a collection. We eventually chose a charming photograph and returned the remainder. The subject of the photograph was working in the War Office and, as she had access to "Top Secret" papers, we were able to tell her that we wanted to use the photograph as that of someone's fictitious fiancée in a deception, and she gave her permission.

None of us had felt up to writing the love letters—after all, ours was not the feminine point of view—and it was a bit difficult to ask a girl whether she could write a first-rate paean of love. So we asked a girl working in one of the offices whether she could get some girl to do it. She took on the job, but never would tell us the name of the girl who produced the two magnificent letters that Major Martin was to carry with him.

I had decided that the first of these should be written on my brother-in-law's notepaper, for I was sure that no German could resist the "Englishness" of such an address as "The Manor House, Ogbourne St. George, Marlborough, Wiltshire"; this letter, dated "Sunday 18th" ran as follows:

THE MANOR HOUSE
OGBOURNE ST. GEORGE,
MARLBOROUGH, WILTSHIRE.
Telephone: Ogbourne St. George 242.
Sunday, 18th.

I do think dearest that seeing people like you off at railway stations is one of the poorer forms of sport. A train going out can leave a howling great gap in ones life & one has to try madly—& quite in vain—to fill it with all the things one used to enjoy a whole five weeks ago. That lovely golden day we spent together—oh! I know it has been said before, but if *only* time could sometimes stand still just for a *minute*—But that line of thought is too pointless. Pull your socks up Pam & dont be a silly little fool.

Your letter made me feel slightly better—but I shall get horribly conceited if you go on saying things like that about me—they're utterly unlike me, as I'm afraid you'll soon find out. Here I am for the weekend in this divine place with Mummy & Jane being too sweet & understanding the whole time, bored beyond words & panting for Monday so that I can get back to the old grindstone again. What an idiotic waste!

Bill darling, do let me know as soon as you get fixed & can make some more plans, & dont *please* let them send you off into the blue the horrible way they do nowadays—now that we've found each other out of the whole world, I dont think I could bear it—

All my love,

PAM

It was followed by two sheets of plain paper, such as was used in government offices for carbon copies; the letter was headed "Office, Wednesday, 21st," and the writing, which started reasonably good, suddenly degenerated into a

scrawl as the letter was hastily brought to an end when the
writer's boss was heard returning. It ran:

OFFICE
Wednesday, 21st

The Bloodhound has left his kennel for half an hour so
here I am scribbling nonsense to you again. Your letter
came this morning just as I was dashing out—madly late
as usual! You do write such heavenly ones. But what are
these horrible dark hints you're throwing out about being
sent off somewhere—*of course* I won't say a word to
anyone—I never do when you tell me things, but it's not
abroad is it? Because I won't have it, I *won't*, tell them so
from me. Darling, why did we go and meet in the middle
of a war, such a silly thing for anybody to do—if it weren't
for the war we might have been nearly married by now,
going round together choosing curtains etc. And I wouldn't
be sitting in a dreary Government office typing idiotic minutes all day long—I *know* the futile sort of work I do
doesn't make the war one minute shorter—

Dearest Bill, I'm so thrilled with my ring—scandalously
extravagant—you know how I adore diamonds—I simply
can't stop looking at it.

I'm going to a rather dreary dance tonight with Jock &
Hazel, I think they've got some other man coming. You
know what their friends always turn out to be like, he'll
have the sweetest little Adam's apple & the shiniest bald
head! How beastly & ungrateful of me, but it isn't really
that—you know—don't you?

Look darling, I've got next Sunday & Monday off for
Easter. I shall go home for it of course, *do* come too if you
possibly can, or even if you can't get away from London
I'll dash up and we'll have an evening of gaiety—(By the
way Aunt Marian said to bring you to dinner next time I
was up, but I think that might wait?)

Here comes the Bloodhound, masses of love & a kiss

from

PAM

We felt that we had been well served, and that the letters
were ideal for our purpose.

We took some precautions before we gave the letters to
Major Martin. The letters, other than the love letters, I
carried in my pockets for the appropriate number of days
to get them into the right condition. But the love letters

were more of a problem, especially as one of them was on
flimsy paper. It was obvious that they would have been
read and reread and would not be in mint condition, but
the proper appearance could not be produced quickly by
scrumpling them up and then smoothing them out again (as
someone foolishly suggested would be the suitable method);
once a piece of paper has been scrumpled no amount of
flattening will erase the act that it has been treated that way
—and the one thing that Bill Martin would never have done
to those letters was to crush them up. So I did what he
would have done; I folded and unfolded the letters again
and again, and in addition I rubbed them carefully on my
clothing to get a little patina onto them.

On the 3rd of May we received a signal from the naval
attaché in Madrid. . . . The body of Major Martin, Royal
Marines, had been picked up off shore (near Huelva) on
the 30th April 1943.

3

Overlord Goes Underground

Editors of the Army Times

Almost every one of the great Allied seaborne invasions of Europe during World War II was preceded by operations which attempted to deceive the enemy as to the place and time of the landings. The deception for "Overlord"—the massive invasion of Normandy—consisted not of any one operation, but of a whole roster of deception maneuvers.

IN MAY, 1944, a distinguished British visitor arrived at Gibraltar in the Prime Minister's private airplane. The beak nose, piercing eyes, and straight posture of the visitor revealed at once to the guard of honor at the small airfield that he was none other than Field Marshal Bernard Law Montgomery. He was, it appeared, swooping in for a fast inspection or even to lead an invasion through France, or possibly, Spain. He returned salutes briskly before being whisked off in an olive-green command car. Enroute to the Governor's house, The Convent, the military leader poked his head out of the vehicle's window to acknowledge the cheers of the garrison:

FROM the book *The Tangled Web.*

"Good old Monty!"

At The Convent, the Field Marshal alighted to more salutes and subdued ovations before vanishing within its heavily guarded portals. Fully aware of the august presence was a Spanish resident of "The Rock," known to British intelligence as a double agent. As had been anticipated when he was tipped off on Montgomery's arrival, the spy lost no time in advising his German employer that the great Field Marshal had come to England's Mediterranean bastion.

There was no question at all, concluded the General Staff in Berlin, that seven German divisions must continue to be held in the South of France, even though Marshal Erwin Rommel, somewhere on the Channel coast of France, was demanding reinforcements. Perhaps "Monty" was merely vacationing at Gibraltar, but, more likely, he was not.

General Gerd von Rundstedt, Commander-in-Chief on the Western front, was one of the few who suspected Monty's visit was a trick. But he never dreamed in his wildest fancies of the possibility that the visitor to The Convent was not Montgomery at all!

The gentleman in field marshal's uniform was a "double," Captain Meyrich Edward James, of the Royal Army Pay corps. He had in fact been "discovered" while impersonating Monty in a service theatrical performance in Leicester.

This visit to Gibraltar was the climax of other ruses to which James had been party. At one point, he could have been located at the Duke of York's School on Swingate Down, not far from Dover. Since this city was a favorite haunt of spies, there could be little doubt that Berlin was kept apprised of almost everything "Monty" did, including sneezing and setting down his swagger stick.

This Gilbert and Sullivan touch, tagged "Operation Fortitude," was one of the plans designed to cloak "Overlord," the impending invasion of the European continent. Actually, it was only one tiny facet of a master plan of deception which was conceived and carried out to a degree that gives it the right to be called the greatest hoax in history. Never before had such effort on such a scale been counted upon to play as important a part in a military operation. And its success was far beyond the most optimistic expectations.

Indeed, many who had access to its secrets suspected afterward that some mysterious, powerful influence caused the German High Command to accept sources of false information as absolutely authoritative. If such a source or sources existed, their secret was never revealed and probably never will be. However, what we do know of the intricate structure of operation, the functioning and effect of its multifarious parts, is intriguing enough.

Early in the year, a high German officer, speculating on the time of the invasion, noted in his diary: "We had a rough guide from a notice in the London *Times* which appeared to have escaped the censor. The item stated that the United States would compensate farmers for damage by tank exercises. It was evident the invasion could not take place before mid-April."

Early in April the Nazis began opening dikes in Holland, threatening to flood some five thousand square miles of the coastal area if the Allies attempted a landing there.

That the Allied intelligence chieftains won their desperate gamble was proved by the complete confusion evident in the positioning of German forces. Rommel himself expected the blow to fall at the Pas de Calais, just a few minutes' cross-Channel dash by torpedo boat. Other German divisions were pinned down needlessly in the South of France, in a reinforced Italian theatre, and even at the Bay of Biscay.

An entire Army Group, the "First United States," had been created on paper to drive Nazi counterintelligence officers further out of their minds and impel them to conclusions they never would have drawn under less confusing circumstances. Lieutenant General Lesley J. McNair was one of the "commanders" of this entirely spurious organization.

The real purpose of the "First Army Group," which appeared to be most careless in announcing "Secret" and "Top Secret" plans, was to convince Hitler that the main Allied invasion thrust would be at Calais, just as Rommel had predicted. To buttress this deception, the Canadian Second Infantry Division set up headquarters in Dover, under the wing of the "First Army Group." Its soldiers, flaunting Maple Leaf shoulder patches, drilled in the fields of Kent.

German Intelligence knew the Canadian troops were normally barracked in Sussex and Surrey. Further, these were the hard-bitten "Empire" fighters from which the commandos had been chosen for the bloody Dieppe raid. It looked as though the Canadians were going to hit that part of the Channel coast once more.

Between ten and fifteen *Wehrmacht* divisions were tied down in this potential Pas de Calais beachhead. They waited . . . and waited.

As Churchill rationalized, the enemy had to be made to think the Allies "were landing somewhere else and at a different moment." Such an attempt, he added in understatement, involved "an immense amount of thought and action."

The pre-D-day deception actually consisted of two plans. "Bodyguard" was the code for the strategic deception plan. It was primarily intended to induce the enemy to make faulty strategic dispositions. The second part of the deception, known as "Fortitude," was tactical: to mislead the enemy, when preparations could no longer be entirely concealed, as to the date, strength and area of attack.

"Bodyguard," a British plan, involved action by both Americans and the Russians. It was based on the principle that false deductions may be fostered from true premises, and its substance consisted of an ingenious assembly of likely facts, presented so as to suggest specious conclusions. "Truth," philosophized Churchill, "deserves a bodyguard of lies."

The landing point for the Allied invasion was decided a year before it took place. The decision on where to invade was made after COSSAC (Chief of Staff to the Supreme Allied Commander) had studied the European coasts for six months. The plans were, of course, an elaborately guarded secret. Up to the end of April, 1944, only a few hundred Allied officers knew the time and place of D-day.

There were seven main ways by which the Germans could see and hear for themselves what was happening in Britain prior to invasion:

Luftwaffe reconnaissance.

Plotting of Allied signal traffic by radio.

Questioning of Allied POW's and members of resistance movements in Europe.

Reports from German diplomats and spies in Eire and other neutral countries.

"Leaks" and careless talk by neutral diplomats in London.

German agents operating in Britain.

Reconnaissance landings by German commandos on British shores.

The Allies were not overly concerned about German agents in Britain or even about commando landings, since the German spy network in Britain had already been smashed. Attempts to land agents by parachute or rubber boats from U-boats had been unsuccessful. *Luftwaffe* reconnaissance was no problem at all.

In fact, one of Goering's snooper planes was unwittingly doing yeoman service for Allied intelligence. Observed frequently over the Kent and lower Thames area, it was obviously photographing much of the deception: the Canadian troops, the spurious "First Army Corps," and hundreds of useless small landing craft (not seaworthy enough even to cross the Channel) packed within the Thames estuary, the Downs anchorage, and southeast coast ports.

Orders were given to shoot at the prying aircraft, but always to miss, and thus encourage a return visit. The German pilot returned day after day to take his misleading photographs.

Wireless became a key part of the hoax. The Germans placed great weight on monitoring Allied radio traffic in Britain in order to determine the strength and location of troops. Allied planners thus decided to make wireless deception the main means of concealing their strategy. The idea originated with British Army Colonel John Bevan, at the War Office. He advocated carefully executed wireless operations by special signal units simulating radio traffic from ground forces preparing for amphibious invasion. This involved the representation on the air of nonexistent divisions and higher commands.

The wireless operations described the formation of the First U.S. Army Group in East Anglia, composed of real and fictitious forces, as a threat to the Pas de Calais. The

Army Group was represented as consisting of the fictitious 14th U.S. Army and the real Fourth British Army in a fictitious location.

In another deceptive use of radio, signals were conveyed from the Portsmouth area by landline to Kent and transmitted from there to conceal the fact that Montgomery's real headquarters were near Portsmouth.

By radio subterfuge, the idea was also implanted that the two follow-up armies, the First Canadian and Third American, were in fact an assault force which would land in the Pas de Calais. To unnerve the Germans further, they were allowed to learn that this Army Group was commanded by General George S. Patton, "an ideal Bogey."

Further radio deception was the work of Double Agent ND98, who worked for the Germans and the Americans. He sent false radio messages to the Germans to the effect that the invasion had been delayed by "a breakdown in the production of invasion barges," and that troops were therefore embarking at English Channel ports for rerouting to the Mediterranean, where they would strike at "the soft underbelly of Europe." *Luftwaffe* reconnaissance confirmed that many troops were indeed boarding vessels, from Southampton to Plymouth. It was anybody's guess whether they were bound across the Channel or for the Mediterranean.

The French Resistance also received false instructions by radio concerning sabotage of the Pas de Calais communications, furthering still more the German belief that this area was to be the invasion target.

One of the most complex uses of radio evolved from the Allied discovery that it was possible, by careful analysis, to build a picture of the directives behind the German radio broadcasts, and thus gain reasonably accurate appraisals of enemy tactical and strategic plans. It was believed that the Germans employed the same analytic methods for Allied broadcasts, so the Allied psychological warfare experts devised broadcasts which would lead the enemy to erroneous deductions.

As the invasion date drew nearer, "Fortitude" was intensified. Off Dungeness, near Dover, small sections of "Mulberry" were temporarily sunk or half-sunk in the shallows.

"Mulberry" was the collection of old barges and surplus freighters used as a breakwater off the open Normandy coast.

This feint, carried out across the Channel from Boulogne, was another "clear sign" that the Allies were to strike from this direction. Seeming to confirm it were dummy landing craft and dummy tanks, most of them inflated rubber. Deflated, a "tank" could be carried along by two men without strain.

There were also rubber trucks, gun tractors, amphibious light landing craft, and larger troop-carrying landing craft. With a few men, several truckloads of equipment, and lots of hot air, the Allies managed to create the illusion of a vast armored force and its transport massed at a beachhead. The whole stage setting was, in fact, so convincing that many American and British cameramen were fooled again.

A party of engineers would drive up to a peaceful wood in southeast England and within a few hours would have built a track connecting the wood with a nearby road. Trucks would leave marks on the trail and mud on the road. Barriers would be erected and MP's placed on duty.

There was nothing but another magnificent hoax to be concealed, but from the air the wood appeared to be the hiding-place of armed men, massed for a major sortie. Gossips in nearby villages unwittingly augmented the illusion.

Unusual activity also sprang up on the cliffs between Folkestone and Dover, between Hythe and Dymchurch, and near Dungeness. The *Luftwaffe* reported seeing pumping stations. For what? Why, for gasoline to be pumped under the sea to invasion beaches in the Pas de Calais.

The Germans were able to see all of these things because the RAF allowed them to. The dummy gliders on coastal airfields were observed by the Germans, but they never saw the real gliders on Wiltshire and Oxfordshire airfields. The *Luftwaffe* could take pictures of dummy landing craft in the Thames estuary, but not of the real ships lying at anchor in the Fal River and in the Bristol Channel.

Reconnaissance aircraft could not easily penetrate to the west coast of Scotland, where heavy naval craft were massing, or as far as the invasion centers of Portsmouth and Southampton, which were heavily guarded by antiaircraft and the RAF. The entire SHAEF operation, as well as "Fortitude" masterminds, moved out of the cosmopolitan atmosphere of Bushey Park, London, to the quiet sylvan tract near Portsmouth.

There also had to be false airfields to engage the interest of the *Luftwaffe*. At night, dummy flare paths were set up in country fields, inhabited by nothing more ferocious than sheep and goats. Sound tracks blared forth the noise of hundreds of heavy motors warming up—just to serenade enemy agents who might be registered in a local Swan or Boar's Head Inn.

As a companion motif to this singular symphony, balloons or light aircraft drifted low over Nazi outposts with recorders and amplifiers that made sounds suggesting the approach of strong raiding forces. Boxes with special electrical apparatus were floated across the Channel to simulate formidable fleets upon the enemy radar screens.

British operatives in Switzerland, Spain, Portugal, and Sweden began inquiring in bookshops for copies of Michelin Map No. 51, which had delineated for prewar tourists the roads and attractions of the Pas de Calais.

It was later established that a German informant in Lausanne was making careful note of this unusual geographical interest.

Major General William J. ("Wild Bill") Donovan's OSS was naturally called upon for many contributions to the pre-invasion deception. One feint involved a suspected German female agent in London, two or more Dutch Resistance fighters, and several American operatives, working together to make Hitler think that plans were afoot to fight ashore in Holland.

Considerable fanfare attended the making of documentary Dutch films in London, the hiring of Dutch-speaking wireless operators and buying of postcards and photographs showing Netherlands scenes much as was being done with respect to the Calais region. Unfortunately, it was necessary to the success of the scheme that even the brave Dutch underground be made to believe that the landing was contemplated upon the flat coast of the Nether-

lands. It was feared that at least one such member of the
Resistance who parachuted back into his native land was
captured by the Nazis, tortured, and shot.

To keep the conquerors of France jumpy and generally
off-balance, Eisenhower broadcast orders to underground
forces at regular intervals, commencing in late May. He
asked that Resistance members observe their conquerors
closely in order to provide information on the appearance
and duties of every German in occupied areas.

An auxiliary project of "Fortitude," known as "Operation Columba," had been initiated with much the same
goals in mind. It grew out of the determination of British
pigeon fanciers to contribute toward Allied victory. A
group of them volunteered the services of their homing
pigeons to American intelligence in London, claiming that
the birds, which were trained to return to their owners'
lofts, could be used to fly information back from Europe.
Uncertain of the usefulness of the scheme, but unwilling to
hurt the feelings of the patriotic pigeon breeders, the Americans adopted a plan to use them, and dubbed it "Columba"
(which designates a genus of pigeon).

It was decided to drop the birds by parachute into
northwest France, Belgium, and Holland, a region which
contained many pigeon fanciers. The birds were crated in
pairs with a letter saying that, if released, they would return to England and might be used to send information to
the Allies.

Hundreds of birds were parachuted into Europe. Only
five or six returned with messages, and the information
they contained was of no value to Allied intelligence.
"Operation Columba" was ruled a failure. But was it
really?

The Germans had picked up a few crates of the parachuted birds, and plotting the points of impact, found that
the drops were all north of the Somme River and the
Amiens-Abbeville line. They regarded this as further evidence that the Allies would cross the Channel near Calais.

Many of the tricks played on Himmler by Canaris' men
played (perhaps deliberately) into Allied hands. At one
point, they put on the war map thirty nonexistent American and British divisions, in a desperate plan aimed at

discrediting Himmler with Hitler and the High Command. In turn, it was hoped this would hasten the war's end.

The thirty nonexistent divisions remained in the German mind until the autumn of 1944 and aided "Fortitude" enormously, although Allied intelligence did not know about it at that time. This was confirmed after the war by General Freiherr Geyr von Schweppenburg, commander of Panzer Group West at the start of 1944. He was responsible for the disposition of the armored division to meet the invasion, but could never get from his Army intelligence a clear picture of the Anglo-American Order of Battle or any reliable information on the positions of the armored divisions massing for attack.

As the climactic hour neared, British intelligence experts cranked up the deception machine full speed. They flooded their German counterparts with such a deluge of false, true, half-true, and unfalteringly conflicting information that it would have taken the enemy an eternity just to sift it all out.

Special copies of books were printed, containing matter which should have been eliminated by the censors. Magazines and technical journals were issued with articles describing scores of new and projected developments in the Allied war machine. Other articles discussed in detail invasion training plans and equipment. Still others had experts debating where and when the invasion would take place.

Hundreds of highly technical diagrams and charts, and hundreds of "authentic" pictures showing military activities were released. Letters began to arrive in Eire from Irish citizens in the United Kingdom with amazing amounts of information which apparently rang true to German agents. Here and there in the letters, passages were blacked out just to show that the censors were on the job.

Travel bans were eased and Irish workers arrived in Eire with more information which German agents picked up. It is doubtful whether any secret operatives had as harrowing experiences as the Germans in Dublin, who had to sort out the mountain of facts they received and send it on to Berlin by means of miniature transmitting sets. Yet, in all this wordage, Britain's real secrets—"Mulberry," "Pluto," etc.—were never revealed.

Until the middle of April—with Rommel in command of Army Group B, under von Rundstedt—the buildup of German forces in the Pas de Calais and north of the Seine continued while Normandy remained static. About April 20, the RAF reported that photo reconnaissance showed the Germans were at last building anti-invasion obstacles behind the Normandy beaches.

There was consternation among the Allied planners until they found that the Germans were also erecting similar obstacles in Brittany and the Pas de Calais. Then came a large movement of troops and equipment into Normandy during the end of April and the beginning of May.

It seemed at first that "Operation Fortitude" had not worked. But this was not the case. Hitler's own intuition was correct, but Rommel still thought the blow would fall between Le Havre and Dunkerque. Certain the landings would come in Normandy and the Cherbourg Peninsula, Hitler ordered the strengthening of the forces in the area. Even so, the defenses in the Pas de Calais were not wholly depleted.

"The ports are bristling—crammed to bursting point—with all the invasions equipment which will have to be ferried to the continent overnight," wrote Dr. Harald Jansen, a "war reporter" in his May 18 English-language propaganda broadcast over Radio Berlin, commenting on the preparations in England. At least sixty Allied divisions, he believed, were poised in the south of England alone.

Starting on the first of June, Allied aircraft began attacking tactical targets between Calais and Le Havre with increasing force, striking coastal guns and beach defenses. To deceive the Germans about the invasion fleet, the remaining radar stations between Cherbourg and Le Havre were jammed. A total of 105 RAF planes and 34 Royal Navy small vessels were used for the three pre-invasion feints: Operation "Glimmer" directed at Boulogne, "Taxable" at Cap d'Antifer, and "Big Drum" at Pointe Barfleur. Soon after dark on June 8, eighteen ships steamed toward Cap d'Antifer, north of Le Havre, towing barrage balloons which would produce "big ship echoes" on enemy radar receivers, of which the enemy possessed many—in 100 posts between Brest and Borkum on the North Sea.

Above this "fleet" a squadron of heavy bombers flew

round and round, dropping bundles of "window," strips of metallized paper which inspired false readings on the German radar. The planes swooped in a continuous orbit, moving gradually nearer the French coast to give the impression of a large convoy sailing across the Channel.

A similar deception was effected by ships and planes off Boulogne, while other bombers patrolling the Channel represented themselves as precursors of an airborne invasion. Dummy paratroops were also dropped in three main areas to confuse the Germans as to the destination of Allied airborne forces. The diversions were successful and allowed the Allied forces to continue far toward Normandy before the Germans could determine their true position.

Now, "Fortitude" entered a new phase, aimed at making the enemy believe the Normandy landings were a secondary action, masking the main attack against the Pas de Calais. Convoys were routed northward past the battered remains of the German radar screen, and dummy signal traffic built up a picture of intense activity centered on the Allied "Hq" in Dover. RAF attacks on V-1 launching sites were extended to include coastal batteries.

As late as June 20 Rommel was still expecting an attack at the Pas de Calais. Seven days later, the entire peninsula behind Cherbourg was in Allied hands.

For weeks von Rundstedt believed the Normandy invasion was nothing but a feint. The continuing stream of radio messages originating from the spurious "First Army Group," firmly and obviously anchored in England, went far to strengthen this illusion in the Marshal's mind. This allowed the true 12th Army Group to move, undetected, to France in July.

After many weeks of fighting in Normandy, the Germans still hadn't weakened their Pas de Calais defenses, and had even reinforced them with two divisions from the Russian front. In fact, some twenty German divisions were there during the early weeks of the invasion, when the outcome of "Overlord" depended on the Nazis not reinforcing the Normandy battle area.

When the Germans finally realized there would be no invasion on the Pas de Calais, "Fortitude" entered its third phase: the Normandy effort had to be made to appear even larger than it was. Dummy landing beaches already established with rubber tanks and dummy landing craft were expanded in magnitude. Among those engaged in this part of the deception was Major Basil Spence (who was later to be architect of the new Coventry Cathedral).

At the Nuremberg trials, Field Marshal Wilhelm Keitel admitted the complete failure of German military intelligence to discover the "Fortitude" deception.

"The invasion of northern France," he testified, "was expected since the spring of 1944, whenever there was favorable weather. The Normandy landing was reported in time, but only the usual alert was given as it had been many times before—an alarm which in its different degrees had become almost a habit with the German troops in view of the frequent Allied commando raids. . . . The German military intelligence knew nothing about the real state of the Allied preparations. When the Allied transports were nearing the Normandy coast, the highest state of alarm was not ordered; the troops in France only received a stand-by order. . . ."

After the war, in the records of the German Admiralty, the Allies found a dossier containing about 250 reports from agents dealing with the time and place of the invasion. Only one report, from a French colonel in Algiers, was correct, but it had been filed away with the others. Most of the agents had predicted the invasion would come in July at the Pas de Calais.

"My appreciation at that time," wrote John Baker White, an English psychological warfare expert, "was that 'Operation Fortitude' had been an eighty percent success, and I have not changed my mind since. It was the greatest deception operation in the history of war, and there may never be a greater."

4

News Made to Order

Subcommittee of the U.S. Senate

*A special form of deception involves the use of
forgeries and fabrications, the purpose of which is
to convince a gullible sector of the public of the
disreputable intentions of the adversary. The
Soviets, who frequently resort to this kind of deception, have a special name for it—disinformation
—and an entire department of the Soviet intelligence service is concerned with producing items of
disinformation and planting them abroad. The
main target is the U.S. Government, and the main
audience the less-sophisticated people of Asia and
Africa.*

*The main purpose of such forgeries is to mold
public opinion in a manner favorable to the per-
petrator of the fabrication, or to create prejudice
and hostility against its opponents. Obviously, one
of the most convincing types of forgery is one that
purports to be an official document. But it is never*

FROM *Communist Forgeries,* testimony of Richard Helms, Assistant
Director, Central Intelligence Agency, on June 2, 1961, at a Hearing
before the Subcommittee to Investigate the Administration of the
Internal Security Act and Other Internal Security Laws, of the Committee on the Judiciary, United States Senate. Printed by U.S. Government Printing Office, Washington, 1961.

easy to explain how an official document has been obtained, other than by theft. When leftist mobs attacked the U.S. Embassy at Taipei, Formosa, in June, 1957, they succeeded in forcing their way into the building, and even in breaking open files and scattering papers about. It was this event which no doubt gave the Soviets the inspiration for a "disinformation" campaign directed against the U.S. in the period following the riots. "Sensational documents" allegedly found in the files of the U.S. Embassy could now be put before the public. These were forgeries modeled on actual State Department telegrams which had presumably reached Soviet hands after the attack on our Embassy. They therefore looked authentic.

One such campaign sought to undermine relations between the U.S. and the Nationalist Chinese by "exposing" an American scheme to assassinate Chiang Kai-shek and members of his entourage. The vehicle for this was a group of articles which the Soviets planted in an English-language newspaper called Blitz, *which has a wide circulation in Asia. One such article, to which the fabricated telegrams are appended, appears below.*

COUP . . . VERSION 3: MURDER BY ACCIDENT

HONG KONG: Further to the news (BLITZ, September 14, Page 7) that Mr. Karl Rankin, U.S. Ambassador in Formosa, was in a crisis following the loss of highly important States documents by the U.S. Embassy in Taipei during the May riots. BLITZ is now in a position to expose some of his documents of a sensationally conspirational character.

The first of these documents—photocopies of which are published below—are the official U.S. Embassy copies of Telegrams Nos. 508 and 561 which apparently refer to an American plot to liquidate Generalissimo Chiang Kai-shek, President of "Nationalist" China, either by means of a palace coup ("Version No. 1") or by murder camouflaged as an accident ("Version No. 3").

These documents, including secret material from the Cipher Department, were lost during the anti-American disturbances in Taipei on May 24, when infuriated Chinese mobs raided the Embassy premises.

The Associated Press of America, in a dispatch dated June 26, 1957, admitted the fact that during the riots, secret documents had been lost and that the U.S. State Department was conducting a special investigation into the loss.

TELEGRAM SENT

To: SECSTATE   Date: April 4, 1957   No.: 508
      WASHINGTON
Code: OTF   Charged to: Embassy
      508, April 4, 5 P.M.
      MOST IMMEDIATE
      TOP SECRET
      Your telegram No. 1348 of April 2, 1957.

At the present moment it would be rather difficult to carry out version No. 1, which you apparently prefer, owing to the lack of people in Gimmo's entourage whom we could trust completely. There is also no certainty that at the last moment some of the successors will not lose heart and tell Gimmo everything.

The situation is further complicated by the fact that Chiang Ching-kuo continues to retain complete control of the secret service. Preparations for version No. 1 might, therefore, be discovered by his agents. Chiang Ching-kuo's uncompromising character makes it likely that he would take immediate countermeasures and ruin the entire enterprise.

I consider, therefore, version No. 3 preferable, although its details must be more carefully worked out. Its execution will depend on proper timing if all suspicion is to be avoided. In any case I agree that a final decision should be taken as soon as possible.

                                    RANKIN

TELEGRAM SENT

To: SECSTATE   Date: April 9, 1957   No.: 561
      WASHINGTON
Code: OTP   Charged to: Embassy
      561, April 9, 5:30 P.M.
      MOST IMMEDIATE
      TOP SECRET

Latest reports from very reliable sources on the attitude of Gimmo's entourage indicate that the plan outlined in your telegram No. 1348 does not solve the problem.

In my opinion, it is necessary to go further and, besides Gimmo, take similar measures against the persons mentioned in my last report. These members of the old guard might seriously interfere with our plans. Representatives of the special services here fully share this view.

Meanwhile we shall continue to "screen" officers and ensure the appointment of reliable individuals to positions in the Army and the Air Force. This has to some extent been done in the Navy already.

In view of the general opinion prevailing here I have drawn up certain measures to be taken before carrying out the actions authorized in your telegram No. 1348.

RANKIN

VII

Codes and Ciphers:

Secrets to Unravel

IN "COMMUNICATIONS INTELLIGENCE," as it is called, two things are necessary: to get one's hands on the other fellow's coded messages, and then to be able to understand what they say. When a group of conspirators was planning to free Mary Queen of Scots from captivity, they sent messages to her in a beer barrel which her warders had no difficulty intercepting. The messages were in cipher, however, and in order to decode them Sir Francis Walsingham, Queen Elizabeth's espionage and security chief, had to employ an expert, Thomas Phelippes, who, in his day, was both a maker and a breaker of codes and ciphers.

Today, when radio is frequently used for transmitting messages, there is even less difficulty in picking up the messages, since anybody with the proper equipment can listen in on the airwaves. Deciphering them is another matter. Until a short time ago such things as book codes were still in use in some quarters, so that the thrilling business much beloved in spy fiction, of "stealing the code books" was still plausible. In World War I, the fixed code groups mentioned in our excerpt from *The Zimmermann Telegram* also made the decoder's job much easier. Once he had established the meaning of a fixed group of symbols he could recognize it in the future. But this is no longer so.

Today, the art has advanced to a point where codes and ciphers have become more and more unbreakable, and science and technology are used both in the making and breaking of codes.

1

A German Blunder

Barbara W. Tuchman

The incident of the famous Zimmerman telegram is generally considered to have been instrumental in bringing the United States into World War 1. Zimmermann, the German Foreign Secretary early in 1917, sent a message to the German Ambassador in Mexico outlining the German plan for the resumption of unrestricted submarine warfare, which presumably would bring the U.S. into the war, and proposing that Mexico enter the war on Germany's side. Mexico was to be rewarded with the recovery of "her lost territories in Texas, Arizona and New Mexico." The coded text of the message was sent via U.S. Government communications facilities, since President Wilson had offered the use of these to the Germans on the understanding that the German messages would be devoted to the furtherance of the peace feelers, which in 1916 were being put out.

In Room 40 at British Naval Intelligence Headquarters in London, a group of cryptanalytical experts working under the famous Admiral Hall had long been intercepting and deciphering certain

---

FROM the book *The Zimmermann Telegram.*

*German diplomatic and naval traffic, and it was
these experts who deciphered the Zimmerman telegram and quietly passed its inflammatory contents
to the American State Department for President
Wilson's perusal. The following excerpt reconstructs the events in Room 40 on the morning the
Zimmerman message was intercepted.*

THE FIRST MESSAGE of the morning watch plopped out of
the pneumatic tube into the wire basket with no more
premonitory rattle than usual. The duty officer at British
Naval Intelligence twisted open the cartridge and examined
the German wireless intercept it contained without noting
anything of unusual significance. When a glance showed
him that the message was in non-naval code, he sent it in
to the Political Section in the inner room and thought no
more about it. The date was January 17, 1917, past the
halfway mark of a war that had already ground through
thirty months of reckless carnage and no gain.

On duty that morning in the inner room, the most secret
in Whitehall, were two civilians diverted to cryptographic
work masked under the guileless name of Room 40. One
was the Reverend William Montgomery, a tall gray-haired
scholar of forty-six, and the other Nigel de Grey, a young
publisher of thirty-one borrowed from the firm of William
Heinemann. Neither knew they were about to midwife a
historic event. De Grey spread open the intercept, revealing
rows of numerals arranged in four- and five- and a sprin-
kling of three-figure groups. Mute and passive on the paper,
they gave forth no hint that a key to the war's deadlock lay
concealed in their irregular jumble. De Grey noticed only
that the message was of unusual length; more than a thousand groups, he estimated.

The gray morning was cold as Britain's fortunes, dingy
as her hopes in this third winter of the war. The ghastly
losses on the Somme—sixty thousand British casualties in
a single mad day, over a million Allied and enemy losses in
the five-month battle—had been for nothing. The Hinden-
burg Line was still unbreached. The whole war had been
like that, regiments of lives spent like water, half a million
at Verdun alone, without either side's winning a strategic
advantage, but only being riveted together like two fighting

elks who have locked horns. Now the French were drained, the Russians dying, Rumania, a late entry on the Allied side, already ruined and overrun.

The enemy was no better off. Germans were living on a diet of potatoes, conscripting fifteen-year-olds for the army, gumming up the cracks that were beginning to appear in the authority of Kaiserdom with ever harsher measures. The German offer a few weeks before to negotiate a peace had been a mere pretense, designed to be rejected so that the General Staff could wring from the home front and faltering Austria yet more endurance and more sacrifice. Room 40 suspected it must have an ulterior purpose, for there was no evidence so far that the German leaders were any less obstinately fixed on total victory than the Allies.

England had fortitude left, but no money and, what was worse, no ideas. New commanders stumbled forward in the old rut, not questioning whether to assault the Western Front again, but merely where along its wall to bang their heads. No prospect of any end was visible.

Montgomery and de Grey examined the close-packed groups of numerals they were supposed to transform into verbal intelligence, expecting no more than another piece in the prolix correspondence they had been intercepting lately between Berlin and Washington about a negotiated peace. This was President Wilson's cherished goal. Bent on stopping the war, he quested after a compromise peace between mental blinkers, blind to both combatants' utter unwillingness to compromise at all. Berlin kept him talking in order to keep him neutral. The talk exasperated the Allies. It was not meditation they wanted from America but her great, fresh, untapped strength. Nothing else could break the war's deadlock. Arms, money, ships, men—everything the exhausted Allies needed was waiting in America, but Wilson would not budge. He remained unmoved behind his eyeglasses, lecturing both sides how to behave. It seemed there was nothing that would bring in the Americans before Europe exhausted itself beyond recovery.

De Grey's eye caught the top group of numerals in the message, 13042, and recognized it as a variant of 13040, title number of the German diplomatic code. He pointed

it out to Montgomery, who unlocked the safe and took
from it a book which he handled as he might have a bottle
labeled POISON! If there was no visible skull and crossbones
on the book's cover, there was more than one in its history,
for the sea bottom had been scraped and blood and life and
honor spilled to assemble it. It was a copy of the German
code book for Code No. 13040. With it Montgomery took
out another book that contained all that Room 40 had
collected on the variants of the code. Through painstaking
filing and collation of hundreds of intercepts, they had
progressed toward a solution of the variants and so had
built up a partially reconstructed key to use in cases like
the present one.

The decoders tried first for the signature, which might
give them a lead as to the nature of the message. A group
in the 90000 range, 97556, appeared as the last group but
two in the last row. High numbers such as this were usually reserved by the encoders for names or special words of
infrequent use which were added as a supplement after the
body in the code was made up. Working from earlier re-
constructions in the code book, Montgomery and de Grey
concentrated upon 97556. Obediently, as if tapped by a
wand, it transformed itself into a name they knew well,
"Zimmerman," the German Foreign Secretary.

Going back to the beginning, they searched for the ad-
dressee, but instead of a name the first words to emerge
were "Most Secret," and then they made out, "For Your
Excellency's personal information." As the message was
directed to Washington, the Excellency in question must be
the German Ambassador there, Count von Bernstorff.

Routine so far, they were just about to decide, when an
unexpected word appeared—"Mexico." Wondering what
the Germans could be saying about Mexico, they worked
on with added interest, decoding the word "alliance" and
farther on, to their astonishment. "Japan," which was repeated in a phrase that came out as "us and Japan." The
decoders looked at each other with a wild surmise. Was it
possible that Japan, one of the Allied powers, was changing sides? Urgently now they renewed the attack, their
muttering dying away into concentrated silence as their
scribbling speeded up. The code book pages flipped back
and forth with an agitated rustle while sheets of paper filled

up with words tested and discarded, with more words fitted together until, after two hours and in spite of many gaps in the sequence, an intelligible version had come clear.

It fell into two parts, for the intercept contained two separate telegrams. The first and longer one, addressed to Bernstorff, informed him of Germany's intention to resume "unrestricted" submarine warfare on February 1, a decision expected and dreaded by the Allies for many months. "Unrestricted" meant that the U-boats were to be permitted to sink without warning all neutral as well as enemy merchant shipping found in the war zones. Bernstorff was instructed not to deliver the notice to the United States Government until February 1, the very day the torpedoes would be let loose. Preparing for the belligerency that they believed would be America's answer to the U-boat, the Germans had added another telegram. It consisted of 155 code groups and was headed, "Berlin to Washington. W 158. 16 January 1917. Most Secret. For Your Excellency's personal information and to be handed on to the Imperial Minister in Mexico by a safe route."

The message for the Imperial German Minister in Mexico, von Eckhardt, was headed "No. 1" and, in the incomplete version so far decoded, read:

> WE PROPOSE TO BEGIN ON FEBRUARY 1 UNRESTRICTED SUBMARINE WARFARE. IN DOING THIS HOWEVER WE SHALL ENDEAVOR TO KEEP AMERICA NEUTRAL. . . . (?) IF WE SHOULD NOT (? SUCCEED IN DOING SO) WE PROPOSE (? MEXICO) AN ALLIANCE UPON THE FOLLOWING BASIS: (JOINT) CONDUCT OF WAR, (JOINT) CONCLUSION OF PEACE . . . YOUR EXCELLENCY SHOULD FOR THE PRESENT INFORM THE PRESIDENT* SECRETLY (? THAT WE EXPECT) WAR WITH THE U.S.A. (POSSIBLY) . . . (JAPAN) AND AT THE SAME TIME NEGOTIATE BETWEEN US AND JAPAN . . . PLEASE TELL THE PRESIDENT THAT . . . OUR SUBMARINES . . . WILL COMPEL ENGLAND TO PEACE WITHIN A FEW MONTHS. ACKNOWLEDGE RECEIPT. ZIMMERMANN.

The significance of the message the decoders could hardly let themselves believe. Zimmermann had given Room 40 the lever with which to move the United States.

---

* Of Mexico.

Mexico was both America's chief foreign investment area and chief trouble spot, where twice in the last three years American troops had gone in shooting and where, at that moment, twelve thousand men under General Pershing were deeply engaged. The United States was also exceedingly jumpy about Japan. In the circumstances, Zimmermann's spectacular proposal, picked out of the endless whispering in the air, must surely dynamite the Americans out of their neutrality.

In the telegram there was a blank passage of thirty groups from which the decoders had been unable to pry any meaning whatever. They could not guess that it contained the most explosive material of all. Only after weeks of patient, unrelenting effort were they able to reconstruct this portion of the code and discover that the missing passage contained Germany's promise to assist Mexico "to regain by conquest her lost territory in Texas, Arizona, and New Mexico."

Enough was at hand to require immediate action. This was a matter for the DNI, otherwise Admiral Hall, Director of Naval Intelligence. Montgomery hurried out of the room to fetch him. He returned, preceded through the door by a small ruddy man with authority in his step and an admiral's gold stripes on his sleeve. The physical presence of Admiral Sir William Reginald Hall frequently nerved in men an impulse to do something heroic. For once de Grey, as he stood up and silently handed the scribbled sheets to the admiral, felt equal to the moment.

"Zimmermann, eh?" said Admiral Hall while his eyes darted over the pages. As he read, the intermittent eyelid twitch for which he was nicknamed "Blinker Hall" quickened, the compact little figure seemed, if possible, to stiffen, the brilliant blue eyes to blaze almost literally, and the tufts of white hair to bristle around the bald pink head until he looked like a demonic Mr. Punch in uniform.

Hall knew instantly that he held in his hands notice of what was at once a deadly peril and a possible miracle. Only the miracle of America's entrance into the war could outweight the peril of the unrestricted submarine, which, once let loose, might well accomplish what the Germans hoped—cut the Allies off from their source of supplies before the Americans had time to mobilize, train, and

transport an army to help them. That was the stake the
Germans were playing for.

Hall had known for months it would have to come to
this, for the submarine was never designed for the gentlemanly role President Wilson seemed to think proper. To
demand that it rise to the surface to warn before sinking,
making itself a sitting duck in case its prey should shoot
first, made nonsense of its function. He knew the Germans
had accepted Wilsonian restrictions not because of the
moral force of the President's notes tapped out on his
private typewriter, but only because they had not enough
U-boats on hand to force the issue. Since then, he knew
too, Kiel's machine shops had been burning day and night,
forging U-boats as fast as they could toward the goal of the
two hundred Germany needed before letting loose a massive naval Verdun she hoped would bring Britain to her
knees. Today's telegram was the signal that the two hundred must be nearly ready.

"Two weeks," Hall said aloud. In two weeks it would be
February 1, the date staring up at him from Zimmermann's dispatch, when Britian's war effort, already hanging
by its thumbs from Persia to the Channel on a lifeline of
sea-borne supplies, would meet its greatest test. "Compel
England to peace within a few months," Zimmermann's
closing words had boasted. Hall knew it was no idle boast.

His mind racing ahead, Hall tried to think like a German. They had taken a desperate gamble, knowing unrestricted warfare might flush the reluctant dragon in the
White House out of his cave. Obviously they must have
made up their minds that the U-boats could sink ships
faster than the Americans could mobilize, and it was even
possible the Americans might not mobilize at all, in which
case the gamble would pay off. But here in Hall's hands
was a persuader, thoughtfully provided by Herr Zimmermann himself, that should help to make up the American
mind.

Hall understood well enough why Zimmermann had sent
the telegram. In case America should answer the U-boat
threat by declaring war on Germany, he wanted to arrange
enough trouble for her to keep her busy on her own side of
the Atlantic. It was the shrewd, the clever thing to do—and
he had done it, aiming straight for Mexico and Japan, the

two whose long hostility to the United States gave most promise of readiness to jump to the attack. How right and proper! How correct!

Ah, yes, the Germans were clever, thought Hall with an inner smile, but just that fatal inch short of being clever enough to suspect that their enemy might be clever too. Sublimely confident that their code was as nearly perfect as human minds could devise—was it not scientific? was it not German?—they had used it unchanged since the first day of the war, assuming its inviolability. In war, never assume anything, Hall reflected, in the happy knowledge that every German wireless message was being grasped out of the ether and read in Room 40.

2

Keeping a Secret

The Editors of Life

*These unusual documents were released for public
perusal just after World War II. There is nothing
quite like them in the whole history of intelligence.
They bear upon still another facet of communications intelligence: the need to avoid any action that
would reveal to the enemy that his codes and
ciphers have been broken and his messages are
being read. This normally means that commanders,
in taking advantage of the information about
enemy forces which comes their way through intercepted and decoded messages, must always
guard against doing so in a fashion which might
tip off the enemy that there is a leak in his communications. In this case, however, the great advantage which the United States held and continued to hold in being able to read certain
Japanese coded materials was threatened from
quite a different quarter.*

DURING THE 1944 election campaign General George C.
Marshall wrote two letters to Republican candidate
Thomas E. Dewey, telling him that Army cryptographers

FROM *Life* magazine, December 17, 1945.

had broken the Japanese "ultra" code. This fact was first revealed in a story by *Life* editor John Chamberlain which appeared in *Life* September 24. Marshall's purpose, Chamberlain wrote, was to forestall Dewey's revelation of that fact in a possible attack on the Roosevelt administration's Japanese policy before Pearl Harbor. The actual text of the letters remained secret until last week [*early December 1945*] when General Marshall appeared before the congressional committee investigating Pearl Harbor and made the letters public. They appear below.

When he had finished reading the first two paragraphs of the first letter, Governor Dewey stopped because, as the Chamberlain article reported, "the letter might possibly contain material which had already come to him from other sources, and that anyway, a candidate for President was in no position to make blind promises." General Marshall sent the letter back again with an introduction which relieved the governor of binding conditions. This time Dewey read the letter and after much thought and discussion decided not to make use during the campaign of any information he previously had.

First Letter
TOP SECRET
(For Mr. Dewey's Eyes Only)
25 September, 1944

MY DEAR GOVERNOR:

I am writing you without the knowledge of any other person except Admiral King (who concurs) because we are approaching a grave dilemma in the political reactions of Congress regarding Pearl Harbor.

What I have to tell you below is of such a highly secret nature that I feel compelled to ask you either to accept it on the basis of your not communicating its contents to any other person and returning this letter or not reading any further and returning the letter to the bearer.

I should have preferred to talk to you in person but I could not devise a method that would not be subject to press and radio reactions as to why the Chief of Staff of the Army would be seeking an interview with you at this particular moment. Therefore, I have turned to the method of this letter, to be delivered by hand to you by Colonel Carter Clarke, who has charge of the most secret documents of the War and Navy Departments.

In brief, the military dilemma resulting from congressional political battles of the political campaign is this:

The most vital evidence in the Pearl Harbor matter consists of our intercepts of the Japanese diplomatic communications. Over a period of years our cryptograph people analyzed the character of the machine the Japanese are using for encoding their diplomatic messages. Based on this, a corresponding machine was built by us which deciphers their messages.

Therefore, we possessed a wealth of information regarding their moves in the Pacific which in turn was furnished the State Department—rather than, as is popularly supposed, the State Department providing us with the information—but which unfortunately made no reference whatever to intentions toward Hawaii until the last message before December 7, which did not reach our hands until the following day, December 8.

Now the point to the present dilemma is that we have gone ahead with this business of deciphering their codes until we possess other codes, German as well as Japanese, but our main basis of information regarding Hitler's intentions in Europe is obtained from Baron Oshima's messages from Berlin reporting his interviews with Hitler and other officials to the Japanese Government. These are still in the codes involved in the Pearl Harbor events.

To explain further the critical nature of this set-up which would be wiped out almost in an instant if the least suspicion were aroused regarding it, the Battle of the Coral Sea was based on deciphered messages and therefore our few ships were in the right place at the right time. Further, we were able to concentrate on our limited forces to meet their advances on Midway when otherwise we almost certainly would have been some three thousand miles out of place.

We had full information of the strength of their forces in that advance and also of the smaller force directed against the Aleutians which finally landed troops on Attu and Kiska.

Operations in the Pacific are largely guided by the information we obtain of Japanese deployments. We know their strength in various garrisons, the rations and other stores continuing available to them, and what is of vast importance, we check their fleet movements and the movements of their convoys.

The heavy losses reported from time to time which they sustain by reason of our submarine action largely results from the fact that we know the sailing dates and the routes of their convoys and can notify our submarines to lie in wait at the proper point.

The current raids by Admiral Halsey's carrier forces on Japanese shipping in Manila Bay and elsewhere were largely based in timing on the known movements of Japanese convoys, two of which were caught, as anticipated, in his destructive attacks.

You will understand from the foregoing the utter tragic consequences if the present political debates regarding Pearl Harbor disclose to the enemy, German or Jap, any suspicion of the vital sources of information we now possess.

The Roberts' report on Pearl Harbor had to have withdrawn from it all reference to this highly secret matter; therefore in portions it necessarily appeared incomplete. The same reason which dictated that course is even more important today because our sources have been greatly elaborated.

As a further example of the delicacy of the situation, some of Donovan's people [the OSS], without telling us, instituted a secret search of the Japanese Embassy offices in Portugal. As a result the entire military attaché Japanese code all over the world was changed, and though this occurred over a year ago, we have not yet been able to break the new code and have thus lost this invaluable source of information, particularly regarding the European situation.

A recent speech in Congress by Representative Harness would clearly suggest to the Japanese that we have been reading their codes, though Mr. Harness and the American public would probably not draw any such conclusion.

The conduct of General Eisenhower's campaign and of all operations in the Pacific are closely related in conception and timing to the information we secretly obtain through these intercepted codes. They contribute greatly to the victory and tremendously to the saving of American lives, both in the conduct of current operations and in looking toward the early termination of the war.

I am presenting this matter to you, for your secret information, in the hope that you will see your way clear to avoid the tragic results with which we are now threatened in the present political campaign. I might add that the recent action of Congress in requiring Army and Navy investigations for action before certain dates has compelled me to bring back the corps commander, General Gerow, whose troops are fighting at Trier, to testify here while the Germans are counterattacking his forces there. This, however, is a very minor matter compared to the loss of our code information.

Please return this letter by bearer. I will hold it in my secret file subject to your reference should you so desire.

Faithfully yours,
G. C. MARSHALL

Second Letter
TOP SECRET
(For Mr. Dewey's Eyes Only)
27 September, 1944

MY DEAR GOVERNOR:
Colonel Clarke, my messenger to you of yesterday, September 26, has reported the result of his delivery of my letter dated September 25. As I understand him you (A) were unwilling to commit yourself to any agreement regarding "not communicating its contents to any other person" in view of the fact that you felt you already knew certain of the things probably referred to in the letter, as suggested to you by seeing the word "cryptograph," and (B) you could not feel that such a letter as this to a Presidential candidate could have been addressed to you by an officer in my position without the knowledge of the President.

As to (A) above I am quite willing to have you read what comes hereafter with the understanding that you are bound not to communicate to any other person any portions on which you do not now have or later receive factual knowledge from some other source than myself. As to

(B) above you have my word that neither the Secretary of War nor the President has any intimation whatsoever that such a letter has been addressed to you or that the preparation or sending of such a communication was being considered.

I assure you that the only persons who saw or know of the existence of either this letter or my letter to you dated September 25 are Admiral King, seven key officers responsible for security of military communications, and my secretary who typed these letters.

I am trying my best to make plain to you that this letter is being addressed to you solely on my initiative, Admiral King having been consulted only after the letter was drafted, and I am persisting in the matter because the military hazards involved are so serious that I feel some action is necessary to protect the interests of our armed forces.

(The second letter then repeated substantially the text of the first letter except for the first two paragraphs.)

VIII

Scientific Intelligence:

The Technology of Espionage

THE SELECTIONS IN this section touch on different aspects of the marriage of science and intelligence.

The use of modern scientific apparatus in the work of reconnaissance in the form of the U-2 and the satellite-in-the-sky, as well as the equipment for detecting atomic explosions, has revolutionized both espionage and warfare itself. Since in an all-out atomic missile attack the attacker hopes to cripple the enemy before he can retaliate, the vigilance with which the intelligence services keep watch on the opponent's missile readiness is partly responsible for keeping him at bay. Thus, the confirmation by the U-2 reconnaissance planes of the Soviet missile buildup in Cuba before it was in full readiness, and the disclosure to the world of the Soviet intention inherent in this buildup did a great deal to deter the Soviets from their purpose. Since then the U-2 has been joined by the Spy-in-the-sky satellite. The improvements in these high-altitude techniques have taken place rapidly since World War II, which saw the beginnings of modern photo-intelligence and in which photo-interpretation played an important role.

An amusing example of early photo-interpretation recently appeared in the *New York Times Magazine* in an article by Peter T. White (April 3, 1966).

He writes, "In World War II, just before the invasion of

Makin, one of the Gilbert Islands, the enemy garrison was estimated at 4,000—correct, as it turned out, within 40. The photo-interpreter produced the figure by counting latrines, then multiplied by the customary Japanese Army ration of latrines to men."

Although in this age of machines new tools will be, and already have been, invented to facilitate the task of the agent in his search for the facts, there will always remain the need for skilled handling of these tools and experienced interpretation of the product, as with the U-2 and its photography, for example.

1

Eyes from the Sky

Constance Babington-Smith

*One great achievement of the combined British
and American air photo-reconnaissance units of
World War II, about which Constance Babington-
Smith writes in her book, was the discovery by
intruding aircraft of the German experimental
rocket establishment at Peenemünde on the Baltic
Sea, and of the various ramps and other installations along the Atlantic coast which the Germans
were building for the launching of the V-1 and V-2
rockets. At about the same time Peenemünde also
was pinpointed in other intelligence which I had
picked up from various German and Austrian
industrialists.*

*A less publicized and even more painstaking
project of the air reconnaissance units was the hunt
from the air, during the last year of the war, for
the widely dispersed and skillfully concealed workshops that were turning out the components of the
Nazis' new jet fighters.*

ALTHOUGH AFTER THE spring of 1944 most of the Germans'
big aircraft production centers were in such ruins that they

FROM the book *Air Spy*.

were hardly worth attacking, yet the new jet fighters, the ME 262 and the ME 163, were already appearing in combat, to the incredulous dismay of Allied aircrews, and plans had to be made to attack jet production. So once again enemy fighter factories were high on the target priority list, which meant a new and urgent demand for our interpretations.

But this time it was different. This time Speer was in charge of the dispersal program—determined to make aircraft production invulnerable. So in the summer of 1944, when once again I and my team set to work to hunt down dispersed aircraft factories, it was a search far and wide throughout Germany, following up reports and scraps of news to the most unimaginable hiding places: to lunatic asylums and chocolate factories, to vast fantastic underground workshops, to firebreaks in pine forests and tunnels on autobahns. The search had a feeling of unreality about it, for one's usual standards of what was possible or impossible had to go by the board; the only thing was to go ahead and report honestly the strange facts that the camera had recorded.

On our photographs we followed the new dispersal up the valleys of the Bavarian Alps, to little villages in Silesia, to the Baltic coast, and the Polish border. In 1943, the Germans had made a habit of plastering camouflage paint over their dispersal factories, which was a great help to us, because we could then see at a glance which plants were being used for war production. But the Speer regime evidently realized that when you convert buildings from other uses the most effective camouflage is no camouflage at all. As they became more subtle in their methods we had to become more subtle too, and we watched for the most tenuous clues: for the smallest new extensions, for the slightest increase in road and rail traffic, for the special look that comes to a factory when it is busy, just as in everyday life a room looks lived in or a house looks inhabited. At the airfields where assembly was rumored we watched for "track activity," the accumulation of faint lines that tells an interpreter where feet or wheels have been passing over the field again and again—faint pale lines which are actually caused by the reflection of light from the myriad flattened blades of grass. And the fading of that tracery of lines at an airfield, when the grass has resumed its upward growth, means that feet and wheels have been absent. It was like the children's game Grandmother's Steps, where Grandmother tries to look round so unexpectedly that she catches you actually moving. Often we could not say more than "possibly" or "probably," but when we *could* establish definitely that a site was working on jet aircraft it was promptly blotted out by the bombers, like the little Bavarian shoe factory at Wasserburg, where we found some ME 262 wings lying about. That little factory was completely destroyed, but the manager was not killed, and when after VE-Day the Allied ground-check team arrived to inspect and measure the damage, his one question was, "How did you know?"

2

The Case of the Wayward Missile

James McGovern

*The fact that the Nazis tested their rockets in flight
in Poland during the latter part of World War II
(since it would have been too dangerous to do so
in Germany itself) gave the Polish Underground,
which was in touch with British intelligence, a
chance to observe German experiments and, in the
incident described in the following account, to do
more than observe them.*

*The A-4 was the German designation of the
rocket which, on the Allied side, was known as the
V-2. Blizna is a town in Poland. General Dornberger was in charge of the German experiments.
His assistant, Dr. Wernher von Braun, since trans-
planted to the United States, has become famous
as one of the leading American rocket experts.*

IN THAT HOT July of 1944, although the field performance
of the A-4 was improving, many of them were still breaking up in the air about two miles before impact. Dornberger suggested to von Braun that he go to southern Poland and "establish headquarters at the exact bull's-eye of
the target area."

FROM the book *Crossbow and Overcast.*

This solution to pin-pointing the A-4's technical short-comings was not as grim as it sounded. No A-4 had yet come within two miles of striking a planned land target. "It was Dornberger's reasoning," von Braun recalled, "that dead center of the target area would certainly be the safest spot." All this changed, however. One day von Braun was standing in an open field looking at a time indicator atop an observation tower which announced when a rocket fired from Blizna, two hundred miles away, was due to arrive. When the time indicator showed that a rocket was coming into the area, von Braun glanced in the direction from which it was expected and saw a thin contrail streaking across the sky. To his "horror," he saw that it was heading right toward him.

"There was varely time to fall on the ground before I was hurled high in the air by a thunderous explosion, to land unhurt in a nearby ditch," von Braun recalls. "The impact had taken place three hundred yards away and it was a miracle that the exploding warhead did not grind me into powder."

The A-4 was improving in accuracy. But von Braun and his crew of evaluators were not alone in observing the improvement from close range. The Polish Underground was watching too. Ever since the Poles had reported the construction of the Blizna range, they had followed the instructions of British Intelligence to find out all they could about what was going on in the area.

The Poles had reported much that was helpful, especially about the V-1 flying bomb that was also tested at Blizna. But the urgent request to capture a long-range rocket, kidnap a German rocket expert, or even to find rocket fragments that had fallen off course proved to be beyond the resources of the Polish Underground. It lacked weapons and mobility. The able-bodied men who had escaped German prisoner-of-war camps, forced-labor battalions, or death were few in number. And those few were now heavily engaged in *Burza* (Storm), the partisan warfare campaign ordered by the Polish Government-in-Exile in London as the Red Army approached the borders of eastern Poland.

Nevertheless, some Underground units patrolled the line of fire of the rockets in southern Poland and noted the reports of the peasants living there. The Underground was informed of each rocket impact. But it was no match for the German motorized patrols which arrived to collect all the fragments, then drove off, leaving empty craters behind. For months the Poles—lacking the fire and manpower to engage the Germans—watched helplessly as their desperately sought-after prize was driven away.

Then late one afternoon an off-course A-4 hurtled into the sandy bank of the Bug River near the village of Sarnaki in the Warsaw District. Its warhead failed to explode. A German motorized unit was sent speeding toward the Sarnaki area. But this time a Polish patrol happened to be passing through and got there first. The Poles saw that the rocket was intact, but they had neither the means nor the time to make off with it before the Germans arrived. It was the most frustrating moment since the search had begun in January, 1944.

Then one of the Poles had an idea. Twenty Underground men strained at the rocket's side and managed to roll it off the bank into the shallow Bug River. It could still be seen, however, in the clear blue water. In a nearby field, a herd of cows grazed peacefully. The Poles dashed into the herd and drove the cows into the river. Five minutes later the German search party arrived and saw only a herd of cows watering in a river. The cows had churned its clear blue surface into a thick, muddy brown. The Germans drove off in another direction in search of the elusive rocket.

The Poles returned at nightfall with tools, three battered trucks, and a team of Underground engineers. The rocket was hauled out of the water and dismantled by the light of flaming torches veiled by blankets. The unexploded warhead presented a dangerous problem. It appeared to contain about a ton of high-explosive Amatol. But the Poles went to work, knowing that the slightest miscalculation could blow them to bits, and defused it. Just before dawn the three trucks moved off with a precious cargo.

British Intelligence was radioed that the Polish Underground was at last in possession of a German long-range rocket. It was in almost perfect condition. Intelligence replied that it wanted the rocket in England at all costs. How a twelve-ton, forty-six-foot-long rocket could be gotten out of an occupied, embattled Poland to the Royal Aircraft Establishment at Farnborough was a question that baffled the Polish Underground, but London advised that a solution was being worked on.

Intelligence finally came up with a plan that might work, if all the factors involved meshed perfectly. The RAF base at Brindisi, Italy, was only six hundred flight miles from Poland. The RAF had already sent one stripped bomber to an abandoned German airfield in Poland with a cargo of guerrilla weapons and supplies. In a space of ten minutes the bomber had landed, unloaded, and taken off for Brindisi, completely escaping the attentions of the Luftwaffe. This small airfield, with the Polish code name of *Motyl* (Butterfly), was chosen by intelligence as the collection point for the long-range rocket. The pickup, London radioed the Poles, would have to be timed to take no more than twenty minutes. After that, the Germans would certainly realize that something was going on and close in on *Motyl*.

The Poles agreed but wondered what type of bomber could carry a twelve-ton rocket. The complete rocket was not necessary, London replied; only its essential parts were needed, supplemented by accurate technical drawings of the whole object. For three weeks a Polish Underground engineer and aircraft designer, A. Kocjan, drew the blueprints while other engineers selected and boxed what they considered essential parts.

On the morning of July 25, 1944, British Intelligence radioed the Poles that the pickup would be that night. In a heavy rain the Poles brought the boxes close to *Motyl*, and four hundred Underground fighters armed with old rifles and carbines staked out positions in the woods surrounding the airfield. They knew that a Luftwaffe ground detachment, four hundred strong, was stationed a mile distant and that a German cavalry squadron was quartered in a village two miles away.

At four-thirty in the quiet afternoon the rain stopped and the waiting Poles were stunned to see a German fighter land on the rutted, soggy surface of what was thought to be an abandoned airstrip. Five minutes later a second German fighter landed as a radio message was received that an RAF Dakota was on its way from Brindisi. The planes sat there until dusk. Then they took off as suddenly as they had come. The Poles decided with relief that they had been on routine training flights.

The dark summer night was fair and quiet. The only sound was the faint rumble of artillery fire from the Russian July offensive to the east. Toward midnight the Poles heard the engines of an approaching plane. They dashed to the boundaries of the airstrip, fired torches to guide the bomber in, and placed an arrow of red lights in the center of the airstrip to indicate wind direction. The Dakota made three passes, then roared in to a perfect landing. Kocjan got aboard with 110 pounds of key rocket parts and the technical drawings. The operation had taken ten minutes. The Dakota's engines, which had been kept running, were gunned for the take-off

But the big bomber did not respond. Its tires had become bogged down in the rain-soaked surface of the airstrip. As the seconds passed, the twenty-minute limit set for the operation became a grim joke. The Dakota, its powerful engines opened to full boost and booming through the quiet night, vibrated helplessly on the ground. After almost an hour had passed since landing, the pilot suggested that the rocket parts be unloaded, hidden again, and the plane burned.

But the Poles persisted. They ran to the neighboring village and returned with shovels and other tools and materials. They dug narrow, gently sloping trenches in front of the Dakota's wheels and filled the trenches with straw and wooden planks. An hour and a half after it had landed, the Dakota moved forward, gained speed, and lumbered off the ground to clear the trees and roar off into the sky. "We of the Underground," one eyewitness later recalled, "melt into the darkness of the woods." Another eyewitness has commented, "The Germans close at hand, almost within hailing distance, were either too tired by their strenuous marches to care for what went on around them or did not want to risk their skins in an armed encounter with the Home Army. . . . They gave no sign of life during the whole operation, by which a military secret of the first importance was transferred to their enemies under their very noses."

The Dakota was not attacked by the Luftwaffe as it

returned to Brindisi, from where Kocjan, his blueprints and rocket parts were flown to England. As the only technician on the Allied side who had ever seen and studied an almost intact German long-range rocket, he was interrogated round the clock for a week at the Royal Aircraft Establishment at Farnborough. Then he was told that he could remain in England, but he insisted upon returning to his homeland; there was still work to be done in Poland.

"The gallant man, Mr. A. Kocjan," Winston Churchill wrote, "returned to Poland, and was later caught by the Gestapo and executed in Warsaw on August 13, 1944."

The information that Kocjan had supplied, however, together with the "Kalmar Specimen," permitted the Allied leaders to know by the end of August, according to Churchill, "exactly what to expect" from Big Ben, the code name now assigned to the long-range rocket by British Intelligence.

3

Spying on the Winds

Lewis L. Strauss

*Entering the nuclear-missle age about 1950, the
United States faced the prospect of having to prepare for the possibility of surprise attack by missiles with nuclear warheads. At that time the danger was still somewhat remote. But the Soviet
Union and then Communist China have since built
up both their nuclear potential and their means to
deliver nuclear weapons. Obviously, preparations
for such an attack could be made in far greater
secrecy than in the days when aggressive war was
preceded by tell-tale activities of mobilization of
great military and naval forces and the concentration of the material and human requirements for
an attack.*

*Intelligence in the age of science has to direct
itself toward the obtaining of vital information on
the nuclear and ballistic progress in other countries, and this has become a prime target for national intelligence. When in the 1950's a reconnaissance vehicle, the U-2, was developed, it was
primarily for the purpose of keeping the West advised of the new Soviet battle order of its guided*

FROM the book *Men and Decisions*.

missiles. How many launching pads had the Soviet Union equipped and where were they placed? Years earlier, those working in the nuclear field and, in particular, Admiral Lewis Strauss, then Chairman of the Atomic Energy Commission, became convinced that we both could and should equip ourselves to monitor any tests of the atom bomb which might be conducted in the atmosphere. How he realized an effective monitoring system is told in his own words in the following quotation, which is the essence of Chapter X of his interesting reminiscences.

IN 1946 THE Soviet delegate to the United Nations let it be known that in peace-loving Communist Russia the facts about atomic energy were "very well understood." But atomic energy was being employed by his country for peaceful purposes only—to change the course of rivers and to remove mountains. This was welcome news to a world bone-weary after six years of the most devastating war in history.

To a surprising degree the world has maintained its wide-eyed and childlike credulity about Soviet pronouncements. It is a state of mind that, astonishingly, survives periods of disillusionment when the actions of the Soviets expose their insincerity and untruthfulness. The phenomenon is unexplained. Not everyone, however, accepted Soviet assurance in 1946 that the development of atomic energy in Russia was solely pacific and humanitarian. The first Atomic Energy Commissioners did not.

The several Commissioners were confirmed by the Senate in April, 1947. At a meeting shortly thereafter we discussed a memorandum I had addressed to my colleagues. The memorandum noted that we had no information as to whether the intelligence arrangements of the Manhattan Engineer District had made provision in the past for continuous monitoring of radioactivity in the atmosphere. "This," it said, "would be perhaps the best means we would have for discovering that a test of an atomic weapon had been made by any other nation. It is to be presumed that any other country going into a large-scale manufacture of atomic weapons would be under the necessity of conducting at least one test to 'prove' the weapon. If there is no such monitoring system in effect, it is incumbent upon us to bring up the desirability of such an immediate step and, in default of action, to initiate it ourselves, at once." There was unanimous agreement, and the Chairman suggested that, having raised the subject, I might like to push it.

At that time there was a general disinclination to engage in any monitoring based upon the feeling that it would be a waste of time, personnel, and money. The experts for the most part believed that the construction of an atomic bomb was simply beyond the immediate competence of Russian science or the capability of existing industrial organization in the Soviet Union. The earliest date any of us had seen estimated for Russian achievement of nuclear weapon capability was five years. Intelligence reports to President Truman varied in estimates of the date when Russian achievement of an atomic weapon could occur, but in general none expected the Soviets to detonate any atomic device before 1952. The majority opinion set the time substantially further in the future, while not a few believed it beyond Soviet capacity in *any* time scale likely to be of much concern to us.

By May of 1947, being satisfied that we had no monitoring program in being, we found it necessary not only to devise adequate technical methods but to fix a responsibility at some point in the operating organization of the Government. Divided responsibility could invite the same circumstances as prevailed at Pearl Harbor. But there were an unusually large number of organizations which seemed to have a special interest in such a monitoring service—the Joint Chiefs of Staff, the Army, the Army Air Force, the Navy, Central Intelligence, the Joint Research and Development Board, the Department of State, and the Atomic Energy Commission. Obviously, all could not operate the project. Operation by committee would guarantee failure. Responsibility had to be firmly fixed.

The next step had been to call on Secretary of the Navy Forrestal. His response when he heard that we had no round-the-clock monitoring to see whether the Russians were testing atomic weapons could be reasonably anticipated. It was, in fact, "Hell! We must be doing it!"

"Well," I answered, "you can be sure it isn't going on in the Navy or you would know it. Why not call Ken Royall and see if the Army or the Army Air Force is?"

Forrestal lifted his phone and called Secretary Royall, who returned the call a few minutes later to say that there was no such project in the War Department and some question as to whether it was necessary. "Jim," I said, "if neither of the Armed Services takes on this responsibility, the Commission will. If we do it, we'll have to buy planes and hire pilots. We'll have to get an appropriation for that. When we ask for the money, that will be the first time Congress will know that monitoring hasn't been going on all this time." Forrestal saw the point immediately. We went together to lunch with Secretary Royall for further discussion.

There was a second meeting on September 15, and on the next day General Dwight D. Eisenhower, as Chief of Staff, placed the authority in the hands of General Carl A. Spaatz and the Air Force. The order called for establishing and operating a system to have as its objective "the determination of the time and place of all large explosions which might occur anywhere in the world and to ascertain, in a manner which would leave no question, whether or not they were of nuclear origin."

Details of the system were closely guarded as a matter of security for nearly ten years—until the scientific conference with the Soviets on the cessation of testing atomic weapons was begun in 1958. In 1947 we had the accumulated experience both from the original test at Alamogordo in 1945 and the two tests on naval structures at Bikini in 1946. There had been recordings at varying distances from the site of these explosions, but the results were inconclusive. It was important that the tests which the Commission was planning to conduct in the vicinity of Eniwetok in the spring of 1948 should be monitored in order that a system for a reliable detection might be perfected.

During the New Year's holiday in 1948, two officers from General Spaatz's command called on me to say that the Air Force found itself short of funds to procure instrumentation for the monitoring program and that about a million dollars would be required to complete it; that certain contracts had to be let at once if the instruments were to be ready in time. Since every day counted and no Commission meeting could be held until the Commissioners returned from the holiday, I volunteered to obligate myself for the amount so that the contracts could be made firm immediately. The Commission met on January 6, and we undertook to supply the shortage from our own appropriation—to my very immense relief.

Our forthcoming test series, with the code name Sandstone, was staged at the Pacific Proving Grounds, which included several atolls in the group known as the Marshall Islands. As it turned out, the series was efficiently monitored and the principle established that an atomic detonation above the surface of the earth and within the atmosphere, under given conditions, could be detected without difficulty.

Even after this event, however, there continued to be an important body of opinion which regarded the operation as unnecessary. As late as June of 1949, a Subcommittee on Atomic Energy of the Joint Research and Development Board of the Department of Defense was reported as expressing the opinion that the amount which the detection program was estimated to cost might be spent more wisely in other fields.

But in that same year, on September 3, not only the cost of the operation but the apprehensions of those responsible for it became chillingly justified. As former President Truman described what had happened:

... one of the planes operating in the long-range detection system collected an air sample that was decidedly radioactive, and the entire detection machinery at once went into high gear. The cloud containing the suspicious matter was tracked by the United States Air Force from the North Pacific to the vicinity of the British Isles, where it was also picked up by the Royal Air Force, and from the first these developments were reported to me by the CIA as rapidly as they became known.

It was hard to convince a number of people who had been skeptical of Soviet success at so early a date that some

mistake had not been made by our monitoring system. The
findings were carefully reviewed, however, and on September 21 it was reported to the President that there was no
room for doubt that an atomic explosion had occurred
somewhere on the Asiatic mainland and at some date
between August 26 and 29. On the morning of September
23, the President gave the news to his cabinet and issued a
statement to the public:

> I believe that the American people, to the fullest extent
> consistent with national security, are entitled to be informed
> of all developments in the atomic energy field.
> We have evidence that within recent weeks an atomic
> explosion occurred in the U.S.S.R.
> Ever since atomic energy was first released by man, the
> eventual development of this new force by other nations
> was to be expected. This probability has always been taken
> into account by us.
> Nearly four years ago I pointed out that scientific opinion
> appears to be practically unanimous that the essential theoretical knowledge upon which the discovery is based is already widely known. There is also substantial agreement
> that foreign research can come abreast of our present theoretical knowledge in time. . . .
> This recent development emphasizes once again, if indeed
> such emphasis were needed, the necessity for that truly
> effective enforceable international control of atomic energy
> which this government and the large majority of the United
> Nations support.

Even after the successful detection of the first Soviet
atomic test (or more properly, as I tried repeatedly to
emphasize, the first Soviet atomic test *we detected*), there
were those who believed that it was not the test of a
weapon at all, that what had probably happened was some
sort of an accident in Russia during an experiment with
this highly sensitive process. These views may have been
responsible for the second paragraph in the President's
statement, in which he referred to an atomic "explosion"
rather than a test of an atomic weapon.

And even after this, there were recommendations to
cancel the research and development program concerned
with long-range detection. "Stop orders" were issued to
cancel contracts for instruments. These orders actually had

to be changed so that our analysis of the debris from the first Soviet test could be completed.

The precedent for the announcement of Russian atomic weapon tests following their detection has been continued. When a sequence of weapons tests in fairly close order was recorded, however, the fact that a series had been detected was announced, although the individual shots were not separately specified.

One of the most dramatic demonstrations of long-range detection was the recording as far away as Washington of the greatly attenuated shock waves originated by the Pacific tests in 1954. The signals initiated by one of these tests were picked up at the National Bureau of Standards, amplified, and the distance between the crest and trough of the waves electronically compressed and recorded. This enabled me to take a recording to the President. The explosion had occurred many thousands of miles away at Bikini, but the unbelievably faint signals had been caught by the most delicate of instruments and were impressively re-created.

It is sobering to speculate on the course of events had there been no monitoring system in operation in 1949. Russian success in that summer would have been unknown to us. In consequence, we would have made no attempt to develop a thermonuclear weapon. It was our positive knowledge of Russian attainment of fission bomb capabilities which generated the recommendation to develop a qualitatively superior weapon—thus to maintain our military superiority. And *that* recommendation nearly failed because of determined opposition to it. The Russian success in developing thermonuclear weapon capability in 1953 would have found the United States hopelessly out-distanced and the Soviet military would have been in possession of weapons vastly more powerful and devastating than those in our stockpile.

The course which events would then have taken can be only conjecture. But to assume that Communism would have used such overwhelming power benignly is belied by history. The effect on the so-called neutral and uncommitted nations almost certainly would have been demoralizing.

Hard decisions would have been before us—to compromise, appease, surrender or fight. The decision in 1947 to undertake the long-range detection of nuclear weapons tests was a fortunate one and far more crucial than we knew.

IX

Evaluation:

Sifting the Evidence

THE WORK OF the best intelligence officers and of the ablest spies may all be in vain if their reports are not properly handled at the receiving end, if they fail to reach the responsible policy makers in time, or if the evaluator, despite the available intelligence, makes a wrong estimate. I have included in this collection instances to illustrate these points. On the two occasions I have cited—Pearl Harbor, 1941, and the Battle of the Bulge, 1944—the particular evaluation of available intelligence had momentous consequences.

The cases of Pearl Harbor and the Battle of the Bulge, while in many respects quite different, have one thing in common: we did not make allowances for the enemy doing something which we regarded as totally unreasonable from his own point of view. We did not estimate that the Japanese warlords, in 1941, with all the alternatives for action in Southeast Asia open to them, would choose a course which proved suicidal in the frontal attack on Pearl Harbor. In the same way, at the Battle of the Bulge we did not impute to the Nazis the determination to carry out a form of attack which, with their limited resources, proved in the long run directly counter to their own best interests. This only shows that our estimators must learn that the opponent will, at times, view the situation very differently than we and, hence, will act in ways which seem to us improvident. This is the hardest estimate to make, and it is against the hard rock of prejudice and preconception that our intelligence processes often founder. Of course, the Cuban Missile crisis of 1962 is another example of this, though here some of our estimators correctly appraised the Soviet intentions.

1

Last-Minute MAGIC

Roberta Wohlstetter

*Pearl Harbor is one of the most startling examples
of a situation in which intelligence was plentiful
and timely, but was either neglected, misunder-
stood, misinterpreted or received just too late by
the responsible policy makers or military commanders. Before one condemns the responsible
leaders receiving the intelligence one must realize
that an oversupply of high-level intelligence pointing in different directions can be almost as be-
wildering to those responsible for political or
military decisions as a lack of intelligence.*

*As the author of the excerpt which follows states
elsewhere: "If our intelligence system and all our
other channels of information failed to produce an
accurate image of Japanese intentions and capabilities, it was not for want of the relevant materials.
Never before have we had so complete an intelligence picture of the enemy. And perhaps never
again will we have such a magnificent collection of
sources at our disposal."*

FROM the book *Pearl Harbor: Warning and Decision.*

To THE LAYMAN, by far the best-known and most fascinating intelligence work done just before Pearl Harbor is the detective activity that resulted from mastery of the Japanese codes and ciphers known as MAGIC. For dramatic suspense the last-minute signals revealed by the officers in charge of this top secret source have no equal. The ability to read these codes gave the United States a remarkable advantage over the enemy—an advantage not likely to be repeated. America's military and government leaders had the privilege of seeing every day the most private communications between the Japanese government and its ambassadors in Washington, Berlin, Rome, Berne, Ankara, and other major Japanese embassies throughout the world. They saw the reports of Japanese military attachés and secret agents in Honolulu, Panama, the Philippines, and the major ports of the Americas. They knew in advance the diplomatic moves that Japan was contemplating and the sorts of information that her agents were collecting on American defense preparedness. Yet even this advantage— alone or in combination with information from other sources, such as British intelligence, aerial reconnaissance, naval radio traffic analysis, radar, and the American Embassy in Japan—was not enough to prevent the United States from being surprised.

There were four main last-minute MAGIC signals. These have become known as the pilot message; the fourteen-part message; the one o'clock, or time-of-delivery, message; and the final code-destruction message.

The first of the four messages, known as the pilot message (Tokyo No. 901), announced that the Japanese government was sending a reply to the American proposal of November 26:

This separate message is a very long one. I will send it in fourteen parts and I imagine you will receive it tomorrow. However, I am not sure. The situation is extremely delicate, and when you receive it I want you to please keep it secret for the time being.
Concerning the time of presenting this memorandum to the United States, I will wire you in a separate message.

However, I want you in the meantime to put it in nicely drafted form and make every preparation to present it to the Americans just as soon as you receive instructions.

This was the reply for which the Japanese ambassadors had been waiting; they had been warned on November 28 that with this reply to the American proposal, "the negotiations will be de facto ruptured." The Japanese obviously regarded their answer and its timing as extremely important, and the length of the message—requiring fourteen parts—was also unprecedented. The pilot message announcing the arrival of the fourteen-part message was intercepted by the Navy at 7:20 A.M. on December 6 and was received by the Army translating unit at noon on that day. SIS and the Navy's Communications Security unit altered all their stations for receipt of the fourteen-part message to come, as well as for a notice regarding the time of presentation.

In spite of this buildup, when the fourteen-part message (Tokyo No. 902) began to come in, it turned out to be a long-winded presentation of Japanese views about their earnest efforts for peace in Asia and the obstructions of the United States and Great Britain. These views had been stated in the same manner many times before. The fourteenth part alone contained some new information. It was the declaration by Japan that she was formally closing negotiations, ending with the following statement:

Thus, the earnest hope of the Japanese Government to adjust Japanese-American relations and to preserve and promote the peace of the Pacific through cooperation with the American Government has finally been lost.

The Japanese Government regrets to have to notify hereby the American Government that in view of the attitude of the American Government it cannot but consider that it is impossible to reach an agreement through further negotiations.

The Navy station on Bainbridge Island (in Puget Sound, opposite Seattle) started intercepting this long message on the morning of December 6; the first thirteen parts came in approximately in order all through that morning, and were forwarded to Washington, D.C., by teletype just before noon and during the early afternoon. Part 14, however, was not intercepted by the Bainbridge Island Navy station until 3 A.M., Washington, D.C., time, on the morning of December 7. [All of these parts were decoded by the Navy and no translation was necessary, since the clear came out in English].

The so-called one o'clock message, Tokyo No. 907, said briefly:

> Will the Ambassador please submit to the United States Government (if possible to the Secretary of State) our reply to the United States at 1:00 P.M. on the 7th, your time.

This message was intercepted at 4:30 A.M., Washington, D.C., time, on December 7 by the Bainbridge Island Navy station and was sent to the Army SIS for translation. The final code-destruction message (Tokyo No. 910) read:

> After deciphering part 14 of my #902, and also #907, #908, and #909, please destroy at once the remaining cipher machine and all machine codes. Dispose in like manner also secret documents.

Tokyo Nos. 908 and 909 were messages to the ambassadors, thanking them for their efforts, and to the commercial attaché and his staff, commending their efforts on behalf of Japan and praying that they continue in good health. Tokyo No. 910 was intercepted by the Navy station at 5 A.M. on December 7, decoded by the Navy, and sent over to the Army for translation.

It might be interesting to recall at this point that on November 28 Tokyo had announced that an unfavorable reply acknowledging the rupture of negotiations would be sent "in a few days," a sort of advance pilot message. Receipt of the later pilot message and receipt of the fourteen-part note were therefore anticipated, and anything except an unfavorable reply was regarded in Washington as extremely unlikely, except perhaps by Kurusu and Nomura. The thirteenth part of the Tokyo reply in fact even used some of the same vocabulary as one of the notices on November 30 to the Japanese Embassy in Berlin on the closing of negotiations. The Berlin notice had referred to "one insulting clause" stipulating that "in case the United States entered the European war at any time the Japanese Empire will not be allowed to give assistance to Germany and Italy." This clause alone, Tokyo claimed, "makes it impossible to find any basis in the American proposal for negotiations."

Since the contents of the note were anticipated, the time of this signal should have been the moment that it started coming over the wires on Saturday morning, not the moment that Marshall and Stark read the fourteenth part, sometime after 9:30 on Sunday morning. On the basis of MAGIC alone, a rupture of negotiations was expected. MAGIC, combined with other signals such as Japanese Fleet and armament movements, should have made that rupture and its date almost certain. If we believe in signals at all, we have to do at least this much anticipating.

For it is extremely unlikely that the unequivocal final signal—in code or in some other form—will be sent, or if sent, that it will be intercepted, or if intercepted, that it will be properly interpreted in time to act on it. The time for action is before that final signal is on the air.

Regarding all these last-minute messages it is less important to determine the exact hour on Saturday or Sunday that the decision makers received them than to determine *the way they handled the evidence available before that time*. If a rupture of negotiations was going to be taken by them as equivalent to a declaration of Japanese intent to go to war with the United States, then the evidence was already in. The only possible exception is the one o'clock delivery message, which we now read as setting the time for attack, even if it did not mention the place. To many top officials the significance of this message was apparent, however, only after the event. And in spite of the prevalent assumption about the criticality of these last-minute signals, they did not function as such before the attack. No one really believed—in the sense of belief implying a course of action—that a diplomatic rupture firmly announced by Japan would mean immediate war initiated directly against the United States. There was absolutely nothing in MAGIC that established such a Japanese intent clearly and firmly. And even if there had been, there would still have been doubt as to whether Pearl Harbor was to be included in the Japanese plan of attack.

We have, of course, to make a systematic distinction between signals of a coming event—first, as seen after the event, and second, as seen before the event. Afterward, when we know the actual physical links between the signals and the event, it seems almost impossible that we could have ignored the now-obvious connection. We forget how matters looked at the time the signal appeared in the midst of thousands of competing indications, the signal itself compatible not only with a single catastrophe, but also with many other possible outcomes.

The puzzle is never complete. The signals that the local commanders later argued were muffled and fraught with uncertainty are the ones they viewed before the event. The signals that seem to stand out and scream of the impending catastrophe are the ones learned about only after the event, when they appear stripped of other possible meanings.

All decisions are made in the face of uncertainty, even those that depend simply on an understanding of natural phenomena. But decisions based on reading the intentions of others, and in particular, the intentions of an enemy, are especially difficult. These intentions are complicated and shifting, and subject to change between the time the intent is signalized and the time of the intended act. Sometimes they are also deliberately obscured, or invented to mislead, as in the case of bluffing.

In spite of these deliberate and accidental ambiguities, however, intelligence can do a great deal to diminish the uncertainty of military decision. MAGIC did have a lot to say, even if it did not tell all. It did not say, "Air raid on Pearl Harbor," but it did support the hypothesis of hostile action by the Japanese in Southeast Asia breaking over the weekend of November 30 or close to that date, involving the British and the Dutch, if not the Americans. It is important to point out that the Pearl Harbor air attack was the only part of the Japanese war plan that took Washington unawares. Washington was surprised that the Japanese chose Pearl Harbor in the first place, and then that they chose an air raid rather than sabotage. The attack on the outlying islands and the Philippines had been entertained as one of many plausible hypotheses by some of our policymakers, beginning on November 26. But no one could be sure. All of the signals were ambiguous. And perhaps one of the important lessons to learn from Pearl Harbor is that intelligence will always have to deal with shifting signals. Its evidence will never be more than partial, and inference from its data will always be hazardous.

2

The Dark December

Hanson W. Baldwin

The intelligence failure on the Allied side that gave the Germans the advantage of surprise in their offensives which opened the famous Battle of the Bulge in December of 1944 was, in large measure, as Hanson Baldwin points out, a failure of reconnaissance. He emphasizes a very special type of reconnaissance, in which patrols venturing close to enemy outposts succeed in capturing prisoners and bringing them back for interrogation.

A much larger issue, however, overshadows this whole disaster, and that is the rightness or wrongness of estimates of enemy intentions, which are also a responsibility of intelligence. We are likely to exclude the possibility that the enemy will do something foolish, that is, something that we would regard as foolish, even when the available intelligence seems to point in that direction. One of the many broader reasons, no doubt, for our intelligence failure just before Pearl Harbor was our conviction that the Japanese would not needlessly antagonize and draw into the conflict the potential power of the United States when there were so

FROM the book *Battles Lost and Won*.

many other targets they could pick off without
endangering their long-range position. In the case
of the Bulge, it was unthinkable that Hitler would
throw away in an offensive gamble the troops he
should have saved for the defense of Germany
proper. Yet this was precisely what he did.

THE BATTLE OF the Bulge is a case history in the "Dos" and
"Don'ts" of intelligence. It provides, in the annals of war, a
remarkable example of deception and surprise, and the
results that can be achieved, even against a more powerful
enemy, by masking intentions.

"The American Army," an Australian critic has written,
"tends to concentrate upon the development of its own
strength and, unlike the British Army, does not normally
seek victory by playing upon its opponent's weaknesses."

"A shocking deficiency that impeded all constructive
planning existed in the field of intelligence [at the war's
start]," Dwight D. Eisenhower wrote after the war. "The
stepchild position of G–2 in our General Staff system was
emphasized in many ways."

The Battle of the Bulge portrayed these weaknesses in
bold relief.

The German armies, with their extreme secrecy and
their carefully prepared security and deception plans, indeed made the task of the combat G–2 (intelligence officer) difficult.

The organization of the Fifth Panzer Army was masked
by keeping many of its divisions engaged in active operations at the front until mid-November. Corps and army
boundaries were shifted gradually and imperceptibly. Units
brought from the East or elsewhere, or newly organized,
were concealed under new names. Radio deception for
some units was practiced extensively, and the Sixth Panzer
Army, the key unit upon which the success of the offensive
depended, observed complete radio silence for at least three
weeks prior to the start of the operation.

Small elements of divisions were left in line to permit
continued identification by the Allies, long after the bulk of
the divisions had been removed (2nd Panzer Division and
12th SS Panzer Division were among the units that used
this deception). Infantry divisions earmarked for the as-

sault did not move into assembly areas until a few days before the attack; during the moves to the assembly area—all at night—unit emblems and vehicular markings were covered and light bulbs in vehicles were removed. Along much of the U.S. First Army front, including the quiet VIII Corps sector, extensive use was made of deception sound trucks. The sound of tracked vehicles was simulated by loudspeaker each night for a month prior to the offensive, so that when the actual concentrations started a few nights prior to jump-off, the actual noise of tanks and halftracks was like the boy's cry of "Wolf, wolf."

Despite all these precautions, there were signs. The Germans could not possibly keep secret, for instance, the existence of the Sixth Panzer Army, which they had started to form early in the fall. The Allies had long known of its existence, and intelligence reports for weeks before the offensive had emphasized it and had discussed its potential. The risk in the Ardennes was known, faced and discussed, but as Lieutenant Colonel Wilbur E. Showalter has demonstrated in *Military Review*, it was not calculated as carefully as it might have been. The Germans, like the Americans, had used the Ardennes front to "break in" new divisions and to rest weary ones. The Allies knew that the enemy strength in the sector had been "beefed up" from three to more than six divisions prior to the offensive.

Another and more basic failure was the inadequacy of collection; the Allies simply did not get all the facts that were available. There were a variety of reasons for this.

In General Sibert's words:

"We may have put too much reliance on certain technical types of intelligence, such as signal intelligence . . . and . . . we had too little faith in the benefits of aggressive and unremitting patrolling by combat troops. We had no substitute, either, for aerial reconnaissance when the weather was bad; and when we came up to the Siegfried Line, our agents had great difficulty in getting through, particularly in the winter."

Dependence upon MAGIC, or decoded signal intercepts, was major—particularly at higher echelons; when the Germans maintained radio silence, our sources of information were about halved.

Our own failures were not only passive and negative;

they were also positive. U.S. security measures were lax, and our communications procedures and methodical and routinized habits at the front greatly helped the German intelligence officers to estimate (with extreme accuracy) U.S. strengths.

The most outstanding failure was in aggressive patrolling, the textbook weakness that is constantly emphasized in every maneuver and in every recent war in which Americans have engaged. This failure to probe deep into the enemy's lines in order to bring back many prisoners and force him, by reaction, to reveal his intentions was particularly pronounced on the VIII Corps front, where the natural letdown of exhausted troops who had been shifted from bloody carnage to a "quiet sector" was a factor. And at higher headquarters too little attention was paid to the few ground patrol reports available.

The reduced reports of agents behind the enemy's lines due to tighter German security measures also reflected, however, a lack of adequate coordination between the Office of Strategic Services, an outfit for which too many of the combat units had little use, and the Army. There was also a misuse of the intelligence sources available to a field army.

The limited success of air reconnaissance was in part due to the atrocious weather, but the night air effort was also handicapped by a major shortage of adequate aircraft. Moreover, the value of visual reconnaissance, as distinct from aerial photography, could not be measured by the numbers of missions flown or the reports made (many of which were erroneous), for the pilots and observers were largely untrained in identification of ground targets.

Martin M. Philipsborn, then a major and S–2 of Combat Command "B" of the 5th Armored Division, in a "Summary of Intelligence Operations from July '44 to May '45" (May 27, 1945), commented on "the absolute and complete failure of aerial reconnaissance." Increased "tank and vehicular recognition courses for the air force" were indicated.

The ground-air organizational liaison also left something to be desired. The official history comments that "the air force was responsible for the initial screening of the results of its own reconnaissance."

Perhaps the chief fault was one of organization, for there seems to have been a twilight zone between air and ground headquarters in which the responsibility had not been sufficiently pinned down.

There was, finally, a failure in evaluation. For no one predicted accurately the German offensive. Colonel Dickson, G–2 of the army most involved, was closest; his estimates just prior to the attack warned clearly of the danger of a heavy German blow, quite possibly before Christmas. But he was wrong as to place; the German security measures were successful in that they made us believe the attack, when it came, would be toward the Aachen area, north of the Bulge. And he was somewhat inexact as to time; Dickson expected the "counterattack" or "counteroffensive" (as he variously called it) when we had crossed the Roer or controlled its dams. Neither Dickson nor anyone else correctly assessed the power of the enemy drive. Moreover Dickson's definite note of warning was diffused, as were the estimates of all other G–2's, by inclusion of numerous "capabilities." We hedged against all bets.

Correct evaluation might have rectified weaknesses in organization, differences in concept, personality frictions and inadequate collection. But it did not do so. As Colonel Showalter demonstrates:

> Aggressive patrolling increased [on the part of the Germans], high-caliber units were reported in the front line, river-crossing equipment was located in the forward areas, troops were recalled from the rear, and a large build-up, including armored divisions, was reported in what previously had been a quiet sector. In spite of these telltale signs, intelligence estimates were *not* materially revised [Colonel Dickson's particularly and to a certain extent the reports of Colonel Koch were exceptions] . . . intelligence did not measure up to the trust of its commanders.

The failures in evaluation were in one sense, a composite of all the weaknesses previously noticed, plus other factors. There was far too much of a "scratch-my-back-I'll-scratch-yours" attitude among various G–2's. Each echelon was eager to pad out and expand its factual output. Bits of information, often reported speculatively, or evaluated as possibilities, not certainties, by lower echelons, would be picked up by higher G–2's, and would appear and reappear in higher-echelon estimates, often with the qualifying factors omitted, until they came to be accepted as facts instead of possibilities.

Higher-echelon G–2's, privy to a flow of information from MAGIC, British Intelligence, OSS, etc., often incorporated so much in their reports that front-line combat units received a plethora of data, much of it of little use to them. The lower-level G–2 had great difficulty in separating the chaff from the wheat.

The deficiencies of much of this "high-level stuff"—which gave, for instance, the strategic situation on the Russian front, and described the psychology of the Rhinelanders—is best illustrated in the official words of Major Philipsborn:

"While it is perhaps an exaggeration, nevertheless there is a certain amount of truth in the statement that while we knew to a nicety where bridges, fords and brothels were located in towns all around us, we rarely—if ever" knew where the enemy's antitank gun was sited.

Cole sums up the intelligence failure as "general," as one which "cannot be attributed to any person or group of persons." It was "a gross failure by Allied ground and air intelligence."

One of the greatest skills in the practice of the military art is the avoidance of the natural tendency to overrate or underestimate the enemy. . . . The enemy capability for reacting other than to direct Allied pressure had been sadly underestimated. Americans and British had looked in a mirror for the enemy and seen there only the reflection of their own intentions.

Such, then, was the case history of intelligence in the Battle of the Bulge.

History, many say, is simply "Monday morning quarterbacking." But the intelligence lessons of the Battle of the Bulge are still pertinent today, in an era when accurate intelligence may mean the difference between national life or death.

From a review of
Battles Lost and Won
by General S. L. A. Marshall

IMMEDIATELY AFTER WORLD War II ended, I applied for a conference between six of my chiefs of section, and the main figures of the Great General Staff, led by General Walter B. Smith, to enter into all unanswered questions. To my surprise, the request was granted, and the conference at Frankfurt went two full days.

Ultimately, we got to the big question: Why had the Ardennes surprise come about? All present defended Strong. He had warned repeatedly (especially in informal staff conversation) that the enemy could be mounting a main offensive that might hit the U.S. VIII Corps front any day. He marked the build-up of enemy divisions as they came into line and continued to repeat that the massed armor could be within six hours of the Ardennes sector. We asked for the evidence—which, on being produced, was convincing.

I then said: "OK, we're satisfied, but if G–2 is blameless, then G–3 must be seriously at fault."

General Harold E. ("Pinky") Bull, the G–3, spoke up: "Since I was a small boy I have believed that when caught with my pants down, it is best to admit it. Yes, it was my fault. But not wholly. I'll take my proportionate part of

FROM *New York Times Book Review*, October 9, 1966.

blame—if those two fellows sitting there will accept their share. We together advised the Supreme Commander that the enemy would not make a main attack in the Ardennes."

He pointed to Generals Smith and "Jock" Whitely, the Britisher who shared with Bull the operations main desk. They nodded in agreement.

The question was then asked:

"Why did you discount Strong's warnings?"

Bull replied: "Because we reckoned we were dealing with the German General Staff mind. It would not be in character for them to take such a gamble. Here they were, comfortably fitted into winter quarters, in some respects better off than our own forces. It was in their interests to prolong the war, hoping for a more favorable settlement."

So there it was, out in the open. What had been missed was that, following the bomb plot in July of 1944, Hitler's grip on the High Command had tightened like a vise. The decisions were his; the General Staff mind was irrelevant. It is hardly strange that men at SHAPE didn't crank his recklessness into the problem. Many German generals did not realize this was the situation.

X

Action:

The Dagger Beneath the Cloak

IN WARTIME ALL intelligence services tend to play rough. In peacetime they usually do not. One reason is the fear of reprisal. If you hit a man he is likely to hit you back. In peacetime a certain decorum is observed even among hostile intelligence services, despite the lurid imaginations of the fiction writers.

There are exceptions to this. The Soviets may play rough even in peacetime if the object of their vengeance is one of their own nationals, for example, a defecting member of their intelligence service, or a person of Russian origin who is politically dissident and sets up a resistance movement against Soviet Russia, no matter how distant from the homeland. The Soviet Intelligence Service has a special section of experts for the jobs of eliminating or kidnaping their antagonists. This is not the sort of thing that is done in a slipshod way by amateurs. Everything is planned carefully, from the highly developed weapons which leave little or no trace to the planned escape of the murderers, who likewise usually leave little or no trace—except for a corpse or two to discourage anti-Soviet activity on the part of others.

1

The Venlo Incident

Walter Schellenberg

Walter Schellenberg, from whose memoirs this account is taken, was the chief of the Foreign Branch of the Nazi Intelligence Service, an organization distinct from the older-line German military intelligence service, the Abwehr.

The "Venlo incident," which took place in Holland in October and November 1939, as Schellenberg explains, was mounted only because Hitler was convinced that the British intelligence service was behind the assassination attempt made on his life in that month. By kidnaping and interrogating two British intelligence officers the Germans would then, so Hitler thought, be able to find out the truth about the British plan.

Before that, the operational contact between Schellenberg and the British officers was of quite a different nature. It was, in a sense, a combined deception and penetration operation on the German side. The British thought they were in touch with an anti-Hitler underground movement in Germany, but this was only Schellenberg and his minions playing the role. On the German side the

---

FROM the book *The Labyrinth.*

*point was apparently to gain an insight into British
intelligence and, beyond that, to get a reading on
British political intentions at a high level.*

FOR SEVERAL YEARS a German secret agent, F 479, had
been working in the Netherlands. He had originally been a
political refugee and by continuing to pose as one after he
began working for us he was able to make contact with the
British Secret Service. He pretended to have connections
with a strong opposition group within the Wehrmacht,
which greatly interested the British. His influence became
so great that his reports were sent direct to London and
through him we were able to infiltrate a continual stream
of misleading intelligence. He had also built up a network
of informants of his own and had managed to establish
contact with the Deuxième Bureau. After the outbreak of
war, British intelligence showed even greater interest in
establishing contact with this alleged opposition group.
They thought they might be able to exploit the activities
of this officers' conspiracy to bring about the overthrow
of the Hitler regime. At the time I was called in, this
operation had reached a crucial stage; the British had been
promised direct discussions with a high-ranking representative of the opposition group.

After careful study of the case, and long discussions
with those who had been conducting it, I came to the
conclusion that it would be advantageous to continue the
game. I therefore decided to go to Holland myself to meet
the agents of the British Secret Service, adopting for this
purpose the identity of Hauptmann Schaemmel, of the
Transport Department of the OKW. I had found out that
there really was such a Hauptmann in the Transport Department and I saw to it that he was sent on an extensive
journey in the eastern areas.

Having secured approval of my plans, I went to Düsseldorf, where I established residence in a small private house.
These "lodgings" had been equipped, however, for Secret
Service work, having direct telegraphic and telephonic
connections with the central office in Berlin.

Berlin was meanwhile to contact our agent F 479 and

instruct him to arrange a meeting between Hauptmann Schaemmel and the British agents. Unfortunately circumstances made it impossible for me to meet F 479 beforehand and discuss arrangements with him, so I had to leave everything to his skill and ingenuity. There was, of course, a considerable element of risk in this, but that is something which cannot be avoided in Secret Service work.

Further information was sent to me in Düsseldorf by airmail from Berlin and I studied it carefully. I had to master the story completely, memorize every detail of the fictitious conspiracy we had planned and the names and relationships between the various people, as well as all the available information on the British agents whom I was to meet. I had also secured an exact and detailed report on Hauptmann Schaemmel—his background, his way of life, his behavior and appearance—for instance, he always wore a monocle, so I had to wear one too, which was not difficult, as I am shortsighted in my right eye. The more inside knowledge of the group I possessed, the more chance I had of gaining the confidence of the British, for, of course, the smallest mistake would immediately arouse their suspicions.

On October 20 at six o'clock in the evening a message finally came through: "Meeting arranged for October 21 in Zutphen, Holland."

One of our agents was to accompany me. He knew the background of the affair well, for he had been in charge of Agent F 479 at various times. We made a final check of our passports and the registration papers of our car (the German customs and frontier police had been instructed not to ask us unnecessary questions). We had very little baggage and I took special care checking our clothes and laundry for any signs that might betray our identity. Neglect of small details of this kind can cause the best-laid Secret Service plans to fail.

In the evening, I received a call, much to my surprise, from Heydrich. He told me that he had secured full authorization for me to carry on the "negotiations" in whatever manner I thought best. I had complete freedom of movement. Finally he said, "I want you to be very careful. It would be too stupid if something should happen to you.

But in case anything does go wrong, I've alerted all posts along the frontier. I want you to call me immediately you get back."

I was surprised by this show of concern. However, I realized that it was based not so much on human feelings as on purely practical considerations.

Early in the morning on October 21 we drove to the Dutch border. It was a dark and rainy day. My companion drove while I sat beside him lost in thought. I could not suppress a feeling of uneasiness, more especially because I had had no chance to speak to F 479, and as we drew near the frontier this feeling of uncertainty increased.

The formalities at the German border were dispatched quickly and easily. The Dutch, however, were more troublesome, insisting on a thorough inspection, but in the end we were passed through without much difficulty.

When we arrived in Zutphen a large Buick was waiting for us at the appointed meeting place. The man sitting behind the wheel introduced himself as Captain Best, of British Intelligence. After a brief exchange of courtesies, I got in beside him and we drove off, my companion following in my car.

Captain Best, who, incidentally, also wore a monocle, spoke excellent German, and we very soon established friendly relations. Our common interest in music—the Captain apparently was a very good violinist—helped to break the ice. The conversation was so pleasant that after a little while I felt I could almost have forgotten the purpose of my journey. But though I may have appeared outwardly calm, I was inwardly tense as I waited for Captain Best to broach the matter that we were to discuss. But apparently he did not wish to do so until we got to Arnhem, where his colleagues, Major Stevens and Lieutenant Coppens, were to join us. When we arrived there, they got into the car and we drove on. The discussion took place while the Buick rolled through the Dutch countryside.

They accepted me apparently without reservations as the representative of a strong opposition group within the highest spheres of the German Army. I told them that the head of this group was a German general, but that I was not free to divulge his name at this stage of the negotiations. Our aim was the forcible removal of Hitler and the setting up of a new regime. My purpose in these conversations was to explore the attitude of the British Government toward a new government controlled by the German Army and whether they would be willing to enter into a secret agreement with our group which would lead to a peace treaty once we were in power.

The British officers assured me that His Majesty's government was definitely interested in our enterprise and that their government attached the greatest importance to preventing a further extension of the war and to the attainment of peace. They would welcome the removal of Hitler and his regime. Furthermore, they offered us all the aid and support within their power. As far as any political commitments and agreements were concerned, they were not at this point authorized to enter into anything of the kind. However, if it were possible that the leader of our group, or any other German general, could be present at our next meeting, they believed they would be able to present a more binding declaration on the part of His Majesty's Government. They assured me that they were in direct contact at all times with the Foreign Office and with Downing Street.

It was clear that I had definitely gained the confidence of the British officers. We agreed to renew our conversations on October 30 at the central office of British Intelligence in The Hague. I promised them that I would be there to meet them at that time, and after we had had a meal together, we parted on the best of terms. The return journey and the frontier crossings were uneventful.

As soon as I arrived in Düsseldorf, I called Berlin to tell them of my return. They ordered me to report there in person at once and discuss further steps in the affair.

I arrived in Berlin in the evening and after a discussion which lasted late into the night it was left entirely to me to work out the further conduct of the negotiations. I was also given a free hand to choose suitable collaborators.

During the next few days I worked out my plans. I was accustomed to spend most of my free time in the peaceful atmosphere of the house of my best friend, Professor Max de Crinis, of Berlin University, and director of the Psychiatric Department of the famous Charity Hospital. It was a most pleasant and cultivated household, and for years I had been received there like a son. I had my own room and could come and go as I pleased.

That day, while I was working out my plans, de Crinis came to my room and insisted that I should go riding with him. The fresh air would clear my head. We were cantering briskly along when I was suddenly struck by an idea. I told de Crinis about the operation in Holland, and asked him whether he could come to The Hague with me. De Crinis, who was a colonel in the Medical Corps of the German Army, was born at Graz in Austria, and was considerably older than I. Elegant, stately, highly intelligent and cultured, he was ideally suited for the role I had in mind, and his slight Austrian accent would make him still more convincing. I would introduce him at our next meeting with the British as the right hand of the leader of our opposition group. De Crinis readily agreed to go with me, and in due course my plan was approved by the central office.

On October 29 de Crinis and I, and the agent who had accompanied me to the first meeting, left Berlin for Düsseldorf, where we spent the night and made our final preparations. I had decided that for the rest of the journey we would not talk about our mission, so that this was our final briefing.

De Crinis and I agreed upon a system of signs by which I could communicate with him during the discussion with the British: if I removed my monocle with my left hand it meant that he was to stop talking at once and let me take over the conversation; if I removed it with my right it meant that I needed his support. The sign for an immediate breaking off of the conversation would be for me to say that I had a headache.

Before we set out I carefully checked de Crinis' luggage. This time we had no difficulty in crossing the border.

At Arnhem we drove to a crossroads where we were to meet our British friends at noon. When we reached the spot at two minutes to twelve they had not arrived. We waited half an hour without anything happening; the half hour became three-quarters of an hour as we slowly drove up and down the street, our nervousness increasing every minute, and still nothing happened. De Crinis, unaccus-

tomed to situations of this sort, was, of course, the most
nervous of us and I tried to calm him.

Suddenly we saw two Dutch policemen slowly approaching our car. One of them asked us in Dutch what we were
doing there. The agent who accompanied us replied that
we were waiting for friends. The policeman shook his
head, climbed into our car, and ordered us to drive to the
police station. To all appearances it seemed that we had
fallen into a trap. The main thing now was to keep calm
and retain our self-control.

At the police station we were treated very politely, but in
spite of all our protests they searched our persons and our
luggage. They were very thorough about it, each article of
de Crinis' toilet kit, for instance, being examined with great
care. While they were doing this I was examining our
luggage even more carefully, for I suddenly realized that I
had been so preoccupied with de Crinis at Düsseldorf that
I had failed to check the luggage of the agent who accompanied us. His toilet kit lay open on a table near me
and now I saw to my horror that it contained a roll of
aspirin tablets wrapped in the official German Army packing with a label on which was printed "SS Sanitaetshaup-
tamt" (Main Medical Office of the SS).

I pushed my own luggage, which had already been examined, closer to the toilet kit, at the same time glancing
round to see whether I was observed. Quickly I grabbed
the roll of aspirins and at the same moment dropped a
hairbrush under the table. As I bent down to pick it up I
put the tablets into my mouth. They were truly "bitter
pills" and some of the paper that was round them stuck in
my throat, so that I had to drop the hairbrush again and
pretend to search for it under the table while I tried to
choke everything down. Fortunately all this passed unnoticed.

Then the interrogation began: Where did we come
from? Where were we going? Who were these friends we
were to meet? What sort of business were we going to
discuss? I replied that I refused to answer anything until
we had had an opportunity to consult a lawyer. I also
complained forcibly about the manner in which we were
being treated. They were going too far, there was no pos-

sible justification for all this: they had seen that our papers and our luggage were in order, and they had no right to detain us. I became intentionally rude and arrogant and it seemed to work. Several of the policemen became visibly unsure of themselves, but the others were determined to continue the examination. We had been wrangling for about an hour and a half when suddenly the door opened and Lieutenant Coppens came in. He showed the policemen some papers—I tried to see what they were, but did not manage to get a look at them—whereupon the attitude of the police changed at once. With the most profound apologies they released us.

When we came out of the police station we saw Captain Best and Major Stevens sitting in the Buick. They explained that it had all been a terrible mistake. They had waited for us at the wrong crossroads and then had spent a long time looking for us. Again and again they apologized, saying what a painfully embarrassing misunderstanding the whole thing had been.

It was immediately clear to me, of course, that the whole affair had been arranged by them. They had used the arrest, the search and the examination as an excellent means of checking us over to reassure themselves about our identity. I felt that we had better be prepared for further tests of one sort or another.

After a fast drive, we reached The Hague, where we went to a large room in the offices of Major Stevens. Here our talks began, with Captain Best doing most of the talking. After a detailed and thorough discussion, we finally agreed on the following points:

The political overthrow of Hitler and his closest assistants was to be followed immediately by the conclusion of peace with the Western Powers. The terms were to be the restoration of Austria, Czechoslovakia and Poland to their former status; the renunciation of Germany's economic policies and her return to the gold standard. The possibility of a return to Germany of the colonies she had held before the First World War was one of the most important subjects of our discussion. This has always been of special interest to me and I kept coming back to it again and again. I pointed out how vitally important it was to everyone that Germany should have a safety valve for her surplus population, otherwise German pressure against her borders in the east and in the west must continue to create an element of danger in Central Europe.

Our partners in the discussion recognized the validity of this, and agreed that a solution should be found to meet Germany's demands. They felt that a formula could be found that would secure for Germany the necessary economic rights and advantages and which could be reconciled politically with the present systems of mandates.

At the conclusion of the discussion we set down these results in the form of an *aide-memoire*. Major Stevens then went to inform London by telephone of our conclusions. After about half an hour he returned and stated that there had been a positive reaction in London, but that the agreement would still have to be discussed with Lord Halifax, the Foreign Minister. This would be done at once and we could count on a definite decision during the course of the evening. At the same time a binding agreement on our part would be necessary, which would represent a definite and final decision of the German opposition and would also include a time limit.

The talks had lasted approximately three and a half hours. Toward the end I developed a genuine headache, mainly because I had smoked too many strong English cigarettes and was not accustomed to them. While Major Stevens was speaking to London, I went to refresh myself in the washroom and let the cool water run over my wrists. I was standing there lost in thought when Captain Best, who had entered without my noticing, suddenly said in a soft voice behind me, "Tell me, do you always wear a monocle?"

It was fortunate that he could not see my face, for I could feel myself blushing. After a second I regained control of myself and replied calmly, "You know, I've been meaning to ask you the same question."

Afterward we drove to the villa of one of Best's Dutch associates where three comfortable rooms had been prepared for us. We rested for a while and then changed, for we had been invited to dinner at Best's home.

Best's wife, the daughter of a Dutch soldier, General Van Rees, was a well-known portrait painter and the conversation at dinner was pleasant and lively. Stevens came in later, explaining that his duties had detained him. He drew me aside and told me that he had received an affirmative reply from London; the whole thing was a great success.

Our agent, F 479, was also invited to the dinner, and for a few minutes I was able to talk to him undisturbed. He was very nervous and could hardly stand the tension any longer. I tried to reassure him and said that if he found a pretext to return to Germany, I would use all my influence to straighten things out for him with the authorities in Berlin.

The dinner was excellent. I have never tasted such marvelous oysters. Best made a brief and amusing after-dinner speech, to which de Crinis replied with all his Viennese charm. The general conversation after dinner proved most interesting and through it I gained a greater insight into the attitude of the British toward the war. They had not undertaken it lightly, and would fight to the bitter end. Indeed, if Germany were successful in invading Britain they would carry on the war from Canada. We also talked of music and painting, and it was quite late when we drove back to the villa.

Unfortunately my headache had not left me, so before retiring I asked my host for some aspirins. Several minutes later a charming young lady came to my room with some tablets and a glass of lemonade. She began talking to me and asked a number of questions. I felt quite relieved when I finally managed to maneuver her out of my room without actually being impolite. After the strain and exertions of the day I was in no state of mind to satisfy her curiosity with safety.

In the morning I met de Crinis for a moment in the bathroom. He was beaming and said in his broadest Viennese dialect, "Well, well—these chaps really can make things move, can't they?"

There was an ample Dutch breakfast to fortify us for the homeward journey. At nine o'clock a car collected us to take us to a brief final meeting, which was held in the offices of a Dutch firm (in reality a cover firm of the British Secret Service) the N. V. Handels Dienst Veer Het Continent [Continental Trade Service] at Nieuwe Uitleg No. 15. We were given an English transmitting and receiving set and a special code with which we could maintain contact with the English Secret Service station at The Hague. The call number was O-N-4. Lieutenant Coppens gave us credentials that instructed the Dutch authorities to assist the bearers to call a secret telephone number in The Hague—I believe it was 556-331—to protect us against any recurrence of unpleasant incidents, such as that of the previous day. After we had agreed to arrange the time and place of the next meeting by wireless, Captain Best accompanied us to the border, which again we crossed without difficulty.

This time we did not stop in Düsseldorf but drove straight to Berlin. The next day I made my report and suggested that I should try to continue negotiations with the aim of going to London.

During the following week on three occasions the British asked us to fix a date for the next talks. We were in daily communication with them by wireless, over O-N-4, which functioned perfectly. But by November 6 no directive had been received from Berlin and I began to fear that we would lose contact with the British. I therefore decided to go ahead on my own initiative. I agreed to meet them on November 7, and we finally arranged a rendezvous in the café near the frontier at two o'clock in the afternoon.

At this meeting I explained to Best and Stevens that my trip to Berlin had taken longer than I had expected and that unfortunately the German opposition had been unable to reach a final decision. I then suggested that it might be best if I accompanied the General (the fictitious leader of the group) to London, where final discussions on the highest level could be held with the British Government. The British agents saw nothing against this and said they could have a courier plane ready the next day at the Dutch airport of Schiphol, to take us to London. In the end we agreed that I would try to bring the leader of the German opposition to a meeting next day at the same time and place.

I returned to Düsseldorf, but there was still no directive from Berlin and no permission to continue the conversations. I sent an urgent request to Berlin, warning that without a decisive step of one sort or another my situation was becoming untenable. I received the reply that Hitler had not yet made a decision, but was inclined to break off the negotiations. He felt that they had gone far enough already. Apparently any discussion about his overthrow, even though it was bogus, made the Fuehrer uncomfortable.

So I sat in Düsseldorf, feeling impotent and frustrated, but the game intrigued me so much that I decided to go ahead. I got through to The Hague by wireless and confirmed the meeting for the next day. I must confess that at that moment I had no idea what sort of story I would tell my British friends. I realized that I was placing myself in a very ticklish position. If I aroused their suspicions in any way they could easily have me arrested again; the whole affair might come to a most unpleasant end. But I was determined to go on with the negotiations at all costs. I was angry with Berlin, although I knew that they had good reason for being hesitant: Hitler had tentatively set November 14 as the date for his attack on the West. The bad weather prevailing at that time may have been the main reason for abandoning this plan, but Himmler admitted later that my negotiations with the British agents might have been a contributing factor.

I spent a sleepless night, all sorts of plans whirling confusedly through my mind.

At breakfast I glanced at the morning papers. The headlines proclaimed that the King of the Belgians and the Queen of the Netherlands had made a joint offer to attempt to negotiate between the belligerents. I breathed a sigh of relif—this was the solution to my immediate problem. I would simply tell the British agents at today's meeting that the German opposition had decided to wait and see how Hitler would respond to the Dutch-Belgian proposal. I would add that illness prevented the leader of the opposition from attending today's meeting, but that he would certainly be there tomorrow and would probably still wish to go to London. That was my plan for today's conversations.

In the morning I had a talk with the man I had selected to play the role of the General, the leader of our opposition group. He was an industrialist, but held a high honorary rank in the Army and was a leader of the SS—in fact, he was admirably suited for the part.

In the afternoon I crossed the border once more. This time I had to wait for three-quarters of an hour in the café. I noticed that I was being watched very closely by several persons pretending to be harmless civilians; it was clear that the British had again become suspicious.

Finally they arrived. It was a rather short meeting this time, and I had no difficulty in presenting the situation to them as I had it planned that morning, thus explaining the delay. Their suspicions were entirely dissipated and when we said au revoir to each other the warm cordiality of the previous meetings had been re-established.

Back in Düsseldorf that evening an SS leader called on me. He was in charge of a special detachment and had been sent by Berlin unobtrusively to safeguard my crossing of the frontier. He told me that in Berlin they were very worried about my safety. He had been ordered to block off the whole sector of the frontier and cover all Dutch border police in the area. If the Dutch had tried to arrest me the situation would have become very difficult, for his orders were that on no account was he to let me fall into the hands of the enemy and a serious incident might therefore have resulted.

It gave me a rather strange feeling to hear this, especially when I thought of my plans for the next day, and what might have happened if I had not been able to speak to this SS leader beforehand. I told him that tomorrow I might drive away with the British agents, as my purpose was to go to London. If I went with them voluntarily I would give him a sign. We also discussed the measures he should take in case my departure with the British was not voluntary. He assured me that the best men available had been selected from his detachment.

I then had another talk with the industrialist who was to go with me and pose as the leader of the opposition group. We went over all the details very carefully, and it was midnight before I went to bed.

I had taken a sleeping pill to insure myself against another sleepless night and had sunk into a deep sleep when the insistent buzzing of the telephone awoke me. It was the direct line to Berlin. Drugged with sleep, I groped for the receiver and reluctantly grunted, "Hullo." At the other end I heard a deep, rather excited voice: "What did you say?"

"Nothing so far," I replied. "Whom am I speaking to?"
The reply came sharply, "This is the Reichsfuehrer SS
Heinrich Himmler. Are you there at last?" My consternation struggling with my sleepiness, I continued. "Do you
know what has happened?" "No, sir," I said, "I know
nothing." "Well, this evening, just after the Fuehrer's
speech in the Beer Cellar* an attempt was made to assassinate him! A bomb went off. Luckily he'd left the cellar
a few minutes before. Several old Party comrades have
been killed and the damage is pretty considerable. There's
no doubt that the British Secret Service is behind it all. The
Fuehrer and I were already on his train to Berlin when
we got the news. He now says—and this is an order
—when you meet the British agents for your conference
tomorrow, you are to arrest them immediately and bring
them to Germany. This may mean a violation of the
Dutch frontier, but the Fuehrer says that's of no consequence. The SS detachment that's been assigned to protect
you—which, by the way, you certainly don't deserve, not
after the arbitrary and self-willed way you've been behaving—this detachment is to help you to carry out your
mission. Do you understand everything?" "Yes, Reichsfuehrer. But—" "There's no 'but,' " Himmler said sharply.
"There's only the Fuehrer's order—which you will carry
out. Do you now understand?" I could only reply, "Yes,
sir." I realized it would be quite senseless to try to argue
at this point.

Thus I was presented with a completely new situation
and had to forget all about my great plan of continuing the
negotiations in London.

I immediately roused the the SS leader of the special
detachment and explained the Fuehrer's order to him. He
and his second-in-command were very doubtful about the
plan and said it would be far from easy to carry it out. The
terrain was not favorable for such an operation and for
several days the whole Venlo sector of the frontier had
been so thoroughly covered by Dutch border guards and
secret police that it would hardly be possible to carry the

---

* Every year, on November 8, the anniversary of Hitler's Munich
Putsch in 1923, he delivered a speech in the beer cellar where the
Putsch originated.

thing off without some shooting; and once shooting began you could never tell where it would end. Our great advantage lay in the element of surprise. Both the SS leaders thought that if we waited until the British agents had joined me at the café and we had sat down to begin our talks it would be too late. The time to act would be the moment Best's Buick arrived. They had taken a good look at the car the previous day and were certain they would recognize it immediately. The moment the British arrived our SS cars would break through the frontier barrier at great speed, arrest the Britishers in the street and haul them out of their own car into ours. The driver of the SS car was skilled at driving backward, he would not even have to turn the car round, and this would give the SS men wider field of fire. At the same time, several men would advance to the right and left of the street to cover the flanks during the retreat.

The SS leaders suggested that I personally should take no part whatever in the affair, but should wait for the British in the café. When I saw their car approaching I should come out into the street as though to greet them. Then I was to get into my own car and immediately drive away.

This plan sounded fine and I agreed to it. However, I asked them to introduce me to the twelve men of the special detachment; I wanted all of them to get a good look at me. Captain Best, though he was slightly taller than I, was of about the same build, had a similar overcoat, and also wore a monocle, so I wanted to make certain that there would be no mistake.

Between one and two o'clock I crossed the frontier as usual. The agent who had accompanied me on previous trips was still with me, but I had left the man who was to play the General safely in the German customs office, for no one could say how the situation might develop.

At the café we ordered an apéritif. There was quite a crowd in the place and unusually heavy traffic in the street, many of them cyclists, as well as some strange-looking men in civilian clothes accompanied by police dogs. It seemed that our British friends had taken unusually thorough security measures for this meeting.

I must admit that I felt pretty nervous, especially as time

went on and there was still no sign of them. I began to
wonder whether they had prepared a similar trick to the
one they played on us at Arnhem. It was already after
three o'clock and we had been waiting more than an hour.
Suddenly I started—a gray car was approaching at high
speed. I wanted to go outside, but my companion grasped
my arm and held me back. "That's not the car," he said. I
was afraid that the leader of the SS detachment might also
be misled, but everything remained quiet.

Having ordered a strong coffee, I had just taken the first
sip and was glancing again at the clock—it was now nearly
twenty past three—when my companion said, "Here they
come." We stood up. I told the waiter that some friends
were arriving and we went out into the street, leaving our
coats in the café.

The big Buick was approaching at speed, then, braking
hard, it turned off the road into the car park behind the
café. I walked toward the car and was about ten yards
from it when I heard the sound of the SS car approaching.
Suddenly there were shots and we heard shouting.

The SS car, which had been parked behind the German
customs house, had driven right through the barrier. The
shots had been fired to add to the surprise and had reduced
the Dutch frontier guards to such confusion that they ran
about aimlessly and did nothing.

Captain Best was driving the Buick and Lieutenant Coppens was sitting beside him. Coppens jumped out of the car
at once, at the same time drawing out a heavy service
revolver which he pointed at me. I being completely unarmed, jumped to one side and tried to present a less prominent target. At this moment the SS car came skidding
around the corner into the car park. Coppens, recognizing
it as the greater danger, turned and fired several shots into
the windscreen. I saw the glass shatter and crystalline
threads spreading from the bullet holes. It is strange how
vividly one notices details on such an occasion and how
indelibly they remain etched in one's memory. I was certain Coppens must have hit the driver and the SS leader
sitting beside him. Yet it seemed like an eternity before
anything else happened. Then suddenly I saw the lithe
figure of the leader leap from the car. He had also drawn
his pistol and a regular duel developed between him and

Coppens. I had no time to move and found myself between them. Both men shot with deliberation, aiming carefully. Then Coppens slowly lowered his gun and sank down on his knees. I heard the leader shouting at me, "Will you get the hell out of this! God knows why you haven't been hit."

I turned and ran round the corner of the house toward my car. Looking back, I saw Best and Stevens being hauled out of the Buick like bundles of hay.

As I rounded the corner I suddenly found myself face to face with a huge SS subaltern whom I had not seen before. He grabbed hold of me and thrust a huge pistol under my nose. It was obvious that he mistook me for Captain Best. Later I learned that against my express orders he had been added to the special detachment just before they left and consequently did not know who I was.

I pushed him back violently, shouting, "Don't be stupid. Put that gun away!"

But he was obviously nervous and excited and he grabbed hold of me again. I tried to fight him off, whereupon he aimed his gun at me, but in the same second that he pulled the trigger his hand was knocked to one side and the bullet missed my head by about two inches. I owed my life to the second SS leader's alertness. He had noticed what was happening and intervened just in time.

I did not wait for any further explanations, but got into my car as quickly as I could and drove off, leaving it to the SS detachment to finish the operation.

The plan was for everyone to return to Düsseldorf as fast as they could. I got there in about half an hour and the SS leaders arrived about the same time. They reported to me as follows:

"Best and Stevens, as well as their Dutch driver, have been secured as ordered. From Lieutenant Coppens' papers it transpires that he is not British at all, but is an officer of the Dutch General Staff. His real name is Klop. Unfortunately he was seriously wounded during the shooting and is at present under medical care."

The other SS leader added, "I'm sorry that I had to shoot Coppens, but he fired first; it was a question of his life or mine. I turned out to be the better shot."

Coppens, or Klop, later died of his wounds in a Düsseldorf hospital. Best, Stevens and their driver were brought to Berlin.

Best and Stevens were held prisoner for the duration of the war and finally liberated in 1945. I tried several times to secure their freedom by having them exchanged for German POW's, but all these attempts were sharply rejected by Himmler, until finally in 1943 he forbade me ever to bring up the matter again. Mention of it would remind Hitler of Elser, the man who planted the bomb in the Beer Cellar. Hitler still believed that there were others behind Elser and considered it one of the greatest failures of the Gestapo that they were not able to uncover anything to prove this. Himmler had been glad that with the passing of time Hitler had forgotten the matter, and did not want to remind him of it by bringing up Best and Stevens, who were linked in Hitler's mind with the Beer Cellar affair.

2

Assassin Disarmed by Love

John L. Steele

*Because the assassin hired by the Soviets, Bogdan
Stashinskiy, defected in 1961, this account of the
planning and execution of two separate but related
murders carried out under the instructions of the
Soviet Intelligence Service in 1957 and 1959 is, in
all likelihood, the most detailed of any such accounts available.*

*Beyond that it is a modern morality tale of a
very high order. The Soviets had obviously tried
to drill any human sensibilities out of Stashinskiy
for years, using a kind of Pavlovian deconditioning
and hardening scheme in order to turn him into a
perfectly functioning robot-murderer. To equip the
human monstrosity they hoped to create they also
had invented new murder weapons whose use was
clearly and solely for assassination purposes.*

*Although, as the author, John L. Steele, has
shown, it was in great measure Stashinskiy's love
for his German wife which made him break away
from the Soviets, the record of his trial in Germany for the murders revealed that there was also
a strong element of moral revulsion in Stashinskiy*

FROM *Life* magazine, September 7, 1962.

*against his employers. After defecting Stashinskiy
confessed at once to the two crimes, knowing he
must then face a German court and pay for them
with the loss of his freedom.*

ONE EVENING OF midsummer 1961, the American Intelligence Center in West Berlin received a phone call from local police with a routine message: a man claiming to be a Soviet intelligence agent had ridden the elevated train into West Berlin, turned himself in and was requesting contact with American authorities. With this last-hope act Bogdan Nikolayevich Stashinskiy, scheduled to go on trial for murder in a West German court early next month, ended his career as a Russian political informer, secret agent and assassin. His timing was, as nearly always, perfect. The following day, August 13, the wall dividing East and West Berlin went up.

The surrender, which caused only a small ripple of interest at the time, eventually produced a priceless store of evidence for the West on the organization and operation of the Soviet espionage system. It also bared the fascinating details of two political assassinations so astonishing in their conception that they make most fictional spy murders seem haphazardly contrived. Agent Stashinskiy was the trigger man in this bizarre method of murder, especially prepared by Soviet intelligence to get rid of two anti-Communist leaders in Europe who for years had been an embarrassing irritation to the Kremlin. The crimes were perfect in nearly every way—until Stashinskiy defected to the West.

Long before the trial date was set Western intelligence officials had checked and rechecked Stashinskiy's story until they were convinced his defection was legitimate, that he was not a counterespionage "plant." The Soviets' numerous attempts to ridicule Stashinskiy's story were made meaningless by their own reaction to his defection: seventeen officials were fired in a major shake-up of the Russian intelligence apparatus.

Stashinskiy's reasons for coming to the West were clearly his own. Time and circumstance had caught up with him. His superiors had become suspicious and were spying on him. He was an unemployed spy—and a dangerous liability to the state he had once served with complete dedication. His chances of survivial were clearly better in the West, even though he knew he would have to go on trial on two charges of murder. Most important, an escape was his only means of preserving his marriage to the German girl whose love had become more important to him than his career.

Except for his apparent dedication to the Communist cause there is little in Stashinskiy's experience as a teen-age trainee in the Soviet espionage system or as a working spy to suggest he would make a deadly efficient assassin. The story of his rise and fall as a spy elicits no sympathy—but it is a weird and fascinating case in the recent history of international intelligence. It also offers testimony that the oldest of spy thriller clichés—spy meets girl, spy falls in love, spy gets in a miserable jam—is very much part of the flesh and blood business of espionage.

To get a start in the Soviet Security Service, Stashinskiy was not above betraying his own family. The Stashinskiys, who lived in the small Ukrainian village of Borshovitsy, had been affiliated with the burning nationalist movement in the Ukraine for many years. Picked up by the police on the frivolous charge of riding the railroad home from school without his ticket, Bogdan was easily lured into the net by the KGB (Soviet Secret Police). After the interrogating officers made veiled threats about his family, Stashinskiy told them what he knew of their activities in the underground; a few months later he was on the KGB payroll with an appropriate pseudonym and was involved in the drive to wipe out the last fragments of the Ukrainian nationalist movement!

In the summer of 1951 he was assigned to a secret police *Spetsgruppa*, a group of toughs that employed strong-arm and sometimes bizarre tactics to round up Ukrainian underground workers. Stashinskiy was particularly adept in one cops-and-robbers charade that sounds as if it had originated on a movie lot. A Ukrainian suspected of being an underground worker was arrested and taken by car to another town for imprisonment or trial. En route the car would "break down" conveniently near a farmhouse where the arresting officers would take the prisoner for security reasons. The farmhouse was occupied by Stashinskiy's *Spetsgruppa*, posing as Ukrainian adherents. A fight would break out, with the Russian agents finally routed by blank cartridges and left for dead or dying in pools of chicken blood. The prisoner would then be spirited off to a bivouac manned by other Soviet agents disguised as Ukrainians. Here the prisoner was told to make a clean breast of his Ukrainian underground activities so that he could be properly protected in the future. Equipped with the written record of his testimony, the "liberators" transferred the prisoner to a "Ukrainian nationalist unit." But alas, they would then fall into a trap and get overpowered by Soviet agents, who would find the incriminating papers. So well did Stashinskiy and his cast play the melodrama that many underground workers were led to their execution believing they had suffered a run of incredibly poor luck.

By 1952 young Stashinskiy, a handsome twenty-year-old who had been through the rough-and-tumble of secret police work, had convinced his superiors that he was dedicated enough to Communism and his job to prepare for a major assignment in the West. For the next two years he went through an intensive training program in Kiev, studying German and Polish and learning the basic skills of undercover work. After he had successfully completed the course a banquet was held in his honor. Then he was sent to Poland to undergo his most assiduous transformation as an agent: he was to assume a new identity, one meticulously tooled to his own background and his future needs by the Soviet counterespionage chief directorate in Moscow.

Unlike previous pseudonyms he had been given, his new one Josef Lehmann—carried a complete biography. From June to October, 1954, Stashinskiy spent his time absorbing the details of the life of this fictitious character. He visited every locality and address that was part of the Lehmann legend; he even learned the routine of a job in a sugar beet factory where Lehmann supposedly worked as a boy. After this painstaking preparation Stashinskiy was finally turned loose in East Germany to assume the identity of Josef Lehmann. He posed as a sheet metal cutter, an employee in the motor pool serving the Soviet delegation to the East German government and a German-Polish interpreter in the East German Ministry of Domestic and Foreign Trade. But his real work as an espionage agent was routine and uninspiring for a graduate of a *Spetsgruppa*. He made contacts with and passed information to other undercover agents. He ran simple courier missions to West Germany. Once he was sent to Munich to copy license plate numbers of all military vehicles he observed. Much of the time he was a bored spy with no anticipation of the events that were soon to transform his personal life—and his career.

At the Tanz Casino in East Berlin he met a girl named Inge Pohl. He asked her to dance and rather suddenly Josef Lehmann had become entangled in a major non-espionage case: love. Inge Pohl, a twenty-one-year-old hairdresser, was hardly the *femme fatale* that walks into the lives of fictional spies. She was of common, sometimes sloppy appearance. Her hairdo was usually awry. Her intellectual interests were limited. Her table manners were wolf-like. But she was plainly dedicated to her man. In return she received his love and loyalty.

Agent Stashinskiy dutifully told his superiors of this change in his personal life. They immediately checked the girl with East German authorities and learned she had no police record and had never been spotted or suspected as an agent for Western intelligence. Stashinskiy's handlers told him he could pursue his friendship with Inge Pohl although social contact between agents and German girls was generally discouraged. He was reminded that she was a German, hence a Nazi, and that her father was a capitalist who employed three workers in his automobile repair shop. He was warned to tell Miss Pohl nothing about his activities except the Lehmann cover story and that he worked as an interpreter for the East German Ministry of Trade.

The dramatic turn in Stashinskiy's professional career came with an order to report to Soviet intelligence headquarters in the Karlshorst compound of East Berlin. There he was given the details of a new assignment: to locate and assassinate two prominent Soviet enemies—Ukrainian *émigré* leaders Lev Rebet and Stepan Bandera.

At that time—spring of 1957—the Kremlin was plagued by trouble throughout the Soviet bloc. There had been unrest in East Berlin, rioting in Poland, open revolt in Hungary, and activities of dissident groups within the Communist structure had assumed dangerous proportions.

The most persistent irritation of all came from the passionate Ukrainian nationalists. Though they had been frag-
mented and mutilated in their battles against occupiers
from Austria, Poland, Germany and Russia, they still
maintained a vigorous underground movement with headquarters in Munich.

Getting rid of Rebet and Bandera were major moves in
Moscow's attempt to obliterate the Ukrainian nationalists.
Stashinskiy's assignment was cold-blooded political assas-
sination, but elaborate preparations were taken by Soviet
Intelligence to avoid the possibility of linking the murder
plots to the Kremlin.

His first target, Rebet, was an ideologically motivated
individual of high intellect. As a successful anti-Soviet
propagandist and as a popular Ukrainian literary figure he
was regarded with extreme distaste by the Soviets. Russian
Intelligence knew that he divided his working hours between two Ukrainian *émigré* offices in Munich. He was
described as a man of powerful build, medium height, a
fast walker; he wore glasses, shaved his head, usually wore
a beret.

Stashinskiy's second target, Bandera, was quite a different man. Called "The Sly Fox," Bandera had been an
elusive target for Soviet assassins for more than five years.
He was the real symbol of the Ukrainian resistance—a
Lenin in exile—and a sharp thorn in the side of the Soviets. Bandera was affiliated with several Western intelligence
services. He led his own organization with a hard fist and
was not above using Soviet tactics. In the chaos of postwar
Munich he ran a "Bunker," named after the hideaways
used by nationalists within the Ukraine, where refugees
who claimed they had come from the underground were
carefully screened—and sometimes shot if they were suspected of being Russian agents. Stashinskiy was given
little information about Bandera's life in Munich except
that he drove an Opel car, that he occasionally attended a
Ukrainian *émigré* church on Sundays, used the alias of
"Poppel," and regularly visited his mistress.

Because Stashinskiy's handling officers decided he had
overused the Lehmann legend, particularly in the Munich
area which he had visited many times, he assumed new
aliases. For the Rebet mission he was given the identity of

Siegfried Draeger, who, unlike Lehmann," was a real flesh and blood citizen of Essen. His identity for the Bandera assignment was that of Hans Joachim Budeit, who lived in Dortmund. Stashinskiy was sent briefly to Dortmund and to Essen to familiarize himself with the surroundings and residences of the two men whose identities he was borrowing without their knowledge.

Using his Draeger alias, Stashinskiy flew to Munich and registered at a hotel near one of the two *émigré* offices which Rebet used. After several days of loitering near the offices, he finally spotted from his hotel window a man answering the Rebet description. A few hours later Stashinskiy followed the man through the Munich streets to the publishing office of the *émigré* newspaper, *Suchasna Ukraina*, on Karlsplatz. In an effort to establish a pattern of Rebet's movements, Stashinskiy followed him for several days. Sometimes his close surveillance became too close. Late one afternoon he boarded a street car behind Rebet. In the rush hour crowd he bumped against his quarry. He got off at the next stop so that Rebet would have little chance to recall his appearance. While Rebet was at work, Stashinskiy studied his apartment building, entering through an unlocked back door. Eventually, Stashinskiy decided that the newspaper office on Karlsplatz, an old masonry building adjacent to one of the city's three medieval gates, would be a favorable spot for murder.

Stashinskiy informed his superiors that he was ready. A Russian intelligence expert in weaponry was sent from Moscow to the Karlshorst compound with a top-secret assassin's gun. It was an aluminum cyclinder weighing less than half a pound and measuring three-quarters of an inch in diameter, just over six inches in length. Its "ammunition" was a liquid poison sealed hermetically into a plastic-type ampule container. The poison was colorless and odorless. When the weapon was fired it ejected a fine liquid spray. The weapon could not be reloaded and was meant to be disposed of after use.

For maximum results, Stashinskiy was told by the Moscow armorer, the liquid poison should be fired directly into the victim's face, forcing him to inhale. However, the weapon might be aimed chest-high since the vapors from the liquid spray rose. Maximum effective range for the weapon was about eighteen inches, but Stashinskiy was urged to use it at an even closer range. The poisonous vapors had to be introduced into the respiratory system through inhalation. The effect was such that the arteries carrying blood to the brain became paralyzed almost immediately, precipitating a form of thrombosis. The Moscow expert said that death would come to the victim within ninety seconds and that long before an autopsy could be performed the effect of the poison would wear off entirely without leaving a trace of the killing agent. (Stashinskiy was never given the identity of the poison vapor.) It was suggested that he carry the weapon concealed in a newspaper and that he catch his target climbing upstairs, which would enable him to point the weapon at the victim's face, fire it, and keep on walking down.

The user of the gun was considered safe from the poisonous vapors provided he kept his own head several inches away from the fumes. However, Stashinskiy was given several tablets to take which would protect him by enlarging the arteries to permit uninhibited flow of blood even if a small amount of poison was inhaled. He was also given the additional protection of a compress inhalant.

The day after he was introduced to the weapon, Stashinskiy drove with his handler and the Moscow armorer to the outskirts of East Berlin, where a dog had been tied to a tree. Stashinskiy held the weapon in his hand and squatted down with his two colleagues on either side of him. He stuck the tube within eighteen inches of the dog's nose and released the catch. A liquid spray shot out and the dog immediately collapsed without a sound. However, the animal continued to writhe in agony for almost three minutes.

In October, Stashinskiy flew out of Tempelhof Airport in Berlin for Munich carrying the weapon concealed in a sausage container in his suitcase. He was given no suicide weapon in the event his mission failed. He had only his wits, his cover story as Draeger, and a reminder from headquarters that his real salvation was to accomplish his mission and then quickly clear the Munich area. He would communicate with intelligence headquarters by means of postcards bearing innocuous messages with prearranged meanings. He was on his own.

At 9:30 of the third morning after he arrived in Munich, Stashinskiy spotted his victim. Lev Rebet was getting off a streetcar at his office. Stashinskiy, with the newspaper rolled in his hand and the weapon's safety catch removed, maneuvered just ahead of Rebet. He started climbing the building's circular staircase. As he reached the first floor, he heard footsteps on the stairs below. He turned and began to descend. He kept to the right of the staircase, thus getting Rebet on his left. When Rebet was a few steps below him, Stashinskiy, with a forward swing of his right arm discharged the weapon, ejecting the poison directly into Rebet's face. Stashinskiy continued on his way without breaking stride. He heard Rebet stumble, but did not look back. He then walked away, and dropped the weapon into the water.

On his way back to the hotel Stashinskiy passed the Karlsplatz. This time he glanced at the scene. Already a police car and an ambulance had arrived and were standing at the door to the *émigré* office—mute confirmation of the success of his mission. As soon as he returned to the hotel Stashinskiy checked "Siegfried Draeger" out at the desk. He proceeded to Munich's main railraod station and boarded an express train for Frankfurt am Main. In Frankfurt he spent the night at the Hotel International and the following morning took a British European Airways flight to Berlin. At Karlshorst he filed a detailed, written report. He was told that the Ukrainian *émigré* press reported that Lev Rebet had died, the victim of "a natural heart attack." But Rebet had lived long enough to struggle up two flights of stairs where he died in the arms of a colleague.

A week or two later Stashinskiy went to the KGB's Karlshorst "safehouse" to attend a banquet, given partially in his honor and partially to mark a Soviet holiday. He was formally congratulated by his superiors and praised by an unidentified Soviet general. He was handed a gift of a Contax camera.

Immediately, Stashinskiy took on his next assignment—to track down and kill Stepan Bandera.

There was no positive identification of Bandera available. Pursuing a report that Bandera was to deliver a graveside eulogy in Rotterdam for a martyred Ukrainian leader, Stashinskiy hurried to the Netherlands to attend the services and to identify him. At the Rotterdam cemetery he spotted the Opel that apparently belonged to Bandera. Stashinskiy stood at the graveside as the memorial oration was delivered. Ukrainian security men beat off attempts to photograph the speaker but the *émigré* press later reported that Bandera *was* the speaker. Stashinskiy had etched that face clearly in his mind. In early 1959, he received his final orders to go ahead with the killing.

Stashinskiy—as Hans Joachim Budeit—made four trips to Munich on the Bandera assignment. On the first run, Stashinskiy drew a blank until it occurred to him to look up Bandera's pseudonym, "Poppel," in the telephone directory. It was listed with the address of an apartment house at Kreittmayr Str. 7. Stashinskiy made various attempts to enter the Bandera apartment building, but always found the door locked. There was no rear entrance. He decided it was too risky to enter the apartment following on the heels of some resident. He needed a key to the lock. Stashinskiy returned to Moscow to pick up the murder weapon. The murder weapon was the same type he had used in killing Rebet, save that it was double barreled and could be fired either singly or in tandem. He carried it back through Berlin to Munich wrapped in cotton and placed in a cylindrical container. He also brought with him a skeleton-type key with five different and interchangeable bits which he hoped would enable him to enter the Bandera building.

Stashinskiy managed to work the five key bits he carried into the building lock. All of them failed to open the door. One of the bits snapped off in the process and dropped into the key housing. (It was later found by German police who learned through the apartment landlord that the key housing never had been taken apart. This became an important bit of circumstantial evidence in validating Stashinskiy's claim that he was the killer.) By using force on one of his remaining keys, Stashinskiy was able to make an impression on the metal, providing a clue for Russian locksmiths in Karlshorst. Despite his failure to gain entry to the building, Stashinskiy tried to get near enough to Bandera to kill him on this trip. But his efforts to corner Bandera in the apartment garage were unsuccessful.

Stashinskiy jettisoned his weapon into the canal after firing both barrels into the air.

On his third trip to Munich, he went without the weapon. He wanted to try a new set of keys against the stubborn apartment building lock. One of the four key bits he brought with him on this attempt partially turned the lock. Stashinskiy went to a nearby Woolworth store in Munich and purchased a file with which he ground down the pressure ridges impregnated upon the key. On his next visit to the apartment, this key bit worked. He entered and found a door on the third floor that carried the card of "Poppel." He surveyed the building in detail, including its modern elevator, and then returned to Berlin. Stashinskiy was convinced he had been cautious enough in his activities around the building. He always worked at night, fiddling around with a key ring as though he were a resident of the building.

In the second week of October, 1959, Stashinskiy made his last trip to Munich on the Bandera mission. He carried with him a new murder weapon, his protective pills and compresses, his false documents. At one o'clock one afternoon Stashinskiy spotted Bandera as he drove into the apartment garage. Using his key, Stashinskiy entered the building just ahead of Bandera. He took the stairs, hoping that the athletic Bandera would also use them instead of the elevator. However, when he heard women's voices in the stairwell just above him, he knew he could not loiter long so he began to descend. At the first floor landing he paused and pushed the elevator button. He was not sure where Bandera was. At this moment a woman walked by him, the elevator arrived, and he spotted Bandera at the front door of the apartment building. Caught between the waiting elevator and Bandera at the door, Stashinskiy could do nothing but turn to walk out of the building. Bandera carried a heavy bag of groceries in his right arm. With his left hand he struggled clumsily to withdraw his key from the door. Stashinskiy moved down the several steps from the entrance hall to the front door level as Bandera, key now withdrawn, held the door open for him with his foot. Stashinskiy grabbed the door with one hand, turned to Bandera and asked in German, "It doesn't work?" Bandera looked at him and replied, "Yes, it's all right." Stashinskiy raised his murder weapon concealed in a newspaper, and fired both barrels pointblank into his victim's face. He saw Bandera lunge to one side as he walked out of the building.

Stashinskiy once more headed for the canal. He dropped the key into a sewer manhole on the way and tossed his weapon into the canal. Then he made a quick departure by train for Frankfurt am Main. After an overnight stay he boarded a Pan Am plane for Berlin.

Bandera was found, not in the entry way where Stashinskiy had assaulted him, but on the stair landing between the second and third floors. The groceries which he had been carrying were in their bag unspilled. Subsequent investigation revealed Bandera had emitted a loud scream. He was found with his face seriously bruised and marked by black and blue welts. He died on his way to the hospital. An autopsy attributed his death to potassium cyanide poisoning. The poison gun had not brought instantaneous death to Bandera.

On his return to East Berlin, Stashinskiy was met by his superiors at the Café Warsaw. After filing his reports he was ordered back to Moscow to be decorated by his superiors. Stashinskiy's honor was one of the highest his country would offer a loyal citizen. On the recommendation of the Presidium of the Supreme Soviet he was given the Order of the Red Banner. The citation referred to his "extraordinarily difficult mission" in killing by poison-gas gun two enemies of the state.

The stag party in his honor had extravagant supplies of food and drink. Stashinskiy reveled in the splendor of the affair in his honor. He was a happy man. He was at the apex of a career which his hosts now promised would take an even more glorious turn. In Moscow he would begin a retraining program which would lead him as a secret agent eventually to England or the United States.

Stashinskiy took the occasion to announce his own personal plans: he and Inge Pohl were to be married. The reaction to the young agent's marriage plans was one of cold opposition. The Russian general in attendance and Stashinskiy's handling officers began to belittle his idea. They told Stashinskiy that they thought the girl was far below him socially. It was all right to enter into an "engagement" with her—but marriage was ridiculous. He was urged to pay her off with several thousand marks and forget about her.

Stashinskiy was stunned. He had somehow expected congratulations and at least a polite tolerance of the marriage. For the first time Stashinskiy began to realize that as a dedicated young agent in the Soviet intelligence system he was considered more a tool than a human being.

Following the celebration that had started so grandly and had ended in anger and embarrassment, Stashinskiy continued to press his campaign to get official permission for the marriage. When he met Aleksandr Shelepin, then chief of the Russian secret police at headquarters in Moscow, to receive his congratulations and the medal, Stashinskiy brought up the subject again. Shelepin argued against the marriage and reminded him that if he needed a companion he could have one of the Soviet girls in the secret police force who traveled as wives of agents. But Stashinskiy was so persistent he was finally given permission to return to East Berlin to tell Inge Pohl that he was associated with Soviet Intelligence—but no more—and to bring her back to Moscow.

On Christmas Eve, 1959, Stashinskiy told Inge that he was a member of the Russian Intelligence. He also explained in general terms the clandestine activities he had been engaged in, and that his identity as Josef Lehmann simply was a cover. Her reaction was one of shock and disappointment. She urged that they get married and immediately go to the West. Stashinskiy flatly refused to consider defecting. He could work the whole business out with his supervisors, he said. Finally, it was agreed that she would at least feign a willingness to help her fiancé and to do anything the secret police asked of her.

This was the first act in Stashinskiy's career which revealed a lack of trust of his supervisors. Soon his life as an undercover agent was crowded with doubts—and fears. Stashinskiy and Inge Pohl—traveling as Mr. and Mrs. Aleksandr Antonovich Krylov—were met in Moscow by Arkadiy Andreyevich, an official in the KGB, and taken to the Hotel Ukraina. When Arkadiy Andreyevich and the hotel clerk wrangled over the room selected in advance, Stashinskiy guessed that a recording device had been hidden in this room. He was placed in the uncomfortable position of trying to halt Inge's critical comments about life in Moscow without appearing to do so.

An attempt by agent Arkadiy Andreyevich to sell Inge Pohl on life in Russia failed miserably. She became even more withdrawn and homesick. Finally, on March 9, 1960, she and Bogdan were told they could go to East Berlin to get married but must return to Moscow as soon as possible so that Stashinskiy could begin his retraining program. KGB was in a dilemma over their prize political assassin. He had just been highly decorated and was regarded as an extremely capable agent. He could hardly be discharged from the service and allowed to go free. Apparently Stashinskiy's superiors decided to let him marry Inge Pohl in the hopes that she would become a satisfied wife and settle down in Russia.

On March 23 Igne Pohl and Stashinskiy (as Josef Lehmann) were married in East Berlin. In May the couple returned to Moscow, where they were quartered in a one-room furnished apartment—a secret police safehouse. Stashinskiy was put through a reindoctrination program. Because of the marriage the original plans to send Stashinskiy to an English-speaking country were abandoned. He was given intensive training in West German customs, manners and speech.

While Igne joined in the German lessons she rebuffed efforts to draw her into an intelligence training program. Her attitude had reached the danger point. She talked openly and indiscreetly to Stashinskiy about breaking with the KGB and defecting to the West. His own relations with the secret police grew worse. He learned that they were intercepting and opening his mail and that their small apartment was rigged with microphones. Furious, Stashinskiy complained to his handling officer, who informed him that it was a big mistake, that the apartment had been used at other times for other purposes. But shortly after the discovery Stashinskiy's training program ceased. It was explained that his instructor was away on a temporary duty assignment; the German lessons would be resumed, sometime. But the political training also stopped. Stashinskiy was told to be patient.

In September, 1960, Stashinskiy informed the secret police that his wife was pregnant. The KGB officers suggested an abortion. Stashinskiy claims that this, along with the bugging of his apartment, the interception of his mail and disregard for his personal life convinced him that he had become a tool—and a useless one at that. Inge, furious at the suggested abortion, drove this idea home time and time again; Moscow, she claimed, had no interest in them as people. Finally, on December 3, 1960, Stashinskiy was summoned for a showdown meeting with secret police General Vladimir Yakovelevich.

The General was a tough, grizzled veteran of the KGB. Bluntly he informed Stashinskiy that he would have to settle down in Moscow. He would not be allowed to leave Russia for seven years at least. He could not even visit East Berlin, although his wife could go any time she wished. Yakovelevich claimed that the KGB had penetrated U.S. and West German Intelligence to learn that an investigation had been opened into the deaths of both Rebet and Bandera. Stashinskiy was a marked man. (American Intelligence sources deny both the claimed penetration and the investigation of the deaths.) The KGB was not summarily firing him, the general explained. In recognition of his past services they would continue to pay his salary of 2,500 rubles a month until he was gainfully employed.

Stashinskiy and his wife were clearly on the defensive— and in trouble.

If there is anything more dangerous than the role of a Soviet espionage agent it is being an ex-spy. The Stashinskiys had to be constantly on guard for sudden, silent attempts to kill them. They had to be cautious of what they ate, where they went and how they traveled. They began to make their plans for an escape to the West. It was agreed that Inge would return to East Berlin so that their child could be born under East German citizenship. They devised a set of code messages to be sent by post card, including the phrase "visited a seamstress" which would mean that Inge had received promises from American Intelligence in West Berlin to help them. In January, 1961, Igne was permitted to return home. Meanwhile Stashinskiy, with KGB assistance, had started an advanced study course at the government Pedagogical Institute of Foreign Languages. The KGB, in a sharp change of attitude, was being conciliatory toward Stashinskiy and even suggesting he might be given future assignments. Stashinskiy suspected that the new approach was an attempt to pacify him and bring his wife back to Moscow.

In East Berlin, Inge's naïve attempts to get her husband's travel ban lifted were unavailing. In early August she made preparations to return to Moscow with her infant son whom Stashinskiy had never seen. One day before her scheduled departure she left her child with a neighbor. During his feeding the baby choked to death. The grief-stricken mother cabled her husband in Moscow.

Stashinskiy appealed through his new KGB handling officer, Yuriy Nikolayevich Aleksandrove, to go to East Berlin to join his wife. The appeal at first was denied. But finally the KGB fearing a desperate act by Mrs. Stashinskiy, permitted the trip. Accompanied by Aleksandrove as custody officer, Stashinskiy was flown to East Berlin by Soviet military plane. After his arrival Stashinskiy was given considerable freedom although he was obliged to report regularly to his handling officer and, with his wife, required to spend the nights in the Karlshorst security compound rather than in her rooming house.

Stashinskiy immediately intensified his plans to defect. He knew that the KGB suspected an escape effort and would insist upon their return to Moscow immediately after the funeral. He knew he was under close surveillance, by agents on foot and by those operating from a car. An escape attempt would have to be made before the funeral. Taking advantage of his own training, he practiced various stratagems to shake off his followers. On Saturday, August 12, Stashinskiy and his wife were driven by KGB car to the home of Inge's father in the suburb of Dallgow to work on the final preparations for the funeral the next day. They spent the entire morning and the early afternoon at the home, several times walking the short distance to Igne's rooming house and to a shopping center to order flowers and make a few purchases.

At four o'clock in the afternoon, Stashinskiy, his wife and her fifteen-year-old brother, Fritz, slipped out the back door of the rooming house. Screened by bushes and the trees of neighboring backyards, they walked unobserved into the center of Dallgow. Then they walked three miles to the town of Falkensee. Arriving there around six o'clock in the evening, they hired a taxi at a garage and headed for Friedrichstrasse in East Berlin. They had no trouble in crossing the border between East Germany and East Berlin; Stashinskiy simply displayed his Lehmann documents and the cab was waved through the check-point. Forty-five minutes later they arrived at their East Berlin destination and discharged the cab. Fritz Pohl's plea to accompany them to the West was turned aside; Stashinskiy gave him three hundred marks—most of his remaining cash—to pay the funeral expenses and sent him home.

After making certain that they were not being followed, Stashinskiy and Inge hailed another cab and rode to an S-Bahn station to take the elevated train into West Berlin. Luck was with them. Although the East German police were checking the documents of passengers on the train, the car in which they sat was not checked. At about eight o'clock, they casually got off the train at Gesundbrunnen, the first S-Bahn stop in West Berlin. They taxied to the home of Inge's aunt and then requested to be driven to the police. Bogdan and Inge Stashinskiy walked into headquarters just as darkness covered West Berlin on the night before the city was split by the wall.

XI

Classic Instances of Espionage

I HAVE ASSEMBLED here a number of accounts of intelligence operations which I regard as unique, either because they describe events which are quite out of the ordinary in a domain in which almost any events are quite out of the ordinary, or because the events were of singular significance at a certain moment in history.

1

The Archtraitor

Richard Wilmer Rowan

Colonel Alfred Redl was chief of counterespionage of the Austro-Hungarian Empire's Military Intelligence Service from 1901 to 1905 and later was its representative in Prague. From around 1902 until he was caught in 1913 Redl had been a secret agent of the Russians (the main target of Austro-Hungarian Intelligence), who had apparently threatened to expose him as a homosexual and had thus blackmailed him into working for them. He was caught by an instrument of his own devising: thoroughgoing postal censorship in the service of counterespionage. A suspiciously large sum of cash sent in the open mail to "General Delivery" in Vienna and not called for (because Redl had begun to fear that his time was up) aroused the interest of the man who had succeeded Redl as counterespionage chief, Maximilian Ronge. Had Redl not gone for the money he might never have been caught, but an insatiable appetite for cash and the good living it bought finally sent him belatedly to the post office. Although the Russians paid Redl amply by any standard, he had also sold secrets to

---

FROM the book *The Story of the Secret Service.*

*the French and the Italians. The Black Cabinet,
also known as the Black Chamber, is the name for
postal censorship.*

ON THE SECOND of March, 1913, two envelopes were
opened in the Black Cabinet. Both had been addressed:
Opera Ball, 13, Poste Restante, General Post Office, Vienna.
And they came, according to their postmarks, from
Eydtkuhnen in East Prussia, on the Russo-German frontier.
One enclosed bank notes to the sum of six thousand
Austrian kronen and the other yielded eight thousand, or a
combined equivalent of more than twenty-seven hundred
dollars. As neither contained any covering letter, it was
natural for the censors to suspect them. Eydtkuhnen,
moreover, was a little frontier station well known to spies
of every nationality. The "K.S."* returned both letters to
Poste Restante and resolved to have a look at the individual who would call for them.

On one side of Vienna's general post office, in the
Fleischmarkt, there was a small police station. Ronge ordered a wire installed between it and the Poste Restante
counter. The clerk on duty there would only have to press
a button to set a bell ringing in one of the rooms of the
police station, and he was to do this the moment the letters
were asked for and be as slow as possible in handing them
over. At the police station two detectives were to be ready
day and night to hurry out when the bell sounded and
detain for questioning the person receiving the letters.

A week went by, everything was ready, but the bell did
not ring. March and April, and still no one had called for
the letters; fourteen thousand kronen lay unclaimed. But
on the eighty-third day of waiting, Saturday afternoon,
May 24, the police alarm began to clamor for attention.
One detective was out of the room; the other was just then
washing his hands. Yet in two minutes' time they had
overcome their surprise and were sprinting across the
Postgasse.

The postal clerk complained of their delay and said the

---

* "K.S." stood for Kundschafts Stelle, the Austro-Hungarian intelligence service.

man had just gone out "to the left." They reached the
street only to see a taxi rolling away, and the only taxi in
sight. The two men stood right there for twenty minutes, as
reluctant as tardy schoolboys to report their failure and
hear their superiors' comment. Hence another choice bit of
irony enters the Redl case, for the detectives' blighted effort
and aimless lingering in front of the post office provided a
major clue. Presently a taxi came by, which one of them
recognized as the cab whose recent passenger had certainly
been the receiver of the letters. Hailing it they asked the
driver where he had driven "their friend"—the man he had
picked up in this very street about twenty minutes before.

"To the Café Kaiserhof."

"We'll drive there too," said the detective. And on the
way he and his partner thoroughly searched the interior of
the taxicab. They found the cover of a pocketknife, a little
sheath of gray suède, and nothing more. At the time of day
the Café Kaiserhof was almost empty; no doubt he had
doubled on his tracks in another cab. There was a taxi
stand not far distant, and here the detectives learned that
a gentleman had taken a cab, about half an hour ago, to be
driven to the Hotel Klomser.

Going to that hotel, they asked the *portier* if anyone had
arrived in a taxi during the past half hour. Yes, several had;
the guests in Number 4 and Number 11, and also 21 and
1—Number 1 was Colonel Redl.

One of the investigators showed the *portier* the pocketknife sheath. "Take it, and ask your guests, as you get the
chance, if any one of them has lost it."

The *portier*, true to his profession, was glad to oblige the
police. One of the detectives stepped aside and began to
read a newspaper. Presently a well-groomed man in
smartly cut civilian clothes came down the stairs and gave
up his key. It was Number 1.

"Pardon me," said the *portier*, "but has the Colonel by
any chance lost the sheath of his pocketknife?" And he
held out the grey suède cover.

"Why, yes," said Redl, "of course that is mine. Thank
you." Then he hesitated. Where had he last used his pocketknife? In the first taxicab—removing the money from the
letters! He glanced at the *portier*, who was hanging up the

key. Another man stood near, apparently engrossed in his newspaper. Redl pocketed the sheath and walked to the door.

The detective who had been reading sprang for a telephone booth and called "123408"—the secret number of the headquarters of the political police in Vienna. And the chief officers of the "K.S." were now hearing what had happened in the past exciting hour. The "Opera Ball, 13" letters had been called for; their recipient had used two taxicabs in trying to throw off possible shadows but had carelessly mislaid the sheath of his pocketknife—which sheath, on his own admission before a witness, had been established as the property of Alfred Redl—the well-known Colonel Redl, Chief of Staff of the Eighth Army Corps, stationed at Prague.

One can imagine the stricken bewilderment of those officers of Austrian Intelligence. Their former leader, their painstaking teacher, and still their model and inspiration! Captain Ronge hurried to the post office to make inquiries. At the Poste Restante counter in Vienna all persons asking for letters had to fill in a brief form:

Nature of packet—
Address on packet—
State (if possible) where from—

He was able to take away the form which had been filled in by the man receiving the "Opera Ball, 13" letters. From a concealed shelf in his office he took down a slim, neatly bound volume. It was in manuscript, a forty-page document written by Redl and considered by him too confidential to be sent to a printer. It represented his advice to his successor at the "K.S." and was the last thing he had done there before being promoted to Prague.

Among numerous subtleties of espionage and secret service, it summed up his five years' experience as a detector of spies and now it was going to detect a master spy.

Ronge placed the little post-office form upon a manuscript page. There could be no question about it—the handwriting was Redl's. He had received suspicious postal packets containing large sums of money. That did not prove him a traitor; he might merely be acting for somebody else in a private matter. But coming from Eydtkuhnen, that border "funnel" of secret-service conspiracies!

The reverie of the intelligence captain was interrupted by one of the two detectives who had been shadowing Redl. Did he bring fresh proofs? "In fragments," he answered grimly. He was taking a number of raggedly torn scraps of paper from his pocketbook. with the anxious Ronge he bent over these pieces, fitting them together.

In half an hour the small puzzles were conquered. Ronge and the detective studied the proofs they had gained. Beyond all doubt Redl was a spy and a traitor.

The bits of paper had been obtained in a curious way. The two detectives had shadowed Redl as he walked away from the Hotel Klomser. Looking back and recognizing the man who had stood in the hall of the hotel reading a newspaper, Redl quickened his pace. This was a game he had often helped to play, but never before as the one pursued. Only seventy yards from the hotel, at the corner of the Strauchgasse, he managed to give his shadows the slip.

A few yards down the street, on the right, the detectives had a view of Wallnerstrasse. No Redl! Taking thought, the detectives agreed he must have entered the old Exchange Building. It had three exits, two into the Café Central, and the other through a passage into a large open square called the Freiung. They gambled on the passage to the Freiung—and there, sure enough, caught sight of their quarry. As Redl reached the square, he looked back, saw the two detectives, and once more quickened his pace.

He was heading down the long Tiefengraben, and as he could not seem to outdistance his shadows, he tried strategy. Drawing some papers from his pocket, he tore them up and threw them down without looking to see what they were. The staff colonel appeared to realize that his being trailed so persistently could only mean his treason had at last been exposed. It was too late to worry about "evidence"; the one thing to do now was to give these men the slip—be alone for a while—try to think of a way out.

Redl hoped the shadows would stop to pick up his papers, but neither of them did. On they came until, at the Konkordia Platz, they reached a rank of taxicabs. Redl did not take a cab, as his pursuers could easily do the same. He walked on. But one of the detectives jumped into a cab and was driven hurriedly away. Redl continued his strained, urgent patrol about Vienna, along the Heinrichsgasse to the Franz Josef Quai—down the Schottenring's mile length —into the Schottengasse and back to his hotel.

Where had the other detective gone? He had driven to the spot where Redl's torn-up papers dotted the pavement, collected all he could find, and hastened with them to Captain Ronge. At the "K.S." it was thus learned that Redl had been carrying in his pocket a receipt for the dispatch of money to an officer of Uhlans, Lieutenant Hovora. And three receipts for registered letters to Brussels, Warsaw and Lausanne. Ronge smiled bitterly as he read the last three addresses. A "black list" of known intelligence bureaus of foreign powers which Redl had prepared was in his file; and it included these three addresses. Ronge now reported his findings to the chief of the Austro-Hungarian secret service, General August Urbanski von Ostromiecz, who was so shocked by the news that he hurried to convey it to his superior, General Conrad von Hotzendorf.

At his hotel Redl had found Dr. Victor Pollack waiting. "Alfred, we dine at the Riedhof," he reminded him, and the colonel agreed, excusing himself to change into evening clothes. Pollack was one of the most distinguished legal authorities of Austria and had often been Redl's collaborator in court proceedings connected with espionage cases. The detective had overheard what was said, telephoned his superior, and then gone to the Riedhof to interview the manager.

When Pollack and Redl sat down to dinner in a private room, their waiter was an agent of the secret police. But he heard little, as Redl could not match his friend's gaiety and hardly spoke except when they were alone. Pollack that same evening had occasion to repeat Redl's private conversation when he went to a telephone and, to the astonishment of the waiter-detective, rang up Gayer, the Viennese chief of police.

"My friend, you are working late," said Pollack.

"I'm awaiting some developments in a rather important case," said Gayer, and listened while Pollack described

Redl's difficulty. The colonel had seemed moody all evening, had apparently suffered a psychological disturbance
—had confessed to his friend of moral lapses, magnified
anxieties, various delinquencies and misdemeanors. But, of
course, nothing about espionage or treason.

"Overwork, probably," Pollack explained. "He asks me
to see to it that he goes back to Prague immediately and
that the journey be made as comfortable as possible. Could
you provide him with a companion?"

Gayer said it would be impossible to arrange anything
that night, adding: "But calm the colonel, and tell him to
come straight to me in the morning. I'll do all I can for
him."

Pollack returned to the private dining room. "Let us go,"
he said to Redl in the "waiter's" hearing. "I am sure we
shall be able to arrange matters for you."

Pollack left the waiter-detective perplexed and worried.
He had heard the lawyer telephone to the chief of police,
and then tell a spy and traitor that something would be
arranged for him. Was the affair to be hushed up? Had
powerful General Staff influences cut in to prevent the
legal processes of retribution? The treason of Alfred Redl
was, if possible, to be hushed up. But not in a way that
would spare the traitor. The detective's worry and perplex-
ity were as nothing compared to the reaction of such responsible commanders as Von Ostromiecz and Conrad von
Hotzendorf. The latter, interrupted while entertaining
friends at the Grand Hotel, was privately advised of the
treason—Redl—the Eighth Corps. "Just the point where
treason may be most deadly! If Plan Three is gone . . ."

The Commander-in-Chief is said to have perceptibly
aged in a few moments, for Plan Three was the ultimate
expression of the technical and tactical skill of himself and
his staff.

"We must hear from his own lips the extent of his treason. Then," said Conrad, "he must die. . . . No one must
know the reason for his death. Call together four officers—
you, Ronge, Hofer and Wenzel Vorlicek. Everything must
take place tonight."

At 11:30 Redl took leave of Pollack and returned to his
hotel. At midnight the four officers, in full uniform, called
upon him. He had been sitting at a table, writing, and now

he rose and bowed. "I know why you have come," he said. "I have spoiled my life. I am writing letters of farewell."

"It is necessary to ask the extent and duration of your— activities."

"All that you wish to know will be found in my house in Prague," said Redl. He then asked if he might borrow a revolver.

None of the officers was armed; but fifteen minutes later one of them returned with a Browning revolver and handed it to the colonel. And now, left alone, and at the end of the somber spiral of his treacheries, he wrote on a half-sheet of notepaper, in his firm legible hand:

> Levity and passion have destroyed me. Pray for me. I pay with my life for my sins.
>
> Alfred
>
> 1:15 a.m. I will die now. Please do not permit a post-mortem examination. Pray for me.

He left two sealed letters, one addressed to his brother, the other to General Baron von Giesl, who had trusted him and recommended his promotion to Prague. Fate had sardonically used that trust and that promotion to work Redl's undoing. If his abilities had not won him the complete approbation of his superior, he would probably have stayed on in Vienna; and while retaining his place at the "K.S." through manifest aptitude for secret-service work, Redl might have continued for years to cover up his treachery by means of subterfuges impossible to the chief of staff of an army corps at Prague.

The officers assigned by the chief of the Austrian General Staff to interrogate Redl and make sure of his immediate "execution" had established themselves in the Café Central, ordered coffee, and, tense and silent, prepared to wait out the night. One of their number had been left to keep watch upon the door of the Hotel Klomser; and every half-hour this man was relieved. Not until five o'clock in the morning did they take any further action. Then, summoning to the café one of the detectives who had shadowed Redl, they gave him an envelope addressed to the traitor and told him to deliver it personally. The detective was warned of what he might find and instructed to return without raising any alarm if the colonel was dead.

Arriving at the Klomser, the detective explained his errand to a drowsy *portier*, then went up and knocked at the door of Room No. 1. When he received no answer, he tried the door. It was unlocked. He stepped into the brightly lighted room, to find Alfred Redl lying in such a position that it was evident he had stood in front of a mirror with a strong light shining upon him when he fired the shot into his brain. The agent of police came away at once, closing the door and going out past the sleepy *portier* on tiptoe.

A few minutes later the telephone rang, arousing the *portier*. It was a request for Colonel Redl to be called to the phone. Whereupon the night *portier* went and discovered the body, just thirteen hours after the two "Opera Ball, 13" letters had been picked up at the general post office.

The hotel management immediately notified the city police; and Gayer, the chief and a physician hurried to the Klomser. No further intrusion of the military authorities was to occur. But Redl's devoted valet, Josef Sladek, a Czech, tried to interest Gayer in a clue he had discovered. The Browning revolver was not his master's. Four officers had paid him a midnight visit. It might be murder! Gayer took the servant aside, however, spoke to him earnestly, thereby sealing his lips so that newspapermen on the following day could not get Sladek to utter a word.

As soon as Conrad von Hotzendorf had been informed that Redl had shot himself he appointed a commission consisting of a colonel and a major to go to Prague by special train. Their search of the dead officer's house was conducted in the presence of General Baron von Giesl; and the results of this investigation were sensational. Redl's home was luxuriously furnished—documents showed that in 1910 he had bought a costly estate—in Vienna he owned a large house—during the past five years he had "bought no fewer than four of the most expensive motor cars."

He had been thought by his brother officers to possess private means; but actually he had lived like a multimillionaire. In his wine cellar were found one hundred and sixty dozen of champagnes of the finest vintages. It was then discovered that in nine months he had received from Russia about sixty thousand kronen. That was ten times his colonel's pay; yet the extravagances of his mode of life hint that the accounts uncovered failed to reveal the full amount. The czarist secret service was always notably liberal; and Redl probably was worth five or six times the sum indicated, or the equivalent of at least sixty thousand dollars.

Perhaps the most curious touch of all to this extraordinary affair was given in Prague, after his death and owing to the investigation of his dwelling. The greatest possible precautions had been taken to keep the treason secret. In all Austria but ten people knew the facts—the Commander-in-Chief, the highest officers of the Secret Service and of the War Office, and chief officials of the Vienna police—and each of the ten took a special oath not to breathe a word of it. Even Franz Josef himself and his heir, the Archduke Franz Ferdinand, were to be kept in the dark. And yet these measures of secrecy failed because the best locksmith of Prague was also a crack football player.

The locksmith Wagner, could not play with his team, Storm I., on Sunday, May 25, 1913, and, as the *Prager Tagblatt* reported next morning, his team had been beaten, score 7–5, largely on that account. The captain of Storm I. was a subeditor of the *Tagblatt*, and when he visited Wagner on Monday to inquire about his absence, he learned how the locksmith had superseded the fullback at the imperative command of ranking army officers.

Wagner, in short, had been employed to force his way into Alfred Redl's house and then to pick or break the locks on all its drawers, cabinets, wardrobes, chests, desks and cupboards. These had yielded up great quantities of papers, photographs, a good deal of cash, and maps and plans. Some of the papers, he had heard, were Russian. And the officers seemed utterly confounded and kept exclaiming: "How is it possible?"—"Who would have imagined it?"

Instantly the football captain was superseded by the journalist. As a subeditor he had handled in that day's issue the message coming from the official Vienna Correspondence Bureau. It told "with regret" of the suicide of

Colonel Alfred Redl, Chief of Staff of the Eighth Corps—
"a very gifted officer who would have risen to the highest
rank." The colonel, having gone to Vienna "on a professional mission, in a moment of depression, brought about
by weeks of insomnia, had shot himself." But Russian
documents—photographs and plans—a commission of officers sent to search Redl's house a few hours after his
suicide! That meant espionage—it meant treason!

The captain of Storm I. had unearthed a sensational
secret; yet now that he had his story, he dared not print it.
So stringent was the censorship in Bohemia, even in 1913,
that the most guarded editorial exposition of "the Redl
case" would have only meant a police descent upon the
newspaper office, suspension of the paper, and jail sentences for as many of the staff as could be incriminated.
But the Czech and German public of Bohemia had taught
themselves to read between the lines and even to peer "behind the paragraph." To let their readers know, then, that
Redl was a spy and betrayer of his country, the captain of
Storm I. and his editor concocted this "denial" for the
Prager Tagblatt of Tuesday, May 27:

> We are asked by a high authority to contradict rumors
> which have been spread, particularly in army circles, about
> the Chief of the Staff of the Prague Army Corps, Colonel
> A. Redl, who, as already reported, committed suicide in
> Vienna on Sunday morning. The rumors are to the effect
> that the colonel had been guilty of betraying military secrets
> to a foreign power, believed to be Russia. As a matter of
> fact, the commission of high officers who came to Prague
> to carry out a search in the dead colonel's house were in-
> vestigating quite another matter.

Moreover, the football captain was the Prague correspondent of a Berlin paper; and by the twenty-eighth all
Europe was reading his exposé of Redl's perfidy and suicide. Austrian officers, when questioned, were at pains to
belittle the importance of Redl the spy. Only since the
World War has it been possible to determine the full impact, the incredible scope and frightful cost of the staff
colonel's decade of treason.

He had begun to spy in 1902 and for ten years had been
Russia's leading foreign spy. He had made a specialty of

aiding Russian counterspies, had denounced scores of persons acting as spies in Russia. Some of these were his personal friends and devoted subordinates at the "K.S." And he had sacrificed them to make more secure his own position as an agent of the Russian service. In order to earn the good will of the Czar's intelligence directors, he had ravaged the empire's archives as well as its secret service. Not only had he denounced his own men on foreign service, but he had contrived to assist Russian spies sent into Austria-Hungary. He had been invaluable when it came to trapping and betraying to the Russians any "Redl" of their own forces who notified Vienna he had secrets for sale.

What—apart from the rifled files of the "K.S."—had he sold of Austro-Hungarian military secrets? The preliminary and hurried examination at his house in Prague developed a tale of unparalleled treachery. From the great mass of copied documents, codes, ciphers, letters, maps, charts, photographs, police records, confidential army orders, mobilization plans, reports on the condition of railways and roads, it became all too painfully clear that there was little he had not betrayed.

Plan Three was assuredly a victim of his rapacious trafficking. The complete scheme for military action against Serbia should war come with that bantam of the Balkans had been sold to Russia, which meant that the Pan-Slavic partisans at Belgrade now knew all about it. Plan Three was the avowed masterpiece of the Austro-Hungarian General Staff and the pride of Conrad von Hotzendorf. Years of thought and strategical study had gone into it; they might modify it here and there, but its main features hardly could be changed. Examining Plan Three would have given the Serbian General Staff an X-ray photograph of the best minds of the Austro-Hungarian Army. Marshal Putnik, a brilliant officer, was at the head of the Serbian staff. It is said that he concentrated upon the copy of the plan which the Russians sent him until he knew it by heart.

With what result? When the war came in 1914 all the world was astonished by Putnik's generalship. He and his heroic little army inflicted terrible losses upon the Austro-Hungarian invaders—who thus were still paying for Redl's champagnes and motors. Thrice the Austrian high command tried variants of Plan Three—now known as Plan B (Balkans) as distinguished from Plan R (Russia)—and thrice the Serbian Voivode checkmated it. It took overwhelming odds and a shortage of all materials to expel him and his gallant troops from Serbia, for to the last he had his mind attuned to enemy conceptions of tactics and strategy.

Examination of Redl's papers shed light upon many a revolting transaction, as, for example, his crafty undoing of a brother officer and a Russian colonel. The Archduke Franz Ferdinand, visiting St. Petersburg, had been so well received by the Czar and his court that on his return journey he asked the Austro-Hungarian military attaché to reduce espionage in Russia to such a degree that it would no longer disquiet the Russians. The attaché left the royal train at Warsaw, stopping there two days, in which time a Russian colonel visited him, offering to sell a complete plan of a Russian offensive upon Germany and Austria-Hungary. Despite the Archduke's recent instructions, this seemed too rare a "bargain" to miss; and so the attaché came to terms with the Russian.

Redl heard of the deal and immediately went into action: a czarist agent who, at need, would put the whole Austro-Hungarian service to work—for Russia. As head of the military secret service he was first to lay hands upon the Russian plans. He prepared and substituted a palpably fraudulent set of plans, to make it appear that the St. Petersburg attaché had not alone disobeyed the Archduke's order but had been ridiculously duped. The attaché was reprimanded and recalled. Redl then returned to Russia the genuine plans, safe in the knowledge that only he and the discredited attaché had seen them, and that the latter had not had time to study them.

Lastly, Redl informed the Czar's intelligence of the guilt of the colonel who had proposed the sale—which officer committed suicide on learning he had been betrayed. Redl's accounts noted proudly that by this odious exploit he had earned one hundred thousand kronen.

No exception can be taken to his suggesting that he "earned" what was then equivalent to twenty thousand dollars. To the Russians he demonstrated his value beyond the peradventure of doubt; for he not only saved their secret plans and all the toil which staff officers put upon such speculative—and highly negotiable—paper, but he prevented both the Austro-Hungarian and German general staffs from learning of the formation of a considerable number of new Russian Army corps. As a consequence it has been argued that the traitor directly influenced the ruin of three empires.

"If," said the late Count Albert Apponyi, "we had known of the existence of those army corps, our General staff—and the German staff also—would have recognized the hazard of a quarrel with Russia, and would have been able to prevent our 'statesmen' from driving us into war in the summer of 1914. Hence our absurd war fever and our crushing defeat. . . . That villain, Redl, denounced every Austro-Hungarian spy in Russia, suppressed reports that leaked through in spite of him, and delivered our own secrets to the Russians."

2

London Calling North Pole

H. J. Giskes

"North Pole" was without question one of the most effective German counterespionage operations of all time—not so much because of the level at which it operated, which was not of the highest, but because of its complexity, extent, duration and the cleverness with which it was executed. It would have been unthinkable before the days of radio.

The British Special Operations Executive (SOE), during World War II, directed intelligence and sabotage operations against Nazi-occupied Europe from London via radio links to underground groups. It frequently air-dropped into enemy territory agents, equipment and munitions, as well as the radio operators themselves who were to work with underground groups. German Military Intelligence, the so-called Abwehr, was able in Holland to capture and "turn" some of the British SOE agents who had secretly been dropped into Holland. By controlling and dictating the messages of these agents in their underground transmissions to London, the Abwehr enticed the SOE to keep dropping further agents and material, immediately

FROM the book *London Calling North Pole*.

apprehended on arrival. Over a period of time (1942–44) a large part of SOE's efforts to support the Dutch Underground was thus neutralized. This operation was called "North Pole" by the Germans. It was directed by H. J. Giskes, an Abwehr officer, from whose book on the subject the following excerpt is taken. "Ebenezer" was the name the Germans gave to the captured Dutch radio operator whom they had forced to cooperate with them at the time our account begins. MID is the Dutch Military Intelligence Service, working out of London with the British SOE. Funk-Abwehr is the German name for counterespionage units engaged in the technical task of locating secret radio transmitters by direction-finding (D/F) methods. And SIPO and ORPO are German police units working in conjunction with the Abwehr.

OUR EXPECTATION THAT Ebenezer would soon be sent new tasks by London was subjected to a difficult test. We had not yet had much experience of this sort of thing and the quiet interval seemed all the more ominous by reason of the fact that we had incontestable proof that the London Secret Service was carrying out operations in Holland without making use of our "good offices."

The first of these occasions was in early April. I received a report from the *gendarmerie* that the body of a parachutist had been found, the man having fractured his skull on landing against a stone water trough. Investigation showed that the dead man belonged to a group of agents who had dropped in the vicinity of Holten. In our efforts to clear up this mysterious affair we turned for help to the local Luftwaffe headquarters which gave out daily reports in map form containing details of all enemy air activity during the previous twenty-four hours. The information on which these maps were based was provided by air-observation posts and radar stations, which plotted the course, height, circling positions, etc., of all single aircraft flying across Holland. We were agreeably surprised by the completeness and accuracy of this information. We found, for example, that details of the operations over Hooghalen and Steenwijk on 28th February and 27th March had been fairly accurately recorded. And we were now able to confirm that the dead agent and his companions must have been dropped near Holten on 28th March. Through the Luftwaffe headquarters in Amsterdam we arranged for closer watch to be kept so as to establish the course of single aircraft, which we described by the word "specialists," as accurately as possible. The evaluation of these daily reports, whose accuracy steadily increased, gave us a useful line on the operations which the Allied Secret Service in England had started without our knowledge. Another indication of secret enemy activity came from Funk-Abwehr and the FuB headquarters, to the effect that a new transmitter had been heard in the Utrecht area, whose radio link had been fixed by D/F as lying close to London. Intercepted traffic indicated that this was the same station as that with which Ebenezer worked. And to add to it all Heinrichs came to me in the second half of April with the news that Radio Orange was once more passing "positive" and "negative" signals.

From all this we concluded that at least one group of agents was working in Holland outside our control and that preparations for further drops had been made. All this made me very uneasy about our play-back on Ebenezer. Had London smelt a rat?

On 29th April Ebenezer received instructions to collect material which would be dropped in the previous area near Steenwijk. I was pretty sure that it would mean bombs this time instead of containers, so I took full precautions. I borrowed against the day of the drop, which was 25th April, three motorized 3.7-cm, flak guns from Hauptmann Lent, the celebrated night flyer and Commandant of the airfield at Leeuwarden, which on the day of the operation were sited round the dropping area after dark. I had the red lights of the triangle fixed on posts so as not to endanger personnel, and arranged things so that they could be switched on from a point 300 yards distant under cover. The same was done for the white light. The flak battery had orders to open fire in the event of bombs being dropped, or if I should fire a red rocket.

We switched on the lights as the British aircraft made its approach at about 0100. "Tommy" flew several times across the area, but clearly missed his direction, as the lights were not being pointed at the aircraft. As he crossed the third time I went to the apex of the triangle and shone my white light at him until he turned on his correct course. I have to thank the absence of bombs for my ability to go on telling this story.

This drop was definite proof that London had not yet discovered our control of Ebenezer. I forgot, in my delight, the lamentation of the young officer in charge of the flak, who had not been able to fire, and who might never again have such a prize held in his sights at a range of two yards.

The development of "Nordpol" reached a decisive stage at the beginning of May. All that we had achieved hitherto could only have been maintained for a short while had not luck, sheer chance and ingenuity caused to fall into our hands at the lines by which the London Secret Service controlled MID-SOE in Holland at that time.

At the end of April London found itself compelled to join up with one another three independent groups of agents and one other isolated individual. Since Ebenezer was included in this link-up, we very soon succeeded in identifying the whole organization.

It happened in this way. In the period February–April, 1942, MID-SOE had dropped three groups of agents in Holland, each consisting of two men and a radio set. We knew nothing of these operations. Another single agent had been landed on the Dutch coast by MTB. The operations consisted of the following:

Operation Lettuce. Two agents, named Jordaan and Ras, dropped near Holten on 28th February 1942. Jordaan was radio operator and was to work in accordance with Plan Trumpet.

Operation Turnip. On 28th February 1942 Agent Andringa and his operator Maartens were dropped near Holten. The set was to be operated in accordance with Plan Turnip. Maartens had an accident and it was his body that was found near the water trough.

Operation Leek. Agent Kloos with his operator Sebes dropped on 5th April 1942. The set was to have been operated in accordance with Plan Heck, but it was rendered useless by damage during the drop.

Operation Potato. On the 19th April 1942, Agent de Haas, using cover-name "Pijl," landed by MTB on the Dutch coast. Pijl had no radio transmitter, but was equipped with a radio-telephony set capable of working at ranges up to five kilometres. He had been sent out from London to contact Group Ebenezer.

Since the Turnip and Heck sets could neither of them establish communication with England, these agents made contact with Group Lettuce, which was operating the Trumpet set, in order to report their mishaps to London. It was not clear whether or not London had told Lettuce to establish these contacts. A signal from Trumpet, intercepted on 24th April and subsequently deciphered, indicated that Trumpet had been in contact with Agent de Haas from Operation Potato, but that the latter had been unable to get in touch with Ebenezer. London thereupon ordered Ebenezer to make contact with Trumpet by a signal passed to the radio set under our control, and the circle was complete.

In our judgment London had felt itself compelled to make this fateful link-up through the loss of transmitters Turnip and Heck, and because of Trumpet's report that de Haas had been unable to contact Ebenezer, which was to pass his signals to England.

A loose contact between different groups of agents had the disadvantage from our point of view that imminent arrests could be quickly reported to London, thus making it difficult to play-back a captured transmitter. But if this contact became a close one, as in the present instance where Trumpet was operating for three other groups, the danger for all of them became very great should one be discovered and liquidated by the German counterespionage. It was highly unfortunate for London that our controlled station Ebenezer had been ordered to make these contacts just at the moment when the groups which were still working at liberty had been linked up directly with one another. (I do not know all the details of how Schreieder and his section in a few days achieved the liquidation of the entire enemy MID-SOE network operating in Holland at that time.)

Without doubt lack of experience and gullibility played

an important part on the other side. The agents were really amateurs, despite their training in England, and they had had no opportunity to work up through practice to the standard required for their immensely difficult task. Generally speaking they could not have reached the standard of a specialist such as Schreieder.

Afu Trumpet had fallen into our hands complete with signal plan, operating and cipher material. The operator Jordaan collapsed when he discovered the extent of the disaster. He was a well-educated young man of good family, perhaps not developed or tough enough for the most dangerous of the jobs known to secret service—agent operating. But that wasn't his fault! Jordaan soon developed confidence in Huntemann and myself, and took the chance which we offered him of operating his transmitter, after we had succeeded in getting him through the nervous crisis which followed his transfer to Scheveningen. On 5th May we used Trumpet to open up a second radio link with London and passed a signal proposing a new dropping area for this group which we had found a few kilometres north of Holten. The line of communication developed smoothly, and evidently gave London no grounds for suspicion, for the dropping area was approved shortly afterward, and we accepted the first drop there about a fortnight later.

A third radio link with London was established in the following manner. The signal plan for Turnip belonging to the dead operator Maartens had been found on the person of the arrested agent Andringa. We signaled to London via Trumpet that Andringa had discovered a reliable operator who would be able to carry out Turnip's signal plan using Maartens' set, and London gave him a trial transmission so as to test the efficiency of this new recruit. The ORPO operator who took the test must have done it excellently, for the next signal from "over there" told him that he was approved. But we soon had new troubles, which worried me a lot.

About the middle of May Heinrichs reported anxiously to me that he and his men suspected Lauwers of having transmitted several additional letters to the end of his last routine period. It was in fact normal to put a series of so-called dummy letters at the end of signals, and his "over-

seer" had consequently not immediately switched off the
set. His mistrust had, however, been aroused. Heinrichs
could not himself be present during every transmission by
Lauwers or Jordaan, and he requested urgently that the
two operators should somehow be replaced by his own
men. I saw the overseer concerned at once. The man declared that he did not know exactly what extra letters
Lauwers had transmitted, but that they had had no meaning. The man knew quite well that any other answer could
have brought him before a military court for treasonable
negligence, but since nothing could be proved one way or
the other we had to await London's reactions.

I brought in Huntemann to try and find out what had
actually happened, as he was on very good terms with both
the ORPO men and Lauwers. It emerged simply that
Lauwers had made some of the ORPO men much too
trusting, had "softened them up" as we put it. The routine
periods had become much too comfortable, and the good
treatment I had ordered for the operators, with coffee and
cigarettes, had broadened into a friendship which was
proving highly dangerous. While awaiting London's reaction, I did not tell Lauwers that our suspicions had been
aroused. Nevertheless, although there were no clear indications of treachery, we soon afterward put an end to the
operating of Lauwers and Jordaan by once more using the
trick of proposing a "reserve" operator—which was immediately approved.

We were now in a position to bring an ORPO man onto
the key in place of either operator without London suspecting anything. The instruction and employment of reserve
operators drawn from the Dutch Underground must have
been quite understandable to them, as it was always possible that a mishap might occur to the No. 1 operator at
any time. Profiting by these events, we did not in general
use agent operators any longer. After the arrest of agents
sent across later on, their sets were operated from the
outset by the ORPO without any turn-over period. In this
procedure we ran the risk that the "handwriting" might
have been recorded in London (on a steel tape or gramo-
phone) and that a comparison might easily give rise to
suspicion. By means of touch, speed of operating and other

individual characteristics of a transmission technique an experienced ear can detect the difference between different operators when on the key in exactly the same way as a musical ear can detect differences between the renderings of different masters.

If the radio organization of MID-SOE had observed proper security precautions we should never have been able to introduce our own ORPO operators. But since our experience hitherto had not disclosed any special degree of watchfulness on their part we took the risk. The carelessness of the enemy is illustrated by the fact that more than fourteen different radio links were established with London for longer or shorter periods during the "Nordpol" operation, and these fourteen were operated by six ORPO men!

In the course of the spring we had amassed a considerable store of knowledge about the enemy's plans, his methods of operating and his radio and ciphering systems. With the help of this experience we could probably even have dealt with blind drops had any more taken place. If the enemy had discovered the truth at this time, he would have had to rebuild a difficult, costly organizational structure, employing entirely new methods. Even making allowance for the fact that MID-SOE had not the slightest suspicion of the true state of affairs, it is a fact that the decision to drop "by arrangement" was the chief reason for the catastrophe which followed. This arrangement, which was carried out rigidly and without variation for over a year, was the really dramatic feature of "Nordpol" amid the many other mistakes of omission and commission made by our enemy.

One single control group, dropped blind and unknown to us in Holland, with the sole duty of watching drops which had been arranged, could have punctured in an instant the whole gigantic bubble of Operation "Nordpol." This unpleasant possibility was always before our eyes during the long months of the play-back, and it kept us from getting too sure of ourselves. We could never forget that each incoming or outgoing radio signal might be the last of the operation.

The decision of MID-SOE was confirmed when the

period from 28th May to 29th June brought three dropping operations, for which the "reliable" groups Ebenezer and Trumpet had to provide the reception parties. The operations were:

Operation Beetroot (via Ebenezer). Agents Parlevliet and van Steen dropped near Steenwijk. Duties—to instruct in the Eureka apparatus, guiding beacons for aircraft. Radio communication in accordance with Plan Swede.

Operation Parsnip (via Trumpet). Agents Rietschoten and Buizer dropped near Holten on 22nd June. Duties—organization of sabotage in Overijssel. Radio in accordance with Plan Spinach.

Operation Marrow (via Ebenezer). Agents Jambroes and Bukkens dropped near Steenwijk on 26th June. Duties—organization of armed resistance in Holland. Radio in accordance with Plan Marrow.

The duties prescribed for parties Beetroot and Marrow were of such importance subsequently that I will discuss them in detail. The Beetroot party was welcomed on its arrival by Underground representatives who were in fact Dutch police working for the SIPO. The arrests were made after dawn, by which time the reception party had had time to find out what the duties of the group were to be. Actually this plan broke down in the case of Beetroot, but was highly successful in all the remaining cases. On subsequent occasions we often discovered important details from the enemy's side, particularly about their secret operational intentions. For example, a single operation gave us precise information about the agent radio schools in England, including the numbers under instruction, their nationality, the teaching staff, standards of ability, etc. Later on our knowledge extended into an accurate picture of the inner circle of leading personalities "over there."

Group Parsnip, which had been dropped on 22nd June near Holten, had a normal assignment, namely, the organization of a sabotage group in Overijssel. Parsnip was consequently played back normally by the customary process of opening up communication, agreeing on dropping points and accepting drops. It was noteworthy that the operator Buizer was, on London's orders, also supposed to transmit for Potato (de Haas), Potato having previously worked through Ebenezer. Ebenezer's burden had been lightened in this way because London considered it to be the most reliable of its links and intended soon to use it for an important special task—the blowing up of the aerial system of the Kootwijk radio transmitter.

At the beginning of July London told Ebenezer to make a reconnaissance to see whether the aerial system could be blown up by a demolition commando under Taconis. In a series of signals exact details were given of the method by which the whole system could be destroyed by means of small charges placed at special points among the mast anchors. I accordingly sent out a reconnaissance party of our people under Willy, who were to conduct themselves exactly as if they were members of the Underground, to find out in what way it would be possible, by day or night, to approach the aerial system, and how the operation could then be carried out. The precise state of affairs as reported by Willy was then signaled to London. We reported a rather small guard, and an inadequate watch over the surrounding area. The demolition of the anchors would not present much difficulty. London signaled back that Taconis must make his preparations in such way that the demolition could be carried out on the night following the receipt of a prearranged signal.

Toward the end of July we reported that Taconis and his men were ready, and were told by London to stand by, but on no account to start anything before receiving the signal. By the time this signal came I had already thought out reasons for "failure."

Two days later Ebenezer passed the following message to London: "Kootwijk attempt a failure. Some of our men ran into a minefield near the anchors. Explosions followed, then an engagement with the guards. Five men missing. Taconis and remainder safe, including two wounded." And the next day: "Two of the five missing men returned. Three others were killed in action. Enemy has strengthened guard on Kootwijk and other stations. Have broken off all contact. No signs yet that enemy is on our track." London signaled back somewhat as follows: "Much regret your failure and losses. Method of defense is new and was not foreseeable. Cease all activity for the present. Greatest watchfulness necessary for some time. Report anything unusual."

A fortnight later London sent Ebenezer a congratulatory message for the Kootwijk party, adding that Taconis would receive a British decoration for his leadership. The medal would be presented to him at the earliest opportunity.

The attack planned on the Kootwijk transmitter was clearly aimed at the destruction of the radio link by which the German Admiralty communicated with U-boats in the Atlantic. When some days later the English made their landing attempt on the French coast near Dieppe we saw another reason why Kootwijk had been intended to be destroyed. Somewhat late in the day, the German Admiralty hastened to carry into actuality the form of defense for the aerial system which we had conjured up in our imagination.

By arrangement with IC of the Wehrmacht staff, Rittmeister Jansen, I had a reference to the Kootwijk affair published in the Dutch press. The article referred to criminal elements who had attempted to blow up a wireless station in Holland. The attempt had been a failure, and captured sabotage material had pointed to enemy assistance. The law-abiding population was warned once again against committing or supporting such acts. I hoped that my opponents in London would receive this report by way of neutral countries.

A description of Operation Marrow which follows covers the decisive phase of "Nordpol" from June, 1942 until the spring of 1943.

We knew from the first conversations on the night of the drop what the tasks were which had been given in London to the leader of Marrow, Jambroes, and his operator Bukkens, in broad outline. The plans of MID-SOE, revealed by interrogation, were on a big scale which underestimated the Abwehr potential on the German side. Typical of this was the lack of understanding of the true position in Holland concerning the morale of the population. There is no doubt that the willingness of the mass of the people to participate directly or indirectly in preparations for underground warfare did not correspond with London's expectations. It was not until one to two years later that morale grew gradually more favorable toward such plans as a result of the military defeats of the Third Reich, the growing Allied superiority and repressive German actions both against the population and against the economy of the western occupied areas.

By the terms of Plan Marrow, Jambroes, who was a Dutch Reserve officer, was to establish contact with the leader of the organization OD (Ordedienst) and get them to provide men to carry out the plans of MID-SOE. Sixteen groups, each of a hundred men, were to be organized all over the country as armed sabotage and resistance nuclei. Two agents from London, a group-leader-cum-instructor and a radio operator, were to take over the leadership, organization, training and arming of these groups. No doubt this plan looked fine from an armchair in London. But its fulfillment was postponed indefinitely by the fact that Jambroes never met the leaders of the OD.

It soon became clear to us that we could not play back Jambroes' task, because as we did not know who were the leaders of the OD we would not be able to tell London what Jambroes had discussed with them—when Jambroes himself was all the time under arrest. So we had to put it to London that the task originally assigned to Jambroes was impracticable, and take action in accordance with what we imagined to be the true state of affairs. We now proceeded to overwhelm London with a flood of reports about signs of demoralization among the leaders of the OD. The leadership, we said, was so penetrated by German informers that direct contact with its members as ordered by London would certainly attract the attention of the Germans. When the replies from London began to show signs of uncertainty and instructed Jambroes to be careful, we started a new line. This proposed that Jambroes should make contact with individual and reliable leaders from OD area groups, so as to form the sixteen groups planned by consultation with the middle and lower OD levels. Our proposal met with some objections, but was finally recognized in a practical manner by the increasing of the support through agents and material given to Group Marrow and its supposed component organizations.

The build-up of the Marrow organization began in August, 1942. Naturally at no time were links established with OD groups or with their leaders. On the contrary, we assured London repeatedly that we were making use of more reliable and security-minded individuals. The development of the sixteen Marrow groups had soon made such apparent progress that between the end of September and November London sent across seventeen agents through our hands in Holland, most of whom were designed for Marrow groups. Five were operators with independent radio links. We had these five lines in working order by the end of November, operating in accordance with Plans Chive, Broccoli, Cucumber, Tomato and Celery. Each of these five groups set to work and were soon able to give dropping points to London, which were approved and supplied continuously with materials. At the beginning of December we signaled a progress report of the existing state of the Marrow groups to London. According to this, about fifteen hundred men were under training, attached to eight Marrow groups. In practice, these training detachments would have had urgent need of such articles as clothing, underwear, footwear, bicycle tires, tobacco and tea. We accordingly asked for a supply of all these articles, and in the middle of December we received a consignment in thirty-two containers totaling some five thousand kilos, dropped in four different areas in the course of one night.

Our information indicated that a new party of agents had completed their training at the secret schools in England about the middle of January, in preparation for action in Holland. From 18th January to 21st April 1943 seventeen more agents were dropped by MID-SOE and met by our reception parties. This time again the majority were group leaders and instructors for Marrow and other sabotage groups. One party of two men had intelligence tasks. Another two-man party was given the task of establishing a courier line from Holland via Brussels and Paris to Spain, and a single woman agent who arrived had been given intelligence duties. The newcomers included seven operators with independent radio links.

The agents supplied in the spring of 1943 fulfilled the

requirements of personnel for the MID-SOE groups which had been planned in Holland. With my few assistants, I was faced with the problem of keeping London's operational maps supplied with information about the multifarious activities of nearly fifty agents, and it seemed impossible that we could keep this up for long. To meet our difficulties an attempt had to be made to get London to agree to a reduction in the number of working radio links which were now available. We accordingly proposed "for reasons of greater security" to close down some of the Marrow transmitters. These sets, we said, would form a reserve in case some of the active transmitters and their operators should be knocked out by German action. We subsequently arrived at the position where of all the Marrow sets only Marrow I to Marrow V remained in operation.

Although several times between the autumn of 1942 and the summer of 1943 we had reported one of our controlled transmitters as having been knocked out by German action, we had been compelled at times to operate as many as fourteen lines simultaneously. A reduction in radio traffic was essential for the one reason alone that we had a maximum of six ORPO radio operators at our disposal for handling the entire radio traffic with London, and these men were being continually worked up to the very limits of their capacity.

This account of how agents were dropped direct into our arms has not yet described any efforts by MID-SOE to get knowledge of the true state of affairs in Holland. Though there was no lack of trying, these attempts never made allowance for the fact that a possibility did exist that the entire communication network and all the agents sent in were in German hands. The most noteworthy enemy attempt at control, which may perhaps have been one of a number which we did not recognize as such, occurred at the time of Operation Parsley on 21st September 1942. There was little doubt that the agent who was dropped, a certain Jongelie, cover-name "Arie," had a control task. Shortly after his arrest Jongelie declared that in order to confirm his safe arrival he must at once signal to London: "The express left on time." by saying this he put his SIPO interrogators in a quandary, a situation which they were meeting for the first time.

I had spent the night of the Parsley operation in the dropping area, which lay a few kilometres east of Assen, and had returned to The Hague at about 0700. At nine the telephone bell roused me from my slumbers, and the head interrogator of Schreieder's section IVE informed me of what Jongelie had just said. He added that this message would apparently have to be dispatched at the first routine period at 1100.

Half an hour later I was sitting opposite Jongelie in the Binnenhof. He was a man of about forty, with a broad, leathery face, who for a long time had been chief operator for the Dutch naval headquarters in Batavia. After a short conversation it was quite clear that Jongelie had developed some Asiatic cunning during his long period of service in Indonesia. With an unnaturally immobile face, he answered my pressing questions repeatedly with the statement that he must pass the message "The express left on time" at 1100 or London would realize that he was in German hands. Finally I pretended to be convinced. Seemingly deep in thought, I said that we would pass his message at 1100—and then, as I suddenly raised my eyes, a gleam of triumph appeared in his. So this was treachery! At 1100 we passed the following message: "Accident has occurred in Operation Parsley. Arie landed heavily and is unconscious. He is safe and in good hands. Doctor diagnoses severe concussion. Further report will be made. All material safe." Three days later we signaled: "Arie regained consciousness for short period yesterday. Doctor hopes for an improvement." And the next day the message ran: "Aire died suddenly yesterday without regaining consciousness. We will bury him on the moor. We hope to give him a worthy memorial after victory is won."

I have related this case in detail as an example of how competent tough agents, who had been appropriately prepared in London, could easily have forced us into the position where a single treacherous report would have blown the gaff. All we could do in such cases was to pretend that the man was dead or that he had been arrested by the Germans. A series of such "accidents" would probably always have been less dangerous than the possibility of treachery. Shortly after the Arie incident London began to press us to send Jambroes, the head of the Marrow groups, back to London for consultation, Jabroes having to name a deputy to act for him in his absence. This request accorded with the man's earlier statements that after three months of preparatory activity in Holland he would be required back in England. A reference to the possibilities of Jambroes' journey was now never absent from our interchange of signals. At first we described him as indispensable due to unforeseen difficulties in the building up of the sixteen groups, and in due course we found new excuses, in which the difficult and lengthy journey by the insecure courier route into Spain played the principal part.

Ninteen forty-two went by in this way. At the beginning of 1943 the requests from London for a personal report became more urgent and were now broadened to include representatives from other groups. Innumerable signals passed. London began to demand information about areas in Holland where land or sea planes could be sent to pick up couriers or agents. We were unable to find suitable areas, or, alternatively, those which we did find and reported did not suit the gentlemen "over there"—or else we would suddenly declare them "unsafe," whenever the organization of a special flight seemed imminent.

On various occasions we reported a number of agents as having departed for France, who were expected every month to arrive, but naturally never did so. Finally we took the only course still open to us and reported Jambroes as missing . . . informing London that our investigations showed that he could not be traced subsequent to a German police raid in Rotterdam. . . .

On 18th January 1943 Group Golf was dropped into Holland. Golf's duties were to prepare secure courier routes through Belgium and France to Spain and Switzerland. The group was well supplied with blanks for Dutch, Belgian and French identity cards with stamps and dies for the forging of German passes of all kinds, and with francs and pesetas. We let about six weeks pass before Golf signaled to London that a reliable and secure route had been established as far as Paris. The courier for the Golf groups would be an experienced man with cover name "Arnaud." In actual fact Arnaud was none other than my Unteroffizier Arno, who had effected an excellent penetration of the enemy courier routes by posing as a refugee Frenchman who made his living by smuggling jewels. We proposed to London that we should dispatch to Spain via the Arnaud route two English flying officers who were living underground in Holland in order to test the reliability of this "escape line." Our proposal was approved, and London confirmed three weeks later that the men had arrived safely in Spain.

Through this exploit, the Golf group and Arnaud acquired much credit in London, and in the spring and summer of 1943 London gave us details of three active stations of the British Secret Service in Paris which were working on escape routes. These were run partly by French and partly by English personnel and had their own radio links with London. Obviously we did not permit the German counter-espionage in Paris to take action against these stations, once more adhering to the principle that intelligence is more valuable then elimination. My section under Major Wieskotter now had a clear view of the inner working of these important escape lines, made possible by the well-sponsored arrival of Arnaud in the organization by reason of a signaled recommendation by London to the stations concerned.

The responsibility for innumerable captures of couriers and espionage material, of incoming and outgoing agents, and of espionage and radio centers in Holland and Belgium during 1943, inexplicable to the enemy Secret Services, must be laid at the door of MID-SOE's confidence in the Golf radio link, which had been in our hands since the day of its arrival in Holland. In actual fact Golf rendered certain services to the enemy in order to increase this confidence.

We had proved once again the truth of the old saying: "Give and it shall be given unto you." Numbers of Allied flying personnel who had been shot down and had gone underground in Holland and Belgium had reached Spain after an adventurous journey without ever knowing, perhaps until the present day, that they had all the time been under the wing of the German counterespionage.

* * *

On 31st August, Queen's Day in Holland, two "Nordpol" agents, Ubbink and Dourlein, broke out of the prison in Haaren and disappeared. I had a short report to this effect on the morning of 1st September from Schreieder's office. Soon afterward Schreieder himself rang up in considerable agitation to give me a seemingly endless description of the measures which he had taken for their recapture. It was clear to me that, through this incident, the bottom had been knocked out of the whole "Nordpol" operation. Even if the fugitives did not succeed in reaching Spain, Switzerland or even England itself, they were at large—though perhaps only temporarily—and would certainly somehow record their experiences since their departure from England and get this report by some means or other back across the Channel.

During the first ten days of December London's signals became so dull and colorless compared with their usual quality that it did not need all our knowledge to enable us to guess that the enemy was trying to deceive us in his turn. Hardly any doubt remained that Ubbink and Dourlein had reached their objective. Nevertheless, we made no move, and gave not the slightest indication that we too realized that the great bubble of the agent network and radio links in Holland had been finally pricked.

In March, 1944, I proposed to Berlin that we should put an end to the hollow mockery of the "Nordpol" radio links by means of a final message. I was immediately told to submit a draft for approval to Abwehr Berlin, which must express confidence in victory. Huntemann and I set ourselves to compose a message which should fulfill not only Berlin's requirements but also our reflections on the two years' hoax which we had carried out so successfully. This message, the first to be transmitted quite openly in plain language, must not in any way fall short of the standard of the thousand-odd cipher signals which had been previously dispatched. We sat at my desk and exchanged our first attempts at a suitable text in order to discover something worthy of this unique occasion. Writing rather as if we were playing "consequences," each of us composing a few sentences in turn, we finally agreed on the following:

> To Messrs. Blunt, Bingham & Co., Successors Ltd., London.
> We understand that you have been endeavoring for some
> time to do business in Holland without our assistance. We
> regret this the more since we have acted for so long as
> your sole representatives in this country, to our mutual
> satisfaction. Nevertheless we can assure you that, should
> you be thinking of paying us a visit on the Continent on
> any extensive scale, we shall give your emissaries the same
> attention as we have hitherto, and a similarly warm wel-
> come. Hoping to see you.

The names given were those of the men whom we knew
to be at the head of the Netherlands section of SOE. We
signaled this draft to Berlin for their approval. They were
evidently occupied with more important matters, however,
and we had to wait a fortnight until, after one or two
reminders, we received permission to transmit the message
without amendment.

I passed the plain language test to the FuB station on
31st March, with instructions to pass it to England over all
the lines controlled by us, which at that time numbered
ten, the next day. It had occurred to me that 1st April
might be particularly apposite.

The following afternoon the FuB station reported that
London had accepted the message on four lines, but had
not answered calls on the other six. . . .

Operation "Nordpol" was over.

The attempt of the Allied Secret Services to gain a foot-
hold in Holland had been delayed by two years. The establishment of armed sabotage and terror organizations,
which might have disorganized the rear areas of the Atlantic Wall and crippled our defenses at the critical moment
of invasion, had been prevented. The penetration of the
underground movement had led to the liquidation of
widely spread and boldly directed enemy espionage services. The complete deception of the enemy about the real
state of affairs in Holland would have subjected him to
the danger of a heavy defeat had he attempted to attack
during 1942 or 1943. The information which we had
gained about the activities and intentions of the enemy

Secret Services had contributed directly to the countering of corresponding plans in other countries.

Operation "Nordpol" was no more than a drop in the ocean of blood and tears, of the suffering and destruction of the Second World War. It remains none the less a noteworthy page in the chequered and adventurous story of Secret Service, a story which is as old as humanity and as war itself.

3

Prelude to Invasion

Stewart Alsop
and Thomas Braden

"Torch" was the code name for the Anglo-American invasion of North Africa in November, 1942. After the fall of France in the summer of 1940 the French Navy and the greater part of the administration of the French colonies in North Africa had come under the sway of the Nazi-installed Vichy government, and therefore would theoretically oppose any Allied move into Africa as faithful minions of the Germans. Not all Frenchmen would feel this way, but it was a question of finding out which ones would and which wouldn't, and which were ready to help the Allied undertaking by becoming a kind of anti-Axis underground in North Africa.

THE OASIS ON the northern edge of the Sahara Desert, extending both west and east of Spain, consists of a long semicircle of coastal countries whose domed cities glare white in the hot sun and succeed in averting the traveler's eye from the festering filth of their native quarters. Tangier, Spanish Morocco, French Morocco, Algeria—theirs

FROM the book *Sub Rosa.*

are comparatively minor ports of call, not particularly beckoning to the American tourist. Probably it is because of their many nationalities and their close yet separate relationship to the governments of Europe that they have frequently been chosen by novelists as the scenes of international intrigue. In the summer of 1941 they became such a scene in fact.

They were neutral. German and American officials passed each other that summer on the streets of Casablanca, Oran, Algiers and Tunis as they did throughout the war in the international zone of Tangier. These officials were not there to decide the major issues of war. Their relationship to each other had been settled or was being settled in the seats of power to the north, in Vichy, Berlin, London and Madrid. In Vichy, Pétain had surrendered to Adolf Hitler. The old man had succeeded, for the time being at least, in keeping French North Africa to the French. The best spies in French North Africa said, however, that it was only a question of time.

In Madrid, Franco was biding his time too. The best spies in Spanish Morocco said that Hitler would attack Africa through Spain with Franco's connivance and aid. Later, they said he would not. It was a question, and certain persons were willing to pay large amounts of money for an answer.

In London, the Churchill government fretted over all of its difficult situations, not the least of which was that in July of 1940, British warships had shelled the French Navy at Mers El Kebir, and as the result of it, Pétain had broken off relations with England. Not that France was then a potent enemy—though its fleet was still worth a good deal —but it meant that all known British agents were being rounded up and thrown out of French North Africa, that there was no adequate communication system there for British spies.

It was indeed a difficult situation, for though nothing was being settled in Africa, much might be, and in any event, there was a great deal to learn there.

There was the question of the French Army. Which way would it swing? Its leadership was conservative to the point of reaction, inclined toward monarchism, extremely anti-

German, almost as anti-British, on the whole loyal to Pétain. If Laval came to power, it might be a different story, or it might not. The younger French officers and men, some of whom had escaped after the fall of France, were beaten, disgraced and angry, anxious to fight against Germany but suspicious of British leadership, or even of British partnership. Most of all they feared the final failure to France which might result from an abortive uprising, a half-hearted Allied attempt, the kind of action which the French spoke of scornfully as "Allied commando raids."

There was the French Navy, jealously guarding the balance of its fleet, and particularly the proud ship, the *Jean Bart*. In the old naval tradition which knows no bars of nationality, it was far more conservative than the Army. Furthermore the shelling by the British in which more than a thousand Frenchmen had been killed still rankled deep.

There were the Riffs of Morocco under Tassels, willing to rise if there were money and arms to be had for it, and there were the Arabs, interested in the power politics around them, anxious to be on the winning side.

There was the Italian Armistice Commission in Tunisia, the German in Morocco, the combined commissions in Algeria. They were there to see that the Hitler-Pétain terms were carried out, and to remind the French that they had been defeated. There was the little group of Spanish republicans who had managed to keep out of concentration camps, and there were the riff-raff spies of no nation who for years had made a good living selling secrets on the open market.

All of these groups and their relationships to each other were discussed and rediscussed in the small waterfront cafés that summer where agents of all nations found that there was much to learn and that it was not very difficult to learn it.

There was, in fact, only one secret which was not for sale on the fringe of the African coastline that summer. The secret was the date, or the approximate date, when Africa would be invaded by the United States.

That it would be invaded was no secret at all. United States officials intercepted a telegram to Germany that summer which read, "There are 10 United States citizens in Casablanca who are there for the purpose of forming a fifth column to pave the way for intended Allied disembarkations in the spring."

After all, the invasion of North Africa was a factor in Allied strategy which the Germans would have been stupid not to consider. Far to the east in Libya, the tiny British Army was battling back and forth between Alexandria and Benghazi and getting nowhere. A pincers movement on Africa was therefore an obvious possibility.

The Germans might even have suspected that the idea was in the mind of Franklin D. Roosevelt before Pearl Harbor, as indeed it was. After Pearl Harbor, the idea became a definite plan which waited only for the recruiting and training of the United States Army.

In the meantime, of course, it was always possible that the Germans themselves would invade. In such an eventuality, the United States hoped that the French in Africa would oppose them. But with Britain and France at swords' points, with British agents and British radios being tossed out of all French North Africa, if any encouragement was to be given the French, and if anything was to be found out from them, it was up to the United States to do it. The opportunity to carry on that work in Africa was the major reason why Franklin D. Roosevelt did not give way to the urgings of well-meaning citizens who wanted him to break off relations with Vichy.

Preparing for the invasion of North Africa was the first big operational task of OSS. On the success or failure of the task hinged much of the future of the organization. Yet OSS did not inaugurate the intelligence-operational program in Africa. What it did was to make use of men whom the State Department had already placed in the field. These men were vice-consuls of the State Department. That was their title. Yet they did little or nothing of vice-consular work, and their superiors, the United States consuls in Africa, did not know the real reasons why they were there or what they were doing. This peculiar situation came about in the following way:

Shortly after the fall of France, the United States had become a party to what were known as the Weygand-Murphy economic agreements. They were negotiated in North Africa between Robert Murphy, who was then counselor of the United States Embassy at Vichy and General Weygand, whom Vichy had delegated to rule North Africa. The agreements provided that the United States ship substantial amounts of coal, cotton, gasoline, and sugar to North Africa. In return the French promised not to export these or similar goods out of North Africa. More important, they agreed to allow a small number of United States officials to enter French North Africa and to oversee the goods, to make sure that they were not reshipped to Germany. Checking these goods should not have been a full-time job for any group of reasonably efficient men, and it was not. The small number of United States officials sent to do the job were given vice-consular status and told that their real mission was to collect information.

"The plotters," they later called themselves, and they were about as amateur a team as has ever faced big-league opposition, about as likely to be successful spies as Mata Hari was likely to be chosen president of Vassar College.

There were Stafford Reid, a construction man from New York; Sidney Bartlett, a California oil man; Leland Rounds, a businessman; John Knox, who had graduated from the French Military Academy at St. Cyr; John Boyd, who had been a Coca-Cola branch manager in Marseilles; Harry Woodruff and John Utter, two bankers who had lived in Paris; Franklin Canfield, a young lawyer; Donald Coster, an advertising man; Kenneth Pendar, a Harvard librarian who was later to write a revealing book based upon his adventures; Carleton Coon, a Harvard anthropologist; Ridgeway Knight, a wine merchant; and Gordon Browne, who had previously traveled in Morocco.

They arrived in Africa in July of 1941 and set to work under Robert Murphy, acquiring maps, charting fields, measuring coastlines, sounding out French and Arab sentiment, watching ship movements, and trying to make up plausible stories for their superiors, the United States consuls, which would explain their so frequent absence from their offices.

Often they got themselves into trouble. Pendar reports that it was a poor week when one of them did not come up with at least one rumor of a German invasion. One of the men fell violently in love with a French girl who turned out to be a German spy. He had to be sent home. Yet by the time William A. Eddy arrived in Tangier to enlist them all in a joint OSS—State Department venture with Murphy and Eddy at the top, they had laid the groundwork for an intelligence system in North Africa. It was not many months after Eddy's arrival that one of them said, in a cable to Washington: "I recommend that when the troops are ready to begin landings I be authorized to arrange for the assassination of the German Armistice Commission at Casablanca." In the training ground of Africa, United States agents learned fast.

Eddy is a man of the highest character. Afterward American Minister to Saudi Arabia, he was born in Syria of missionary parents, became a war hero, a professor of English at Dartmouth College, and president of Hobart College.

When he arrived at Tangier, Eddy had been told that the United States planned to invade Africa as soon as it was strong enough to do so. In aid of the landings, he was to set up intelligence posts in the principal cities. He was to establish a chain of communications between them, and with America. He was to prepare the beachheads and landing fields, and he was to try to nullify French opposition, or if possible win French support. In the meantime Eddy was to encourage the French to resist the Germans in the event that Hitler beat the Allies to the draw by invading North Africa himself. To do the job, Eddy was to have the services of the vice-consuls working under Robert Murphy, and he himself was to direct their efforts in cooperation with Murphy.

In this difficult dual role, Eddy and Murphy worked excellently together. They ran the OSS group much in the manner of one of Eddy's college seminars. Together they set up five secret radio stations, Pilgrim in Tunis, Yankee in Algiers, Franklin in Oran, Lincoln in Casablanca, and Midway in Tangier. Eddy spent much of his time traveling back and forth between them. At each post he would call together the OSS men who worked there, and they would sit for hours discussing the latest information and each others' plans. At the end of the discussion, Eddy would give further orders.

The intelligence-operational mission which Eddy and

Murphy set out to accomplish brought them immediately
into close touch with high officers of the French Army.
Everything in French North Africa centered around the
French Army and Navy. Eddy and Murphy soon discovered that the Navy was a closed corporation which would
have nothing to do with the Americans so long as Americans had anything to do with the British. It was the French
Army, or certain high leaders in it, which was willing to
share intelligence of value, and it was the Army which
would resist the Germans most effectively if any resistance
were to be made.

The head of the French Army in Africa was General
Maxime Weygand, a strongly conservative and immensely
popular leader. All the evidence which can now be gathered points to the conclusion that Weygand, who had
fought the Germans unsuccessfully in 1940, was secretly
planning the opportunity to fight them again. Murphy
seems to have been in close touch with him. It is certain, at
any rate, that Weygand's sympathies did not appeal to the
Germans, who were able to have him recalled to France
in the late fall of 1941. He left behind him various staff
officers who held themselves ready to lead the French
against the Germans, provided they were armed and supplied, and that any American effort in Africa was a major
effort and not an abortive raid. Murphy was certainly in
touch with these men, and when Eddy arrived he learned
about the plan too. Both wanted to accept the French
proposal.

Neither Murphy nor Eddy knew when the United States
landings would take place—indeed at this time no definite
date had been set. But both were convinced that a German
invasion was a distinct possibility, and that if the French
were armed, they would resist it. Thus they believed that
by arming the French, the United States might save North
Africa for the Allies.

It was this conclusion, and its logical consequences,
which led to Murphy's castigation in the United States
press as a dealer with Fascists, and even as a Fascist. It
was this conclusion which led to Eddy's fruitless arguments
with Donovan, as he begged for supplies for the French.
The whole matter of United States policy in respect to the

African landings has been so heatedly debated that it may be well to review the basis for Eddy's and Murphy's decision.

The French whom Murphy and Eddy found at the helm in Africa were about as liberal a group as might be assembled at a cocktail party given by the Chase National Bank. They represented the sympathies of the conservative colonials among the French population, a large number of whom were of Army and Navy families. There was not in the whole of French North Africa a single cell or unit which owed allegiance to Charles de Gaulle. The French Army was loyal to Pétain because they were Frenchmen and Pétain was the chief of France. It was a strange sort of logic which allowed many of the leaders in the Army to insist upon their loyalty to Pétain and, at the same time, agree to aid the Americans, even if the *maréchal* did not go along. "It is what the Marshal would do if he could," one of them said.

The Underground in Africa then, in the sense of a powerful, organized group which could be used against the Germans, consisted of certain leaders within the French Army. Whether they liked it or not, the French Army was the only resistance which Murphy and Eddy could find.

As soon as they had completed arrangements with the French, Eddy wired Donovan for tons of supplies. Donovan was amazed at their quantity and said so. Eddy countered with beautifully worded arguments, the essence of which was that if the French were willing to risk their lives in unloading and hiding the supplies, the Americans ought to be willing to send them. "It is my conviction," said Eddy, "that failure on our part to give this support will be fatal to our plans to keep Morocco and North Africa strong enough to resist enemy aggression. We will not find such leaders elsewhere, and we dare not lose them now. . . ."

Donovan countered with talk of Australia. A fleet had been assembled for Africa in January, but had been diverted to Australia, so that nothing could be done now.

To Eddy in Africa, mention of Australia was merely an annoying change of subject. Every Allied sympathizer in Africa was excited and impatient, and Eddy and Murphy not least of all. In April, 1942, Laval had come to power. The Germans planned to enter Tunisia the moment that Malta fell. Laval would undoubtedly then surrender North Africa, and the whole French Army, still weak, would fall into Axis hands.

But it was not necessary to look into the future in order to feel downhearted. With Laval's coming to power, the French Fascist, Doriot, began a huge campaign of collaboration in Africa. The leaders in various units of the Army with whom Eddy and Murphy had made their plans were being gradually removed and replaced by Laval men. The Axis grip on North Africa was growing tighter by the moment.

"They are taking all the risk. They will receive, distribute, and use the supplies, every step being taken with the threat of execution as traitors if they are uncovered. The least we can do is to help supply them on their own terms, which are generous and gallant . . . we have days, not weeks," Eddy said, and begged for help.

His prayers were doomed. Donovan turned the matter over to the Joint Chiefs of Staff, who decided in that same month of April, 1942, that if the Axis intended to occupy North Africa, there was nothing in the world the United States could do to prevent it. In the meantime, they thought it best not to arm the French. Anticlimactically, they proposed that Eddy and Murphy leave the radio stations behind as listening posts and organize guerrilla bands to harass the enemy if the Axis should invade. It seemed to Eddy when he heard that decision that the Allies had already lost the war in North Africa.

History would seem to have proved that Murphy and Eddy were wrong in their proposals to arm the French. Eddy did not realize at that time what few arms America had. The Germans did not beat the Allies to an invasion date, as Eddy and Murphy feared they would. That they did not, however, was due in large part to the work of Eddy and Murphy.

After the decision had been made, the OSS group in Africa continued to work on the French Army, trying to neutralize it, to make American friends and German enemies even without the inducement of American arms. On a low level, the OSS methods on this job have been recorded by an Austrian black marketeer known as Pinkeye, who helped the Americans:

"I would talk with people of the current situation," Pinkeye has said, "and we would reminisce of France and speak of the French Army. After a while, I would make some slight observation uncomplimentary to the Germans. If that was taken up, I would go a little further, making the bridge between the Germans and Vichy. After a meeting or two I would begin to form an idea of whether a man was worth something."

In the meantime OSS men scattered throughout Africa at the various radio stations continued to watch shipping and cargoes, sketch defenses, and pass back their information. Frequently ships were spotted and sunk by British submarines on the information of OSS men who watched the harbor and the ships which sailed.

The United States consuls, who did not know of these clandestine activities on the part of the men whom they considered their assistants, sometimes caused trouble. Once, the radio station which had been secreted on the roof of the consulate in Tangier had to be moved because the consul's wife complained of "tapping noises on the roof at night." Another time Murphy had to intervene with the State Department to save an OSS man whom the consul had proposed to dismiss because he was not "paying any attention to the affairs of the consulate."

Always the OSS men were asked by the French, "When are the landings coming?" Always they said there would be no landings. As time went on people began to believe them. Eddy himself first learned of the approximate date of the invasion on July 24 in a hotel room at Claridge's in London.

He had been ordered there to meet General George V. Strong, chief of the Military Intelligence Service. He was introduced to Strong and to General George Patton by Colonel Edwin Buxton, Donovan's executive officer.

As chief of G-2 Strong had always been anything but partial to OSS. It was up to Eddy to impress him. Eddy must have been an impressive figure. He was wearing his Marine Corps uniform with the five rows of ribbons he had won in the Fifth Marines during the last war, and he had a noticeable limp from old wounds. Even Patton did not yet have five rows of ribbons. "Do you know Bill Eddy?" Buxton said, introducing him to Patton.

"Never saw him before in my life," said Patton, shaking hands, "but the son of a bitch's been shot at enough, hasn't he?"

They took chairs in the room, and Eddy began to talk about Africa. Before he could get fairly under way, Strong interrupted him.

"Now wait a minute, Eddy. I'm G-2 of this Army, and I'm going to tell you something. If you're going to tell us what you think instead of what you know, you might find yourself contributing to the murder of thousands of your own countrymen. Now for God's sake, tell us the facts."

Eddy began again. He told about the French Army, the possibility of its nonresistance to a landing and of its support. He named the groups he had trained outside the Army, and his plans for them. He told of his own organization and of the intelligence on ship movements and defenses which his group had already assembled. Halfway through his explanation, Patton rose and dashed out of the room, saying, "I want Jimmy to hear this."

He came back in a few minutes with General Doolittle, and Eddy continued, telling, for Doolittle's benefit, all about the airfields in Africa, and estimating the possibility of their delivery intact to a landing force.

He talked without interruption until one o'clock. When he had finished, Strong rose and held out his hand. "I am very much impressed with you," he said. "I think you know what you're talking about."

The next day Eddy saw Eisenhower. He returned to Africa with more definite plans in mind than he had ever had before. The date set for the landing was now four months away.

The kind of work which the OSS group was to do from that time on, the organizing and training of special forces to take over key points, the gathering of every conceivable piece of information about landing points, the smuggling out of Africa of various persons who might be useful to the Allied plan, the encouraging of the German belief that the landings would take place at Dakar—none of this lends itself readily to description. Perhaps two incidents which involved only three of the men will best describe the field work accomplished during the last four months before the invasion. The first has to do with the Dakar Cover Plan.

The idea that the Allies would land at Dakar and then proceed westward had widespread credence in Africa. It had some logic in itself. Dakar was strategically important and a previous attempt to take it by a British-French force under the leadership of de Gaulle had failed miserably. What was most important about the idea, from the OSS standpoint, was that Dakar was many, many miles from the point where Allied troops would first touch French soil in Africa. OSS men did everything possible to encourage the rumor. One such effort was made by the husky, immaculate Donald Coster, of the J. Walter Thompson Advertising Agency, and Radio Station Lincoln at Casablanca.

Coster had been asked by an acquaintance in London to look up two French friends who had escaped from France to Africa. They were known to Coster as Freddie and Walter. As soon as he met them, Coster decided that they were interesting. Freddie was blond and romantic. He had been a moving-picture star in France. Walter was dark and muscular but smoothly so. He had once been middleweight boxing champion of Austria. Both had fought in the French Foreign Legion and in the Loyalist army in Spain. They had been placed in a Vichy concentration camp, and had escaped through a remarkable coincidence. Freddie was an extremely good friend of the German diplomat Teddie Auer. They had met in the salons of Paris before the war when Auer had been a military attaché. In Africa, Freddie remarked, Auer had arranged for both of them to be released from prison. Seated across from the two Frenchmen at the Café de la Gare in Casablanca, Coster heard the fact and blinked. Teddie Auer was attached to the German Armistice Commission.

Coster cultivated his new friends. Eventually, on instructions from Eddy sent through Coster, Freddie and Walter were sent to General Auer to sign on as his spies. It was easily done. They told him that they knew Coster, who was an American spy, and that they could get valuable information from him. Auer agreed to hire them and to pay them well. Coster began to feed them correct information, little things such as the numbers of the American agents' license plates, the dates when Eddy or Murphy would be in Casablanca. Freddie would go off at night to see the German general, and the next morning would call Coster to say, "Your friend from the hospital wants to see you."

The three would meet at noon for coffee in the Café de la Gare and Coster would receive and give information. Freddie and Walter lived well on the money Auer paid them. Not once did they ask Coster for so much as a franc.

Once, the scheme which Coster had in mind nearly fell through. He received a frantic telephone call from Freddie saying that Auer was acting up. He had told Freddie that he had never seen him in the company of Coster, and that he suspected Freddie was getting his money for nothing. Walter suggested a plan. He, Freddie and Coster would meet that night at a large café and have dinner in public where the Germans could see them. Coster agreed.

That night at a center table in the café, the three men had blackmarket steaks and quantities of wine, while they told loud stories and slapped each other's backs. "As a matter of fact," Coster recalls, "we got pretty fried." From a side table, the entire German Armistice Commission, with Auer seated in the center, watched in comparative silence. Herr Auer was evidently convinced. Next day, Freddie presented him with the bill for the dinner. He paid it with thanks.

It was in August that Coster planted the information to which all his work had been leading. "Tell Herr Auer," he said to Freddie, "that you have just learned from me that the final invasion plan has been settled. American and British troops will land on Dakar sometime this fall." Freddie passed the information on to General Auer that night. Auer was delighted with it. Next morning Freddie reported that he had sent off a special message to German headquarters at Wiesbaden.

The Dakar Cover Plan was a huge success. Three months later, the largest armada the Allies had ever assembled landed in Africa. Yet it was not once attacked by submarines until four days after the landings had been made. Those four days constituted the exact time that it took the entire German fleet in the South Atlantic to rendezvous off the coast of Dakar and then return to Africa again.

How much Coster's plotting had to do with his success and how much should be attributed to others, to the invading fleet's feint toward Dakar, and to the mistakes of the German Intelligence will probably never be known. Nevertheless, for the rest of his life Coster will delight in remembering the first conversation he held with a Frenchman on his return to Africa. He had gone back to England and come in again with the invasion forces: When he landed at Oran, he walked up to an old acquaintance, the Vichy French colonel in command of the Oran airfield. Coster extended his hand. The colonel grew red and angry. "Pourquoi êtes-vous ici?" he asked. "Nous vous attendions à Dakar."

Another example of OSS work in the field was known later as the "Malverne Exfiltration." Eddy had received a request from invasion headquarters for a pilot to guide the Allied convoys to the beaches. Such a man had been previously offered to David King in Casablanca. His name was Malverne and he was the chief pilot of Port Lyautey.

Malverne had been expelled from France for anti-German activities. He was perfectly willing to be exfiltrated. The question was how to get him across the border, past the French and Spanish authorities into Tangier. Eddy wired King to put him in the baggage compartment, meaning that King should smuggle him out, and not try to bring him through under false passports. King delegated Gordon Browne and Franklin P. Holcombe, who happened to be in Casablanca at the time, to make the trip in their Chevrolet, and hide Malverne in the trailer.

Malverne was fitted in behind some gasoline drums. Two gunny sacks and a Moroccan rug were thrown over him, and across the whole a heavy canvas cover was lashed down, with just enough slack to let in the air. Malverne took up his position and with Browne and Holcombe in the front, set out for Tangier.

It is a long journey from Casablanca to Tangier and the roads are rough. Browne and Holcombe knew that their passenger was taking a terrible beating, but what they worried about most was the monoxide from the gasoline drums and the exhaust in the rear. At frequent intervals, Browne would draw up on the side of the road, and walk leisurely to the back of the trailer, pausing to kick the tires as though making a cursory inspection. When he reached the right rear tire, where there was a large gap in the canvas cover, he would inquire in a low voice for Malverne. As though from the bottomless deep, the answer would come. "Tout va bien, pas trop de monoxide." Browne would go back to his seat and start out again.

They reached the border-control post at dusk. The French post was run by a friend of David King's, so the Spanish post was the dangerous one. Holcombe went up to the office with the passports for Browne and himself to have them stamped, while Browne walked casually around the trailer, getting some exercise and keeping an eye on the canvas cover.

One of the customs officers asked him what was in the back, and Browne answered easily, "Gasoline." It was at that very moment that he noticed the black and white bird dog which belonged to the customs officials. The dog had taken up a position in the rear of the trailer and was pointing Malverne in championship style. Browne picked up a rock and threw it at him; then patted him until Holcombe appeared.

A few minutes later they were driving past the control posts ahead, and eventually they reached Holcombe's house, high over Tangier. Malverne was let out of the trailer and remarked that such journeys were all very well for the *type sportif*, but he made an even more dangerous journey later when he took an American destroyer up the Sebu River to Port Lyautey, a task which most Navy men thought could not be done, and for which he received America's Navy Cross.

Browne has written a report on his journey that night which ends with a note on his own feelings: "It turned out to be an easy job," he says, "but it wouldn't have been so good if we had been caught. It would have meant the recall of the vice-consuls in Africa, but worse than that, it would have pointed a sure finger to the landings. That is what we thought about on the dark road to Tangier."

While all this was going on, Eddy and Murphy were still working hard to ensure as little resistance as possible to the landings. The outlook was not altogether bright. At German insistence, the French Navy and its air force were being given larger defense areas, areas which at the time of the invasion were to cover in some places as much as forty miles inland.

However, the Army leaders with whom Murphy and Eddy had constantly been in touch were still trying. Not long before the invasion, they put forward General Giraud as their logical leader, and again asked that they be taken into full partnership in the invasion. Giraud had escaped from prison and secretly established communication with Murphy from France. He suggested to Murphy that the main force land in the south of France, where he would prepare the ground, and that the African expedition be a sideshow. General Mast, Giraud's representative in Africa, also pleaded the case to Murphy.

Allied headquarters stood firm, however. On the grounds of security, it would not reveal to the French the time nor the place of the invasion. Eisenhower was willing, however, to send representatives to meet with Giraud or Mast if it would help to neutralize resistance by the French, and if headquarters could get some intelligence from them. But not until the invading fleet had already sailed were Giraud and Mast told even that there would definitely be an invasion.

On October 20, Eddy received a message from Gibraltar: "General Clark and four officers will rendezvous at point agreed on 21 October. Reception party should be at rendezvous, 2100 hours, prepared to remain until dawn. In the event weather fails, arrange alternate plan to meet aboard submarine. . . ."

Murphy had arranged the meeting, and had set its location. It was to be held at the farmhouse of Jacques Tessier, near the shore, seventy-five miles west of Algiers. General Mast, Colonel d'Astier de la Vigerie, Murphy, and Ridgeway Knight, Eddy's OSS representative, arrived at the farm on October 20. At dusk, the signal light was lit, a white electric bulb hanging in a window looking out on the sea. Knight spent the night on the beach, waiting to guide Clark's party from the submarine, but no one came. In the morning Murphy and the French went back to Algiers, and the next night they tried again.

At midnight, halfway through another lonely vigil, Knight saw a kayak bobbing in the water, a little way offshore. He waited until it beached and he saw a man get out of it; then he stepped forward and identified himself. The man was a British commando officer, and he winked a flashlight to signal three more kayaks out of the darkness. They carried Clark, General Lemnitzer, Colonel Hamblin, Colonel Holmes, Captain Wright of the United States Navy, and two more British commando officers. The party shouldered their kayaks and carried them into the house.

The next morning the French arrived and Clark held staff talks with them until evening. Mast gave Clark details on the ports, tonnage capacities, the dispositions and strengths of the French Army. He insisted that the Americans hold off the invasion for six weeks or more because Giraud's organization in southern France was not yet ready. It was a difficult situation for Clark because he could not tell Mast that the fleet had already sailed, that it was going to land in Africa and not in France, and that the troops were British as well as American. When Mast outlined the French preparations in France and Africa, Clark could only say that they were satisfactory.

The two staffs had just finished their talks and were sitting down to dinner, when a young French officer burst in at the door. "Gendarmes, gendarmes!" he shouted, waving his hands in a circle. The French officers seemed to vanish. Clark and his staff ducked into a wine cellar. The civilians immediately emptied their pockets of money, laid it on the table, and poured themselves glasses of wine. Somebody produced a pack of cards, and in a moment the farmhouse was the scene of what looked like a drunken poker game.

Someone had told the police to investigate the suspicious arrivals at the lonely farm. It was Murphy who thought of a plan to forestall them. "Go and tell the police," he told the young French officer, "that there is a member of the American State Department here who is buying a little black-market wine. Tell them he has a girl friend, and is having a little party. Tell them if they break it up, it will create an international incident."

The French officer left armed with that story, and in an hour was back again. He had convinced the police. General Clark, somewhat cramped and damp, was let out of the cellar.

At four that morning, after three attempts which failed, Clark and his party succeeded in launching their kayaks in a rough sea. By that time, everyone was wet to the skin, and most of the group had taken off their clothes. When the last kayak was lifted onto the waves, with the officers inside, Murphy was so happy he did a dance in the sand. Then everyone went back to Algiers, leaving the French farmer to rake the beach of footsteps.

The meeting between Clark and the French was in a sense the last of the preparations for the invasion. Gaining French support, or at least nullifying French opposition, had been Eddy's and Murphy's primary concern from the beginning. They were not to be completely successful. But the principal opposition to the invasion was to be furnished by the French Navy and its air force, and this opposition had been a foregone conclusion from the beginning. Wisely or unwisely, Eddy and Murphy had not been allowed to make as much use of the French as they had desired. Nevertheless, the fact that only 900 men were killed out of the 109,000 soldiers who landed on the beaches was largely due to the fact that most of the French Army did not fight.

There were still jobs to be done after the Clark meeting. Eddy had arranged a commando force of 132 men to eliminate the German Armistice Commission, but the order to do so was canceled at the last minute. Murphy was to get in touch with Admiral Darlan in a final effort to silence the guns of the French Navy. The OSS infiltration of Spanish Morocco to contact native chiefs and help ensure the left flank of the invading troops still went on. A guerilla force was alerted to seize the key points in Algiers. Men were nominated to stand on the beaches and guide the landing parties in to the shore. And intelligence still poured in from Yankee and Franklin, Lincoln, Midway and Pilgrim.

It continued to come in up to the very last moment, ensuring that every Vichy ship and every Vichy outpost was spotted for the landing of troops. There was only one slip-up. At the last moment, OSS men learned that the French Army command in Oran had decided to fight. By radio, they tried to warn the ships to prepare for action and come in fighting, but the message was never received, or if received, was not acted upon.

On the night of November 8, Eddy was in Gibraltar. So was General Eisenhower, who had arrived under the name of "Howe," and General Clark whose alias was "Mark." Murphy was in Algiers arguing with Darlan. Everything was as ready as it ever would be. The secret had been well kept. The Germans had not even tried to close the strait of Gibraltar. Allied ships had long been at sea.

On that night, Eddy and Carleton Coon and several others went to the United States Consulate in Gibraltar, where they sat up late with Colonel Holcomb, the military attaché, who did not know what was about to happen, and was a little surprised at the lateness of the visit. They ate sandwiches and drank beer and listened to the radio.

Coon said he remembered the German most clearly, for it broke a sudden silence in the room: "Achtung, Achtung, Achtung! Ein amerkanisches Kraftsheer ist auf der nordwest Küste Afrikas! Achtung, Achtung, Achtung!"

Then, before Franklin Roosevelt made his broadcast to the world, came the final message for the secret radio stations which OSS had began operating in Africa fifteen months before. It was a fitting last word: "Ecoute, Ecoute, Yankee, Franklin, Pilgrim, Midway, Lincoln. Robert arrive. Robert arrive.

"Robert" was arriving. America's first big invasion had begun.